SUSTAINABLE AND RESILIENT COMMUNITIES

SUSTAINABLE AND RESILIENT COMMUNITIES

A Comprehensive Action Plan for Towns, Cities, and Regions

STEPHEN COYLE | Foreword by Andrés Duany

WILEY

John Wiley & Sons, Inc.

Published by John Wiley & Sons, Inc., Hoboken, New Jersey.

Published simultaneously in Canada.

For general information on our other products and services, or technical support, please contact our Customer Care Department within the United States at 800-762-2974, outside the United States at 317-572-3993
or fax 317-572-4002.

Wiley also publishes its books in a variety of electronic formats. Some content that appears in print may
not be available in electronic books.

For more information about Wiley products, visit our Web site at www.wiley.com.

Library of Congress Cataloging-in-Publication Data:

Sustainable and resilient communities : a comprehensive action plan for towns,

cities, and regions / [edited by] Stephen Coyle.

  p. cm.

 Includes bibliographical references and index.
 ISBN 978-0-470-53647-6 (cloth : acid-free paper); 978-0-470-91872-2 (ebk); 978-0-470-91873-9 (ebk);
978-0-470-91874-6 (ebk); 978-0-470-95022-7 (ebk)
 1. City planning--Environmental aspects. 2. Regional planning--
Environmental aspects. 3. Community development, Urban—Environmental
aspects. 4. Sustainable urban development. 5. Sustainable development. I.
Coyle, Stephen.
 HT166.S9125 2011
 307.1'2—dc22

                                    2010025646

Printed in the United States of America

10   9   8   7   6   5   4   3   2   1

Contents

Foreword

THIS BOOK IS NOT a silver bullet. It does not offer the magic shot that cannot miss—and for that we must be grateful.

Steve Coyle takes urbanism very seriously indeed. He and his colleagues do not underestimate the patient and skillful work that must be done to recover our lost cities and their dismal suburbs, and by so doing salvage what remains of our natural areas. It is the distinct absence of shortcuts that gives me confidence that the advice provided here will actually be effective.

The lifestyle of the American middle class—how we occupy our land, how we circulate, and how large we live—defies easy solutions. We endure brutal commutes and drive even short distances. To buy petroleum we have effectively shoveled overseas the accumulated wealth of three centuries, the only permanent result being the impoverishment of our citizens and the polluting of our environment. We have mitigated for the absence of neighborhood and public realm by building retirement villages and Disney Worlds. What good are silver bullets against this monstrous stupidity?

Despite generous allocations of hope, money and political will, most cities and their surrounding countryside have declined. Conventional wisdom assumes causes that range from misgovernment to disinvestment, inattention, and incapacity for vision to just plain bad luck. Not so! Generations of professional consultants offered their very inventive ideas and too often, alas, their plans were implemented. Recent American planning is not the conventional historiography of a sequence of planners' intelligent proposals that were tragically ignored. Actually, it consists of the dutiful implementation of their simpleminded recommendations. The people and the government did their job—it was the planners who failed them.

To explain my aversion to any simplistic proposal, it is enough to list the catastrophic sequence of ideas that has constituted remedial urbanism for the past seven decades. Most of these have proven to be either duds mercifully forgotten or spectacular backfires, the consequences of which are still quite visibly undermining our society.

Chronologically the first and also the worst was the imposition of single-use zoning: the notion that the separation of the places where we dwell from those where we shop and those where we work was necessary. The resultant cartoon of urbanism requires an immense amount of public subsidy to provide the roads and services and an even larger amount of private capital to assure that every adult has an automobile and its fuel. Nothing has ever equaled zoning in idiocy, but there are close contenders. Among these was the rather large mistake of rerouting of the interstate system through the cities, in defiance of President Eisenhower's conception that high-speed highways should skirt the urban areas. Each highway extension reamed out the delicate urban fabric, eased the escape into the suburbs, and spread dependence on the automobile.

Then, close upon that mistake came the HUD program that demolished and replaced "slum" neighborhoods with superblocks of town houses and high-rises and the promise of "greenery, light and air." The resulting social damage is nearly incalculable. Then, apparently to raise our spirits and distract us from things going wrong, along came the festive space needles topped by rotating restaurants (now usually closed); then came the sports stadiums, many now obsolescent, the hulking convention centers and dont forget the aquariums, all of which are still losing money today. There were also the trashy public plazas and river walks, empty except during the festivals that artificially induce attendance. The "pedestrianized" main streets that emulate suburban malls, of which almost two hundred desiccated their shops and have already been ripped out. There then came the defeatist secessions from the inner city: the indoor "Rouse" malls, today depressingly downmarket and the equally dowdy underground passages and elevated bridges, now used only under threat of climatic extremes. Even the ultimate silver bullets, the Olympics and the World's Fairs, would now be utterly forgotten but for the lingering physical and financial holes that are their legacy to the host cities.

But what about the "Bilbao Effect," that famous attempt to recreate the Guggenheim Museum that put that unknown Spanish City on the map? Unknown to whom? Only to those ignorant of Spain. The charlatans who still propose "starchitecture" always fail to point out that Bilbao was already a very livable, prosperous, sophisticated and beautiful city before the Guggenheim landed. The building did alert the world to the fact, but that is all it did. A new "Bilbao" in, say, dismal Phoenix, would have had no effect at all. Most subsequent "Bilbaos" have not lived up to their billing as "catalytic projects." A good city supports a cultural institution and not vice-versa. Even small benevolent interventions like the now popular subsidized "artist's housing" do little beyond putting roofs over the artists' heads.

The same goes for ubiquitous "open space" projects—the current darling High Line in New York attracted pedestrians not alone for its terrific design, but because it is embedded in the superb and affluent urban fabric of Manhattan. Elsewhere, scores of highly designed new parks stand quasi-abandoned because of the lack of supporting urban context.

The effect of such projects on their cities has been no greater than the ancient cave paintings of antelopes on the next day's hunt.

But enough wishful thinking! Enough pushing silver bullets on hopeful municipalities! Wherever planning has succeeded, it has involved the patient reweaving of the urban fabric into whole cloth: socially, physically, economically, and administratively. That is what makes the difference, and that is precisely what this book is about.

ANDRÉS DUANY

Acknowledgments

THIS BOOK REPRESENTS the combined efforts of contributing authors, editors, illustrators, researchers, and others who supported my work during a yearlong endeavor. At the top of the list, I remain ever grateful to my associate Daniel Dunigan, who co-managed the book development process and authored two brief but important sections.

First, I wish to thank the following people whose contributions appear throughout these pages: urbanist, architect, and retail expert Seth Harry; sustainability-savant Michael Mehaffy; building efficiency guru Erin Cubbinson; innovative architects Gaither Pratt and Sara Hines; attorney, regulatory expert, and author Dan Slone; Rick Pruetz, author and authority on transfer of development rights; form-based code master Sandy Sorlien; co-authors Dana Perls and Daniel Dunigan; transit-oriented development specialist Sam Zimbabwe; transportation planning experts Trent Lethco, Jim Daisa, and Professor Norman Garrick; sustainable streetscape and watershed engineer Paul Crabtree; masters of alternative energy Jon Roberts, Cyane Dandridge, and Jeannie Renne-Malone; Light Imprint development designer Tom Low and the supporting Duany Plater-Zyberk and Company crew; and decentralized wastewater proponents Eric Lohan and Will Kirksy.

My gratitude extends to sustainable landscaper John Harris, green landscape architect Katie O'Reilly Rogers, and architect Jane Martin; sustainable food authority Lynn Peemoeller; and organic agriculturists and educators Raoul Adamchak and Sibella Kraus; doctor of waste recycling and reuse Daniel T. Sicular with associate Jeff Caton; economic revitalization authorities Dave Leland and Chris Zahas; and our sustainable return on investment John Williams; deputy city manager and community educator Susan J. Daluddung; air quality authority Anthony Bernheim; and progressive public health experts Karen Mendrala and Karen Shore. Not all contributors survived the final editing process, including sustainable agriculture and ranching leader Ann Adams and foreign contributors Jaydean Boldt, Steven Branca, Stephen Goldie, and Frank Schaffarczyk. I remain indebted to you all just the same, and hope for an opportunity to work with you in the future.

A volunteer in our early, internal editing effort deserves my exceptional gratitude. Corey Limbach used his practical development experience to transform content-rich but often disorganized materials into worthy contributions; his edits were invaluable. Editor/contributors Dana Perls and Daniel Dunigan worked tirelessly sorting and reviewing text and images, helping to organize and assemble the manuscript, assisted by editor Robin Silberman. Daniel Dunigan graciously rendered some hand-drawn images in Chapter 1 and led the research, selection, and photo-customization of appropriate images. He provided countless suggestions for improving the book's form and substance. The development of this book would have been impossible without him. I extend special thanks to Senior Editor John Czarnecki, Assoc. AIA, Editorial Assistant Sadie Abuhoff, and Production Editor Amy Odum at John Wiley & Sons, for editing and publishing this book. Wiley provided a rare opportunity, based on my simple outline.

I am especially grateful to Andrés Duany for his own collaborative publications on building resilient and healthy urbanism, his continued leadership and generosity in sharing ideas, designs, regulatory codes, and plans for repairing our towns and cities. Finally, I remain in the debt of my wife, Jane, my daughter Leiko, and son Nick for their continual encouragement and inspiration, even as they forge their own tangible efforts to make our world better, brighter, and more resilient.

Introduction

How to Use this Book

This book explains how to develop and implement an action plan to make your neighborhood, community, or region more environmentally and economically healthy, habitable, and resilient. The book introduces two basic development patterns and supportive systems that constitute our built environment, and describes their features, benefits, drawbacks, and performance characteristics.

The built environment—villages, towns, cities, counties, and townships—includes seven essential supporting systems:

1. Transportation—mobility of people, goods, and services
2. Energy—community and building electrical power
3. Water—supply, waste, and stormwater
4. Natural Environment—biological resources and landscapes
5. Food Production/Agriculture—urban/urban edge cultivation and production
6. Solid Waste—garbage, refuse, and sludge
7. Economic—industries, jobs, and financing

The Action Plan

From the built environment through each supporting system, we describe the people and processes necessary for moving from low-performance, high-carbon places and supporting systems to the high-performance, low-carbon models. We instruct you on creating, refining, and implementing an actionable **plan**—a set of policies, programs, codes, projects, best practices, technologies, and tools. We identify the people and other resources necessary to create and activate the plans with an involved public. This customizable **process** enables you and your community to assemble a planning team; research and assess your current state of **sustainability,**[1] both collectively and by each individual element; set timely and measurable performance goals and objectives for each; and propose, evaluate, and select the best methods before launching an implementation plan and monitoring its results. With this process, the plan will be reflective of and supported by the community.

---

1. Achieving full dependency on, and maintaining the health of renewable resources—biological, land, water, air, energy, and people—indefinitely.

We use the following steps to organize these strategies:

1. Define the Project Type
2. Determine the Means
3. Prepare the Team
4. Select the Tools
5. Prepare the Place
6. Prepare the People
7. Develop Goals, Objectives, and Performance Metrics
8. Develop the Strategies
9. Develop the Action Plan
10. Implement the Action Plan
11. Funding, Policy, and Technical Resources

Chapter Organization

Each chapter includes detailed approaches, methodologies, strategies, or interventions consistent with each chapter's theme, followed by a set of concise **actions** that describe specific strategies, programs, and best practices; its features, performance expectations, benefits, rewards, risks and drawbacks; first and lifecycle costs; and propensity for support or resistance to adoption and implementation.

A Synthesized Approach

Virtually every city and county across the country will, sooner or later, need to plan for its sustainable future or its very economic, environmental, and social survival. As one approach, this book will assist jurisdictions, large or small, to plan for economic, environmental, and energy resiliency, health, and appropriate self-sufficiency by informing and instructing. By targeting those responsible for directing, advising, planning, managing, implementing, and monitoring sustainable policies, strategies, programs, and actions, the book will enable jurisdictions to assess their current state of sustainability; set timely performance goals and metrics; propose, evaluate, and prioritize or select appropriate measures; and produce implementable action plans, reflective of and supported by the larger community.

The Built Environment and Its Supporting Systems

Defining the Built Environment

Stephen J. Coyle, AIA, LEED
Town-Green, Townworks + DPZ

The **built environment** consists of the physical structures and organization patterns of buildings, blocks, neighborhoods, villages, towns, cities, and regions. The built environment requires the support of each of the seven essential systems of physical infrastructure, resources, and operational components essential to the survival and health of each place.

Figure 1-1
The City of Santa Barbara, from its 1786 Mission dedication and acquisition by the United States in 1846, remains a vital center of education, tourism, technology, health care, finance, agriculture, manufacturing, and local government.
Katie O'Reilly-Rogers

Defining the Supporting Systems

The **supporting systems** consist of the following:

- Transportation

  The technologies, infrastructure, and vehicles that comprise the system responsible for the circulation or mobility of people, goods, and services

- Energy

  The system for the design, management, and supply of energy sources required to power devices, equipment, industries, buildings, infrastructure, and communities, and includes its generation, storage, conveyance, conservation, and efficiency

- Water

  The technological and infrastructure system that supplies, treats, and conveys potable water; collects, treats, and disposes and/or recycles wastewater; and collects, treats, and discharges and/or recycles stormwater from regional watershed to the plumbing system

- Natural Environment

  The ecosystem of biological resources, landscapes, habitat, and other natural resources providing a continuous state of environmental health and sustenance

- Food Production/Agriculture

  The system that plans and manages the community food supply produced by local and regional agricultural, ranching, and forestry sources

- Solid Waste

  The technologies, facilities, and vehicles that comprise the system that collects, treats, disposes of and/or recycles residential, commercial, industrial, and institutional waste

- Economic

  The economic system that supports the health, maintenance, and survival of the built environment, defined in this context as the economic strategies, policies, programs, and activities administered in support of the other systems

The Two Fundamental Types of Built Environments

Across the country, our built environments are generally composed or organized in two fundamentally different ways.

Sustainably designed communities serve multiple functions—shelter, commerce, education, food production—within a walkable or drivable context. Their resilience extends to adaptive and durable buildings accommodative of changing uses to meet shifting market and societal demands. At risk or conventional communities provide multiple uses accessed by auto only. Single-use buildings confined within single-use pods, subdivisions, or strips require replacement or significant renovation in order to repurpose. The resilient and adaptable community was the only type built through the first half of the twentieth century.

The **conventional/high-carbon (CHC) community,** also known as conventional suburban development,[1] emerged in response to the gradual adoption of separated-use zoning, and the decline of mass transit and walking as mobility choices. Over the last 60 years, this development type, fueled by cheap oil, flourished with highway funding relying on a continuous supply of land to develop by building on existing farmland, forests, and drainable swamps.

Figure 1-2
Sprawling Southern Beaufort County, South Carolina, consumes land through the broad separation of residential, commercial, and industrial uses. *Josh Martin, AICP, CNU3*

The CHC moniker should not be applied to the pedestrian-oriented, pre–World War II suburbs; railroad, subway, and streetcar suburbs; the resort and even industrial suburbs; the single-family house on a tree-lined street, with walkable town center. Automobile dependency defines the CHC.

Resilient/Low-Carbon (RLC), or traditional city, town, and neighborhood development,[2] describes historic settlement patterns that developed throughout the United States from the eighteenth to the mid-twentieth century. RLC settlements developed local commerce, managed available resources, exploited rail and water access, adapted to population growth, and endured from Charleston, South Carolina and Nashville, Indiana to Pacific Grove, California and Forest Grove, Oregon. The RLC most often reflects a continuum or morphing of attributes, as communities outgrew or jumped beyond their original boundaries.

Figure 1-3
A diagram of traditional neighborhood development includes a fine-grain network of connected streets, small blocks, a mix of uses and graduated densities from edge to center, access to transit, and movement of goods.
John Massengale, Anglo-American Suburb

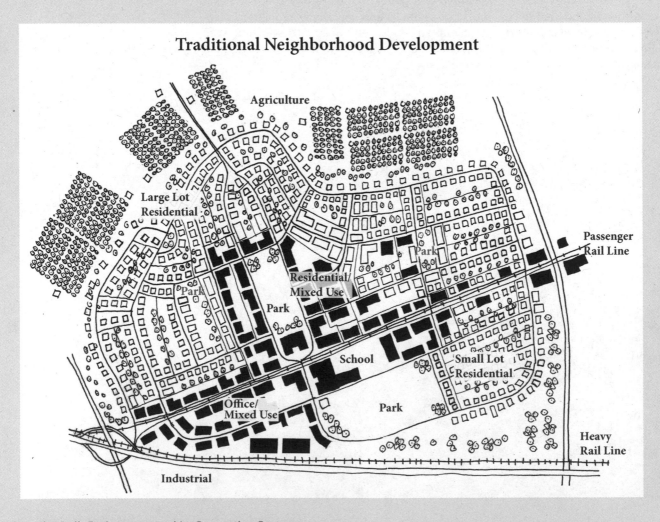

Traditional Neighborhood Development

Agriculture

Large Lot Residential

Passenger Rail Line

Park

Residential/Mixed Use

Park

Park

School

Small Lot Residential

Office/Mixed Use

Park

Heavy Rail Line

Industrial

Conventional/High-Carbon Built Environments

CHC built environments consist primarily of segregated, low-density (less than four dwelling units per acre), auto-oriented development. Typically organized into clusters of single-use buildings, the single-family residential pods, higher-density apartment complexes, retail strip centers and malls, office and industrial parks, and campus-type school sites are generally scaled to the size and spacing of the local and regional thoroughfare system. The dendritic, or branching, street system yields large "superblocks," with the undevelopable land or left over property set aside for park land or the "open space" required by regulations or demanded by the public.

Places that exhibit the following development patterns and qualities are typical of CHC:

Figure 1-4
A diagram of conventional suburban development, bisected by a highway and arterial roadway, which separates and segregates land uses except for the old neighborhood area at lower right. *Daniel Dunigan*

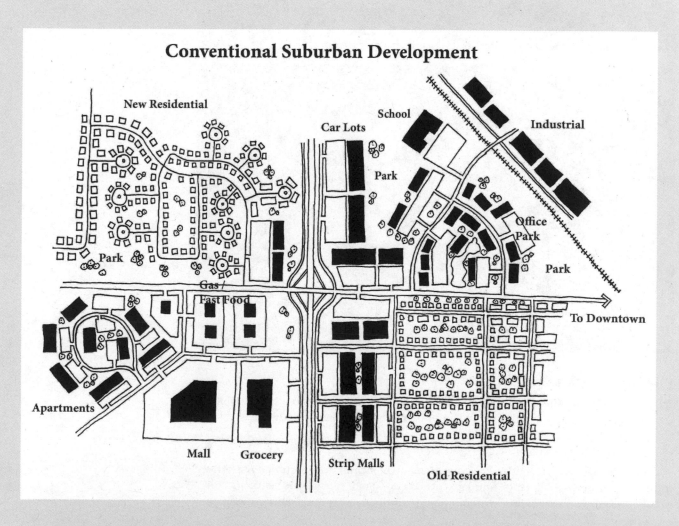

Figure 1-5
The "Edge City" of Oak Brook, Illinois, incorporated as a Village in 1958, represents the suburban development patterns that emerged in force after World War II. *Payton Chung*

Figure 1-6
An example of low-density residential sprawl in Southern Beaufort County, South Carolina, accessed primarily by long roadways. *Josh Martin, AICP, CNU3*

URBANIZATION OR DEVELOPMENT PATTERN

Dispersed, Uncontained Growth: Predominately auto-oriented urbanization lacking clearly defined boundaries between the built and natural environments

CIRCULATION PATTERN

Automobile-Oriented: Dendritic, or hierarchical, branched transportation patterns of highways, arterials, collectors, and local streets designed, scaled, and managed primarily around motor vehicles, with minimal pedestrian, bike, and transit amenities

LAND USE PATTERN

Use-Based Zoning:

- Zoning of land and buildings based primarily on the control of uses, with minimal power over the forms or sequence of urbanization

- High-density apartment sites abutting strip commercial development separated from single-family subdivisions by a multilane arterial

PUBLIC RIGHT-OF-WAY/"OPEN SPACE" SCALE AND FORM

Roadway-Oriented:

- Public streets and other urbanized rights-of-way scaled for automobile convenience

- Motor vehicle–oriented corridors formed by multiple lanes, narrow sidewalks, with little or no spatial enclosure for the public space by buildings

- Parks and other public space scaled to adjoining arterial or regional thoroughfares, and the residual parcels between development pods, or as required by jurisdictional regulations or as a condition of entitlement approval

▲ **Figure 1-7**
Conventional development often yields "no-man's" parcels between paving and buildings. *Stephen Coyle*

◄ **Figure 1-8**
The consumption of land south of Kansas City, Missouri, continues through low-density development patterns and roadway access. *Stephen Coyle*

BUILDING AND LANDSCAPE SCALE AND FORM

Roadway-Oriented:

- Buildings, landscapes, lots, and blocks primarily scaled to the adjacent thoroughfare system with extended block lengths; sprawling building complexes; and identical, subdivided home tracts, with abundant parking sized for peak periods

- Buildings typically set back from the thoroughfare with little or no spatial enclosure

- Buildings and landscapes developed in relation to the thoroughfare's physical scale rather than to adjacent structures, local conditions and building traditions, or landscape

Resilient/Low-Carbon Built Environments

RLC built environments, generally compact in form, comprised of pedestrian-scale blocks and streets, boast a diversity of necessary and desirable functions. The residential, employment, shopping, and civic uses functions are integrated into mixed-use buildings and blocks. The location, scale, and design of squares, plazas, and parks reflect their importance and value as cultural, commercial, and natural resources. Boundaries between built and natural environments are clearly defined to protect both habitats.

Figure 1-9
The typical big-box retail format requires visible, easy access to roadways and automobiles. *CNU.org*

The following text labels appear within the map:

N.E. HALSEY STREET

N.E. 207th CONNECTOR

N.E. GLISAN STREET

223rd AVENUE

FAIRVIEW VILLAGE

HOLT & HAUGH, INC.
DEVELOPER

LENNERTZ & COYLE   SPENCER & KUPPER
TOWN PLANNERS   CITY PLANNERS

ALPHA ENGINEERING   KITTLESON & ASSOC.
PROJECT ENGINEERS   TRAFFIC PLANNERS

WAYNE CHEN   BRAD HOSMAR   GARY REDDICK
STEVE COYLE   BILL LENNERTZ   BRUCE ROBINSON
BILL DENNIS   JERRY PALMER   MIKE STEFFEN
MIKE GATES   STEVE POLLARD   HIESUR STEFFEN
SARAH HOLT   ERIC SEIPER   SAM YODER
                                CARY DASENBROCK

11 MAY 1994

5 MINUTE WALK   1300 FT

Figure 1-10
The masterplan for Fairview Village,
a new development by Holt & Haugh,
Inc. in Fairview, Oregon, and designed
by Lennertz & Coyle with Bill Dennis.
Lennertz & Coyle

URBANIZATION OR DEVELOPMENT PATTERN

Places that exhibit the following patterns and qualities are typical of RLC built environments.

Compact and Bounded: Physically contained, pedestrian- and transit-oriented urbanization with graduated densities and clearly defined boundaries between development and nature, though agriculture can be integrated into both

CIRCULATION PATTERN

Connected and Multi-Use: A fine-grained, interconnected, multimodal transportation network with a balance of motor vehicle, pedestrian, bike, and transit amenities

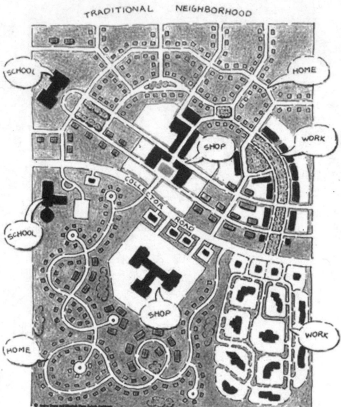

▲ **Figure 1-11**
The traditional neighborhood at top contains a fine-grain network of "complete" or multiuser streets as opposed to the suburban pattern of disconnected roadways below. *Duany Plater-Zyberk and Company*

◀ **Figure 1-12**
The New York City Highline, a linear park built on the former Westside elevated rail bed, provides an attractive, convenient, and cool walking experience. *Shulie Sade*

Figure 1-13
A rendering of a proposed mixed-use redesign of Main Street, Mercer Island, by Bill Dennis, was part of a downtown planning charrette by Lennertz & Coyle.
Lennertz & Coyle

LAND USE PATTERN

Form-Based Zoning: Allocating land uses based primarily on the control of or influence over the physical form, intensity, and arrangement of buildings, landscapes, and public spaces that enable land or building functions to adapt to economic, environmental, energy, and social changes over time

PUBLIC RIGHT-OF-WAY/"OPEN SPACE" SCALE AND FORM

Pedestrian Scale and Form:

- Public streets and other rights-of-way scaled around the pedestrian and transit systems
- Multifunction, multimodal transportation corridors with transit, motor vehicle, bike, and pedestrian facilities, spatially enclosed by buildings and, where appropriate to the urban context, trees

- Parks and other public open space connected to, informed by, and in a hierarchical relationship with the surrounding physical context, development intensities, and natural and landscaped parcels required for normative "place-making," food production, and/or federal, state, or local regulations configured into environmental resource areas.

BUILDING AND LANDSCAPE SCALE AND FORM

Pedestrian Scale and Form:

- Buildings, lots, and blocks primarily scaled around the pedestrian and transit-oriented thoroughfare or right-of-way, and for non-motorized activities

- Buildings that front on and align themselves along the pedestrian and transit-oriented thoroughfares, creating a human-scale spatial enclosure

- Buildings informed by the surrounding physical context, the adjacent landscapes, structures, local conditions, building traditions, and the microclimate

▲ **Figure 1-14**
A pedestrian plaza provides multiple uses scaled for people: a pedestrian way, outdoor seating, and shopping plus emergency vehicle access. *Stephen Coyle*

◀ **Figure 1-15**
The landscape along Delancy Street on Rittenhouse Square, Philadelphia, exemplifies a context-appropriate response to an urban environment. *Sandy Sorlien*

The Two Fundamental Types of Supporting Systems

Both the CHC and RLC require the support of seven essential systems of physical infrastructure, resources, and operational components which are essential to the survival and health of each place.

Conventional/High Carbon Support Systems

Support systems for the CHC environment are conventional economic, energy, water, natural environment, transportation, food production/agriculture, and solid waste systems that exhibit the following qualities:

1. Nonrenewable resource-based systems that are wholly or largely dependent on the extraction, processing, consumption, and/or distribution of nonrenewable resources.
2. Inflexible systems that are incapable of or resistant to expansion, contraction, or modification over time.
3. Inefficient systems that directly or indirectly generate waste as a development or operational byproduct.
4. Nonvirtuous systems that directly or indirectly generate harmful byproducts, or are hazardous as a consequence of their development or operations.
5. Temporary systems that are intentionally built for obsolescence or replacement.

CHC TRANSPORTATION SYSTEM

The conventional conveyance system relies primarily on the use of motor vehicles for the mobility of people, goods, and services. This system has directly or indirectly caused or contributed to air pollution, the destruction of cultural and natural resources, the consumption of land for low-density development, and the rise in asthma, obesity, and other maladies resulting from personal motor vehicle dependency.

Figure 1-16
Throughout the country, thousands of deteriorating, auto-dominated corridors require conversion into "complete streets" or multi-use places. *Stephen Coyle*

CHC ENERGY

Conventional energy systems encompass: the planning, financing, development, acquisition, construction, operation, and maintenance system for the generation, supply, transmission, and management of primarily fossil fuel–generated (coal, petroleum, natural gas) electric energy, with limited renewable power sources. Conventional energy relies heavily on nonrenewable sources, finite resources that will eventually become too expensive or too environmentally damaging to retrieve, as opposed to renewable sources such as wind, biomass, hydropower, and solar energy.

CHC WATER SYSTEMS

Conventional water supply systems deliver water (potable and nonpotable) via engineered hydrologic and hydraulic components. They tend to increase supply volumes to meet expanding demand, rather than to first decrease demand, and require intensive energy demands for pumps and other supply-related equipment.

Conventional stormwater systems collect surface runoff into surface waterways or storm sewers for eventual discharge into the watershed. This process can cause ecological damage from inadequate removal of contaminants (e.g., petroleum products) or sewer overflow flooding, contributing to soil erosion and habitat destruction. Runoff from artificial fertilizers, industrial discharge, and sediment from development degrade and contaminate groundwater. Conventional watershed or drainage basin management

▲ Figure 1-17
Conventional coal power plants produce major quantities of greenhouse gas—up to three times as much as natural gas—and emit particles that adversely affect human health. *Arnold Paul*

◀ Figure 1-18
The Arizona Aquaduct, a water-to-the-desert scheme, and the adjacent, water-use-intensive development, reflect conventional water management strategies. *Paul Crabtree*

attempts to remove, restrict, or prohibit the quantities, rates, and concentrations of chemical, physical, biological, and other harmful constituents that are discharged from point sources into the stormwater.

Conventional wastewater systems: (1) separate inorganic solids from the wastewater; (2) gradually convert dissolved biological matter into microbial biosolids or sludge; (3) neutralize, dispose, and/or reuse biosolids; (4), chemically or physically disinfect effluent; and (5) often discharge the treated effluent into the watershed (i.e., aquifers, rivers, lakes, or oceans) causing potential ecological damage. Conventional processes may not adequately sequester heavy metals, and the sludge can contain manmade organic compounds of which even low levels can have an unpredictable adverse impact on the environment and the potential for reuse.

Figure 1-19
Conventional stormwater infrastructure often channels runoff rather than managing the water for reuse or recharge. *UCSC Storm Water Management Program Environmental Health and Safety Department*

Figure 1-20
The conventional wastewater treatment plant consumes water, power, and chemicals. *Paul Crabtree*

CHC NATURAL ENVIRONMENTAL SYSTEM

The spread of wasteful resource extraction practices and low-density and single-use urbanization has reshaped and destroyed natural landscapes, biological resources, and environments. The expansion of human activities into the natural environment has reduced, fragmented, damaged, and isolated water habitats and other natural resources.

CHC FOOD PRODUCTION/AGRICULTURE SYSTEM

Conventional food production consists largely of monolithic crop production that relies heavily on petroleum-based fertilizers, pesticides, fungicides, and other chemical and technological advances, including mechanization, which has directly and indirectly damaged the health and resilience of the natural environment from water supplies to air quality, harmed the health of human and other biological resources, and may threaten the economic viability of smaller-scale farming and ranching.

Conventional agriculture has damaged the ecology and productivity of approximately 24 percent of worldwide land, including topsoil depletion, groundwater contamination, the decline of family farms, farm laborer health problems, increasing costs of production with rising oil costs, and the decline of the integrity of rural communities. The practice of transforming diverse ecosystems into agricultural monocultures limits an environment's resilience and health immunities without continued human intervention. Both the scale of the intervention of industrial agriculture and the variety of species grown, like sugar cane, can deplete huge areas of rich soils and spread harmful chemicals into the air, the surrounding soils, the watershed, and beyond.

◣ Figure 1-21
Poor logging practices degrade the natural environment, the watershed, and destroy wildlife habitat. *Jim Reeve, May 26, 2007*

▼ Figure 1-22
The agricultural sprawl in the San Luis Valley of Colorado diverts water and power from traditional crop-growing areas. *Paul Crabtree*

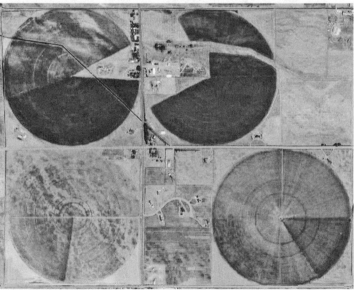

Figure 1-23
Conventional landfill practices degrade the underlying soils and watershed, and emit large quantities of methane. *Stephen Coyle*

Conventional livestock production consumes 70 percent of all land used for agriculture worldwide, generates 18 percent of the world's greenhouse gas emissions, and represents a significant cause of deforestation and reductions in biodiversity in the Amazon basin and Africa.[3]

CHC SOLID WASTE SYSTEM

A solid waste system collects, separates, transports, and disposes of residential, commercial, industrial and institutional solid or semi-solid, nonhazardous waste with minimal waste recycling, reduction, or reuse efforts. The conventional approach treats most waste as materials destined for disposal through landfilling, with the recognition of the adverse consequences of the conventional practice, both up and down the waste stream. The conventional generation, collection, treatment, and disposal of waste contributes to environmental pollution, the accumulation of toxic wastes, the degradation and depletion of natural resources, destruction and depletion of soils and water, the generation of harmful airborne particulates, and the release of methane and other greenhouse gas emissions.

CHC ECONOMICS

The municipal economic system focuses on increasing community prosperity by increasing the production, distribution, and consumption of goods and services. Economic growth implies an increase in quantitative output measured by the rate of change of gross domestic product per year—the aggregate value-added by the economic activity within a city or county's borders. Conventional economic growth requires the generation of waste and fossil-fuel dependency to maintain economic output, with emphasis on maintaining or growing both land development and tax base and personal income rather than focusing on conservation, adaptation, and self-sufficiency.

> "Economics explores the choices people make when resources are limited. Urban economics studies the intersection of economics and geography."
>
> —*Arthur O'Sullivan, Urban Economics, 7th ed.*

Resilient/Low-Carbon Support Systems

Support systems for the RLC environment include economic, energy, water, natural environment, transportation, food production/agriculture, and solid waste systems that exhibit the following qualities:

1. Renewable resource-based systems that, over time, are capable of achieving full dependency on, and supporting and enhancing the health of its renewable resources.

2. Flexible systems that are capable of or responsive to expansion, contraction, or modification over time.

3. Efficient, zero-waste systems or systems that directly or indirectly generate renewable waste as a development or operational byproduct.

4. Virtuous systems that directly or indirectly generate beneficial impacts as a consequence of their development or operations.

5. Durable systems that are built to last.

RLC TRANSPORTATION SYSTEM

The sustainable transportation system makes a net positive contribution to the environmental, social, and economic health of the community by providing safe, convenient, efficient, and diverse means of mobility. The resilient and healthy mobility system reduces tail pipe emissions and improves vehicle energy efficiency; employs intelligent thoroughfare design; facilitates the use of public transit, low/no-carbon fuels and vehicles, and transportation demand–management technologies; promotes low/no-tech/healthy modes like walking and biking; provides economic and environmental alternatives that encourage more efficient passenger and freight movement; and reduces consumption of nonrenewable fuels. At the scale of the corridor, neighborhood, and block, the "complete" or multi-modal street provides mobility choices capable of accommodating changing functional demands.

Figure 1-24
Del Mar Station designed by Moule Polyzoides Architects and Urbanists represents a pedestrian- and transit-oriented development. *Tom Bonner Photography*

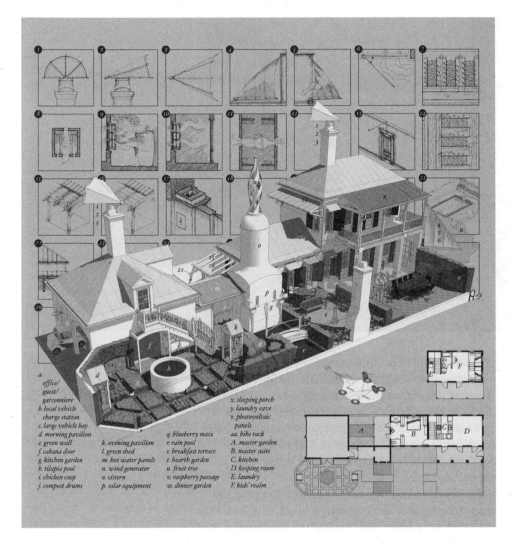

◀Figure 1-25
The Wall Street Journal Green House of the Future design by architect Steve Mouzon incorporates both traditional and contemporary resource -conserving and -producing features. *Steve Mouzon*

▼ Figure 1-26
The Fresno Water Tower symbolizes a water management tradition of conservation and efficiency. *Paul Crabtree*

RLC ENERGY

The sustainable energy system serves the municipality and community primarily through renewable and limited fossil fuel–generated electric power. The sustainable/low-carbon energy system focuses on conservation and efficiency measures to reduce demand before the development of renewable power, such as solar, wind, geothermal, hydro, and microbial, as well as interim power storage.

RLC WATER SYSTEMS

The sustainable/low-carbon water supply system focuses on conservation measures to reduce water demand, and on increasing the efficiency or performance of infrastructure and plumbing fixtures and devices, plus the reclamation of wastewater to meet nonpotable demand.

RLC FOOD PRODUCTION/AGRICULTURE SYSTEM

Sustainable agriculture produces food both within and beyond the built environment without damaging or depleting renewable resources or polluting the surrounding environment, integrating environmental health, economic profitability, and social and economic equity. It employs crop rotation, green manure, composting, biological pest control, water-conserving irrigation, and non-fossil-fueled mechanical cultivation to enhance soil productivity, control pests, cultivate fields, protect the water supply, and exclude or limit the use of petroleum-based fertilizers and chemical pesticides, plant growth regulators, and livestock feed additives.

Sustainable agriculture and ranching, to the extent feasible, produces food for local consumption, in the form of home, business, school, and community gardens, and appropriately sized, diversified farms, supplying the majority of their region's food without resource depletion.

Figure 1-30
Fruit and nut orchards can provide a source of food, habitat, rainwater recharge, and minimal carbon sequestration. *Blaine Merker, Royston Hanamoto Alley & Abey, Landscape Architects*

> "Organic agriculture is a production system that sustains the health of soils, ecosystems and people. It relies on ecological processes, biodiversity and cycles adapted to local conditions, rather than the use of inputs with adverse effects. Organic agriculture combines tradition, innovation and science to benefit the shared environment and promote fair relationships and a good quality of life for all involved."
>
> —*International Federation of Organic Agriculture Movements*

RLC SOLID WASTE SYSTEM

The sustainable solid waste system returns materials to the economic mainstream for reuse, recycling, and composting, and residual materials are used as resources to create clean renewable energy. Sustainable waste management ranges from planning for "zero waste," waste energy management and energy efficiency, to renewable energy generation and water conservation. Best practices include the reuse and recycling of building materials, and the reduction or elimination of non-recyclable materials from manufacturers, distributors, and other upstream sources, through materials recovery and recycling facilities (MRFs), and the composting of renewable waste.

Food, Soiled Paper, Yard Trimmings

Comida, Papel Sucio y Desechos del Jardín   食物、沾污的紙張、剪草和細樹枝

QUESTIONS?

Sunset Scavenger
(415) 330-1300

**Golden Gate Disposal
and Recycling**
(415) 626-4000

SFRecycling.com

For toxic product recycling information, please visit:

Para información sobre el reciclaje de productos tóxicos por favor visite:

查詢含毒廢物回收的資訊、請上網或致電:

EcoFinder at SFEnvironment.org or call (415) 355-3777

SF Environment
Our home. Our city. Our planet.
A Department of the City and County of San Francisco

People • Service • Environment
SUNSET SCAVENGER COMPANY
GOLDEN GATE DISPOSAL
& RECYCLING COMPANY
Proud to be Employee Owned

A food, soiled paper, and yard trimmings recycling and composting poster helps promote and educate the public in this best practice. *Golden Gate Disposal and Recycling*

RLC ECONOMICS

The sustainable/low-carbon municipal economic system focuses on increasing community prosperity through the production, distribution, and consumption of goods and services that minimize or eliminate waste and reliance on nonrenewables. This system enhances the health of renewable resources both in municipal operations and in the community as a whole through conservation, efficiency, adaptation, and self-sufficiency. A sustainable economy relies on maintaining an adequate supply of renewable resources as well as reducing energy consumption and greenhouse emissions.

The Next Step: The Step-by-Step Process of Transformation

Exaptation describes shifts in the function of a trait or feature during evolution. Bird feathers initially evolved for temperature regulation then later adapted for flight. The exaptational traits of RCL communities described above include connectivity, compactness, diversity, and completeness. Planning or transforming communities in the face of uncertainty—economic upheavals, climate change, the auto's demise or the rise of electric vehicles—demands the inclusion of qualities or traits capable of shifting functionality to accommodate change over time. These assets would ideally scale from roofing materials to entire buildings, blocks, and neighborhoods.

Chapter 2 delineates a customizable process for developing and implementing a sustainable community plan. The sequence of steps include assembling a planning team; researching and assessing the current conditions by category or system; setting timely and measurable performance goals and objectives for each; and proposing, evaluating, and selecting appropriate actions. The team then forges an implementation or action plan, reflective of and supported by the community.

Our current economic pattern, to paraphrase attorney and energy blogger Jeff Vail,[5] is fundamentally unsustainable because a hierarchical structure requires perpetual growth. A resilient, adaptive community economy should be less hierarchal and more locally self-sufficient by leveraging developments in distributed, open-source, and peer-to-peer building, manufacturing, and food production.

Chapter 2
The Process of Transformation

Sustainable Plan-Making

Stephen J. Coyle, AIA, LEED
Town-Green, Townworks + DPZ

Transforming a low-performance, high-carbon community into the high-performance, low-carbon place requires a rigorous process and a comprehensive plan. We've organized the **process** into a series of sequential steps, each comprised of tasks, methodologies, examples, and other supporting information. This sequence can be modified and tasks rearranged or deployed concurrently in response to local conditions and desires. The process can and should be customized and calibrated to fit each application and context to most effectively improve, reconfigure, and repair the built and natural environments and the systems that support them.

We first assemble the **planning team**—those individuals and organizations that represent the key disciplines and practices necessary to advise, draft, and activate a plan. Each, according to their area of expertise and focus, commence their research and help establish performance targets consistent with jurisdictional goals and objectives. The team recommends a set of **actions,** or strategies, policies, programs, codes and ordinances, best practices, and tools that best accomplish goals and objectives, with concise descriptions of individual features, plus the benefits, drawbacks, and performance expectations for each.

In order to solicit ideas and build support for each action in the activation of the plan, the team engages and educates the public. Through an iterative process of refining, synthesizing, and combining actions, the team develops an **action plan** and recommends examples and instructions for developing and launching demonstration projects that best illustrate the innovative ideas and actions, to educate and inspire by example.

Finally, the team creates an **implementation plan**—a series of methods for activating each intervention. To evaluate the efficacy of each action over time, the team proposes methodologies for monitoring and assessing the performance of each action, and optimizing for maximize results.

The Plan-Making Steps

We suggest ten steps to organize these strategies. While not every step may be necessary or appropriate for every jurisdiction, the following provide a "roadmap" for commencing, developing, and activating the plan:

1. Define the Project Type
2. Determine the Project "Pathway"
3. Prepare the Team

4. Select the Tools

5. Prepare the Place

6. Prepare the People

7. Develop Goals, Objectives, and Performance Measures

8. Develop the Strategies

9. Develop the Action Plan

10. Implement the Action Plan

Step One: Define the Project Type

Begin by defining and describing the **project's planning framework, consisting of one or more of the following:**

1. A jurisdictional comprehensive or general plan update or amendment;

2. A "climate action," "carbon-reduction," or "sustainability" plan;

3. A specific set of state, regional, or local policies, development standards, or programs;

4. A regional, sector, or community plan or system;

5. A master or specific plan or system;

6. A site or development plan or system; and

7. A specific building(s) or support system.

Figure 2-1
Hayward, California's Climate Action Plan, final 11-6-09 version, represents a jurisdictional approach to sustainable community actions. *City of Hayward, California, Climate Action Plan*

general regulations apply to all districts and to all uses pe... tended to amplify and to supplement district regulations. In the district regulations, whichever regulations are more restrictive shall a... by the Planning Director.

Recommended Changes to Chapter 10: Article 1 - Zoning Ordi...

Municipal Code Section		Recommended Change...
Sec. 10-1.2720 Special Lot Requirements a. Minimum Lot Frontage Except as provided herein, each lot shall have a minimum frontage of 35 feet.	1.	In order to allow a wider ra... for single-family detached including reduced lot size housing and 18 feet for vert... town homes or condos are min. specified in Code).
Yard Exceptions - Accessory Buildings and Uses (1) In conjunction with single-family development located on parcels zoned for same, and in zoning districts where single-family homes are permitted: (a) Accessory buildings not used for parking and not exceeding 14 feet in height and 120 square feet in area and detached from the main buildings, when located in area other than the required front yard (i.e., in side or rear yard area), shall be placed no closer than 3 feet from the side and rear property lines.	2.	In order to facilitate the a... housing, correlate the allowa... Buildings with the lot size, u... rear and side setbacks as d... on larger lots.
q. Front Yards - Driveway Width and Coverage (1) Driveway width, regardless of the number of driveways, shall not exceed 20 feet in front of the garage, except for 3-car garages where the width shall not exceed 26 feet. In addition, for access to a recreational vehicle storage area adjacent to a dwelling, a maximum 10-foot-wide driveway may be located on the opposite	3.	In order to reduce the... surfaces, limit drive... paving, with except... paving materials... aesthetics notwi...

187

Next, outline the project's physical and jurisdictional context, consisting of one of the following:

1. Regional (e.g., multiple counties)
2. County or township
3. Metropolis (over 500,000)
4. City (50,000 to 500,000)
5. Village (under 50,000)
6. Neighborhood or corridor
7. Street, block, or parcel

Finally, consider the project's primary goals, consisting of one or more of the following:

1. Greenhouse gas emissions reduction;
2. Climate change adaption (e.g., plan for reduced water supply);
3. Economic renewal and/or improvement (e.g., increase business diversity);
4. Reduce nonrenewable energy dependency;
5. Protect and enhance the natural environment;
6. Improve quality and health of the built environment; and
7. Improve social health and well-being.

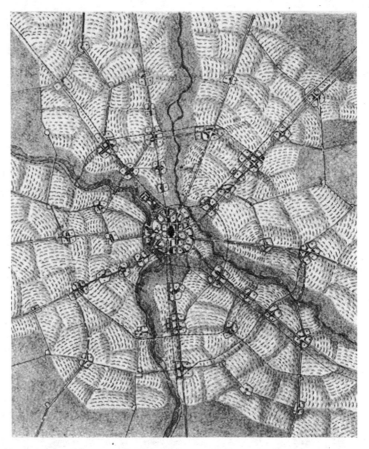

Figure 2-2
Sustainable planning demands actions at the scale of region, cities, towns, villages, and hamlets.
Duany Plater-Zyberk and Company

Step Two: Determine the Project "Pathway"

Determine and describe the primary means for accomplishing the goals. Typically, most efforts require at least two or more of the following, at the jurisdictional or governing level:

1. General plans (or comprehensive plans), consisting of a jurisdiction's document for guiding growth and operational principles, goals, objectives, and policies.

2. **Codes** or **ordinances,** describing the jurisdiction's **development and building standards,** statutes, zoning policies, or other measures for implementing the comprehensive or general plan. Include supporting maps and diagrams.

3. **Plans** and **projects**, describing the legal vehicle or specific action for implementing the policies of general plans and jurisdictional codes, consisting of community, master, area, specific, and precise plans, and specific site and/or building designs, plans, maps, diagrams, and code modifications that typically require legislative or administrative review, adoption, or approval. For example, a **climate action plan** (CAP), a jurisdictional plan for achieving a measurable reduction in greenhouse gas (GHG) emissions and reducing dependence on nonrenewable resources, describes specific policies, strategies, tools, and best

practices for implementing the plan to reach the targets, and a process for measuring progress.

4. **Programs** outlining specific series of steps, operations, actions, or curricula necessary to achieve the goals and objectives.

5. **Best practices,** introducing techniques and methodologies recommended as most effective at delivering a desired outcome in a particular condition or circumstance, based on peer-reviewed and/or field-tested procedures that can reliably provide the most efficient and effective results.[1]

The specific policies, programs, codes, regulations, best practices, technologies, and tools are presented as actions.

Step Three: Prepare the Team

The team's composition should consist of those disciplines, both technical and nontechnical, necessary to function as expert consultants and advisors. Identify and solicit the best available experts and supporting organizations and agencies capable of developing an action plan. Begin with those jurisdictional staff members responsible for or tasked with proposing, evaluating, directing, managing, executing, and/or operating the existing built environment and supporting system. Identify the local champions and leaders capable of gathering support and moving the plan from concept to implementation, from elected officials to citizen representatives.

Figure 2-3
Assemble the key members of the planning team for a kick-off meeting.
Stephen Coyle

KEY DISCIPLINES

1. *The built environment:* policy-makers, architects, city and community planners, landscape architects, urban designers, developers;

2. *Energy:* energy management groups; conservation, efficiency, financing, and procurement specialists;

3. *Water supply:* professional engineers and water conservation specialists;

4. *Wastewater:* professional engineers and wastewater system specialists;

5. *Stormwater:* professional engineers and regional and local watershed managers and specialists;

6. *Natural environment:* biological resource and natural habitat managers and specialists; environmental engineers, biologists, and ecologists;

7. *Transportation:* professional and traffic engineers, transportation planners;

8. *Food production/agriculture:* agricultural production specialists; environmental engineers and ecologists;

9. *Solid waste:* professional solid waste engineers and waste management specialists;

10. *Economic:* urban, employment, and real estate economists; finance and market specialists;

11. *Public engagement and education:* public engagement or involvement specialists; and the professional educator;

12. *The generalist:* a team leader with sufficient expertise or working knowledge of the key disciplines to direct and manage the team.

THE "SUSTAINABLE PLANNING COORDINATOR"

The jurisdiction may employ a "sustainable" project manager or coordinator, dedicated to directing and managing the planning and implementation process, seeking and applying for grants, administering funded projects and programs, and collaborating with other agencies and organizations to leverage their assistance and investment in the plan. Qualifications include adequate project management skills with sufficient technical background to perform a "generalist" function demanded of the position.

Step Four: Select the Tools

Sustainable plan-making requires both low- and high-tech "tools" for the preparation and execution of the process. Each tool application offers benefits and drawbacks including purchase or use costs, technical competency requirements, and thresholds of effectiveness. The planning process requires the deployment of evaluative tools that enable the participants—the public, government staffs, elected or appointed officials, and other stakeholders—to understand the consequences and assess the efficacy of proposed actions.

HIGH-TECH TOOLS

The high-tech tools may not fit neatly into a single category. For example, a GIS-based scenario-making and assessment tool such as PLACE3S provides a way to create, compare, and communicate the features and impacts of alternative use, transportation, and resource scenarios. These tools may include performance-measuring software applications that can evaluate the quantitative and qualitative attributes of alternative place types and support systems.

Visual mapping and data gathering tools for development types and support systems include census and GIS-based survey and data analysis programs. Data gathering tools can explore and yield information on plan-relevant data such as the quantities and sources of greenhouse gas emissions and other environmental conditions, economic trends, and employment numbers. A "data model" consists of generalized, user-defined views in text and numbers that reflect the real world. The best data methods help set "user-defined" parameters that represent the field of study.

A growing number of states, regions, universities, and nonprofit and for-profit firms support, produce, test, and deploy performance modeling tools including impact analysis and environmental and economic forecasting software such as PLAC3S, Urbemis, UPLAN, Community Viz, and INDEX. The more sophisticated programs perform computational functions: calculating baseline emissions from mobile and stationary sources; estimating performance from sets of carbon-reduction actions; and comparing environmental, transportation, and building energy performances from alternative scenarios.

GREENHOUSE GAS EMISSIONS INVENTORY, FORECAST, AND MODELING TOOLS

Emissions inventory software calculates the amount of total greenhouse gas emissions for a given area and year by a jurisdiction. It allows local governments to systematically estimate and track greenhouse gas emissions from energy, transportation, and waste-related activities at a communitywide scale as well as at a municipal or county level. The inventory forecast predicts emissions for a target year using population, employment, transportation, and other relevant data projections.

ICLEI's Cities for Sustainable Community Protection or other accepted inventory methodologies and software form the basis for creating an emissions forecast and reduction target, and enable the quantification of emissions reductions associated with implemented and proposed measures. Emissions inventories are typically organized into four categories: transportation, energy efficiency, renewable energy, and solid waste management, though water also can be included.

Figure 2-4
A high-tech tool such as Community Viz by Placeways, LLC allows the creation of 3D scenarios that describe the impacts of alternative development strategies. *Aviva Johnson, Placeways, LLC*

Typically designed as a spreadsheet connected to a database, an emission modeling tool can estimate greenhouse gas emissions and reduction potentials for various scenarios. For example, ICLEI's Climate and Air Pollution Planning Assistant (CAPPA), an Excel-based decision support tool, will calculate greenhouse gas emissions, establish targets to lower emissions, and monitor, measure, and report ongoing performance.

LOW- /NO-TECH TOOLS

Good planning communication requires appropriate conveyance mediums, applications, and content. While both high-tech communication tools and techniques help engage, educate, and build relationships with those who might impact or be impacted by the plan—the stakeholders—relatively low-tech, low-cost communication tools can create shifts in peoples' thinking and behavior. Use the cell phone for community polling on proposed actions; the homemade Wii remote, a handheld, 3D pointing device that can illustrate actions on projected maps; and simple Internet connections employing Skype's free software for audio/visual communications platforms between team members, staff, and the public.

As long as communities continue to vote with wallets and feet, low-tech and qualitative assessment tools may offer solutions sufficient for local decision-making. Choosing time-tested energy and environmentally efficient plans, codes, transportation networks, and buildings may offer the most efficacious set of remedies that require the fewest software "runs." The spreadsheet still provides a ubiquitous means to propose multiple variables and values and iteratively compute the various outcomes.

The team should always maintain the ability to improvise in the event of a power or equipment failure that undermines the carefully organized digital presentation. Projector malfunctions, broken power and Internet connections, laptop crashes, and lost data follow accidents, brownouts, or intense solar flares. Good preparation should include contingency planning even when extension cords go missing from that equipment box.

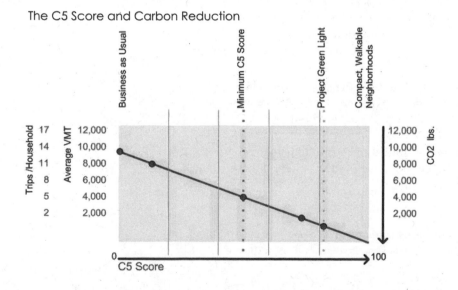

The C5 Score and Carbon Reduction

Figure 2-5
The "C5" place-performance scoring system, a low-tech tool by Townworks + DPZ, assesses five key measures of sustainability: how connected, compact, complete, complex, and convivial is your community or neighborhood?
Stephen Coyle

DATA QUALITY

The quality of tools, like energy assessment software, depends on the quality of data upon which the measured information is based. This data varies with the scale of the measurements or modeling, and on the assumed impacts and implications, intended and otherwise, resulting from the actions proposed. None of the tools are comprehensive enough to assess the impacts of transforming high-carbon, nonresilient development patterns into low-carbon resiliency. However, some mapping tools will illustrate and compare the variations in measured/modeled emissions from household motor vehicle trips across neighborhoods and regions.[2]

While modeling tools can predict with reasonable accuracy the energy return on money invested in alternative renewable energy sources like solar, none incorporate the cost and availability of nonrenewable energy required to produce and maintain the alternatives, a key externality.

Step Five: Prepare the Place

EXISTING CONDITIONS RESEARCH

Research the place to develop a situational understanding of the existing built environment, and the physical, social, aesthetic, and functional attributes, showing patterns, scale, and features. A rigorous investigative process is necessary to explore and evaluate the efficacy of the existing conditions, both quantitatively and qualitatively. The information should be formatted and organized by each team member relative to their area of expertise and assembled into a master document in an easily accessible and adjustable format.

PROJECT BOUNDARIES

With the jurisdiction's direction, clearly define and document the project's physical, economic, and other **boundaries.** Then clarify what will *not* be attempted or included in the project. Often, the jurisdiction's policies, activities, and impacts will extend outside of the political or geographical boundaries, so a decision relative to the breadth and depth of the plans should be made as early as possible in the project.

Within the boundaries, research the supporting systems to develop an understanding of each, quantitatively and qualitatively. The investigation should study the relationships of each of the parts to the whole built environment, and identify the opportunities and constraints.

The research should yield an opportunities and constraints matrix of the existing built environment and supporting systems, and produce the preliminary benchmarks necessary to begin to develop the plan.

BUILT ENVIRONMENT INVESTIGATIONS

Depending on the scale of the project, focus research on buildings, lots, and block patterns, rights-of-way and corridors, neighborhoods, districts, communities, and regions.

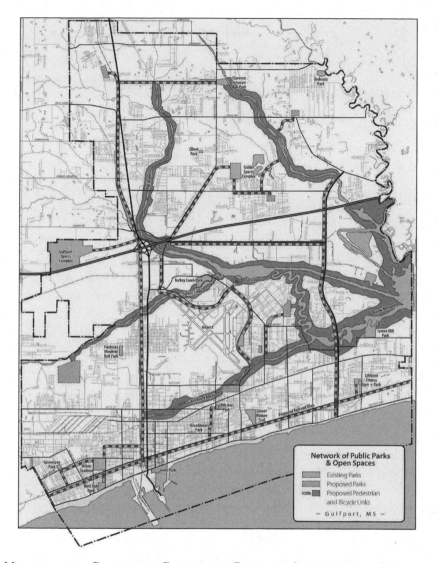

THE MUNICIPAL AND COMMUNITY GREENHOUSE EMISSIONS INVENTORY AND FORECAST

An emissions inventory estimates the amount of greenhouse gas emitted to and removed from the atmosphere by human activities within the jurisdictional boundaries. It establishes a baseline of greenhouse gas emissions to calculate proposed reduction measures against current emissions and to track the progress following the implementation of those interventions, and to better understand the sources and emission trends. The inventory combines emissions from multiple greenhouse gases into a single weighted value of emissions, the amount of equivalent carbon dioxide, or CO_2e.

An emissions forecast projects the inventory results into the future using several sources, including population and economic growth data, projections of changes in vehicle miles, electricity and other energy consumption, and other appropriate growth factors. A typical forecast might target emission at year 2020,

2030, and 2050, sector-by-sector. These future emissions are projected in the absence of any policies or actions that would reduce emissions and are based on practices of "business-as-usual." The resulting estimates are compared to the baseline emissions to determine the total reductions desired. More information on the greenhouse gas inventory can be found in Chapter 3: The Physical Built Environment.

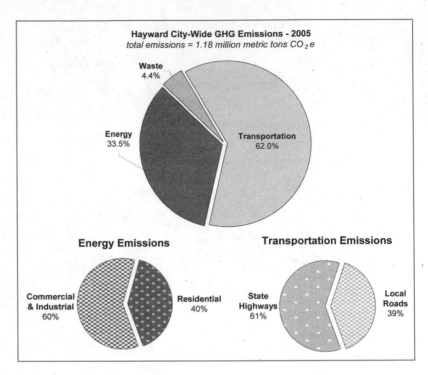

REVIEW OF THE JURISDICTIONAL GENERAL PLAN AND CODES

Review those sections of a regional, county, township, or municipal general or comprehensive plan and the codes, (the *development and building standards*, statutes, zoning ordinances, or other measures for implementing the general plan) that will directly impact or be impacted by the sustainability plan.

Subsequent to the review, the urban planning/coding team member should complete the following:

1. Identify potential weak, incomplete, or outdated polices, ordinances, and standards in the general or comprehensive plan and code for subsequent modifications or amendments.

2. Facilitate a means to compare and provide consistency between the set of proposed interventions or actions with the existing policies and codes.

3. Create a platform to upgrade the general or comprehensive plan and code, as a seamless part of the overall community plan, or deliver a set of recommendations.

Proposed general plan modifications:

- Incorporate any changes into the sustainability plan as a stand-alone set of policy recommendations for future adoption as a general plan amendment or update.

- Integrate a guiding policy into each appropriate element of the general plan. Inconsistencies with the existing general plan may be subsequently amended or updated.

- Include an amendment or update process as part of a concurrent general or comprehensive plan.

Proposed jurisdictional code modifications:

- Incorporate amendments into the sustainability plan as a set of requirements that replace the existing codes.

Figure 2-7
Hayward, California's Climate Action Plan, final 11-6-09 version, summarizes the City and community's Greenhouse Gas Inventory Results for the base year 2005. *City of Hayward, California, Climate Action Plan*

- Integrate changes into each appropriate element of the sustainability plan so that each relevant action is empowered by a code requirement.
- Incorporate into the sustainability plan as a set of code recommendations for a future code amendment or update.
- Include proposed changes as part of a concurrent code amendment or update process.

Appendix H: Recommended Changes Municipal Code

Hayward's Municipal Code, in relation to the climate change plan, is intended to achieve the following relevant goals:

- To protect the public health, safety, and welfare of the citizens of the City of Hayward;
- To gain compliance with state Codes, ordinances, and regulations in a timely and efficient manner.

This sections lists a number of recommended changes to the Municipal Code to successfully:

- Address the CAP's environmental, social and economic goals relative to applicable sections of the Code.
- Describe Climate Change Plan-applicable laws and ordinances for reducing greenhouse gas (GHG) emissions and its reliance on non-renewable resources for existing and future development.

The recommended changes impact the following sections of the Municipal Code:

Chapter 10: Article 1 – Zoning Ordinance
Chapter 10: Article 2 – Off Street Parking Regulations
Chapter 10: Article 3 – Subdivision Ordinance
Chapter 10: Article 11 – Historic Preservation

The general regulations apply to all districts and to all uses permitted in the districts. The provisions are intended to amplify and to supplement district regulations. In the event of conflict with the specific district regulations, whichever regulations are more restrictive shall apply, unless otherwise determined by the Planning Director.

Recommended Changes to Chapter 10: Article 1 - Zoning Ordinance

Municipal Code Section	Recommended Change
Sec. 10-1.2720 Special Lot Requirements a. Minimum Lot Frontage Except as provided herein, each lot shall have a minimum frontage of 35 feet.	1. In order to allow a wider range of housing, permit narrow lots for single-family detached homes that are alley-loaded, including reduced lot size widths of 30 feet for detached housing and 18 feet for vertically attached housing. Attached town homes or condos are allowed to have narrow lots (no min. specified in Code).
Yard Exceptions - Accessory Buildings and Uses (1) In conjunction with single-family development located on parcels zoned for same, and in zoning districts where single-family homes are permitted: (a) Accessory buildings not used for parking and not exceeding 14 feet in height and 120 square feet in area and detached from the main buildings, when located in area other than the required front yard (i.e., in side or rear yard area), shall be placed no closer than 3 feet from the side and rear property lines.	2. In order to facilitate the addition of more cost-effective housing, correlate the allowable height and area of Accessory Buildings with the lot size, using the overall lot coverage and rear and side setbacks as determinants, to permit large units on larger lots.
q. Front Yards - Driveway Width and Coverage (1) Driveway width, regardless of the number of driveways, shall not exceed 20 feet in front of the garage, except for 3-car garages where the width shall not exceed 26 feet. In addition, for access to a recreational vehicle storage area adjacent to a dwelling, a maximum 10-foot-wide driveway may be located on the opposite	3. In order to reduce the amount of impervious and low albedo surfaces, limit driveway widths to 18 feet for impervious paving, with exceptions for greater width only for pervious paving materials approved by the City Building Official, aesthetics notwithstanding.

Figure 2-8
The Hayward Climate Action Plan recommends changes to the City's Municipal Code to improve environmental, energy, and economic performance. *City of Hayward, California, Climate Action Plan*

GENERAL SUPPORTING SYSTEMS RESEARCH

Once the steps discussed above have been performed, the team will investigate and collect data relevant to the development of the plan's supporting systems as each relates to the development of plan strategies and tactics, including reports, studies, and other sources of information.

The following types of specific data should be collected and reviewed:

1. *Transportation:* Review community and regional contextual transportation conditions, patterns, and modes including the amount, origination, types, and frequency of vehicle miles traveled daily for public and private motor vehicles. Include the amount of transit ridership, commuter biking, and pedestrian-accessibility to daily destinations. Research the convenience, safety, and attractiveness of streets for pedestrians, bikes, transit, and motor vehicles, and the level of congestion-reducing infrastructure such as signal coordination. Develop a circulation analysis to identify opportunities and constraints to increase connectivity, pedestrian improvements, and alternative transportation amenities for all mobility modes.

2. *Energy:* Research indirect and direct community energy sources, performance, and conditions, including building, infrastructure, and equipment energy consumption, and other direct and indirect sources, and existing and proposed energy conservation and efficiency measures. Gross energy demand data, rather than more detailed data developed from an assessor's parcel data, should be used to develop the energy profile.

3. *Water:* Research community water demand in the local or regional water management plan or program, including existing water conservation and efficiency measures.

4. *Natural Environment:* Review the community's plan and/or programs to protect and enhance biodiversity, including reports, studies, and other sources of information. Assess the impacts including climate and noise; cultural and biological resources; and geology, soils, and geohazards.

5. *Food Production/Agriculture:* Review the community's agricultural policies, plan, and/or programs for the protection and enhancement of agriculture both within and immediately surrounding the community.

6. *Solid Waste:* Research the jurisdiction's waste management system, including landfills, transfer stations, and waste processing and handling facilities, and demographic conditions affecting the waste stream trends, including residential, commercial, and industrial customers.

7. *Economic Conditions:* Research the jurisdiction's economic background reports, development strategies, industry and market studies, and relevant capital improvement plans and financing programs. At a minimum, research three conditions:

   - *Businesses:* Evaluate the community's economic data and employment position within the greater region, and the local economy's existing strengths, synergies, and competitive advantages and disadvantages moving forward. This analysis should include private employers—small and large—and institutional employers like universities and hospitals. Identify existing and emerging industry clusters to guide the plan's economic development strategy.

- *Residents:* Study the relationship between local jobs and housing, which may include the community's jobs-housing balance, the match between resident skills and local jobs, and commuting patterns. In areas of substantial work trips, study local, noncommutational trips by auto, transit, and other modes.
- *Finances:* Analyze the community's current fiscal position and diversity of revenue sources to understand the balance between different land uses and their contribution to the jurisdiction's general fund, using quantitative and qualitative baseline measures of success for each.

RESEARCH COMPILATION AND ANALYSIS

Based on the research and findings, the team typically prepares the following documentation:

1. A Strength and Weakness/Opportunities and Constraints analysis, categorically
2. A quantitative compilation of the built environment, and the supporting systems
3. A qualitative summary of the findings about the built environment and each supporting system

The research and analysis yields the essential information and situational or contextual understanding of the place sufficient to move to the development of goals and objectives.

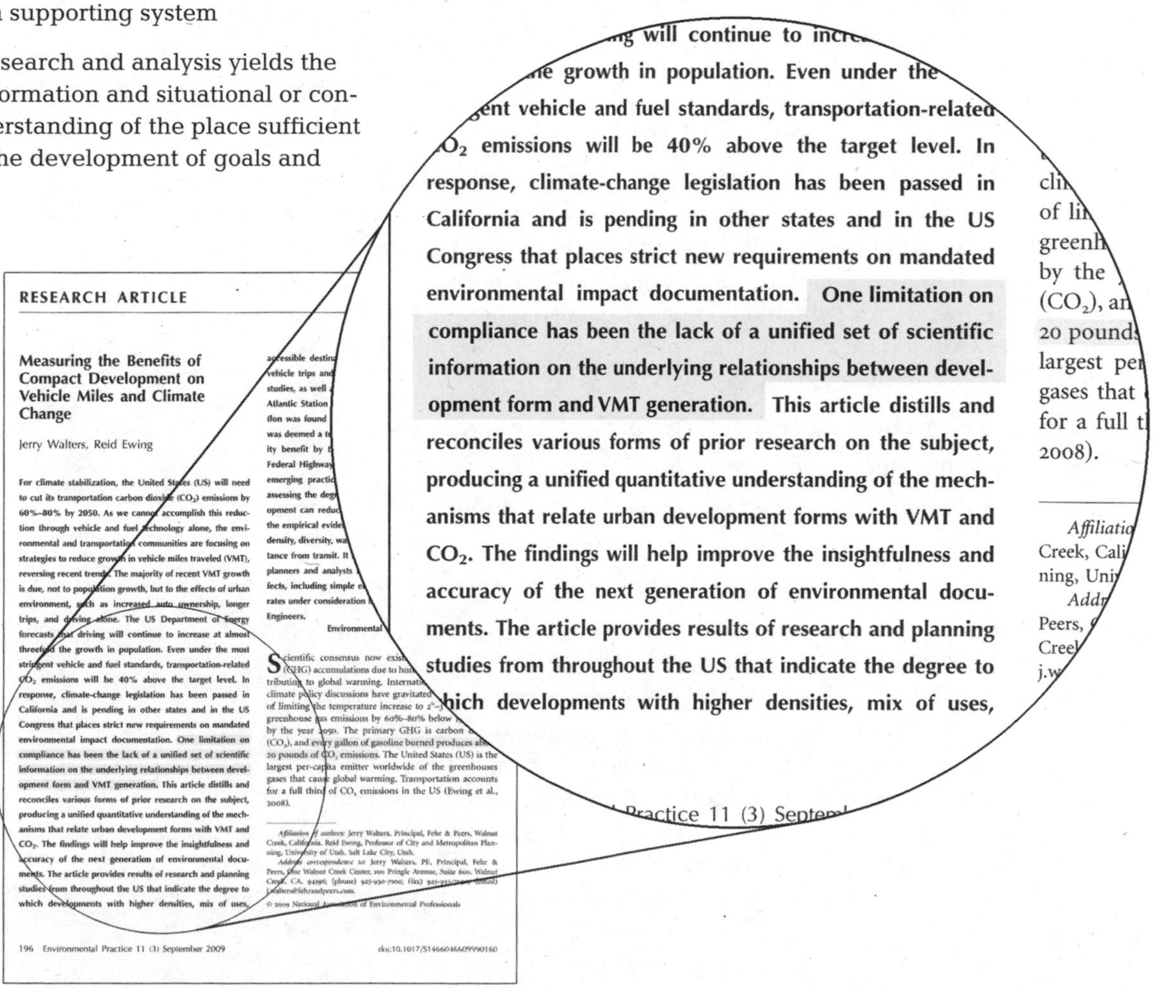

RESEARCH ARTICLE

Measuring the Benefits of Compact Development on Vehicle Miles and Climate Change

Jerry Walters, Reid Ewing

For climate stabilization, the United States (US) will need to cut its transportation carbon dioxide (CO_2) emissions by 60%–80% by 2050. As we cannot accomplish this reduction through vehicle and fuel technology alone, the environmental and transportation communities are focusing on strategies to reduce growth in vehicle miles traveled (VMT), reversing recent trends. The majority of recent VMT growth is due, not to population growth, but to the effects of urban environment, such as increased auto ownership, longer trips, and driving alone. The US Department of Energy forecasts that driving will continue to increase at almost threefold the growth in population. Even under the most stringent vehicle and fuel standards, transportation-related CO_2 emissions will be 40% above the target level. In response, climate-change legislation has been passed in California and is pending in other states and in the US Congress that places strict new requirements on mandated environmental impact documentation. One limitation on compliance has been the lack of a unified set of scientific information on the underlying relationships between development form and VMT generation. This article distills and reconciles various forms of prior research on the subject, producing a unified quantitative understanding of the mechanisms that relate urban development forms with VMT and CO_2. The findings will help improve the insightfulness and accuracy of the next generation of environmental documents. The article provides results of research and planning studies from throughout the US that indicate the degree to which developments with higher densities, mix of uses,

196 Environmental Practice 11 (3) September 2009

Figure 2-9
A research article, "Measuring the Benefits of Compact Development on Vehicle Miles and Climate Change," describes the high-leverage relationship between the form of development and travel behavior. *Jerry Walters and Reid Ewing, Environmental Practice, September 11, 2009*

Step Six: Prepare the People

The people preparation phase begins by employing one of two approaches for developing action plans:

1. "The black box" method consists of participation limited to jurisdictional staff, consultants, and others deemed strictly essential to drafting the plan. Though the legal adoption process typically requires one or more public hearings, it may not demand "public involvement." The military or other organizations requiring restricted involvement might choose the black box approach.

2. "The public involvement process" describes the practice of engaging "stakeholders"—anyone who can influence, impact or be impacted by the plan, and general interested citizenry.

Though the choice between the two rests with local officials, most regional, community, or neighborhood plans benefit from involving a diversity of stakeholders (e.g., residents, businesses, and agencies). Planning for sustainability requires sufficient citizen participation for both plan-making and to maintain support throughout implementation.

SECURING COMMUNITY REPRESENTATION

The people preparation process should compel the public to exchange information critical to the project, empower them to make or recommend good choices, and support actions that don't necessarily reflect their preferred selections. Address the most significant challenge in public engagement: gathering credible input over the course of the project from a sufficiently representative sampling of stakeholders. Though largely citizen based, community planning often relies on those citizens who may not represent the broader community:

1. Those with a direct personal, commercial, or political stake in the outcome;

2. Those attempting to control or direct the outcome;

3. Those citizens with the time and inclination to attend public forums and public hearings;

4. Those with a stake in one part of the plan but with little concern for the whole.

By selecting citizens at random for participation in the input and deliberative process, the team can secure a more diverse and comprehensive cross-section of community representation. Depending on the size of the budget and sample, the results of a random engagement should provide a relatively accurate picture of community sentiments, albeit less than a scientific representation of the entire public's considered opinion on plan-making. Besides its ability to involve those without a direct interest in the outcome, the random or stratified sample can gain a proportional representation of citizens who usually avoid public events: youth, minorities, and others who either will not or cannot participate.

STAKEHOLDER ENGAGEMENT PLAN

Consider a two-pronged approach when gathering stakeholders:

1. Deploy a random sample of citizens able to participate in the investigation and deliberation process using the Internet, phone calls, and face-to-face surveys and interviews, and/or enlisting a diverse group of citizens to participate in a project advisory council or commission. This secures a more diverse and comprehensive cross-section of community representation.

2. Concurrently, seek as wide and diverse participation as possible, and directly engage those willing to participate, treating all willing or eager to engage with the same respect and consideration.

If the jurisdiction employs a "sustainable project manager," this individual may lead or at least assist in the people preparation process. One outcome of the preparation could include the procurement of this position during the initial engagement effort.

STAKEHOLDER ENGAGEMENT PROCESS

The engagement process consists of the following actions:

1. Develop and update a comprehensive stakeholder identification list that describes the name, contact information, and specific stake or position relative to the project of people capable of supporting or resisting the planning process.

2. Complete a stakeholder engagement plan with the assistance of the jurisdiction, and refine and update it during the planning process. The plan should describe the most effective means to engage the stakeholders and maintain their involvement throughout the project, including the need for bilingual members who can communicate with non-English-speaking stakeholders.

3. Create a public relations and promotion plan that includes developing media strategies and tactics and drafting the first press release.

4. If politically or technically essential, help organize an action plan management or advisory commission or committee composed of representative stakeholders to guide the process through the arc of the project.

5. Develop and launch an interactive project website with a concise project description, questionnaire, and an introduction to jurisdictions' participating staff members and consulting team. The posting should describe, in text and graphics, the process and desired outcomes.

6. Hold confidential interviews with key stakeholders, including jurisdictional officials, to explore planning goals, ideas, issues, and concerns, and build trust. Omit attributions unless permitted while sharing key concerns and the apparent support for or resistance to the effort.

7. Identify, clarify, and prioritize long-term goals and interim objectives, and develop measures for evaluating estimated performance of strategies that emerge during the project. Place each goal and objective into its appropriate category—energy, economic, transportation, and so on.

8. Prepare a promotional-quality, two-sided flyer with a project description and questionnaire on the back. Ask no more than four questions if written comments are solicited. Distribute printed flyers through the jurisdiction's departments, civic, and business organizations, and concurrently, post the flyer on the website.

9. Indentify, engage, and support project champions, unelected and/or elected, willing and capable of helping lead the community and build support for the process and the outcomes.

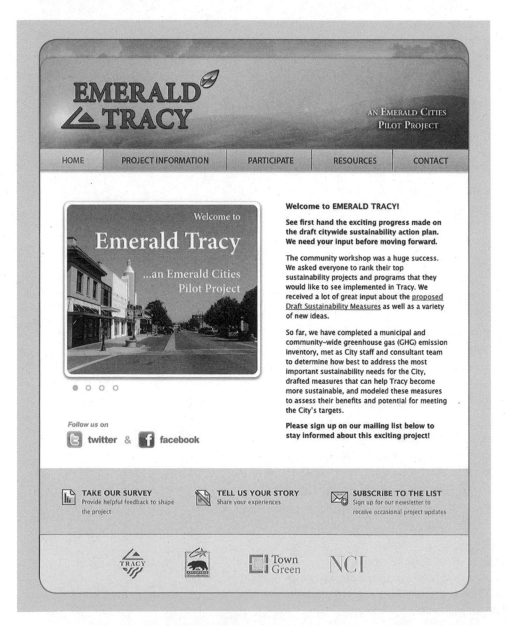

Figure 2-10
The Emerald Tracy website for Tracy, California's sustainable action plan uses the open source web software Drupal to maximize user accessibility. *City of Tracy, California*

RANDOM STAKEHOLDER ENGAGEMENT

If the engagement process includes a random or stratified sample of citizen participation:

1. Gather information from the participants through a one-time or periodic process, based on a series of questions and opportunity for comments using surveys or interviews;

2. Enlist willing participants to engage in the planning process and include opinion polling at critical decision points in the process. Encourage attendance and feedback at workshops or other key public events, and provide briefings and documents to the public and make them available to the press as well.

3. Prepare a survey that targets and captures the appropriate population segment. The process may be limited to a Web-based survey and random telephone interviews or include interviews and meetings, depending on the political and social context and budget.

4. Compile and sort the results into a database with Web responses and summaries of responses to telephone surveys. The telephone survey, though limited, will provide an alternative to those who may not have Web access. Common concerns and frequently asked questions can be included in hard-copy newsletters, printed and circulated at community events or gathering areas.

5. Periodically report results to the jurisdiction of the survey and questionnaires, and incorporate into a Web-post summary with both text and graphic representations of preferences, trends, and opinions.

WEB ENGAGEMENT

If the engagement process includes surveys and other interactive elements, consider developing and hosting an interactive project website, employing a user-friendly format such as Drupal.[3] The advantages to a jurisdictional website include the following:

1. The Web content can be quickly updated by nontechnical staff using simple instructions;

2. The Web provides the jurisdiction with a secure online project website, and gives their staff with a convenient means for content control;

3. The team can develop, launch, and modify the website without the use of specialized programming language or the need to assess a webmaster for each update. This allows maximum flexibility and security for interactive Web activities.

4. The team maintains the website for the duration of the project and then turns it over to the jurisdiction for hosting or incorporation into their specific website.

   The Web pages might be organized or subdivided as follows:

   Project Overview

   Goals, Objectives, and Performance Measures

   News and Updates—dynamically generated, but only headlines and teasers

Current Jurisdictional Efforts

Process and Schedule

Online Surveys and Questionnaires

Downloads

Consulting Team

Proposed Strategies, Policies, Programs, and Actions

Draft and Final Plans and Comment on Draft

Comment Forms

General Feedback

Project Contacts

Ways to Assist

Champions—Individuals/Residents, Businesses

Links to Resources

PUBLIC ENGAGEMENT AND EDUCATION VENUES

THE PUBLIC WORKSHOP

The public workshop, held during evening hours or preferably a Saturday morning, is a team-led event which provides a great way to engage the public directly and facilitate an educational exchange. Introduce the project, the people, the tools, the timelines, and the major milestones. Describe the communication protocols, procedures for notifications and documentation, and explanation of goals, objectives, and "performance measures" necessary to evaluate proposed ideas and strategies. Finally, the workshop offers the public an opportunity to brainstorm ideas, discover common ground and differences, and begin a fair and equitable resolution process.

Three simple ways to attract attendees are as follows:

1. Invite a "featured speaker" to kick off the event;
2. Host a panel of articulate stakeholder representatives to discuss relevant issues;
3. Focus on those relevant topics. For example, economic health issues may attract far more interest than environmental concerns.

The best workshops, after the initial introductions, housekeeping, and speakers, break the assembled participants into groups of 10 or less, a threshold size for eliciting questions and comments from those uncomfortable with speaking publically, followed by a reporting out and comparison of the results. Hosting two events on the development of a sustainability plan is usually sufficient to raise awareness and elicit feedback. The first public engagement includes a brainstorming session to gather ideas for building resilience and reducing fossil-fuel dependency. This tees up the second workshop, an opportunity for the participants' evaluation and discussion of proposed action measures.

Figure 2-11
The best public involvement process actively engages a diversity of stakeholders in the planning process. During a charrette workshop, Steve Coyle leads stakeholder groups through a design exercise. *Stephen Coyle*

THE PUBLIC CHARRETTE

The National Charrette Institute (NCI) Charrette System™, a results-based, accelerated, collaborative planning system, spans the entire engagement, educational, and project time horizon. It employs a multiple-day, collaborative process as an extended transformational event that harnesses the talents and energies of all interested parties to create and support a feasible plan for a resilient/low-carbon built environment. The charrette provides the maximum opportunity to work with the public "at the table" through multiple highly organized iterative feedback loops that will culminate in a plan that reflects a high degree of community authorship.

For a two-charrette or extended workshop alternative, in the first event, "out of the box" ideas are considered and tested, giving the public an opportunity to explore options without the risk of "locking" into one approach or another. The second event focuses on plan refinement, while the time between permits critical research and analysis.

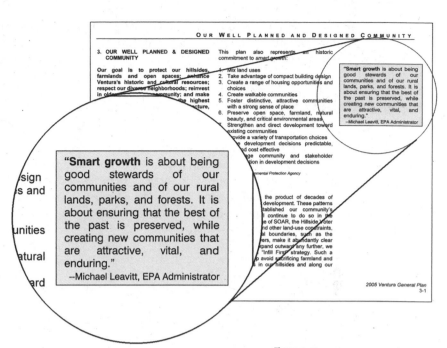

Figure 2-12

A community goal for the City of Ventura general plan includes the promotion of the principles of smart growth. *City of Ventura General Plan, Ventura, California*

DIGITAL PARTICIPATION

The public workshop can include external website participation through standard video connections and polling devices. A digital audio/visual (A/V) program like Skype allows remote participation by key individuals and organizations with just laptops, pug-in speakers, a webcam, and a digital projector for audience viewing. A booth erected for community events allows face-to-face polling, recorded via laptop audio, for feedback on proposed actions.

In fact, A/V connections can be deployed across a community to allow groups of stakeholders to collaborate in the planning process without traveling, drawing rural residents, senior citizens, and otherwise "offline audiences" into the process. This increases the likelihood that people will offer meaningful input.

EQUITABLE DECISION-MAKING

Community residents and other public and private citizens may not easily reach consensus regarding the development of the plan unless differences are resolved through a fair and transparent decision-making process. Cynicism, mistrust, and deeper disagreements may erode participation and undermine support for the plan's adoption.

By the establishment of a set of core goals and objectives that are both quantitative and qualitative, the team can design a framework capable of evaluating the performance of proposed interventions that can allow the stakeholders to measure the impacts against the benefits and drawbacks, iteratively. The alternatives can be prioritized or simply scored, with a subsequent decision by a jurisdictionally appointed or elected body.

Step Seven: Develop Goals, Objectives, and Performance Measures

The goals, objectives, and performance measures should be developed, ratified, and revisited throughout the plan-making process. Methods for obtaining the information include questionnaires, surveys, and interviews described earlier, with periodic updates at key planning milestones. Generally, jurisdictional staff tasked with developing the plan initiates the goal- and objective-setting process, assisted by the consulting team.

EXAMPLE OF CONCEPTUAL GOALS

- Achieve economic, environmental, and social health and resilience
- Reduce vehicle miles traveled
- Decrease the carbon-intensity of vehicles
- Improve the energy performance of existing and new buildings
- Develop renewable energy sources
- Increase waste reduction and recycling
- Sequester carbon in open spaces
- Engage and educate the community

DEVELOP GOALS AND OBJECTIVES

Start by asking the jurisdiction and community the following:

1. What are the goals, generally and categorically? The goals should describe a desired outcome or end result such as building community-wide environmental—air, water, and soils—health.

2. What are the **objectives**? The objectives should describe achievable, specific results, or intermediate steps necessary to attain the goals within a set time span, such as reducing community-wide greenhouse gas emissions 25 percent by 2030 from current rates, or securing 20 percent of energy from renewable sources. The objectives are sometimes referred to as targets.

3. What are the **performance criteria** or **metrics** necessary to measure the qualitative and quantitative potential for proposed strategies, programs, and other remedies? For example, greenhouse gas emissions are typically measured as CO_2e emissions, and fossil fuels can be calculated as electric power in kilowatt (kW) hours/year from nonrenewable resources.

Distill the goals and objectives into a vision or mission statement as the "message." For example, "Our neighborhood, community, or region will, over time, achieve full dependency on, and support and enhance the health of our renewable resources—biological, land, water, air, energy, and people." Since the objectives and performance measures are often technical, such as improving energy efficiency in public facilities, the appropriate level of expertise (e.g., a facility engineer) should be included in the goal and measure-setting process.

Each desired outcome, target, and performance indicator should be reviewed and critiqued by the stakeholders, from elected officials to impacted citizens though some goals, objectives, and measures may reflect statutory requirements. For example, California's Assembly Bill 32, the Global Warming Solutions Act of 2006, codified statewide greenhouse gas emissions—CO_2e—reduction goals. If necessary, revise or refine objectives (e.g., deadlines, target numbers) during the planning as actions are proposed, evaluated against targets and performance measures, and accepted, modified, or eliminated.

SETTING TARGETS

Goals require milestones to evaluate progress over time. Clearly defined jurisdictional targets provide decision-makers with both direction and political cover. Long-term targets should include milestones to drive immediate actions, such as California's goal of reducing statewide GHG emissions to 80 percent below 1990 level by 2050, and 15 percent by 2020. This clearly defined emissions reduction goal defines the target, provides a quantifiable result, and states a specific time period for achieving the goal.

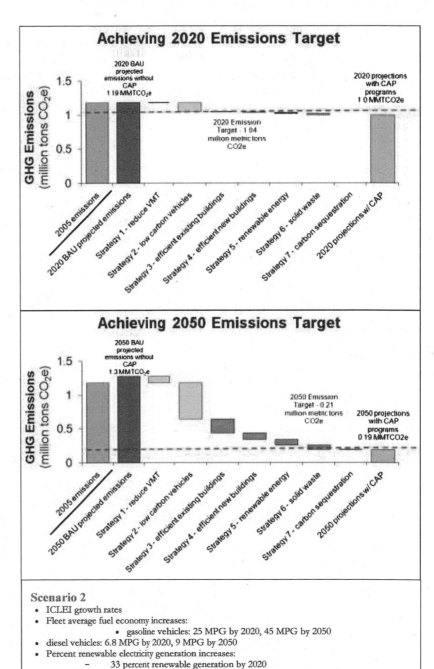

Scenario 2
- ICLEI growth rates
- Fleet average fuel economy increases:
    - gasoline vehicles: 25 MPG by 2020, 45 MPG by 2050
- diesel vehicles: 6.8 MPG by 2020, 9 MPG by 2050
- Percent renewable electricity generation increases:
    - 33 percent renewable generation by 2020
    - 40 percent renewable generation by 2050.

Figure 2-13
The Hayward Climate Action Plan set greenhouse gas emission targets for years 2020 and 2050. *City of Hayward, California, Climate Action Plan*

Targets are useful only if and when a community commits to their achievement through action. Without effective, implementable action plans, goals and objectives become little more than wish lists. Targets require a starting line. One example, the GHG emissions baseline inventory, estimates CO_2e emissions for the base or starting year. The inventory calculates total jurisdiction and community emissions by source, establishing evidence to compare current and target emissions. With a baseline inventory, the jurisdiction sets reasonable reduction targets and prioritizes actions to reduce emissions.

Figure 2-14
An "action sheet" describes the features, benefits, and costs of a Safe Routes to School Program. *Stephen Coyle*

DEVELOPING QUANTITATIVE AND QUALITATIVE PERFORMANCE MEASURES

Greenhouse gas emissions, the primary coin of the climate change realm, comprise the metric for quantifying the anthropogenic causes of climate change. A proverb warns, **"We almost always get what we measure."** Comprehensive evaluation of proposed remedies warrants both appropriate qualitative and quantitative measurements. For example, reductions in building energy and tail pipe emissions employ CO_2e in metric tons as a measure of carbon emission. However ubiquitous, CO_2e represents a single performance metric. For example, though electric vehicles reduce CO_2e, their proliferation could increase auto dependency, reduce walkability, and increase childhood obesity.

The goal of "walkability" requires a quantitative and qualitative assessment of pedestrian mobility, for example:

- Quantified in terms of the walking environment: the presence of safe and attractive streets and paths, maximum block lengths or street connectivity, and the location, diversity, and frequency of destinations—shops, parks, and schools
- Qualitatively, walkability is "the extent to which the built environment is friendly to the presence of people living, shopping, visiting, enjoying or spending time in an area."[4]

Since meeting qualitative targets may be difficult to verify, always include objective criteria. For example, achieving a "sense of place" downtown can be partly quantified as the visual enclosure of public space at a minimum building height to street width ratio of about 1:3.

Step Eight: Develop the Strategies

Develop the jurisdictional and communitywide strategies, policies, codes, programs, tools, and techniques for the built environment and each supporting system to achieve the goals and objectives. Concurrently, assemble a list of performance criteria or metrics for evaluating the efficacy of each proposed action.

DRAFT PRELIMINARY ACTIONS

For each stated goal and objective, generate a draft list of proposed measures, beginning by asking the following questions:

1. What existing actions are already underway by the jurisdiction? These interventions can serve as a starting point for identifying new measures, and as a means to expand, leverage, or improve existing actions.

Categories:

Transportation
Built Environment

 Safe Routes to School Program

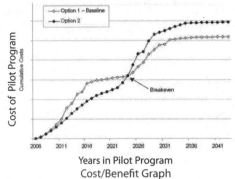

Years in Pilot Program
Cost/Benefit Graph

Description

Safe Routes to School consists of an international, national and State program that increases the number of children who walk or bicycle to school by funding projects that remove the barriers that currently prevent them from doing so within a collaborative community framework.

Those barriers include real and perceived safety, lack of infrastructure (e.g., no crosswalks), unsafe infrastructure (e.g., walkways invisible from the street), and lack of programs that promote walking and bicycling through education encouragement programs aimed at children, parents, and the community. Most students can easily walk a mile and bike up to 3 miles, depending on age, location, and fitness.

Supports Goal/Objectives

Reduce VMT of passenger vehicles to 30 percent below business-as-usual projections by 2030

Conceptual Strategy

Reduce motor vehicle miles traveled (VMT)

Performance Characteristics

GHG Emissions Reductions: From 2-6% of Community Transportation Emissions from private vehicles, and .02% from dedicated bus transit.

Potential Synergism

The Program can or should be coordinated with transportation demand management programs that address traffic calming, "intelligent" signalization, and similar improvements to the safety, convenience, and efficiency for pedestrians, bikers, and motorists.

Implementation Time

The Program can be planned and implemented with six to nine months, if necessary mprovements are limited to crosswalk striping and other adminstrative actions.

Benefits

1. The program has been widely used throughout the US with demonstrated success.
2. Walking or biking to school decreases both private and public motor vehicle use and related costs, and improves health by increasing walking which reduces childhood obesity.
3. Gradually increasing fuel costs will incentivize support for the progam.
4. Reducing VMT will result in a smaller amount of fuel burned within

Drawbacks

1. Without supportive infrastructure and adequate, demonstrated security, a proposed program will flounder.
2. The program will not function in suburban development patterns with remote school locations, or schools built beyond neighborhoods and other urbanized areas.

First Costs

Majority of cost result from the removal of physical, regulatory barriers. Cost depends on the following pirmary variables:
1. Number of schools considered
2. Distance from school to students' residences
3. Route(s) physical, security, and social conditions, and existing transit service
4. Cost of infrastructure improvements

Estimated costs of at least $50,000 and up for a pilot program, depending on grants and efforts required to create safe routes to school, and the number, location, the surrounding circulation context, and types of schools.

Life Cycle Costs

Estimated $50,000 and up, depending on grants and efforts required to create safe routes to school, and the number, location, the surrounding circulation context, and types of schools.
1. Decrease in auto and bus costs
2. Decrease in health-related student care

2. What are the potential "big picture" **strategies** for achieving the goals and objectives? Each strategy should describe a method for achieving one or more particular objectives:

- Develop a freshwater conservation strategy to help save water and energy, preparing the community for any potential decrease in the water supply.

- Develop strategies to reduce vehicle miles traveled (VMT) and reduce emissions per mile traveled, through a combination of policies, codes, plans, programs, and best practices that increase the use and convenience of public transportation, bicycling, and walking.

3. What are the **policies** that could lead to achieving the objectives and goals? These policies could modify or replace existing ones, and enable changes in the municipal codes.

- Neighborhoods shall not be bisected by a significant physical barrier, such as an arterial street, a railroad track, or a major drainage way.

- Encourage infill development on vacant and underutilized commercial and industrial areas through regulatory (e.g., zoning, development standards) and economic incentives.

4. What are the **codes** or zoning ordinances necessary to achieve the objectives? These codes could modify or replace existing ones, and might necessitate policy changes for consistency.

- Permit compatible live-work occupancies in existing neighborhoods at the corners of arterial and collector streets.

- On-street parking shall be required on a minimum of 80 percent of the length of both sides of all new streets including the project side of bordering streets.

5. What are some potential **plans** and **projects** that could manifest the codes as specific site and/or building designs?

- Develop a mixed-use, corridor redevelopment plan that incorporates the new pedestrian street standards.

- Create a public/private renewable energy project for achieving a measurable reduction in kW consumption.

6. What are the **programs** required to achieve the objectives? A specific program could result from a recommended policy and code, or emerge as an independent action that supports the goals and objectives.

- Institute a "Safe Route to Schools" program to promote walking and biking to school through education and incentives that provide safer and more pedestrian-friendly streets.

- Create a comprehensive "Transportation Demand Management" (TDM) program for new projects that reduces weekday peak period motor vehicle trips consistent with project objectives.

Figure 2-15
A public planning process should empower the participants to develop, present, and assess potential alternatives. *Stephen Coyle*

7. What are the **best practices** that could deliver the most efficient and effective results? The best practices could result in modifications or replacements to the jurisdiction's codes and practices.

- Implement a stormwater retention best management practice (BMP) that consists of pervious pavement systems and rain gardens designed to drain down within 24 hours.
- Limit new construction on slopes no greater than 15 percent, and avoid disturbing portions of project sites that have preproject slopes greater than 15 percent.

DEVELOP EVALUATIVE CRITERIA

The draft list of proposed measures should include a simple description of each, and an order-of-magnitude estimate of the expected benefits and drawbacks. If not completed in the Goal, Objectives, and Performance Measures, develop a set of qualitative and quantitative measures and metrics to enable an objectives assessment of each proposed intervention. For example:

QUANTITATIVE CRITERIA

1. GHG emission in CO_2e metric tons;
2. *Energy savings:* Estimated kW/hours saved annually following implementation;
3. *VMT and VT/D reductions:* Reductions in vehicle miles traveled and vehicle trips per day;

The Plan-Making Steps   49

4. *Implementation costs:* Estimated cost to activate the intervention;

5. *ROI or lifecycle cost:* Estimated return on investment following implementation;

6. *Walkability:* Measured in number, diversity, and distance of destinations and route amenities like continuous sidewalks and short block lengths;

7. *EROEI:* The ratio of renewable energy returned on nonrenewable energy invested.

QUALITATIVE CRITERIA

1. *Strategic:* The capacity to create long-term value and benefits;

2. *Leveragability:* The potential for leveraging other programs and actions;

3. *Visibility:* The promotional capacity for an action's visibility;

4. *Phasing:* The ability to incrementally implement or deploy the action;

5. *Reliability:* The ability to remain operational and effective through its estimated life;

6. Control: Whether the jurisdiction controls the actions required for its implementation;

7. Adaptability: The action's capacity to adapt to changing conditions over time.

OTHER PERFORMANCE CONSIDERATIONS

1. Will the action expand an existing action or measure or develop a new program?

2. Health benefits can be measured both qualitatively—improved quality of life—and quantitatively—reductions in incidents of childhood obesity and asthma, for example.

3. While the most common metric for evaluating an investment is simple payback/time, it ignores the time value of money by estimating the time for an investment to pay for itself. The simple payback period is equal to the investment cost divided by the annual savings. A $1,000 investment that saves $500 each year has a two-year simple payback. In comparison, a lifecycle cost analysis considers the economics associated with a particular investment throughout the investment's useful life.

4. A strategic investment adds value well beyond its initial payback period, even for subsequent generations. Will the action provide collateral benefits to the community such as local air quality, improved public health, lower health-care costs, and improved worker and student performance, and can these benefits be assessed and used to support the introduction of the program?

MODELING THE ACTIONS

A transparent and objective assessment of each proposed action requires modeling or estimating their performance using the qualitative and quantitative criteria. Deploy both low- and high-tech tools including those that enable the stakeholders to compare the benefits and drawbacks of proposed actions. Communicate the modeling results with user-friendly formatting and a minimum of technical jargon. Most importantly, for each action, describe all calculations, assumptions, and variables in an appendix or supplemental document—they represent the methodology and evidence behind the modeling.

For example, a Department of Energy (DOE) grant program provides a "calculator" for estimating job creation for specific energy-related actions. Whether or not one agrees with DOE's numbers, they include their methodology with other calculations, assumptions, and variables.

REVIEW AND EVALUATE THE PRELIMINARY ACTIONS

The team must explain often complex, technical policies, codes, programs, regulations, best practices, or tools to staff, officials, and the general public, and articulate estimated performances. In order to clarify the process, the following practices should be implemented:

1. Organize information by function (e.g., solid waste), topic (e.g., renewable energy), or department (e.g., transportation).
2. *First draft:* If appropriate, post a spreadsheet draft list of proposed measures on the website, or post it after the internal jurisdiction review described below.
3. *First review:* Circulate the spreadsheet draft list of all proposed measures to the key stakeholders—typically jurisdictional staff—digitally and/or in print for their initial review and comment. Focus feedback on recommending measures to clarify, retain, revise, or eliminate. Develop a second draft list noting comments, proposed additions, deletions and revisions, and submit for a second review.
4. *Second review:* Lead the stakeholders through a second review and evaluation of the proposed actions and solicit written comments. Develop subsequent drafts that incorporate proposed additions, deletions, and revisions and complete refinements.
5. *Public review:* Either concurrent with or subsequent to initial reviews, lead a communitywide effort to solicit feedback on proposed actions, and record questions, comments, and new ideas for consideration. Employ a series of workshops, online surveys, and other appropriate venues, and post the results on the website. Post the draft action list on the Web prior to and after the event and in prominent locations to allow public examination of the proposed strategies and feedback results.

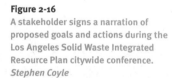

Figure 2-16
A stakeholder signs a narration of proposed goals and actions during the Los Angeles Solid Waste Integrated Resource Plan citywide conference. *Stephen Coyle*

1. AT THE URBAN EDGE: FARMSTEADS (ONE ACRE HERE)

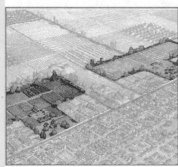

2. AT THE URBAN EDGE: SMALL FARMS

3. AT THE URBAN EDGE: TRACTOR FARMS

Extra-Urban Agriculture:
The Corrugated Edge of Agricultural Urbanism

The plan for this agricultural community provides a variety of ways for different scales of agriculture to plug into the urban fabric. This maintains open viewsheds into the agrarian lands and allows an economic and social interchange between the active agricultural lands and the town.

Figure 2-17
"Agricultural Urbanism," by planners Duany Plater-Zyberk, carefully fits numerous food-related activities, including small farms, shared gardens, and farmers' markets, and agricultural processing. *Duany Plater-Zyberk and Company*

PRIORITIZE AND/OR SELECT A SET OF PREFERRED ACTIONS

Lead the jurisdiction in prioritizing and/or selecting a set of jurisdictional and communitywide actions in preparation for the development of the action plan:

1. Facilitate an iterative process to "score," prioritize, and/or select a list of preferred remedies, based on the estimated performance relative to the goals, objectives, and performance metrics. The numerical values can be weighted for and against the economic, political, and social considerations.

2. Present a set of recommended actions to officials for their consideration, deliberation, and/or decision to adopt, reject, or modify the list.

3. Post interactive Web and circulate print prioritization and/or selection forms. While the public may lack the power to select the final list, public workshops or charrettes can provide stakeholders the opportunity to render opinions or weigh the value of each action.

4. Post the results on the jurisdictional project website and in prominent locations to continue the community education and feedback process.

As a result of a deliberative process, produce a final set of prioritized or selected policies, codes, programs, plans, best practices, and tools, and assemble into an action plan for building resilience, health, and enduring sustainability.

Step Nine: Develop the Action Plan

Create a plan for activating each selected action over time. Before drafting, consider designating or employing a manager/director to guide the actions or projects through implementation, and to monitor and report on the progress of each action. Each strategy, policy, code, plan, program, and tool will comprise a "project" or activity, each nested in a completed action plan.

Complete the following:

1. Finalize the scope of each action, adjusted for any anticipated conditions at the time of activation.

2. Describe the methodology for activating each action (e.g., energy retrofit program).

3. Identify and develop funding necessary to launch and operate each action.

4. Create a human resource list that identifies the person, organization, roles, responsibilities, and contact information for each action, including administrative, managerial, and technical staff; activation and operational labor; and regulatory/legal and economic advisors.

5. Identify and secure political support for each action.

6. Determine commencement dates and operational time trajectories for each action.

7. Set up command and control systems to manage cost, risk, quality, communications, time, changes, procurements, and human resources.

Figure 2-18
California's Contra Costa Centre/
Pleasant Hill BART Transit Village, the
implementation of the second phase
of a resilient, transit-oriented development. *Doug Johnson, MVE & Partners,
Inc., Architects*

8. Develop a monitoring and control program for each action that illustrates the procedures for evaluating, adjusting, and improving the desired outcome and performance of each.

9. Draft a contingency "plan B" for each action in consideration of changing economic, environmental, social, and political conditions.

10. Assemble the documents into a digital action plan, and submit to appropriate staff, team members, and others for peer review and response.

11. Refine and produce the final documents in digital and printed formats.

THE FUNDING CHALLENGE

To effectively implement the action plan, each jurisdiction requires an adequate, reliable, and consistent funding stream necessary to meet the long-term targets. When funds for energy, transit, and solid waste programs, for example, are viewed as amenities rather than necessities, support will fluctuate with national and local politics and economies. Develop a comprehensive financial plan with long-term budgetary needs and specific means to secure funding, independent of annual fluctuations in federal, state, and local constraints, which includes:

1. Action plan management and coordination costs, such as a salaried or contract position

2. Staff and/or consultant fees and expenses

3. Plan, code, program, or technology activation and maintenance costs

4. Monitoring and reporting costs

5. Promotion and education costs

6. Funding, grant-writing, and expense management, tracking, reporting, and oversight

THE FUNDING SOURCES

Public and private grants, awards, and loans offer sources of funds that can cover or help defray the up-front costs of activating measures, though often not for long-term operations. Jurisdictions can respond to long-term funding needs through the development of public reinvestment mechanisms, taxes, and bonds. For example, San Francisco, Berkeley, and Emeryville, California, obtained voter-approved public bonds for solar investments and a property tax assessment for energy efficiency programs.

Public investment in value-building regulations and long-term infrastructure reduces the risk for private capital and, therefore, attracts private investment. For example, Portland, Oregon's commitment to build and operate streetcar lines helped attract high-quality and high-value private development and has made the city one of the most walkable in the nation.

ADAPTABLE ACTIONS

Over time, each action may require modifications to accommodate external changes. For example, the development of more efficient, less expensive photovoltaics, or the discovery of product unreliability, could change the choice of materials and methods of installation. The action plan should describe a protocol for this situation.

The potential for both technological improvements and the emergence of unintended, adverse consequences illustrate the value of employing time-tested actions like resource conservation and urban forms that enhance pedestrian mobility. The discovery of a carbon-free fuel may be most valuable by enabling an easier transition to the development of renewable energy sources that will require the considerable consumption of fossil fuels.

The projects or actions can now be implemented in accordance with each individual plan.

Step Ten: Implement the Action Plan

The action plan's implementation requires key people and organizations for its success. For example:

1. A jurisdictional finance department is useful in providing assistance on budgetary, accounting, and economic analysis of projects and in securing long-term financing.

2. A public works department or agency provides expertise on transportation, energy, and solid-waste-related activities.

3. Local and regional transportation and transit agencies help advise on, regulate, and facilitate motor vehicle mileage reduction actions, thoroughfare modifications, and transportation demand management programs.

4. A planning, building, or development services department reviews and implements building and zoning code upgrades, and reviews development proposals for compliance with new requirements.

5. An economic development or city manager's office assists in the evaluation and management of economic impacts of the programs.

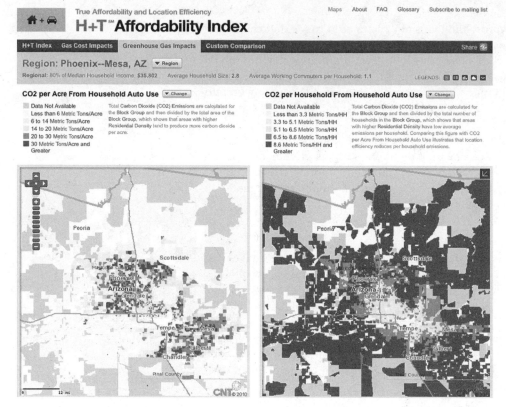

Figure 2-19
One resource for monitoring greenhouse gas emissions from household auto use nationwide is provided courtesy of the H+T Affordability Index, Center for Neighborhood Technology, www.cnt.org. *Center for Neighborhood Technology, Inc.*

6. A parks and recreation department or agency advises on the implementation of programs for walkers and bikers, and landscaping and tree-planting programs.

7. Neighborhood organizations and libraries can help communicate the value of programs and projects.

8. Schools and training facilities provide project-related educational opportunities for students, teachers, and the community.

9. Local service, retail, and manufacturing businesses and business organizations can offer goods and services such as energy-conserving products and audits, and mechanical equipment to optimize adjustments and installations, thus adding to the employment of local tradespeople and service providers.

10. Local and regional developers and builders can help implement and test the energy- and resource-conserving policies and codes.

IMPLEMENTATION CONSIDERATIONS

The implementation process should consider the following:

1. Each action's implementation requires supervision, management, and organizational oversight. Though staff or a sustainability manager can fulfill all or part of this role, certain tasks—developing a renewable energy district—may require the assistance of one or more technical specialists.

2. Long-term actions with years between cause and impact require enduring support and investment to avoid the adverse consequences of short-term thinking. An action plan committee or an oversight commission, organized during the plan's development, can provide both continued support and third-party monitoring.

3. Education provides the most durable means for maintaining and building community support. Those managing the plan's implementation should assume responsibility for developing the means to educate those impacted, and whose support or resistance could buttress or undermine the plan's success.

4. Each action offers an opportunity for promotion, using the Web, flyers, and the press. At a minimum, create a promotional plan with targeted information for the key audiences, a task best initiated during the development of the actions.

5. Demonstration projects and programs present excellent opportunities of educating by example. Targeted demonstration projects help generate and maintain community support and illustrate the value of action and observing the results.

6. Develop and launch high-profile demonstration projects such as a "Safe Routes to School Program" or tree planting. High-visibility projects attract media attention and provide classroom and independent teaching prospects. However, a multifamily recycling program offers direct benefits to both participants and the broader community when the effort includes press coverage, personal testimonies, and images of children recycling.

The action plan functions as an implementation guide and, as necessary, offers detailed instructions. Significant obstructions—lack of funding—may require revising a schedule, the scope of intervention, or adjusting targets. A comprehensive monitoring, assessment, and reporting system helps identify these hurdles and obstacles, and facilitates the generation of solutions.

DEVELOP THE MONITORING AND REPORTING PROGRAM

A monitoring program delineates the methods for observing and reporting on the progress and performance of actions. Timely identification of the potential need for corrective action allows better control of outcomes. Projects monitored regularly can avoid deviations from the action plan and permit "field" modifications, such as adjusting building cooling equipment to optimize energy savings. The development and deployment of a monitoring and reporting program and manual requires the following tasks:

1. Assign a program director or manager the responsibility for monitoring and reporting on the actions, assisted by appropriate experts.

2. Draft a methodology for assessing the performance of each activity over time against the objectives, measures of success, and the action plan.

3. Describe the commissioning processes required after installation or modification of a facility, equipment, process, or system to verify its compliance with the technical specifications and record functionality.

4. Delineate action-specific monitoring procedures and necessary human, equipment, and budgetary resources.

5. Specify periodic reporting protocols that describe performance results, obstacles encountered, actions taken or proposed, and time and funds expended.

6. Identify each project's progress—time, cost, scope, and scale—against the action plan's performance baselines, and the need for corrective or preventive actions necessary to reach or maintain compliance and a desired balance between reward and risk.

7. Recommend interim modifications only as necessary to maintain momentum only until changes are approved and implemented.

8. Establish a voluntary reporting protocol such as the Climate Action Registry[5] or EPA's Climate Leadership program. Participation offers a mechanism for obtaining independent, third-party verification for performance on, for example, greenhouse gas emission inventories. These third-party organizations provide a source of comparable, accurate, and consistent review, and an incentive to monitor and report on a regular basis.

9. In addition to specific monitoring and reporting, the jurisdiction should develop an oversight review process to periodically evaluate and communicate to the community at large, the effectiveness of each specific action and the action plan in general. The process should describe progress without time-consuming details that could detract from its educational value.

Next Steps

Each step described in this chapter delineates a plan for implementing a set of strategies, policies, programs, codes, plans, best practices, and tools by assembling a team; conducting research on the people and place; setting timely and measurable performance goals and objectives; proposing, evaluating, and selecting the best actions; and developing an action plan, reflective of and supported by the community. In the following chapters, the contributing authors recommend a range of methodologies, processes, and actions for achieving resilience and health.

Figure 2-20
The Mississippi Renewal Charrette attracted over two hundred professionals, including the author, from around the world to participate in a week-long charrette (12-18 October 2005) to plan for the rehabilitation of areas destroyed or damaged by Hurricane Katrina. The outcome of this charrette consisted of redevelopment schemes for 11 devastated communities along the Mississippi gulf coast, and recommendations for a host of technical, design, economic, environmental, and regulatory interventions.

Chapter 3

The Physical Built Environment

Sustainable Community Commerce

Seth Harry, AIA
President, Seth Harry and Associates, Inc., Architects and Planners

Retail Dynamics and Context

The nature and role of commerce as an integral part of the human habitat, belongs at the forefront of any discussion on a vital and sustainable urbanism. Traditional urbanism's rational structure and diffuse, fine-grained street networks encourage retailers to locate close to where their customers live or work, and at frequencies and increments of scale proportionate to the frequency and scale of consumer demand, relative to the types of goods and services offered.

Figure 3-1
Meriam Parks, a LEED-ND pilot program mixed-use development in Chico, California, is a good example of a strategically planned suburban infill project intended to encourage and support the sustainable, context-based commercial activity.
Seth Harry and Associates, Inc.

Unlike traditional urbanism, where consumer markets are defined by density and proximity, suburban consumer markets are dictated almost exclusively by the size of the road in front of the box. Suburban retailers exploit anomalies in the suburban road network to locate their boxes where the greatest number of potential customers will pass by, often with little proportional relationship to the surrounding densities or land uses.

Suburban retailers follow "Reilly's Law of Retail Gravitation," which says, in essence, *consumers will drive to the largest concentration of retail most easily reached.* Given that, suburban retailers are encouraged to build their boxes not only to the maximum size that can be sustained at any given time by the traffic volume passing by, but *to continue to expand in size with every incremental increase in said volume, lest their competitive advantage be eroded.* Every increase in road capacity intended to relieve congestion, more often than not, results in even bigger retail boxes, in a never-ending feedback loop of ever bigger roads and boxes, with little regard for long-term consequences. Furthermore, each incremental jump in size tends to further isolate the merchant from the local consumer, while promoting business models which use the resultant economies of scale to access global production and supply chains which tend to externalize many of the social and environmental costs effectively managed through more locally based, sustainable alternatives.

Fundamentally changing this dynamic must begin by addressing the spatial anomalies that enable its existence in the first place, and by reconstituting finer-grained thoroughfare networks, which include transit, that more equitably balance land-use and density allocations to the commerce with which it is associated. This provides an efficient, systemic foundation for human habitation, one which encourages and supports an equally fine-grained and diverse regional network of smaller-scale, independent and locally owned enterprises and community serving agriculture, supported by locally capitalized, community-lending institutions, such as wKREDA in Western Kansas. But—like any self-sustaining ecosystem—its long-term health depends on achieving a minimum threshold of autonymous viability, relative to those local resources. Neither suburbia, nor ad hoc urbanism, can ever function in a similarly sustainable fashion since, by nature, it relies primarily on external inputs to maintain itself.

Achieving sustainable commerce, then, requires a mechanism that will allow jurisdictions to accurately define and evaluate appropriate metrics for retail size and performance, relative to the nature of the urban fabric within it. Empirical models based upon the performance of successful retail venues in vibrant urban settings can be used to set specific planning criteria tied to real consumer market potential, and calibrated to a particular community's goals and objectives. This type of exercise can help bring a regional economic system closer to that of a self-regulating collective enterprise, able to maintain an efficient equilibrium of commercial activity for an indefinite period of time, without excessive or ongoing supplemental inputs.

Locally produced and consumed basic commodities provide greater economic resilience and regional vitality in comparison to the net costs of securing those resources from outside a region. Only essential products that are otherwise incapable of being locally sourced on a competitive basis should be considered for importation from beyond the immediate regional market context. To achieve this goal, first conduct a comprehensive inventory of existing demand for fundamental goods and services, and establish a baseline scenario for assessing the level of localized production necessary to achieve a balanced production/consumption model.

Second, inventory the existing retailers within the region, and document their size and location and the types of merchandise they carry. Third, analyze the locations of those retailers relative to the sources of both their supply and demand, and compare to benchmark indicators for comparable communities/regions determined to have achieved a reasonable level of sustainability. Develop a comprehensive strategy for spatially rebalancing the system in terms of land-use and transportation networks to provide a more efficient model of production and consumption consistent with those benchmarks, such as food miles, regional vehicle miles traveled (VMT), and economic multipliers related to locally sourced products.

Finally, identify and secure new rights-of-way (ROW) that can mitigate the unintended consequences associated with dendritic road networks, institute regulatory policies that require the credible documentation of localized market demand to support commercial zoning entitlements, or consider the creative use of land-use allocation strategies such as transfer of development rights (TDRs) to help bring the mix of retail and commercial activity into better balance. This could be done on the basis of their strata within the "Transect," to bring local food and goods production closer to the consumer. Finally, provide appropriate market incentives, based on credible standards that look at overall net impacts, to encourage the introduction of local equivalents for basic goods and services that are currently brought in from outside the region.

Preparing the Team

Urbanism is, by definition, a dynamic system. Therefore, it is important to have a consultant team which has detailed knowledge of retail dynamics and market criteria, in both conventional (suburban) and urban spatial contexts. The consultant team must be capable of translating contemporary retail standards into a comprehensive, regionally based urban design and place-type strategy that reflects the specific goals and aspirations of the community in question, while also meeting minimum thresholds of market capture and consumer demand. The following professionals often possess the specific skills required to produce an effective market rationalization strategy:

- Market Analysts
- Economic Development Director/Development Consultant
- Leasing Consultant/Main Street Director
- Local Business Coalitions
- Architecture/Urban Design Team
- Planning Staff and Public Works Officials
- Elected Officials

Preparing the Tools

Remediation strategies require qualitative and quantitative representational and regulatory tools to help articulate and define key issues and objectives. Basic graphs and spreadsheets can document relative performance characteristics and other attributes in evaluating existing sprawl-based settlement patterns relative to any proposed remediation.

Insights derived from these evaluations can then be used to inform that application of traditional urban principles and techniques to help achieve the target outcomes.

Relevant spatial metrics can be measured and documented through a variety of means, while qualitative attributes and features can be illustrated through renderings, 3D models, and visual-preference surveys. Visual mapping tools, such as GIS, or INDEX, can be used to help provide a statistical frame of reference to measure the spatial performance of the existing conditions, relative to any proposed interventions. These tools can be tailored to specific audiences, but one should use the best tool for the task, to accurately convey the information in the most readily understood fashion.

Figure 3-2
This proposed neighborhood commercial center is scaled to support locally serving commercial enterprises in new mixed-use development, based upon sustainable principles. *Seth Harry and Associates, Inc.*

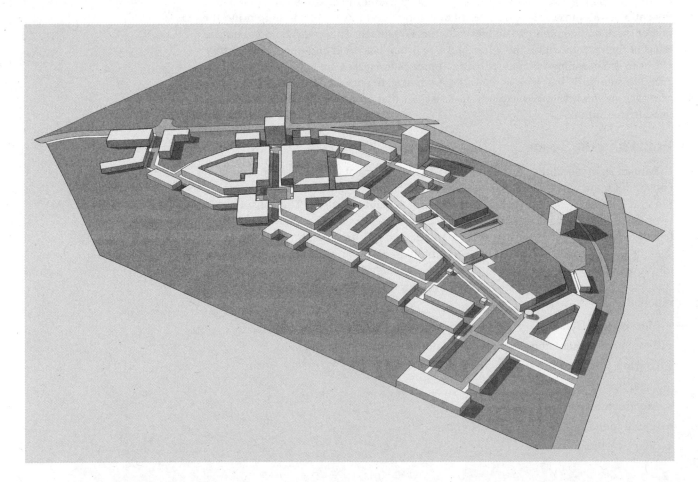

Form-based codes, including regulating plans ideally informed through a public-participatory planning process, should be an integral component of any regulatory mechanism. However, proactive, market-based calibration tools can be used to incrementally change land-use allocations over time in the form of a successional code. The SmartCode Module for Sustainable Commerce defines specific benchmarks for rebalancing existing conditions relative to an idealized model. These changes can be realized through market incentives that allow the normal dynamics of self-interested business activity to move consistently toward a more sustainable future.

Finally, visual representations of any proposed changes—precedent images and analogues, and associated statistical and performance data—help the community understand the rationale and tangible benefits behind such an initiative.

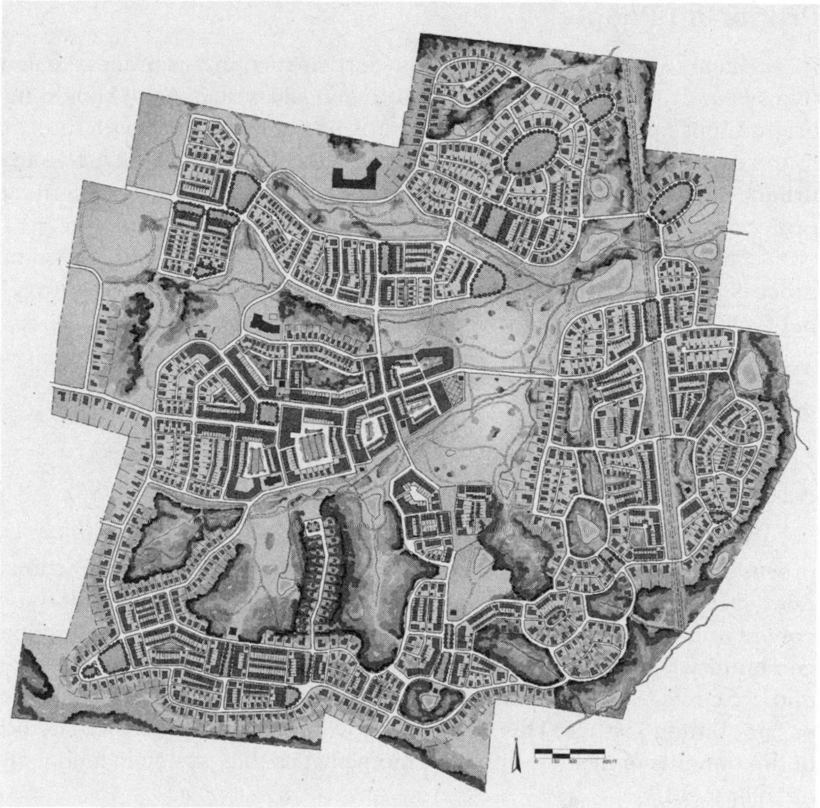

Figure 3-3
This new mixed-use, transit-ready development represents a serviced, urban extension within greater Metro Nashville, which used compact development to restore natural habitat and surface hydrologies, while supporting community-serving agriculture and small-scale neighborhood services.
Seth Harry and Associates, Inc.

Preparing the Place

The research phase, aided by appropriate analytical tools, should focus on generating the necessary data to fully inform the project. Produce a detailed inventory of the existing place and building types represented in the study area. Include their physical, spatial, and regulatory relationships to each other, as well as the prevailing market context, relative to the surrounding regional transportation network. Evaluate and compare against empirical precedents to produce performance benchmarks consistent with the community's stated objectives. Employing measures of net impacts and relative efficiencies, define a set of criteria and measures weighted to reflect the desired outcomes. These outcomes can be used to measure the larger net implications of a local goods and services–based economy as compared to conventional models, for the particular application. This could be accomplished through the cumulative layering of individual spreadsheet analyses, such that the net systemic performance of an urban-based regional settlement pattern can be measured against the preexisting sprawl-based model.

In order to calibrate new models, preliminary studies that compare retail format size, trade areas and sales productivity to urban form, including proximity to product sourcing for agriculture and manufacturing, should be conducted. These will help quantify relative greenhouse gas (GHG) emissions and net economic impacts based upon the spatial relationships of production and delivery of retail goods and services to human settlement patterns and transportation infrastructure.

Preparing People

It is critical to have key stakeholders' participation in this process to achieve effective systemic change. Stakeholder outreach and engagement should be organized around those personal, political, and business relationships with direct connections to the project—i.e., producers, consumers, retailers, and those active in defining urban form—regulatory and administrative personnel in government agencies, and professionals in real estate, market, and economic development.

Stakeholders should be engaged prior to participating in a dynamic planning process, such as a charrette, and before using the tools outlined above. The principal tools and techniques for engaging/informing public officials are:

- Proactive outreach
- Education
- Participation
- Demonstration

Proactive outreach means that public officials are knowledgeable about your process, including what's at stake and the consequences of their actions or inactions related to those issues. Education ensures that they fully understand the forces involved and their relationships to each other, and their collective implications for the community. Participation is fundamental to their awareness of ongoing discussions and concerns, and the community's position on them, as well as any controversial or "hot button" issues. This will help provide a clear and credible demonstration of the benefits in moving toward a more sustainable, systemic model of community development.

Developing Goals, Objectives, and Performance Metrics

Develop goals and objectives on a case-by-case regional basis, reflecting the inherent attributes of that particular place from a climatic and resource perspective. Establishing historical causal relationships based upon spatial configurations of urban structure and retail form and types, will require detailed empirical analysis, including a statistical analysis of production and distribution models and methodologies. It is anticipated that this work will incorporate recent innovations and ongoing work by many disciplines, to add further depth and value to process.

Developing the Strategic Plan

After establishing the goals and objectives, generate a strategic plan that uses the statistical insights gained from the analysis of traditional place types to more fully understand how urban form influences the net inputs necessary to sustain one type of system versus the other.

Based on this information, develop a useful set of principles and associated techniques to effectively mediate the unintended consequences of sprawl. These techniques should produce measurable improvements in the performance indicators associated with sustainable urban settlement patterns. The purpose of this effort is to codify a rational series of steps that will measure and document existing conditions, and define a clear set of tasks, processes, and guidelines intended to achieve measurable improvements in efficiency and sustainability. Base these steps upon established benchmarks of performance, and include an outline set of policies and replicable actions to implement.

Developing the Action Plan

In developing a preferred action plan, identify the performance metrics needed to assess the efficacy of the proposed measures, based upon the specific application. These should demonstrate a systemic relationship between urban form and the efficient use of natural and renewable resources. Therefore, establish performance measures based upon this relationship, which might include:

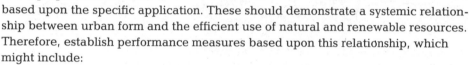

Figure 3-4
This creek-side commercial area provides an attractive setting within walking distance of most residents. *Seth Harry and Associates, Inc.*

- The relative proximity of the production of a generic "basket" of daily goods and services to the point of sale
- The spatial relationship between the consumer base and the retail outlet, relative to the level of sales productivity (gross sales)
- The level of profitability relative to gross sales (net to gross)
- The net return on investment of the retail outlet relative to gross sales (efficiency of investment measured in rate of return).

Relative to urban form, a number of emerging form-based metrics and determinants associated with urbanism might be considered for comparative analysis:

- Block size/perimeter dimension
- Density
- Connectivity factor
- Relative box size (format)
- Diversity of merchandize/services offered per area or square foot
- Index of mix of uses
- Ratio of vertical lot coverage to impervious surface

Pursue strategies which help secure political, technical, and funding support for implementing the proposed measures. The most expedient approach—engaging the community and its elected official—helps them to understand the value in

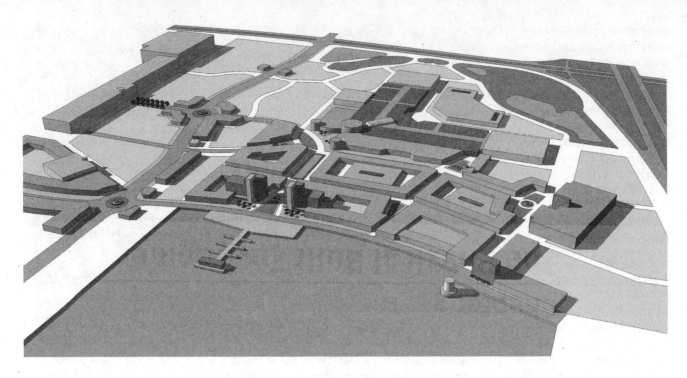

pursuing such an effort, and may include securing public grants and other funding sources aimed at promoting sustainability. Other tools that use development-oriented mechanisms may include tax-increment financing (TIF) and public-private joint initiatives to attract investment. Requests for Proposals (RFPs), or other competitive selection processes, provide effective tools for attracting both technical resources and related professional disciplines with a vested interest in helping to demonstrate the viability of these concepts and ideas to your process.

Implementing the Action Plan

Identify short-term actions which can effectively demonstrate the scalable benefits of sustainable commerce, based upon the measured performance of a range of comparative metrics established in the action plan, and use this to further educate the community and elected officials about the benefits of sustainable commerce from both a consumer's and an environmental perspective.

Figure 3-5
This conceptual scheme for a proposed mall development in Sarasota County looked at adding both dense residential housing and a fuller range of merchandising and center types to encourage a more diverse array of retail formats. The intention was to better leverage the nearby transportation assets while capturing local vehicular traffic. *Seth Harry and Associates, Inc.*

Figure 3-6
Seth Harry and Associates, Inc.

Focus longer-term actions on more regional issues such as transportation infrastructure and updating comprehensive plans using a cumulative, criterion-based planning approach which employs market-based zoning incentives to encourage infill development and suburban retrofit. Incentives might target right-of-way acquisition, commercial zoning entitlement standards, and other means for creating a balanced, spatially modulated urban mixed-use and commercial fabric. Specific resources for establishing and monitoring ongoing performance evaluations provided by professional or trade associations, or through publicly monitored data sources, include the Food Marketing Institute, U.S. Census Bureau, Department of Transportation, National Research Bureau, AASHTO, Household Travel Survey, and Urban Land Institute.

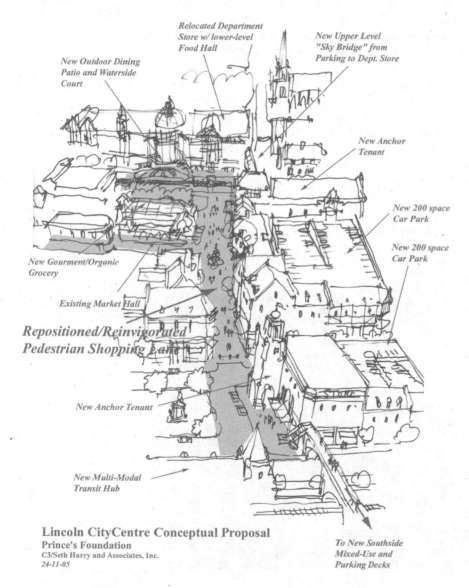

Relocated Department Store w/ lower-level Food Hall

New Upper Level "Sky Bridge" from Parking to Dept. Store

New Outdoor Dining Patio and Waterside Court

New Anchor Tenant

New 200 space Car Park

New 200 space Car Park

New Gourmet/Organic Grocery

Existing Market Hall

Repositioned/Reinvigorated Pedestrian Shopping District

New Anchor Tenant

New Multi-Modal Transit Hub

Lincoln CityCentre Conceptual Proposal
Prince's Foundation
C3/Seth Harry and Associates, Inc.
24-11-05

To New Southside Mixed-Use and Parking Decks

Figure 3-7
This repositioning/redevelopment strategy for Lincoln's High Street, in Lincolnshire, UK, is intended to help bolster and protect local, indigenous retailers from the competitive influences of suburban retail centers encroaching on their market. *Seth Harry and Associates, Inc.*

Building Sustainable Communities:
The Ecological Toolkit

Michael Mehaffy, CNU-A
Structura Naturalis Inc.

Changing the Patterns

Most of us are aware that sustainable development requires more than just boosting the energy efficiency of devices like cars and heating systems. The real change has to come in the ways we shape settlements, and the ways they in turn shape our patterns of consumption. That means creating much more efficient settlement patterns that allow us to live well, while using resources in a much more sustainable way.

This goal is difficult, but achievable. After all, we created our current unsustainable patterns when we created the current system of rules, incentives, and design standards over the last century, and made it over-reliant on cheap oil and disposable resources. We can change that pattern by changing the rules of this "operating system."

This won't happen overnight—but as the best examples show, we can make significant and even dramatic progress sooner than we might think. Conversely, we literally can't afford to continue the current unsustainable pattern. The global financial crisis of 2008–2010 which started in America's sprawling suburbs represents a sign that reality has caught up to us: What is nonecological is ultimately uneconomic.

Figure 3-8
The shape of settlements affects patterns of consumption. Imagine trying to bicycle or walk in this neighborhood of San Antonio, Texas (left). By contrast, European settlements like Amsterdam offer a highly livable pattern—with roughly half the level of resource consumption and greenhouse gas emissions. *Mehaffy, www.tectics. com/IARU.htm*

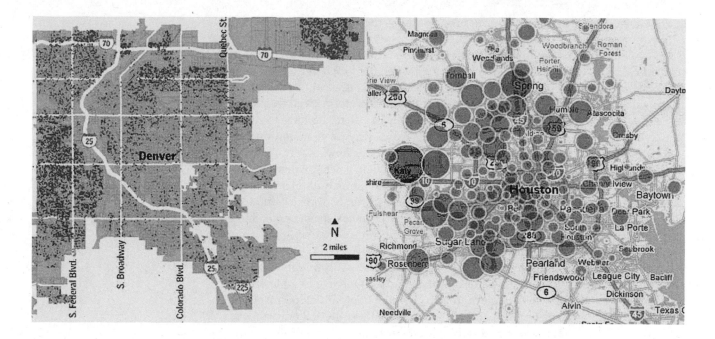

Figure 3-9

In city after city, a strong pattern of foreclosures shows the beginning of the current economic crisis in the far-out "drive 'til you qualify" suburbs of the United States. *Denver Post, Houston Chronicle*

    Making this change doesn't mean we have to go back to a primitive standard of living. On the contrary, the evidence shows that we can dramatically increase the efficiency of our settlements—and reduce the ecological footprint—while actually increasing our standard of living. That's because much of what is wasted now can actually go directly to improving our quality of life, using sustainable methods.

    For example, many of our conventional suburban neighborhoods are planned at very low residential density. That seemed like a good idea at the time—but it has backfired. The pattern forces us to do a lot of driving, whether we want to or not. More than that, it also contributes to increased per-capita rates of infrastructure-embodied energy, operating energy, albedo effects (heating caused by dark paved surfaces), building exposure (reduced common walls and floors/ceilings), impact on the surrounding ecosystem, and loss of so-called "ecosystems services" (for example, water purification, or removal of CO_2 from the air).

    There's also evidence that the shape of the neighborhood profoundly influences our other patterns of consumption. If it's not convenient, safe, and attractive to walk, we may walk less, or get out of the habit altogether. If there are no places to gather and recreate, we may stay in our homes and use high levels of energy from our TVs and other appliances. We may go on to buy much larger homes, and furnish them with cheap imported goods.

    Our conventional settlement technology can be said to be efficient in one sense, because it takes advantage of economies of scale. That's why it has also been relatively cheap—up to now. But in the long term, this technology is highly inefficient: It destroys large quantities of the natural resources on which our well-being depends. It wastes land, and causes excessive amounts of travel. It isolates people, and creates chronic social and even health problems. These are very costly problems for all of us.

These costs are called "externalities," because they are external to our usual calculation of what it costs to develop a settlement—or perhaps we should say, what it has *appeared* to cost up to now. But these externalities gradually catch up with us, and cause us to pay a high price later, often when it is much harder to reverse the even more serious problems they cause. For example, if we cut down too many trees, we will lose the ecosystem services that the trees perform for us—cleaning the air, preventing soil erosion, and so on. It may cost us dearly to have to replace these services later—*if* we can even do it at all. This is why it's so important to develop more efficient, more sustainable settlement patterns now.

The overriding goal we must set for ourselves, then, is what we might call "settlement efficiency." This efficiency must be in both the pattern of settlement—much more compact, well-organized, walkable, and served by transit—and in the systems that generate, service, and maintain it: the technical, social, legal, and especially, economic systems. They must efficiently deliver a sustainable settlement pattern, in a way that is economically feasible.

If we are going to build—or, in most cases, rebuild—sustainable communities, we must therefore meet two closely related goals. One, we need to ensure that future patterns of growth and regrowth are much more efficient, resource-conserving, ecologically benign, and socioeconomically vibrant. And two, we need an economy that reflects and reinforces the economic value of these efficiencies. That means, we need to "monetize the externalities," that is, find monetary value for the previously disregarded factors, like damage to natural resources and ecosystem services. When we damage those externalities, it is only fair that we should pay the true cost of that damage. When we preserve or enhance the externalities, it is only fair that we should be financially rewarded. This will help to provide crucial economic incentives for sustainable projects to "pencil"—for income to exceed costs. That's a crucial ingredient of sustainable development.

Today, there are evolving toolkits available to accomplish each of these goals. For the first goal, we might use new design standards and typological patterns to plan and build transit systems, particular street types, walkable geometries, higher-density and mixed-use communities. We might install specific technologies—district power and heat, recycling systems, and waste heat and methane recovery. This can be done through comprehensive plans, master plans, form-based codes, performance and "generative" codes, best practice guides, technical guides, and other similar tools.

For the second goal, we might use economic tools. These might include pricing signals (like tolls and congestion charges), tradable credits, tax credits, grants, carbon taxes and/or credits, "system development" charges and credits, feed-in tariffs, and variable metering. They might also include financial instruments that capture the value of future benefits, and bring them to the present. An example is tax-increment financing: This is often a municipal bond that is paid off with higher tax revenues from the value created.

We might pursue a sustainable economic development strategy that provides local living-wage employment doing conservation activities, for example, historic renovation/restoration, repair or adaptation of existing buildings, energy retrofits, community power systems, and other "green collar" jobs. These will often require funding incentives, perhaps through tax-increment financing or similar financial

Figure 3-10
At Orenco Station, a transit-oriented development in Hillsboro, Oregon, residents and the local grocer helped to set up a Farmers' Market that now brings fresh produce in regularly from surrounding farms. The grocer, New Seasons, is often exceptionally busy on market days, proving that farmers' markets can be complementary to existing grocers. *Michael Mehaffy*

instruments. The funds can also come from permits to demolish buildings, or construction waste tipping fees, or surcharges on high energy use.

Or we might want to provide more sustainable sources of food, say, by creating a Farmers' Market, or a local community-supported agriculture system. We might finance those with the funds from fines for violation of soil erosion statutes, or other unsustainable activities. In this way, it is the unsustainable activities that pay a fairer share of cost, and more sustainable activities that receive the benefits.

Drawing from these and other new tools, we can develop a customized "toolkit" to accomplish our own specific local goals. Along with the locally calibrated tools we would employ a "diagnostic" process, telling us how to assess the current situation, and how to build on it to improve performance. Lastly, we might develop a Resource Center to guide our tool users to work in a "bottom-up" way. At the same time, the center would serve as a collection point to gather feedback, learn about what is working and not, and adjust and refine the tools.

Prepare the Team

The team composition will vary according to local requirements, but will almost certainly start with one lead organizer—a "sustainability engineer." This is not an engineer in the narrow sense of technical systems like energy production, but an interdisciplinary professional who oversees the mix of strategies and tools to create more sustainable developments. Such a role requires knowledge of sustainable planning principles and standards, and also familiarity with key economic tools: government fee structures, SDCs, TIFs, tax credits, grants, and so forth.

The person must have a broad understanding of energy systems and how they work within building and urban systems. They, or another member of the team, should have expertise in economic modeling, carbon modeling, and knowledge of metrics for VMTs. It will also be important for someone to have knowledge of emerging certification programs like LEED (Leadership in Energy and Environmental Design) and LEED-ND (LEED for Neighborhood Development).

Prepare the Tools

In order to create custom toolkits for each situation, it is helpful to survey the tools that already exist, and that can be easily incorporated in your toolkit. For example, LEED-ND is one very helpful example of a recommended qualitative and quantitative performance-measuring tool that incorporates many other useful metrics. You can offer LEED-ND as an incentive for local developers, and offer them a streamlined approval process or other regulatory incentives.

For visual mapping tools, Google Earth is a powerful tool that allows a number of custom and local features to be added. The Google Earth software code is "open," which allows very useful local capabilities to be added. For example, it has a potential to do a "mashup" that allows other data to be imported, including 3D models of local buildings created in Google's SketchUp drafting program.

SketchUp, in turn, is a powerful 3D drawing tool that allows a range of photo-realistic options. It can be used to develop a "typological library" of preapproved buildings and urban features that can then be used to create photo-realistic 3D models for collaborators to view and modify. (SketchUp also has a "3D Warehouse" of sharable models that can be developed and applied.) There are other similar tools that can be employed (e.g., Rhino, Revit, AutoCad, and various GIS systems). The cost of the software is usually not the most significant element. Google Earth is free, and SketchUp and other programs range from several hundred to several thousand dollars each. A much more significant direct expense is likely to be personnel time in developing and using the software.

While software tools are helpful for many tasks, it is essential to include tools which involve public decision-making. Some of these tools include:

- The Charrette (a collaborative professional and public workshop)
- Open Space (a collaborative technique for soliciting creative ideas)
- Wiki (an easy-to-use collaborative computer site)
- "America Speaks" technique, with "condorcet voting." This technique uses small moderated panels that are then pooled electronically. Condorcet voting allows users to vote for each option in relation to all of the other options, instead of just a single option with majority preference. (This avoids the "lowest common denominator" problem.)

Any decision-making process needs to consider actual costs, so it is important to model costs and compare them in real time, especially in collaborative design processes. Participants can even play a "costing game" to evaluate the balance between cost and desirability of a series of options.

Prepare the Place

As the team moves into the research phase of the project, there are a number of techniques for collecting the required data. Besides the examples described in Chapter 2, consider the following:

- Perform diagnostic assessments of key urban elements and their performance relative to aspirations
- Develop "feeling maps"—maps that show the qualitative evaluations of many people about the different areas of a neighborhood or city. These can help to identify existing under-appreciated resources that can be leveraged, or problem areas that can be targeted for repair.

The budget for this process depends on each scope, but may range from $10,000 to $50,000.

It's also important to have an evidence base to substantiate the needed reforms to the current "operating system." Many of these changes are hard to make, because existing constituencies often benefit from maintaining the status quo. Therefore, good data is crucial for building a case for change. Here are a few examples of reports and studies that are crucial to have at hand:

- Transit ridership and modal split
- Energy efficiency and inefficiency studies (e.g., in generation, distribution, and so forth)
- Waste management efficiency (percentages of recycling, quantities of waste per capita, and the like)

Prepare the People

For the success of any project, key stakeholders should be involved at all stages of the process, from planning to implementation. Examples of these key stakeholders' range in levels include:

- Political leadership and institutional representatives
- Business owners, key property owners, and residents

These key stakeholders will participate in the most important stages of your public process, which can include:

- A charrette process
- Public presentations and discussions
- America Speaks methodology (Small panels, electronic uploading)
- Open Space meetings

In addition to the more formal tools for engaging the public in the project, organizers should not undervalue the importance of more casual relationship-building, including:

- Face-to-face meetings and dialogues
- Early partnerships with key local allies

Figure 3-11
The Mississippi Renewal Forum, a charrette for the reconstruction of the Mississippi Coast after Hurricane Katrina, developed an action plan for the reconstruction of the coastal region, including a proposal for Neighborhood Resource Centers. *Michael Mehaffy*

- Public presentations and discussions
- Ongoing informal contact and dialogue

Develop Goals, Objectives, and Performance Metrics

During all of the initial stages of planning, team members should refer to the strategic objectives for the project. What are the larger goals? What are the more tangible "deliverables," and how will success be measured?

Some existing standards that might help guide the goal and objective developments are:

- Legislative standards (e.g., California's AB32, Kyoto, or Copenhagen treaties)
- Voluntary commitments (e.g., Architecture 2030)
- Certification standards (e.g., LEED-ND)

The budget for these processes varies greatly according to scope, but may be in the range of $5,000 to $25,000.

The metrics will vary according to your goals, but might include:

- Ridership, modal split (e.g., car, transit, walking, biking)
- Household energy use reductions and recycling rate increases
- "Location efficiency" (mix of daily needs and services)
- Certification eligibility (Energy Star, LEED-ND, and so forth)
- Economic performance (volume of sustainable businesses)
- Social indicators (e.g., mental and physical health)
- Environmental indicators (water and air quality)
- Footprint calculations per person (carbon, resource use, and so forth)

Figure 3-12
To build resilient communities, the resources have to be carefully coordinated. The reconstruction of the U.S. Gulf Coast after Hurricane Katrina succeeded best when such resources were brought together into neighborhood-level centers. *Michael Mehaffy*

Develop the Strategic Plan

After the goals and objectives have been solidified, you should develop a strategic plan. Here are some possible steps:

1. Review model strategies/policies/regulations/tools and so forth.
2. Customize a proposed "toolkit" using evaluation methodology (predicting benefits, approving cost).
3. Use public consultation methods to refine and optimize the mix for local needs.
4. Run pilot projects to test the toolkit in operation.
5. Do postoccupancy research to measure effectiveness using multiple overlapping metrics (e.g., household VMT counts, personal carbon footprints, and so forth).
6. Based on the results, compile the written strategy for the use of the tools, together with timeline, metrics, deliverables, assessment, and so forth.

Develop the Action Plan

Once the strategic plan has been completed, the team will develop an action plan that describes the implementation process. To best prioritize and select the measures to implement and the times to do so, teams should use a local charrette that will identify, research, and rank the proposed tools, including those in this book. The charrette will develop its own local decision matrix, with its own ranking criteria, for example, cost, benefits, local availability, local appeal, and so forth.

The local community charrette (discussed previously) is an important method to refine action plans for political support and regulatory approval, if local regulatory staff and elected officials are included. As discussed, a sense of collaborative

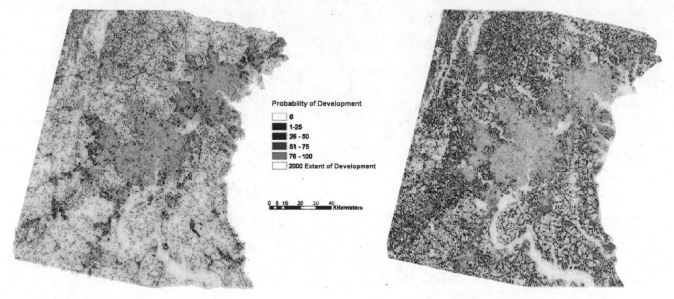

Probability of Development

- 0
- 1-25
- 26 - 50
- 51 - 75
- 76 - 100
- 2000 Extent of Development

0 5 10 20 30 40 Kilometers

Ecological Development Scenario: 20% Expansion

Business as Usual Scenario: 80% Expansion

partnership can be crucial in finding effective paths to implementation. The budget will vary depending on jurisdiction or other client specifics, but may be in the range of $50,000 to $500,000.

The actions taken under the action plan must be monitored for follow-up and revision, using the tools and metrics previously discussed.

Implement the Action Plan

The first implementation step is to identify the sponsors and agencies, both public and private, for the various proposed action projects. Some projects can commence immediately (e.g., by government, say, as infrastructure projects); others will emerge as proposals for others to take up.

The next step is to identify the mechanisms for funding, and make them available for qualified projects. This may require creation of an independent legal entity to administer and follow up.

An invaluable tool in implementing the action plan is a "Neighborhood Resource Center" (see action description). Such a center brings together all of the tools, and guidance for their use by the local people who are responsible for implementing them, into a single "one stop shop."

An action plan manager, who functions as a kind of "research librarian," operates the center. (The manager can be the "Sustainability Engineer," or a deputy.) The center has computers, databases, and other tools for implementers, as well as informational guides. Actions are assisted and monitored by the manager, and conflicting information or requirements are resolved with the manager's assistance. The diagnostic tools developed in the toolkit are used to monitor, follow-up, and revise the action plan or plans accordingly.

Figure 3-13

Existing unsustainable "business as usual" patterns are the result of a complex mix of existing economic incentives. In Maryland, sprawl is projected to increase by 80 percent by 2050, further damaging ecosystems and their services. A more ecological pattern of 20 percent growth, closely following population growth, will require a careful mix of regulatory policies and economic incentives, using a toolkit approach. *Claire Jantz, University of Maryland*

Bioclimatic Building Design

Erin Cubbison, Assoc. AIA, LEED Associate, Gensler

Introduction

The buildings within a "resilient community" individually must be sustainably designed and, ideally, work *together* to create a balance in resource consumption and generation. Each building must minimize its consumption of energy and water, and this should begin with the use of bioclimatic design strategies. Bioclimatic design strategies can be defined as: Strategies that provide thermal and visual comfort by making use of a specific site's environmental conditions, such as temperature, humidity, solar access, wind, precipitation, soil, and vegetation. Bioclimatic design strategies apply to both indoor and outdoor spaces. Buildings should also minimize the generation of waste, and, at the same time, reframe the concept of waste as a potential resource. Although buildings should strive to be as sustainable as possible, each one individually need not be energy-neutral, water-balanced, or zero-waste. Rather, each building should play a role in helping the community as a whole reach these goals.

Support for green building has moved into the mainstream, but there is still significant room for improvement. Conventional design practices often ignore the opportunities and constraints of a building's climate. Currently, architecture, landscape, engineering, and other building disciplines work in silos rather than collaboratively, losing the opportunity to discover synergies around the site's physical context. So many building decisions are short-sighted and simply based on the way things were done by convention and previous generations. Many building owners are not willing to invest in sustainable strategies if the payback is longer than a few years. Also, project timelines often do not allow enough time or sufficient fees for preliminary design phases to fully explore and quantify the benefits of sustainable strategies. These conditions have produced the majority of our current buildings. Since new construction represents only about 2 percent of the total building stock in the developed world [Energy Information Administration, DOE], making our existing buildings more sustainable must also be a critical goal.

Prepare the Team

There are several broad considerations relative to the implementation of green buildings. First, highly innovative, sustainable systems for energy, water, and materials are often community-scale systems. When individual buildings are being designed, built, or retrofitted on different schedules and/or by different parties, this coordination can be very challenging or even impossible. Second, developers who will sell buildings in the near term and tenants who do not pay for energy, water, or materials/waste have little incentive to invest in sustainable strategies. Third, a fundamental shift is needed on the part of both owners and designers to make building performance a key factor in design decisions.

Figure 3-14
Older buildings can provide an excellent opportunity for reuse, especially buildings with high floor-to-floor distances and structural systems that accommodate a variety of uses. *Sherman Takata*

The most successful green buildings are created by an integrated, multidisciplinary team and often involve a variety of expert consultants. A strategist assists the owner in developing the organization's goals and program needs. A planner analyzes the context and proposes key connections of the building to its site. A civil and/or environmental engineer evaluates the opportunity to incorporate sustainable infrastructure. Scientists, such as hydrologists or ecologists, provide expertise on specific environmental conditions. Architects and mechanical/electrical/plumbing engineers collaborate to maximize energy efficiency in heating and cooling, daylighting, renewable energy, and innovative water strategies, and with contractors to identify and source healthy, sustainable materials.

Prepare the Tools

Energy model: A computer simulation that estimates the energy performance of an entire building or systems within a building. It is usually performed for an entire year and uses typical climate data. A key benefit of an energy model is that it captures the interaction between different elements of the design and building program. For example, it evaluates the impact and allows comparison of different orientations, massing, shading devices, spaces uses, daylighting versus electric lighting design, and various heating and cooling systems. It also allows the team to estimate operating costs, evaluate the payback on different strategies, and plan alternative energy options. Energy modeling is described further in Chapter 6: Energy.

Daylight model: A computer simulation that assesses the behavior of daylight within a building, specific interior design condition, or outdoor space. It may be performed for an entire year or for specific days and times and uses typical climate data. A key benefit of a daylight model is that it evaluates the impact of building footprint, window-to-wall ratio, glazing type, material selections, light shelves, skylights, and shading devices. It allows the team to estimate when daylight may be used instead of

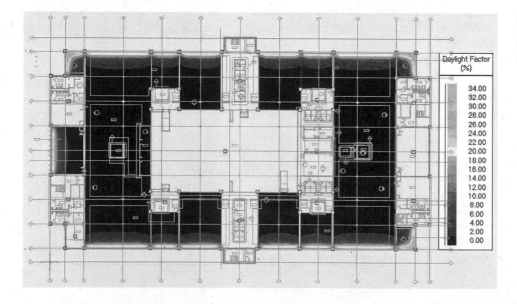

Figure 3-15
Computer simulation allows the design team to evaluate the penetration of daylight into a space. *Gensler*

or in combination with electric lighting, to develop smart building response systems, and to quantify the potential energy and dollar savings of daylighting strategies.

Building information modeling (BIM): A platform for a highly integrated design process, leveraging three-dimensional and, in some cases, four-dimensional tracking. This capability enables the different members of a project team to stay coordinated and greatly improve accuracy. This also spurs decision-making to take place earlier in the design process.

Leadership in Energy and Environmental Design (LEED) has become a widely adopted tool for evaluating sustainable design in buildings. As described by the U.S. Green Building Council, it is "an internationally recognized green building certification system, providing third-party verification that a building or community was designed and built using strategies aimed at improving performance across all the metrics that matter most: energy savings, water efficiency, CO_2 emissions reduction, improved indoor environmental quality, and stewardship of resources and sensitivity to their impacts."

Many cities have incorporated LEED into their building requirements. For example, San Francisco has a green building ordinance that requires nearly all new construction and major renovation projects to achieve LEED certification, with increasing achievement levels between 2009 and 2012. Many companies and organizations have also adopted LEED into their corporate social responsibility commitments.

The state of California has also adopted Green Building Standards (CALGREEN), effective January 1, 2011. CALGREEN requires:

- 20 percent mandatory reduction in indoor water use, with voluntary goal standards for 30, 35, and 40 percent reductions
- Separate water meters for nonresidential buildings' indoor and outdoor water use, with a requirement for moisture-sensing irrigation systems for larger landscape projects
- Diversion of 50 percent of construction waste from landfills, increasing voluntarily to 65 and 75 percent for new homes and 80 percent for commercial projects
- Inspections of energy systems (i.e., heat furnace, air conditioner, mechanical equipment) for nonresidential buildings over 10,000 square feet to ensure that all are working at their maximum capacity according to their design efficiencies
- Low-pollutant-emitting interior finish materials such as paints, carpet, vinyl flooring, and particle board.

Prepare the Place

Implementing sustainable strategies in new and existing buildings requires distinct research methods.

For new buildings, a *program study* should be performed to first assess what activities will take place within the building and how much space they will occupy. People are working, playing, learning, and living in different ways than previous generations. We can no longer assume that certain activities require the same amount of square feet as they used to. Reducing the sheer quantity of built space is the most cost-effective and carbon-effective strategy.

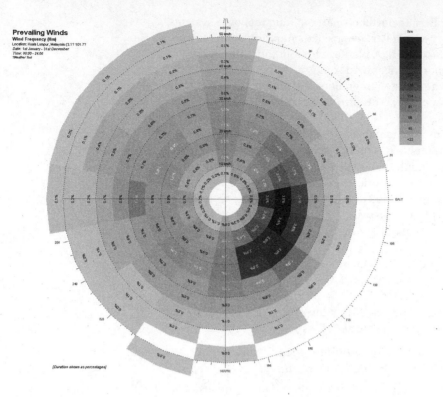

Prevailing Winds
Wind Frequency (Hrs)
Location: Kuala Lumpur, Malaysia (3.17 101.77
Date: 1st January - 31st December
Time: 00:00 - 24:00
[Weather Tool]

[Duration shown as percentages]

A *site environmental analysis* should be performed for a new building to determine solar access, annual and diurnal temperature swings, rainfall, humidity, wind speeds, soil conditions, water table, native and native-adapted vegetation, and surrounding ecosystem health. All of these factors will influence building and site design.

A *survey of comparable buildings* in the new project's local area will reveal useful information about typical building practices (including vernacular design), which have succeeded and failed, what sustainable strategies are already common, and what community resources might be available to the project.

For existing buildings, a *utilization analysis and occupant survey* should be performed to determine how well the building is currently being used. For the same reasons that a program study is needed for new buildings, described above, this activity is essential for maximizing building performance. For example, through extensive research in this area, Gensler has found that most office spaces are highly underutilized, many reaching 60 to 70 percent of unused space.

An *analysis of energy consumption* in existing buildings will help identify targets for energy conservation measures. It may also identify unusual spikes in consumption that indicate a need for system maintenance or replacement. The analysis will also establish a baseline, which is a critical step in performing evaluations of design scenarios.

A *waste audit* will reveal what types and quantities of waste are coming out of the existing building. In addition to tracking material destined for landfill, the audit also tracks waste streams such as recyclables, compostables, electronics, hazard-

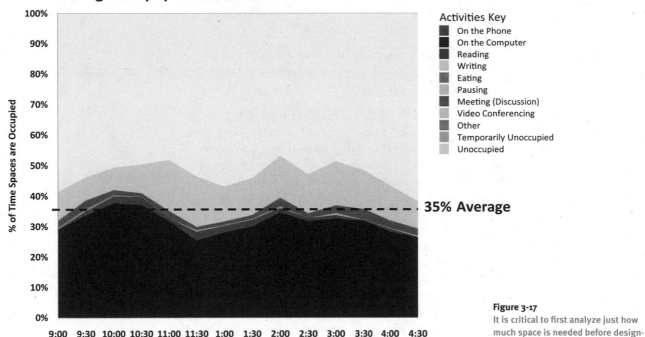

Average Daily Space Utilization

Activities Key
- On the Phone
- On the Computer
- Reading
- Writing
- Eating
- Pausing
- Meeting (Discussion)
- Video Conferencing
- Other
- Temporarily Unoccupied
- Unoccupied

35% Average

% of Time Spaces are Occupied

9:00 AM, 9:30 AM, 10:00 AM, 10:30 AM, 11:00 AM, 11:30 AM, 1:00 PM, 1:30 PM, 2:00 PM, 2:30 PM, 3:00 PM, 3:30 PM, 4:00 PM, 4:30 PM

Figure 3-17
It is critical to first analyze just how much space is needed before designing and building new space. *Gensler*

ous materials, and materials able to be donated. This activity will reveal if different waste streams have contamination and how it might be avoided. Often cities provide financial incentives to divert material to landfill through reduced collection fees or other rebates.

The research needed to analyze the context and conditions surrounding green buildings falls into two categories: infrastructure research and market research.

The infrastructure research required when implementing sustainable building strategies includes evaluating the existing:

- Capacity of municipally supplied power
- Capacity of municipal potable water sources or groundwater sources
- Capacity of municipal wastewater treatment
- Roads, traffic, and parking conditions
- Bicycle and alternative transportation system
- Open space network and appropriate vegetation

The required market research involves collecting data on comparable conventional versus green buildings, specifically related to:

- Rental rates
- Occupancy rates
- Sales prices

- Time/ability to obtain permit
- Insurance rates
- Contingency budgeted for construction
- Occupant productivity (or other metrics as appropriate, such as test scores for schools, or recovery time for hospitals)
- Occupant turnover (or other metrics as appropriate)

Many of the emerging opportunities in green building are related to developments in technology. In addition to energy modeling, daylight modeling, and BIM, smart building management systems allow building engineers to track resource consumption and ensure levels of efficiency. Technology can guide comfort controls, such as automatically adjusting light levels, sunshades, and outside air flow. Improvements in technology also drive higher efficiency and affordability of many sustainable products and systems.

Green building constraints vary widely. An emphasis on first costs often stops a sustainable strategy in its tracks. Instead, lifecycle costs should be used in decision-making. As described earlier, our stock of existing buildings can be thought of as both an opportunity and a constraint, specifically buildings built after the advent of modern air-conditioning. These buildings, almost never designed to use passive strategies, can prove difficult to retrofit. Our human tendency toward the status quo can add years to a full shift to our building systems, products, construction techniques, comfort targets, and space planning to be fully sustainable.

Prepare the People

Key stakeholders relevant to building research focus are as follows:

Building owner

Building occupants/tenants

Building facilities and management teams

Building visitors

Building neighbors—immediately adjacent and larger community

Engage all of the stakeholders who will manage, lease, occupy, maintain, promote, or otherwise spend time in and money on the facility, to develop community support for a building project. The following are key sustainable design issues related to each stakeholder:

Building owner
- Capital costs
- Lifecycle costs
- Project timeline
- Health and safety
- Pride/reputation

Building occupants/tenants

- Support of programmatic requirements
- Comfort conditions
- Adaptability to future needs
- Pride/reputation

Building facilities and management teams

- Systems durability and dependability
- Ease of maintenance
- New training requirements

Building visitors

- Engagement and education

Building neighbors—immediately adjacent

- Shadows
- Views
- Stormwater runoff

Building neighbors—adjacent and greater community

- Traffic impacts
- Potable water burden
- Wastewater burden
- Energy burden

Develop Goals, Objectives, and Performance Metrics

In most cases LEED certification (described earlier) is not a regulatory requirement and is often a goal of the building owner. It provides a point-based framework with clear methods for achievement. There are four different levels of achievement: certified, silver, gold, and platinum.

Achieving the Living Building Challenge is another example of a green building goal. The Living Building Challenge is more aggressive than LEED in its sustainability requirements. It has 20 "imperatives," which cover the areas of site, water, energy, health, materials, equity, and beauty. Examples of a few of these imperatives are zero-net water and zero-net energy.

A common performance measure for sustainable buildings, energy-use intensity is typically measured in energy consumption per square foot. However, for office space, for example, this is beginning to be replaced by energy consumption per headcount or energy consumption per unit revenue. This is because more and more people are working in new ways, using less space overall, but using it more intensively. Other performance measures include water use per occupant per day, percent area daylit, and percent waste diverted from landfill.

Develop the Design

The design process must integrate all of the previous steps. During this process, the architect typically pulls together the technical resources to implement a sustainable building project, including technical experts who are part of the architecture firm or specialized consultants who are contracted by the architect. Funding resources may be available through grants, rebates, and other incentives at the state or federal level. They typically apply to energy conservation, water conservation, waste reduction, and on-site renewable energy.

The design process considers the future life of the building, from both the point of view of the building systems, as well as the occupants. Regarding the building systems, it is very valuable to include a monitoring strategy, especially regarding energy consumption. Typically, energy monitoring is accomplished through a building management system that provides regular reports to building engineers. For example, the reports will help indicate when systems are not performing properly because they are wasting energy. Also, in the most recent version of the LEED rating system, buildings must make ongoing energy consumption data available as a requirement of certification.

A building's design should inspire sustainable behavior in its users. Use the building as an effective way to communicate sustainability, engaging occupants and visitors. Examples include creating a live display of building energy consumption in a public space, like a building's lobby, or installing signage throughout the building that explain why certain design decisions were made or materials selected.

Figure 3-18
Signage can be a very effective method for both educating building users, as well as inspiring sustainable behavior.
Gensler

Ideally, the design process is thought of as a cycle and not just a linear activity. A project moves through strategy, design, implementation, and use, and, as feedback is gained during a building's lifetime, it can continue to improve and respond to the needs of the users and the greater community.

Figure 3-19
Often a design team only engages in the design and implementation of buildings. By including both strategy and use into a design team's approach, projects are much more able to integrate sustainable strategies. *Gensler*

THE REAL ESTATE LIFE CYCLE

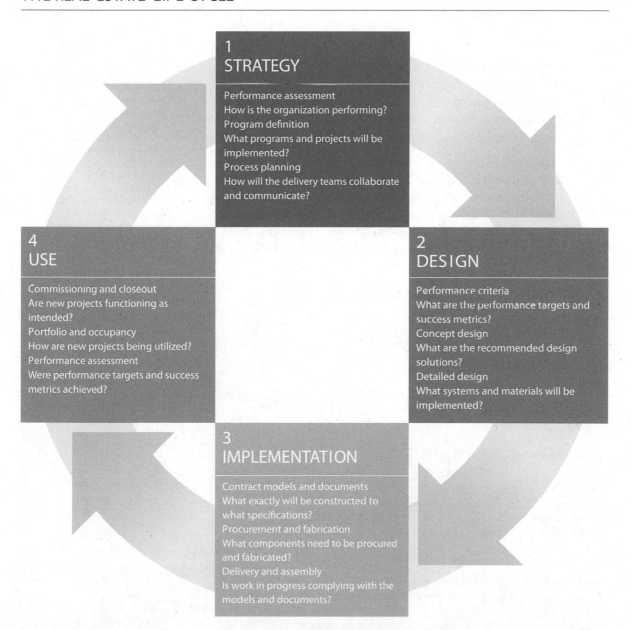

1 STRATEGY

Performance assessment
How is the organization performing?
Program definition
What programs and projects will be implemented?
Process planning
How will the delivery teams collaborate and communicate?

2 DESIGN

Performance criteria
What are the performance targets and success metrics?
Concept design
What are the recommended design solutions?
Detailed design
What systems and materials will be implemented?

3 IMPLEMENTATION

Contract models and documents
What exactly will be constructed to what specifications?
Procurement and fabrication
What components need to be procured and fabricated?
Delivery and assembly
Is work in progress complying with the models and documents?

4 USE

Commissioning and closeout
Are new projects functioning as intended?
Portfolio and occupancy
How are new projects being utilized?
Performance assessment
Were performance targets and success metrics achieved?

A SUSTAINABLE COMMERCIAL FRAMEWORK

Seth Harry
Seth Harry and Associates, Inc.

INTERVENTION TYPE: STRATEGY

Description

Recent changes in human settlement patterns have facilitated a shift toward global commerce based primarily upon competitive advantages gained through scalar exploitation. This means a retailer can control a larger share of the consumer market than they might otherwise have been able to, by leveraging spatial anomalies endemic to single-use zoning and dendritic road networks such as those found in suburbs.

Sustainable commerce, on the other hand, describes a rational and sustainable framework for the local production and distribution of goods and services necessary for daily life. Inherent to that framework is the idea that externalization of human, environmental, or social costs associated with the production of basic goods or services should not be enabled or allowed, either directly or indirectly, as an unintended consequence of the way in which we plan and build our communities.

Figure 3-20
This conceptual 3D diagram shows how conventional highway-related development, including big boxes, can be reconfigured into walkable, compact, mixed-use urbanism, supporting a broader spectrum of retail types, while reducing GHG emissions through a "park once and shop" approach, which still recognizes and responds to its immediate highway frontage condition (suburban infill, Richmond, VA). *Seth Harry and Associates, Inc.*

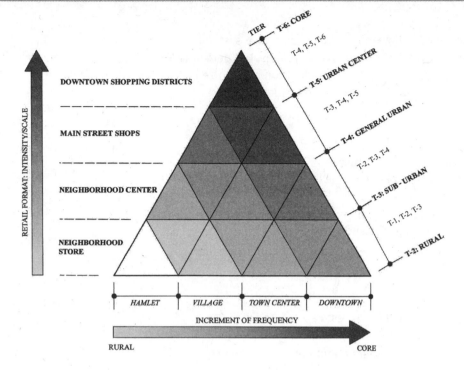

Figure 3-21
Seth Harry and Associates, Inc.

SUPPORT GOALS AND OBJECTIVES

- Support local goods production and small-scale, independently owned retail and commercial enterprises.

- Help communities retain and reuse the highest percentage of their gross economic benefits related to commercial activity (multiplier effect), encouraging a robust regional economy, and reducing demand for long distance transportation of goods.

PERFORMANCE CHARACTERISTICS

The performance indicators for these objectives should measure:

- The distances between where typical consumer items are produced, purchased, and consumed

- The number of local jobs associated with production and distribution of goods

- The net economic activity associated with the prescribed spatial parameters

POTENTIAL SYNERGISM

This program is consistent with other aspects of sustainable development, in that it engenders higher levels of intrinsic efficiencies within the system of human habitation. These include a hierarchical thoroughfare network supporting a range of mixed-use urban densities, housing types, and transportation options that provide an efficient distribution network for goods and services, and the local sourcing and production of those same goods and services.

IMPLEMENTATION TIME

A sustainable commerce program will take time to produce substantive systemic benefits because it requires land-use and societal behavior changes, but perceptual changes can occur relatively quickly. This will require a combination of short-term policy initiatives and long-term regional planning and transportation policies.

BENEFITS

The benefits of this approach can be substantial:

- Greater support and patronage of locally owned business, which contribute up to 300 percent more of their gross revenues back into the local economy than global enterprises
- Minimize environmental impacts associated with excessive VMT and long-distance transport of remotely produced goods and services (food miles)
- Reduce overall traffic congestion which reduces economic and human efficiency, and degrades the environment

DRAWBACKS

- Political resistance to change, and entrenched interests associated with the status quo
- Large need for outreach to help inform consumers about impacts of their choices
- Short-term economic impacts associated with systemic changes

FIRST COST

Initial costs would relate primarily to the development and implementation of regulatory and policy tools which encourage new and infill development in spatial patterns which support program goals and objectives, and could be accomplished in incremental stages ranging from $15,000 to $150,000.

- Comprehensive inventory and market analysis of study area
- Comprehensive strategic regulating plan which rebalances land-uses relative to optimal proportions of mixed-use areas
- Form-based code to ensure supportive building types and formats
- Funding to improve and enhance connectivity in heavily developed suburban centers

LIFECYCLE COSTS

Most lifecycle costs can be measured in terms of positive effects:

- Decrease in number, frequency, and duration of automobile trips generated
- Enhanced local tax base through the growth in locally owned businesses
- Reduction in infrastructure costs associated with high volumes of vehicular traffic, traveling longer distances

- More resilient, robust local economy
- Reduction in negative human and environmental impacts associated with sprawl

ESTIMATED QUANTITATIVE PERFORMANCE
Economic models that focus on metrics of long-term performance, such as job creation, income multipliers, and minimized environmental impacts should be used to more accurately quantify and assess the net economic performance.

IMPLEMENTATION SUPPORTS AND CONSTRAINTS
The primary implementation support necessary for immediate action is political, not economic. However, a lack of supportive economic activity can present a formidable obstacle toward short-term realization, by reducing the effectiveness of incentives. Regardless, public-sector funds can be used to "seed" supportive infrastructure and to encourage private investment.

INFORMATIONAL SOURCES
- "Reilly's Law of Retail Gravitation," *ULI Shopping Center Development Handbook*, 2d ed. (1985)
- Graph of Growth in Shopping Centers, *ULI Shopping Center Development Handbook*, 2d ed. (1985), p. 16
- VMT/Number of Shopping Centers
- VMT/Box Size (Based upon a generic retail type—grocery stores)
- Sq. ft. of retail per capita
- Retail sales per sq. ft.

REPORTS AND STUDIES
One study currently in progress by the author (Seth Harry) focuses on a number of empirical indicators including the frequency and scale of locally owned businesses in extant urban fabric. Feedback suggests that a more traditional urban development pattern typically results in a more diverse, fine-grained retail ecosystem with a higher proportion of locally or regionally owned retail enterprises. Sustainable at a lower threshold of gross sales, this model generates higher net benefits to the community deriving a greater percentage of inventory from more locally available sources. This results in a generally healthier local economy with less GHG emissions than one based upon more generic, global enterprises.

NEIGHBORHOOD RESOURCE CENTER

Michael Mehaffy
Structura Naturalis Inc.

INTERVENTION TYPE: PROGRAM

Neighborhood Resource Center

Many of the most important sustainability projects happen at a neighborhood level, from people working locally, from the "bottom up." These include individual home retrofit projects, business upgrades, neighborhood streetscape improvement projects, neighborhood public space improvements, neighborhood application of city-wide planning reforms, and similar grassroots projects. These projects require the resources to support and coordinate such efforts.

An outgrowth of the work in recovery of New Orleans after Hurricane Katrina, the "Neighborhood Resource Center" model delivers information and other resources directly to the neighborhood, and in a way the residents can use. It provides information tailored for the local neighborhood conditions and its unique characteristics with periodic classes, presentations, and guidance on taking advantage of more regional or national programs and funding opportunities. It creates a point where residents can come together and learn, "peer to peer," about meeting their local challenges, and providing a library of information and a "research librarian" who can look into specific resources and advise on requirements.

Figure 3-22
A neighborhood Resource—
A HOME AGAIN house on
Lizardi Street in the neigh-
borhood of Holy Cross.

A typical resource center might have the following resources:

- Information about household and small business projects, and how to complete them
- Information about financing sources (grants, credits, loans, partnerships, and so forth)
- Guidance in the steps needed to access them
- Information about low-carbon plans
- Preapproved low-carbon plans, and other "incentivized" choices
- Regular educational events and meetings
- Itinerant consultants, designers, assistants, making regular visits to offer free assistance
- Lists of locally available contractors and consultants, together with Angie's List–style customer rankings.

SUPPORT GOALS AND OBJECTIVES

- Provide implementation tools to shift lifestyles at the neighborhood level, reduce domestic CO_2 equivalent emissions to 80 percent below 1990 levels by 2050
- Provide implementation tools to shift lifestyles at the neighborhood level to dramatically reduce other nonrenewable resource consumption patterns

PERFORMANCE CHARACTERISTICS

- Qualitative rather than quantitative, the information and coordination can reduce carbon and waste, and increase recycling and other positive actions.

POTENTIAL SYNERGISM

- The program has close synergism with "economic toolkits" and other toolkits adapted for local use.

IMPLEMENTATION TIME

- The program can be implemented partially within six months, and fully within two years.

BENEFITS

- Provides distributed resources at the point of greatest need
- Educates local citizens on the issues
- Provides a forum for citizens to come together on local grassroots efforts

DRAWBACKS

- Management-intensive; carries a significant cost (though an even greater potential benefit)
- May be abused by those with self-interests, such as salespeople or lobbyists

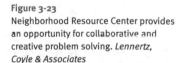

Figure 3-23
Neighborhood Resource Center provides an opportunity for collaborative and creative problem solving. *Lennertz, Coyle & Associates*

First Cost

- A "shoestring" operation can be done with in-kind donations (as was done for a number of centers in New Orleans). However, we recommend a properly staffed and resourced center, which may cost $50,000 to $250,000, and the development of synergies with local libraries, schools, or other institutions to reduce this cost.

Lifecycle Costs

- Depending on staff and synergies with other institutions (libraries, schools), the program may run between $50,000 and $150,000 per year.

Estimated Quantitative Performance

- If an aggressive outreach program is in effect, and funding is available for retrofits and other small-scale implementations, then with full implementation, the neighborhood can be on track to achieve 80 percent reductions in CO_2 emissions in buildings from 1990 levels by 2050.
- Similar magnitudes of reduction should be feasible for rates of consumption of other nonrenewable resources.

Implementation Supports and Constraints

- Because people may misunderstand the importance of this type of resources since their benefits are not immediate, it's important to make the benefits clear with simple examples, and to demonstrate the centers' usefulness through a pilot project.
- Political controversies may emerge about the location of a center, so we recommend taking a neutral position, such as the intersection of several neighborhoods.
- Partner with existing institutions that may have sharable resources, such as libraries, schools, and other institutions. These institutions may become possessive of the centers or some institutions may be seen as shutting out those who are not already affiliated with them, for example, churches.

Informational Sources

- For an example of Neighborhood Resource Centers developed for New Orleans, visit www.tectics.com/NRCs.htm.

Reports and Studies

- Report on Neighborhood Resource Centers for New Orleans:
- http://willdoo-storage.com/Plans/D6/District_06_Appendix_C_Charrette_Report.pdf
- Report on pilot Neighborhood Resource Center in New Orleans: www.lakewoodbeacon.org/

GREEN RENOVATION

Gaither Pratt, Architect
Principal and owner of Limehouse Architecture

INTERVENTION TYPE: BEST PRACTICE

Description: Nalle Street Renovation

802 Nalle Street is a two-story 2,400-square-foot frame residence built around 1900 in Charlottesville, Virginia. Prior to renovation, the building was in very poor structural condition and conventional practice suggested that the building be demolished and hauled to a landfill. The decision was made to save the building in order to demonstrate the possibility of preserving and restoring a structure in poor condition.

Green renovation strategies included the salvage and reuse of an existing structure, and the implementation of high-efficiency foam insulation, high-performance windows, energy-efficient lighting and HVAC, on-demand hot water heater, low-VOC paint and materials, durable finishes, and salvaged flooring and building materials. Financing was through EcoBanc, a Green Lending Institution dedicated to sustainable design.

Figure 3-24
Porches, shade trees, and cross-ventilation are passive cooling techniques that complement the energy-efficient construction and green materials of these townhouses. *Limehouse Architects*

Support Goals and Objectives

- The goal of this project was the use of green building practices in the renovation of an existing residence.

Performance Characteristics

- The use of green renovation strategies for this project has resulted in lowered annual energy use.

Potential Synergism

- This project demonstrates various green building techniques for residential renovation. These techniques are similar to those used for new construction, and can be easily applied to any renovation project.

Implementation Time

- These green renovation techniques can be implemented immediately, concurrent with any renovation project.

Benefits

- Employing green renovation techniques provides all the benefits of sustainable design and construction: increased energy efficiency, lower energy costs, improved indoor air quality, and decreased GHG emissions. Renovation of existing structures offers additional advantages through reduced landfill contribution. Older buildings are typically located in walkable, urban communities providing decreased dependency on the automobile for transportation.

Drawbacks

- The initial costs of green renovation strategies add additional expense to base renovation costs, which must be recouped over time through reduced energy costs.

First Cost

- The green strategies added approximately 10 percent to the base cost of conventional renovation techniques.

Lifecycle Costs

- The use of green renovation techniques provides significant annual savings in utility and energy costs. These long-term savings offset the increased first costs.

Estimated Quantitative Performance

- The reduction in energy use is estimated at 20 percent, comparable to similar reductions achieved in new green construction.

Figure 3-25
The John Street Townhouses combine traditional design with green building strategies. *Limehouse Architects*

IMPLEMENTATION SUPPORTS AND CONSTRAINTS

- Implementation supports include city, state, and federal initiatives for green building, historic preservation, and neighborhood revitalization.
- Implementation constraints include higher first costs of green renovation strategies and a potential real estate market bias toward new greenfield construction.

INFORMATIONAL SOURCES

- Earthcraft building guidelines: www.earthcrafthouse.org
- LEED Criteria: www.usgbc.org
- Original Green: www.originalgreen.org
- Local, state, and national green building initiatives

ATTAINABLE AND RESILIENT HOUSING

Sara Hines, AIA
Principal and owner of Hines Architecture, Ashland, MA

INTERVENTION TYPE: STRATEGY

Description

A sustainable community requires an adequate supply of affordable, durable, and resource-efficient housing. Resilient housing should aim for zero-net energy consumption by using conservation strategies for energy, land, and water use to lower operating costs and environmental impacts. The mix of housing types and sizes should align with income levels, family unit size, and individual needs. Projected housing needs should include job growth, demographics, transportation networks, and the capacity of the watershed to support the projected population.

One new example, the John Street Townhouse project, developed by the Piedmont Housing Alliance, a local nonprofit housing organization dedicated to affordable and sustainable housing, employs the Earthcraft Virginia guidelines, the Virginia green building program. Green building strategies included: traditional and passive design; engineered lumber; high-efficiency foam insulation; high-performance windows; energy-efficient appliances, lighting, and HVAC; water-efficient fixtures; low-VOC finishes; and durable, sustainable materials.

Figure 3-26
Renovations to 802 Nalle Street reused the shell of a 100-year-old house by employing green building strategies including new windows, insulation systems, and interior finishes.
Michael Bailey

SUPPORT GOALS AND OBJECTIVES

- Create a baseline sustainable housing inventory with clear goals for future expansion or contraction, and establish goals for alternate energy generation
- Whenever possible, preserve existing housing that meets standards for energy performance, location efficiency, historic significance, and ability to accommodate future needs; build only new low/zero energy housing
- Establish targets for creating pedestrian sheds with connectivity to transportation, civic, shopping, recreation, and work opportunities
- Maximize potable water use through conservation and graywater systems; evaluate electric, gas, and oil utilities for capabilities now and in the future

PERFORMANCE CHARACTERISTICS

- New housing: Comply with zero-net energy standards. Zero-net energy means that a building will have no energy bills on an annualized basis; this implies that alternate energy will be generated on-site or nearby.
- Existing housing: Upgrade for energy conservation. An affordable upgrade should pay for the cost, amortized over the 30-year life of a mortgage, with energy cost savings. Units of sufficient aesthetic, historic, or locational value should be incentivized with grants sufficient to upgrade units.
- Energy savings for the John Street Townhouses are estimated at 15 to 30 percent over comparable conventional houses.

POTENTIAL SYNERGISM

- Form coalition with utilities for regional capacities and changing loads
- Coordinate with public transportation systems to reduce VMT
- Work with retrofit and replacement programs for dwellings
  - The John Street Townhouses demonstrate various green building techniques for traditional residential construction. These techniques can be easily applied to any new residential construction project.

IMPLEMENTATION TIME

- Initial assessment of housing stock: Approximately one year depending on availability of assessment teams and data
- Adoption of green building codes and revised land use plans: Approximately one to two years, depending on the political will
- Retrofit programs: May take up to three years, and could require grants, tax credits, loan programs, and assessments
- Individual septic systems: New localized waste treatment centers with local aquifer recharge require larger capital investments and may take five to ten years
- Green new and renovation techniques can be implemented immediately, concurrent with any renovation project.

BENEFITS

- Fossil fuel usage will be controlled.
- The community's dependence on automobiles will be reduced.
- Housing costs will be a fixed amount, providing continued value for the owners and community.
- Green construction techniques yield increased energy efficiency, lower energy costs, improved indoor air quality, and decreased GHG emissions. Location of the buildings on an infill site in a walkable, urban community provides decreased dependency on the automobile for transportation.

DRAWBACKS

- The cost to retrofit existing housing or to build new housing may be too high for existing homeowners, and funds may not be available. Existing housing that is well sited for a pedestrian plan may not be suitable for upgrade.
- The initial costs of green renovation strategies adds additional expense to base renovation costs, which must be recouped over time through reduced energy costs.
- Owner education about energy and water conservation and new energy-saving technologies requires time and monetary investment.
- Economic revitalization contributes to an increase in rental rates and property costs, negatively impacting low-income residents.

FIRST COST

- First cost for new construction may be 10 to 20 percent higher than typical construction (at the time of this writing), but payback periods will be shorter as codes are upgraded and fossil fuel costs escalate.
- First cost to upgrade existing housing may not be amortized over the life of a mortgage and must be considered as part of lifecycle costs.

LIFECYCLE COSTS

- New construction costs, when amortized, assume that these structures will always perform at predictable and controllable energy costs.
- The use of green renovation techniques provides significant annual savings in utility and energy costs. When amortized, retrofits should provide predictable costs. Additional savings may be realized as technologies continue to improve.
- After the cost of zero-energy for housing is fully amortized, the house should not have an energy cost over its lifetime except for maintenance and replacement.
- Urban infill contributes to savings in the cost to own/operate an automobile, and savings to the community in reduced auto pollution through the use of public transportation, resulting in reduced driving.

Figure 3-27
Interior renovations used reclaimed flooring and paneling, low-VOC finishes, sustainable lumber, and energy-efficient lighting and appliances.
Michael Bailey

ESTIMATED QUANTITATIVE PERFORMANCE

- New housing will not increase energy use. Energy use in existing housing will decrease by target amounts.
- Water use will be controlled and its quality improved.
- Waste treatment will be part of the total function of the existing watershed.
- The reduction in energy use in the John Street Townhouses is estimated at 20 percent, comparable to similar reductions achieved in new green construction.

IMPLEMENTATION SUPPORTS AND CONSTRAINTS

Implementation strategies include available tax credits, local utility supports, and low-interest loans. Implementation supports include city, state, and federal initiatives for green building, historic preservation, and neighborhood revitalization. However, sometimes the very own political will of the community will prevent individuals from adopting programs, codes, or enforcing new legislation. Implementation constraints include higher first costs of green renovation strategies and a potential real estate market bias toward new greenfield construction.

- International Energy Conservation Code (IECC), 2010 Edition
- International Building Code (IBC), 2009 Edition
- U.S. Green Building Standards (USGB)
- Energy Star standards

Web information

- Boston Science Consulting, Westford, MA: "Building America," U.S. Department of Energy; Energy efficient affordable housing for all climate zones, as presented at Build Boston. www.buildboston.com/
- Earthcraft building guidelines: www.earthcrafthouse.org
- LEED Criteria: www.usgbc.org
- Original Green: www.originalgreen.org
- Piedmont Housing Alliance: www.piedmonthousingalliance.org

Workshops

- New England Sustainable Energy Association Conference—Retrofitting for Energy; Case Study for Wind Energy at Jiminy Peak
- Build Boston, AIA Convention—Getting to Zero, Zero Net Energy Building, Solar Energy Workshop
- Factory Tour: Evergreen Solar; Subdivision Tour: Zero-net energy houses with developer/contractor Carter Scott.

Chapter 4

The Regulatory Environment

Sustainability Planning and the Law

Dan Slone, Esq.
Partner, McGuireWoods LLP

Challenges and Solutions

There are many legal and regulatory challenges to providing sustainable communities, and there are multiple appropriate solutions:

Challenges	Solutions
Leverage private capital to provide community solutions	Adjust regulatory policies and increase system flexibility to permit interventions of private capital in utilities and transportation
	Obtain private funding of building efficiency for a portion of operating costs
	Obtain private funding of stormwater capture and wastewater treatment and private ability to sell this water
	Sell rooftop-generated electricity into a micro-grid of local buildings
Make higher-density redevelopment possible without requiring major infrastructure improvement	Create citywide bicycle programs
	Increase efficiencies of new and existing residents so that new density can be accommodated within existing capacities
Build-out current structures to match current market conditions, while preserving economical ways of increasing density in the future	Planned "densification" to create supportive physical as well as business arrangements
	Building site-design should anticipate reuse and retrofit conditions, including additional floors on buildings and development in former parking lots
Curtail expenses and inputs on "single-purpose" solutions	Sustainability should balance multiple goals:
	Streets should allow safe passage of fire trucks and pedestrians
	Street trees should provide shade, food and habitat
Manufacturing must be located in urban areas, but NIMBY and environmental concerns make this difficult	Choose the right industries: green chemistry and industrial symbiosis make industry more palatable
	Create green infrastructure and appropriate transportation networks, and reduce industrial use and employment friction
Small-wheeled vehicles (e.g., scooters, bicycles, or golf carts) in urban areas will increase as gas prices rise; planning for this environment has been negligent	Create dedicated pathways as well as lanes and parking spaces for users within public right-of-ways

How to Use This Information

- Give a copy to key community leaders
- Form community reading circles to discuss the book
- Get local college architecture, planning, law, and public policy classes to "try out" solutions on the community

Laws and regulations maintain the following unsustainable problems in many planning and design systems:

- Fire codes require a 20-foot (or more) clear street and excessively wide turning radii creating traffic which is too fast for pedestrians
- Department of Transportation (DOT) regulations that establish overly wide right-of-ways, preclude street parking, and prevent normal urban sidewalk encroachments
- DOT regulations focus on moving cars quickly rather than pedestrians and bicycles safely
- Building codes are often conservative, with regulations blocking new green materials and sustainable techniques
- Lighting ordinances built into local laws focus on light impacts at property boundaries instead of preserving night skies and treat all lighting the same, whether in the urban core, or the edge, and parking-lot light-curfews are prohibited
- Zoning codes may require use separation, too much parking, and landscaping requirements appropriate for suburbia but not urban areas.

Ordinances and rules can also include the following challenges:

- Subdivision ordinances built into laws may use "setbacks" instead of "build-to lines," allowing too much separation between buildings and precluding creation of appropriate public spaces.
- Natural resource laws may require protection of manmade wetlands, to the detriment of good connectivity.
- Stormwater regulations can reduce available density by applying inappropriate rules.
- Utilities are empowered to require large easements, creating inappropriate setbacks of urban buildings.
- Homeowner associations can block seasonal grasses, urban gardens, and rooftop photovoltaics.

Moving toward comprehensive sustainability, we need to refine and integrate our land use and transportation systems, develop new paradigms for integrated systems of sustainable agriculture and sustainable industry, and develop a new system of utilities where we combine new net-zero users with retrofitted efficiencies and redesigned community utility systems.

Figure 4-1 outlines a more sustainable relationship between transportation and land use. The city is connected to the interstate, or city-to-city connector, by a

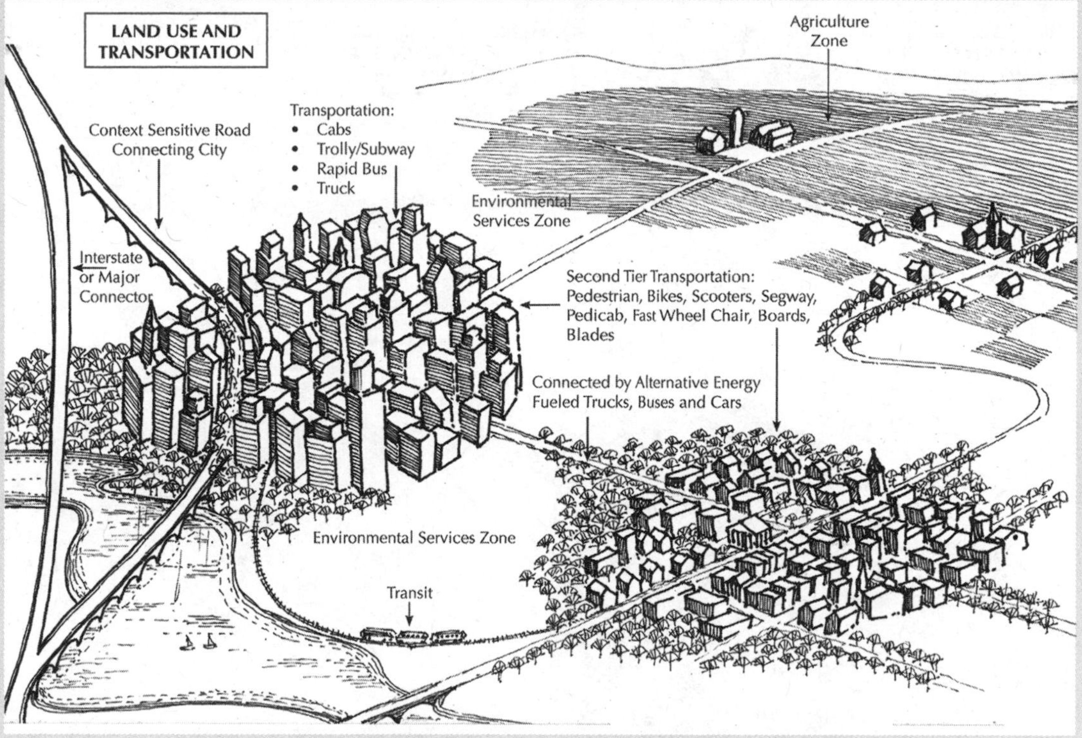
LAND USE AND TRANSPORTATION
Agriculture Zone
Transportation:
• Cabs
• Trolly/Subway
• Rapid Bus
• Truck
Context Sensitive Road Connecting City
Environmental Services Zone
Interstate or Major Connector
Second Tier Transportation: Pedestrian, Bikes, Scooters, Segway, Pedicab, Fast Wheel Chair, Boards, Blades
Connected by Alternative Energy Fueled Trucks, Buses and Cars
Environmental Services Zone
Transit

Figure 4-1
Sustainable cities, towns, and villages should be defined not just by their forms but by their internal transportation networks and the ways that they are connected to one another and related to the surrounding open spaces. *Drawing by Dan Slone and Dhiru Thadani*

context-sensitive road that drops from an exit ramp to a boulevard, instead of piercing the city. Cars are parked immediately and movement is achieved through a mix of walking, transit, bikes, cabs, and other devices that move around in neighborhood streets and separated sidewalks. Population is dense and is surrounded and constrained by an environmental services zone, where natural systems are used to provide flood control, water treatment, pollinators, carbon sequestration, and other services. Towns lie beyond these zones, connected to these centers by transit and traffic fueled by the renewable energy generated by the town. These towns are less dense, but still appropriate to absorb regional growth. In the towns, cars are rarely used because of easier options. These towns connect to villages that provide services for themselves and surrounding farms.

Sustainable agriculture and sustainable industry are woven into this model, responding to their transect zone. In Figure 4-2, the agriculture in T2 includes "industrial crops"—those grown for bulk use as fuel, lubricants, animal feed, or plastics. Closer to the city, "Tuscan Integrated Agriculture" provides sustainable crops for human consumption. These crops are grown closer to the houses in the large lots that were created in T2, but they are also grown in yards, right-of-ways, and common areas of the T3 suburban zone. Agriculture continues into the urban areas, but not through the farming of broken urban spaces. Urban spaces are repaired, and agriculture occurs throughout productive tree-lined streets, green roofs, green walls, private gardens, and community gardens.

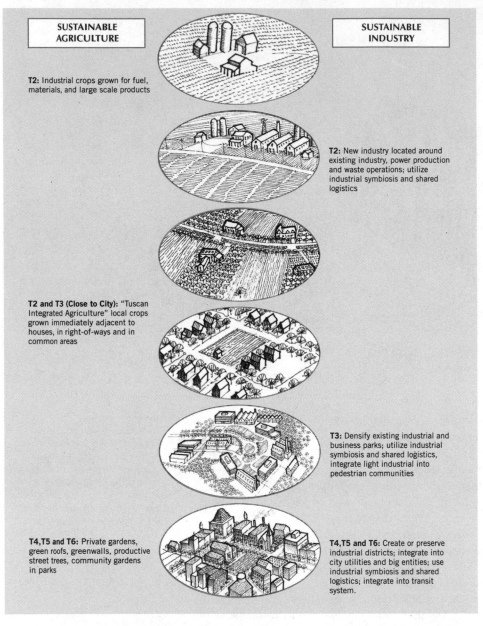

SUSTAINABLE AGRICULTURE

T2: Industrial crops grown for fuel, materials, and large scale products

SUSTAINABLE INDUSTRY

T2: New industry located around existing industry, power production and waste operations; utilize industrial symbiosis and shared logistics

T2 and T3 (Close to City): "Tuscan Integrated Agriculture" local crops grown immediately adjacent to houses, in right-of-ways and in common areas

T3: Densify existing industrial and business parks; utilize industrial symbiosis and shared logistics, integrate light industrial into pedestrian communities

T4,T5 and T6: Private gardens, green roofs, greenwalls, productive street trees, community gardens in parks

T4,T5 and T6: Create or preserve industrial districts; integrate into city utilities and big entities; use industrial symbiosis and shared logistics; integrate into transit system.

Figure 4-2
The way that sustainable agriculture and sustainable industry should be integrated into their community depends on where on the transect the integration occurs. *Dan Slone*

Industry and its employees are integrated into the plan. Industries within the area are connected, and share common utilities to gain the economic benefits of industrial symbiosis. Shared logistics help keep these industries competitive. Industries are clustered around power plants, quarries, wastewater facilities, or existing factories in the T2 rural areas. In the T3 suburban areas, industries are retrofitted into the industrial and business parks as well as into new transit-oriented pedestrian communities. In the urban areas, T4 through T6, industries are located in preserved industrial districts or retrofitted into the mall and shopping center sites.

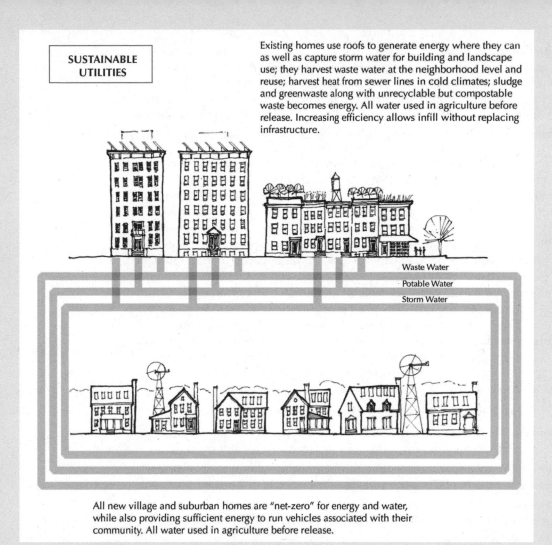

SUSTAINABLE UTILITIES

Existing homes use roofs to generate energy where they can as well as capture storm water for building and landscape use; they harvest waste water at the neighborhood level and reuse; harvest heat from sewer lines in cold climates; sludge and greenwaste along with unrecyclable but compostable waste becomes energy. All water used in agriculture before release. Increasing efficiency allows infill without replacing infrastructure.

Waste Water
Potable Water
Storm Water

All new village and suburban homes are "net-zero" for energy and water, while also providing sufficient energy to run vehicles associated with their community. All water used in agriculture before release.

The entire environment is supported by utility systems that are created with certain assumptions:

- New construction will be net-zero.
- Retrofit of older buildings will allow increases in density by reducing utility use by existing users to create infrastructure capacity.
- No material will be treated as waste; every resource will be fully utilized before being returned to the ecological systems.

Sustainable efficiency must define the multiple systems that drive the economic models of human habitat. Currently, urban systems are defined by what they utilize as well as by what they waste. Buildings are designed so that they must be destroyed in order to accommodate change and density increases. Money and energy are applied for clean-water use in the city, while falling rainwater is the subject

Figure 4-3
Sustainable communities will have sustainable utility systems. New areas will be built as "net zero" but existing areas will harvest from the existing shared systems to reduce their resource use. *Dan Slone*

of energy and expense to transport it out of the city. Process-water and graywater are barely used before they are cleaned and removed. Some environmental solutions focus on removing stormwater with less expense—through rooftop evaporation or infiltration systems—but these solutions do not reduce water use. Similarly, heat and biomass generated in the city are considered "costs" in conventional economics instead of "opportunities." The surface area of the built environment serves as a platform for graffiti or advertisers in the current model.

In a sustainable economic model, positive economics of the systems provide parallel gains in the sustainable social and environmental elements. Buildings are designed to retain value by enabling low-cost changes in use and "easy densification." Adaptation and retrofit of existing buildings is the norm. All water, whether stormwater, process-water or graywater, is captured and used. Uses compete for every inch of building and land surface in the city—a warehouse rooftop may be used for a solar array as well as a point of capture for stormwater that is used in rooftop vegetable gardens. It also can be available for multiple additional floors. Building walls can generate energy or they can support green walls, that clean air and help grow food. Heat from sewers, yard-waste, and composting vegetation becomes energy. Industry and commercial operations integrate transit into smart logistics, to move their products in the region through shared pallets and co-use of mass transit. The urban areas use the heat and bioproducts of industry just as the city's wastewater is used by industry. Multiple pathways allow for various transportation choices, and use every street, alley, and passage for efficiency.

The following principles can be used for creating a sustainable future:

- Regulatory systems must reflect the range of significant differences in human habitat through the use of tools such as the Transect for codes and regulations.

- The codes and regulations that control construction and maintenance of urban space must allow flexibility and not impede sustainability.

- Existing regulatory utility systems—such as water and energy—must be rewritten to establish a mandate for efficiency, and allow interventions where existing utilities fail to achieve sustainability.

- No "single purpose" agency should own the last word on any element of the public good. Optimize every element of complex systems to balance its multiple roles.

- Make by-right mechanisms available for developers who are in accordance with identified public goals. To encourage development, complete those aspects of the regulatory process identified as for the public good without shifting the burden to developers. Studies and regional permits should be obtained by localities to enable development in line with the public vision.

- Support planned densification and transferable development rights with innovations that do not make density more expensive, but transfer the externalities of excessive land consumption.

Preparing the Legal Team

Many localities do not have their own attorneys. Local outside attorneys frequently lack land use expertise. Localities often obtain legal services from outside specialist providers—an expensive proposition. In lawyers employed by jurisdictions, conservatism can act as an impediment rather than a benefit, since they have little incentive to take risks. While unlikely to lose their job for saying "no," if they approve a progressive coding approach, they could face a suit by a stakeholder and have their decisions examined in court. To overcome this problem, the governing legislative body needs to give their attorneys a mandate to move toward sustainable solutions and to openly discuss the possibility that breaking new ground will have risks. When risks are shared, counsels are free to be creative in achieving what is desired. Showing that another locality has undertaken a similar regulatory approach often overcomes legal resistance as well.

There are several other challenges:

- Many municipal agencies involved in obtaining sustainable urban systems have their own lawyers, each with completely different expertise.

- Complex system changes can involve land use lawyers, municipal law experts, and municipal finance experts, attorneys for utilities and attorneys representing traffic or fire expertise; many systems involve state or federal agencies—roads, natural resources, and housing.

- These agencies and their counsel may have separate legal or regulatory concerns; if regulatory changes are necessary, they can take a long time.

- Change can be difficult when national building or fire codes or national flood regulations are involved.

- For legal and regulatory systems, stakeholders can slow the process by going to court.

Attorneys for the localities are subject to political forces. The politics of changing current legal systems can be difficult, because the conventional approaches have been optimized for current political administrations. Planners can resist by-right approaches, because it removes projects from their control. Politicians can resist because it eliminates their ability to negotiate neighborhood benefits, a means of gaining voter support. Neighborhood associations can resist because they prefer their present negotiating strengths.

Typical tasks require different skill sets at different stages of a project. The "systems integrator" represents one with the greatest knowledge of appropriate tools and of legal and regulatory systems and municipal and private development. This knowledge is used to identify impediments and potential solutions—a consultant role that requires experienced-based skills. Through the charrette and implementation process, legal skills are required to test implementation strategies, draft ordinance changes, address legal issues created by others, assess threats and infeasibility arguments, and suggest alternative strategies that may be necessary. Depending on the implementation, understanding the legal aspects of the following is necessary:

- Zoning—conventional, hybrid, form-based performance, and SmartCode
- Comprehensive Plans
- Subdivision—utilities and road-placement regulations

- Utility-provider regulations
- Historic and natural-resource regulations
- Environmental and health-impact assessment regulations
- Private mechanisms—codes, covenants, restrictions, and homeowner association laws
- Real estate financing and transactions
- Common-law issues of tort liability and constitutional issues
- Common national building and fire codes
- Mechanisms for sustainability-standards programs such as LEED

All of these skills need to be inherent in the team, and they can come from different participants, depending on the presence, experience, and scope of other team participants. If the city attorney has land use expertise and is supportive of the project, the outside consultant has less of a role. An experienced planner who has participated in a full impediments analysis might manage this aspect of the project.

Preparing the Tools

There are many regulatory or legal tools that are useful, but there aren't many performance-measurement tools or visual-mapping tools appropriate for this discipline.

We use a wide array of tools and important mechanisms to convey desired project endpoints. For example, "One Planet Living" graphics communicates the consequences of a nonsustainable lifestyle. These graphics convey ecological footprints. The goal is to generate rough dashboards to emphasize that sustainability cannot be obtained by system changes alone; behavioral changes are required to achieve the bulk of sustainability. We employ variations on mind-mapping to outline the search for impediments, and sketches to discuss complex systems that can be represented with icons. Renderings or computer simulations of expected conditions can be vital for obtaining community support.

We use many tools for coding sustainable urbanism. Voluntary standards such as LEED® or Earthcraft™ can be cross-referenced by either a point-of-reference for standards or with implementation through the building code. Localities can choose to impose voluntary standards on themselves, but to impose these requirements on third parties can require integration of the standards into the building code in order to avoid creating competing standards. LEED-ND® represents a product that balances the competing strains of SmartGrowth, New Urbanism, and green-building development in a comprehensive measurement system.

Form-based codes such as the SmartCode and other models contain regulating graphics that make them easier to understand and implement. These codes regulate the form of the building more than the use, and provide for more sustainable communities. We can use other model codes to address particular resources or the introduction of technologies, such as wind turbines or photovoltaics. In almost all instances, our coding is based on some version of the "Transect," since it allows us to modulate the code for the difference in the urban, sub-, and ex-urban intensities, scale, and location, which is more appropriate than context-sensitive codes.

Preparing the Place

We need a broad understanding of the existing physical landscape, but not a lot of detail, because what we are looking for is an understanding of the types of situations we will encounter, not detailed solutions for them. Questions and concerns relate to the following:

- Is the community built out or does it have infill, redevelopment, or greenfield prospects?
- Is it characterized by its proximity to natural resources? Farmland?
- Are trees a significant part of the landscape?
- Does it have road and sidewalk connections in place?
- Is it rural, urban, suburban, hamlet, village, town, or city?
- Does it have an urban core? A historic or other specialized district?
- Is parking an issue?
- What is water availability?
- What are the existing development pressures?

We can receive a report with this information or conduct interviews.

The elements that are needed to assess projects include the following:

- Access to a number of legal documents to understand existing systems. Many of these are available online for localities, but if they aren't, someone is needed to supply them.
- Review zoning, subdivision, and resource protection ordinances for barriers and context.
- Scan the balance of the code provisions for possible impediments, as well as for implemented solutions.
- Scan regional guidebooks or standards for roads, utility installation, and design.
- Review contextual documents such as "Comprehensive or Specific Area Plans," transportation and capital improvement plans, and any recent environmental impact assessments.
- Obtain copies of the state-enabling statutes.
- Review the fire code, building code, and flood code.

Develop some general understanding of the desired level of advance work as well as the general direction of intent before beginning any analysis. If a conventional code is being replaced by a form-based code, extensive analysis of the existing code is unnecessary and a scan for the provisions to remain would be sufficient.

One constraint is cost. Absent a budget for appropriate adjustment of or tailoring of their ordinances, many localities obtain their ordinances by copying them from other localities. If the team is experienced, the planners can narrow the scope, and costs, of legal review. Focused "triage" can remove many impediments, allowing a budget for new-code support of provisions necessary for a sustainable approach. Another constraint is the gap between how laws are read and the procedures that are followed. The law can require that a "Comprehensive Plan" show realistic development areas, but a locality can leave these areas designated as agriculture. This is not done because it disagrees with the appropriateness of their development, but to secure a better negotiating position when property owners try to rezone the property.

We calibrate form-based codes and conduct the following:

- Review the authority for components of form-based codes such as graphics or "unified code"
- Determine which portions of the code to retain to meet state requirements
- Determine which portions of code are necessary to address federal or state requirements—e.g., floodplains, ADA, wellhead protection
- Determine portions of the code that respond to historic circumstances that could recur, and retain these codes—e.g., zoning status of vacated streets
- Check all retained provisions for impediments and coordinate the integration of new and existing definitions

Preparing the People

In many of our projects, we use newspapers, churches, and civic organizations and Internet sites to disseminate information on the process and to create community-input opportunities.

Neighborhood meetings—particularly if they are accompanied by food and are conducted on tables with sheets of paper for people to record their ideas—can be used to develop and harvest ideas, as well as generate community leaders to participate in the project.

Public and private opportunities for questions regarding impacts to individual properties must be created to develop support for changes in ordinances. These may be created with a website.

Developing Goals, Objectives, and Performance Metrics

There is a difference between the goals we help advance for the project and the measures that we use for the product of our work within the project. We advocate a project goal of triple-bottom-line sustainability, with elements of the project examined from the perspectives of environmental, social, and economic sustainability. Parks can be advanced because of their social benefit, and for these to be economically sustainable, their maintenance costs must be taken into account. To make these costs more affordable, seasonal grasses can be substituted for lawns. A similar analysis can be applied when asked whether a green roof should grow useful produce or whether street-trees and right-of-ways should produce habitat or food.

Because our discipline involves the creation of implementation tools, the strategy for their creation and use begins with understanding what the locality wants to accomplish. The difficulty begins when many localities do not know how certain tools affect the nature of their community; they cannot make informed strategic decisions without specific knowledge. For example, the *design* of their zoning code may affect the results. As a part of goal development, objectives, and performance metrics, the community must be exposed to the desired end and the tools so that they can make strategic choices.

The process must occur in advance of a charrette which is more likely to focus on the actual application of the tools. Localities are often unsure about adopting a form-based code, even if they are sure about their vision of how they wish to look in 20 years. They might not be sure whether they want to combine their water, sewer, and stormwater agencies into one department, or provide for third-party intervention to increase efficiencies.

Advance workshops facilitate a discussion of the different tools and approaches available to the locality and the consequences of their use. If held during a charrette, more post-charrette production meetings are required to allow the choice of tools necessary to inform the strategic plans.

Codes and legal/regulatory system changes should result in ordinances and systems which accomplish the following:

- Achieve planning goals and stakeholder visions
- Are designed for active implementation, providing few opportunities to be changed on an ad-hoc basis
- Minimize costs to engage in the process while maximizing available information for decision-making
- Avoid control of critical design decisions by single-purpose agencies
- When power is vested in separate decision-making bodies, align authority toward shared community visions
- Make sure legal tools are clear and easy to use
- Make sure the tools are fair and provide appropriate due process

Developing the Strategic Plan

Strategic plans can be developed as the goals are identified and the appropriate tools or techniques are selected. A community with a goal of pedestrian orientation requires examination of the choice of coding techniques necessary to achieve this result, and may result in a selection of transect-supported form-based code as the best tool to achieve this goal. The strategic plan must address how the code will be developed, stakeholder buy-in obtained, mapping completed, and final legislative approvals obtained, as well as funding and timing issues. Depending on the goals, this process must be applied to each of the necessary implementing codes and changes to contextual documents. Different team members can develop different products, but decisions must be made on task divisions and their integration, both at an individual level and at a jurisdictional or regional level.

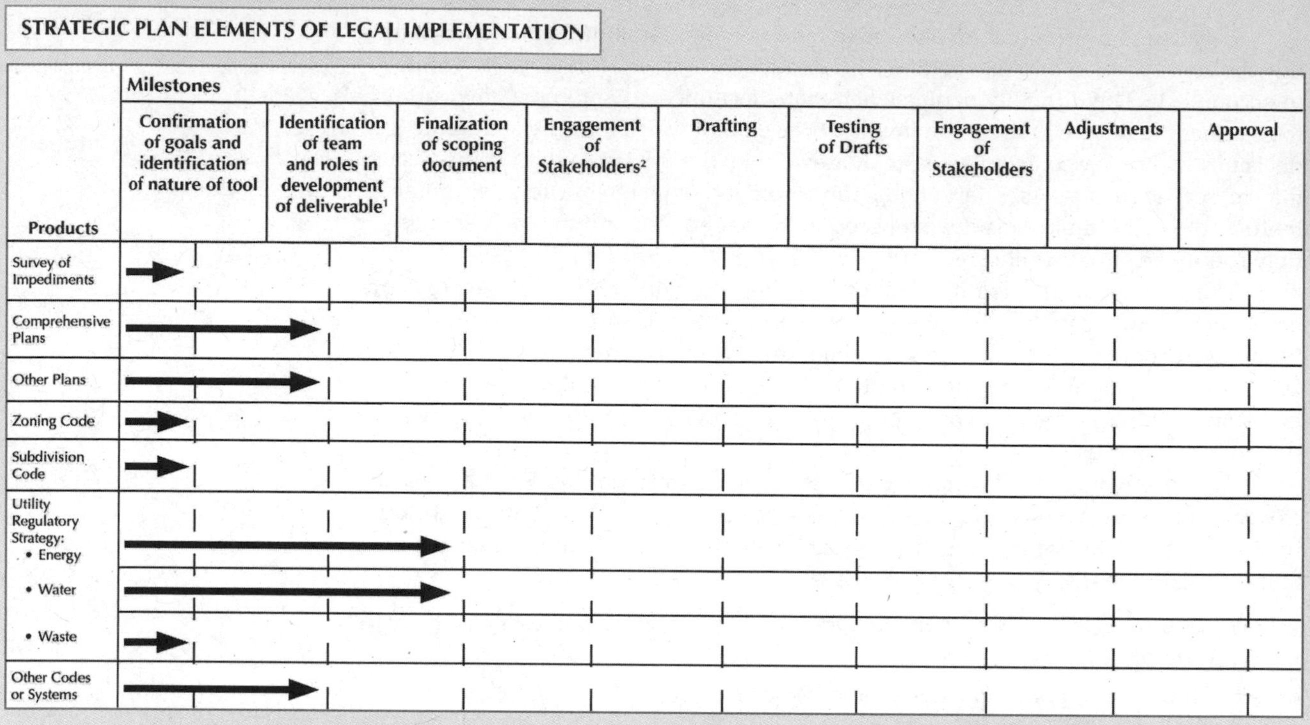

STRATEGIC PLAN ELEMENTS OF LEGAL IMPLEMENTATION

Products	Milestones								
	Confirmation of goals and identification of nature of tool	Identification of team and roles in development of deliverable[1]	Finalization of scoping document	Engagement of Stakeholders[2]	Drafting	Testing of Drafts	Engagement of Stakeholders	Adjustments	Approval
Survey of Impediments	→								
Comprehensive Plans	——→								
Other Plans	——→								
Zoning Code	→								
Subdivision Code	→								
Utility Regulatory Strategy: • Energy	————————→								
• Water	————————→								
• Waste	→								
Other Codes or Systems	——→								

1. A different order may be necessary when components are being provided through an RFP process. This step may be preceded by a preliminary scoping and RFP.

2. Stakeholders may have already been involved in the choice of tools. This step is to engage them in the actual application of the tool to calibrate it to local circumstances.

Key questions for strategic plan development elements might look like those shown in Figure 4-4.

We have successfully used websites to solicit ideas and gather private and public feedback. Various elements of the Internet are important tools:

- Use of bulletin boards
- Posted graphics
- E-mail contacts
- The ability to record oral comments and questions with toll-free numbers
- Bloggers, willing to present and explore positive components, can stimulate discussion, though this requires a significant commitment of personal time.

Developing the Action Plan

Before new ordinances are presented to stakeholders as near final drafts, we recommend a testing process to check for unintended consequences or conflicts. Those most appropriate to conduct this testing depends on the type of ordinance, though usually not a person who has had a major role in creating the ordinance. Where a form-based code has been prepared by outside consultants, the planning staff might create and test scenarios; a local engineering firm might test proposed changes in water regulations. Often volunteer groups or university classes are re-

Figure 4-4

This chart shows the milestones in the process of implementing the changes in legal documents or creation of deliverables for the implementation process. The arrows shown on this chart are merely examples of how it would be used to track the progress of each of the products. *Dan Slone*

sources for testing though regulatory approaches may require testing and evaluation by outside experts. Land-development regulations may need to be assessed by engineers for water-quality consequences by market analysts for their viability, and by fiscal-impact specialists for their economic sustainability.

Smaller jurisdictions may have difficulty dealing with the costs of multiple analyses. Some jurisdictions create regional groups to develop model versions of ordinances and then seek funding for shared costs of studies of these ordinances. Localities can tailor the ordinances to their jurisdiction with substantially less risk and cost; localities also could develop a code jointly, and divide the costs of collateral studies.

Often jurisdictions make the mistake of engaging a third party to prepare a proposed ordinance without specifying progress feedback loops. They usually do not see the consultant again until the final product is presented. If the product is seriously off-base, the budget and timetable may not support the adjustment, and the jurisdiction is then forced to pass an inappropriate product, turn it down and sacrifice their investment, or conduct triage and fix it to the best of their ability. None of these solutions is palatable. The action plan must include progress feedback loops to assess the product as it is being produced.

Implementing the Action Plan

Generating renderings, models, or computer animation from proposed codes provides low-cost feedback and proposed regulatory-schemes testing. Engineering models can create examples that can be shared. Many jurisdictions have needed on-the-ground examples in order to create the political will to fully implement a regulation. The easiest way to accomplish this is to visit a built example model. If the result is positive, it can be easy to share by posting reports or videos. If examples do not exist, the locality can find a way to "try out" the code. Some jurisdictions have done this by implementing the code only on their own municipal or county projects, so that a development authority, a school, or other civic building or area is the test site. Many jurisdictions have partnered with a local developer and applied potential codes through the Planned Unit Development (PUD) process to that developer's project. Sometimes codes are implemented either in greenfield edges, or in the urban core itself, but not in surrounding areas; the development community, the public, and the politicians can assess the results before more broad applications are made. The urban core is often already built-out so the usefulness of this approach is limited as a model, but the impact can be extremely important over time.

For the most part, the physical results eclipse the discussion of the legal tools. The launch of most legal-tool actions will not attract fanfare unless they have been controversial. There can be activity as stakeholders try to gain political advantage and undo or water-down changes that have been made. Any launch should be accompanied by an educational campaign for the staff, elected officials, monitoring activists, and users. For the long term, feedback loops need to be created to share concerns, good results, and questions. A staff member—who is a point of contact—should be created to monitor the application of the ordinance for developing issues.

For most of the legal systems, the only way they can be assessed is based on whether the results in either the built environment or the regulatory environment meet the goals and the performance values. As part of the monitoring plan, milestones should be created to assess performance. The performance results should suggest necessary evaluation for the legal and regulatory process.

Transforming the Built Environment Through Form-Based Coding

Stephen J. Coyle, AIA, LEED
Town-Green, Townworks + DPZ

Jurisdictional Code and Ordinances

The jurisdictional land development code or ordinance consists of a set of laws passed by the governing body—the municipality, county, or township. The state's constitution or statutes or its legislature grants the jurisdiction the power to enact ordinances, referred to land development codes, but also *development standards,* statutes, and zoning ordinances, as opposed to building, structural, and life safety codes.

Many jurisdictional codes encompass public safety, health, and general welfare; we focus on those that directly or indirectly improve or degrade the environmental, energy, economic, social, and aesthetic resilience, health, and adaptability of the built environment and its supporting systems. For example, a county or municipal code typically prescribes the design and maintenance of local streets, landscaping, and sidewalks. Sidewalk widths and crosswalk distances can greatly affect the degree of convenience and safety of the pedestrian, and the walkability of the environment. Street travel lane widths directly impact the travel speeds of motor vehicles, despite posted speed limits.

However, since a jurisdiction is typically divided into land use "zones" or districts, zoning codes and the zoning maps that describe the permitted use areas provide the most significant power of jurisdictional ordinances. While zoning historically attempted to conserve the value of property and to encourage the most appropriate land uses and separation of incompatible uses, this sensible approach was undermined to the extreme with the emergence of motor-vehicle-dominated planning and development that enabled the creation of far-flung, auto-oriented, single-use zones: residential pods, office and industrial parks, and shopping centers.

Conventional, Euclidean Zoning

Euclidean zoning, a convention for almost 80 years, regulates land primarily by use and usually dictates lot size, dimensions, and building lot coverage and height. Use-based or segregated zoning systemically undermines the spatially connected combinations of daily human functions—working, shopping, learning, socializing, governing, and housing—that form the patterns of walkable neighborhoods, villages, towns, or cities. The ubiquity of conventional zoning results in frequent modifications to permit mixed-use zones, a work around for a regulatory system that controls building uses rather than forms that can accommodate changing functions over time—a timeless mark of community resilience.

Performance-Based Zoning

Performance-based zoning employs outcome-based or objective-oriented criteria to establish review parameters for proposed development projects in any area of a

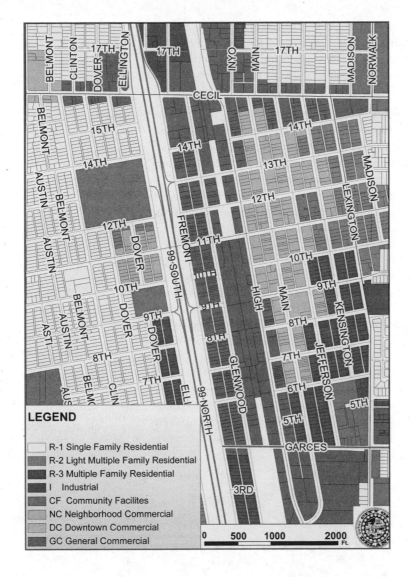

LEGEND

R-1 Single Family Residential
R-2 Light Multiple Family Residential
R-3 Multiple Family Residential
I   Industrial
CF Community Facilites
NC Neighborhood Commercial
DC Downtown Commercial
GC General Commercial

0   500   1000   2000 Ft.

Figure 4-5
Conventional or Euclidean zoning primarily regulates land uses and densities. *Town-Green*

municipality. Performance zoning may employ a numerical rating system to calculate the expected performance of a development application. For example, an applicant might obtain bonus points for increasing the area of undeveloped space or adding other public amenities in a development plan. The additional points might result in an administrative rather than public review of the application.

While performance-based zoning theoretically reflects a market-driven, incentive approach for attracting superior development where the applicant can choose the desired means and level of compliance, even the highest zoning or performance tier may not yield the desired results. The system's fundamental constraint, an essentially discretionary plan review and approval process, stems from qualifying criteria that consist of targets rather than specific development standards. For example, an incentive to increase the amount or ratio of open space to development may ignore environmental performance or proximity to residents. This condition necessitates a high level of discretion by the administering authority. The process can sacrifice flexibility for the predictability of securing the desired environmental, energy, economic, social, and aesthetic performance.

Form-Based Codes

Form-based codes (FBC) consist of land development regulations that emphasize the desired physical form—the design, scale, and relationships—of buildings and public space, and place less emphasis on building or land uses. FBCs integrate environmental, energy, economic, social, and aesthetic performance into the code standards. *They permit by right the rules for making compact, diverse, walkable, and connected development or redevelopment—the key elements of resilient, healthy built environments.*

Form-based codes regulate land, infrastructure, and building development, but do not replace state and local building codes. They seek to achieve a specific urban form and to shape a higher-quality built environment that integrates rather than separates compatible uses. As a supplement, modification, or replacement to city or county zoning and development ordinances, FBCs help create a predictable public and/or private realm by controlling or regulating its physical form as well as the building intensities and uses. The codes enable the implementation of a community's vision by coding desired outcomes appropriate to specific zones or areas, from the natural landscape through the urban center.

Unlike design guidelines or performance-based zoning, form-based codes specify rather than recommend, entice, encourage, or suggest by prescribing a desired or intended outcome rather than proscribing what's prohibited. In place of or in addition to controlling building densities through formulas such as floor-area-ratios (FAR), dwelling units per acre, and parking formulas, FBCs may control densities by regulating the total permitted building volume.

Form-based codes may be applied at the scale of the region, community, neighborhood, or site, and deployed at the general or comprehensive, sector or community, and specific or precise plan level. Like conventional codes, form-based codes should maintain consistency with jurisdictional general or comprehensive plan policies. Similar to conventional codes, FBCs can encompass land zoning and subdivision regulations, and incorporate urban de-

Figure 4-6
Unlike conventional zoning codes and land use maps, form-based codes and plans regulate the physical, urban form and only as necessary, building uses. FBCs establish the regulations that enable resilient communities and neighborhoods to adapt to changes over time, as our traditional buildings once did. *Town-Green*

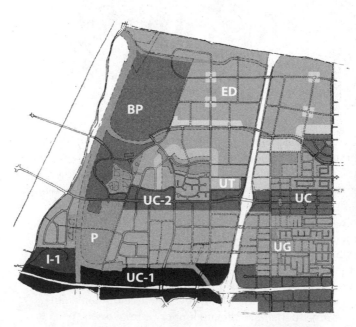

I-1	Heavy Manufacturing District
ED	Employment District
UC-1	Urban Corridor 1 (T6)
UC-2	Urban Corridor 2 (T6.1)
UT	Urban Employment Transition (T5-E)
UG	Urban General (T4)
UC	Urban Center (T5)
BP	Balloon Park District
P	Parks & Open Space

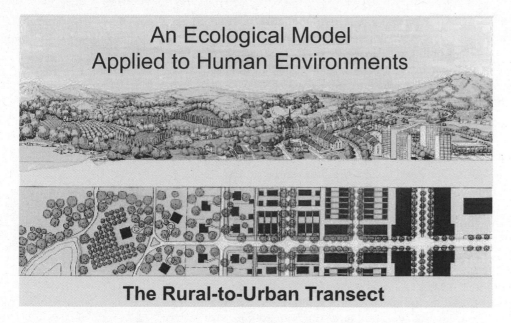

An Ecological Model
Applied to Human Environments

The Rural-to-Urban Transect

Figure 4-7
The transect organizes development patterns into six rural-to-urban zones. *DPZ & Associates, Inc. and Eusebio Ascuy*

sign, architectural and landscape standards, street and open space standards, and environmental, energy, and aesthetic requirements, though not building-scale fire and life safety codes.

A conventional zoning or land use map can morph into a FBC regulating plan that defines the boundaries of various urbanized zones, the natural and/or agriculture and future development areas, and the trajectories and connections of major thoroughfares. Each jusrisdiction defines the range and complexity of plan elements and details, from identifying incompatible uses that require separation or other restrictions, to determining whether to specify or constrain architectural typologies or styles. Progressive environmental and energy standards should be incorporated into all code approaches, but only a form-based code can be "sustainable by design" by its underlying "DNA" that codes in for resilience, diversity, and walkability,

Transect-Based Codes

The transect-based[1] FBC incorporates the rural-to-urban transect zones developed by the architectural and planning firm Duany Plater-Zyberk and Company. Since the transect is based on the physical form of the built and natural environment, all transect-based codes are form-based. The DPZ Transect was drawn from the work of Alexander Von Humboldt at the close of the eighteenth century, whose transect presents a geographical cross-section of a region intended to reveal a sequence of environments and analyze natural ecologies.

For the purpose of coding the built environment and its supporting systems, the transect facilitates the observation and documentation of the key elements that contribute to a resilient and healthy human habitat. That process illuminates those elements and distinctive features within a sequence of habitats, in six rural-to-urban zones, T1—natural, to T6—urban core. The urban-to-rural transect provides a visual, functional, and organizational format for form-based coding, since each sequence or transect zone can be described by text and through imagery as a set of normative forms. The transect helps organize development patterns as six rural-to-urban zones, or T1— rural, to T6—city center, with single- or special-use districts where necessary for airports, ports, or existing office parks and subdivisions.

Prepare the Team

Code drafting begins with the selection of a consulting team with a diversity of backgrounds and significant experience in developing authentic form-based codes: urban designers, architects, landscape architects, planners, civil engineers, and land use attorneys familiar with FBCs. The practitioners should demonstrate, by example, adequate regulatory and design competency with an understanding of fundamental building and spatial design principles.

Conventional planners and code writers, limited to two map dimensions and text, rarely exhibit this skill but can be retrained. Architects intuitively grasp the visual elements of coding but usually have no training or experience in regulating at the block and neighborhood scale. Landscape architects often lack the design and technical knowledge of building design professions. Superior form-based code-makers demonstrate a mastery of building and space design, and regulatory savvy. Since FBCs are best developed in public processes that build off a community vision, coders should demonstrate the ability to engage the public in code-making. Two excellent sources of information about form-based code practitioners are: The Form-Based Codes Institute[2] and the Center for Applied Transect Studies (CATS).[3]

Selecting the Tools

At the beginning of the coding process, the team and/or jurisdiction will decide on a coding format. Form-based codes may be generated from scratch, borrowed and modified from other adopted form-based codes, or adapted from "open source" templates such as the SmartCode mentioned before. As a model code, the Smart-Code, a transect-based code, represents an open source or "freeware" code that provides a template or model for local calibration or customization by the code-making team. Most other codes are proprietary.

THE SMARTCODE

The SmartCode,[4] a complete alternative form-based code system developed by the architectural and planning firm Duany Plater-Zyberk and Company (DPZ), incorporates Smart Growth and New Urbanism principles into a unified development ordinance. It regulates the form of development from regional and community scale to the building and frontage, requires calibration or customization for regional and local conditions, preferably with the participation of the local citizens. The model Smart-Code is freeware, available in an editable format from the websites www.smartcode-central.org and www.Transect.org, packaged into a concise seven-article[5] document released in 2003 which is continually updated. Refer to the SmartCode STEP sheet that follows. SmartCode includes Modules,[6] multidisciplinary guidelines, recommendations, best practices, and development standards, each transect-based.

Prepare the Place

Code research begins by reviewing the relevant documents—the general or comprehensive plans, the jurisdictional codes and zoning maps studies, and development plans, and studies provided by governmental agencies. The investigation continues by reearching the area's physical form, from building, streets, landscapes, parking lots, and open space, to studying the intensity and patterns of the built environment.

Depending on the scale and code type, the research may include the following:

- Natural environmental resources, features, and conditions
- Existing and proposed infrastructure and environmental support systems
- Architectural building types and patterns
- Landscape types and patterns
- Economic and market conditions and trends
- Relevant parcels and ownership, developed, undeveloped, and pending, and assessment of land available for development or redevelopment
- Previously conducted plans and studies for the area

CALIBRATING A FORM-BASED CODE

Form-based codes, including the transect-based, require a calibration or local context customization process so that each code incorporates or reflects the cherished principles and practices, local character and form. Though nearly every town exhibits some rural-to-urban gradient or distinction, the code calibrators, "urban scientists" in the field, research and analyze the local physical context and building practices to extract a type of generative DNA of the built environment, to yield a code "of the place." Coding elements include the disposition, configuration, and function of buildings, thoroughfares, and civic spaces. The combination of elements in each identified transect zone reflects the attributes of an "immersive environment," or the distinctive character of the range of human habitats within the coding zone.

A form-based code calibration may center along a single corridor, a neighborhood, community, or region; the depth and breadth of investigation will depend on the scale of the coding intervention. The coding effort may focus on the design of public rights-of-way, the streets, parks, and building frontages, or the reconfiguration of existing development patterns. Thus, the calibration should adjust to the physical conditions, scale, and range of the coded elements.

When preparing a transect-based code, the calibrator begins by identifying and documenting the features of each of the "T" zones or sequence of physical environments, using aerial, topographical/drainage, geological, and climatological maps, images, and physical tours. Depending on the location and scale of intervention, the research may yield fewer than six T zones. For example, most communities do not contain a T-6 Urban Core Zone, a downtown Kansas City. Since most regions and communities contain a range of development patterns from traditional to post-1950s suburbia, research will help determine the appropriate genesis and combinations of coding forms. Transect-based sprawl repair/retrofit tools are available for the latter areas when desired.

The calibration should qualitatively and quantitatively document the form and spatial character, and numerical indices, using a ground-level visual survey by the coding team and spatial research to tabulate street width and other measures of the urban form. Code calibrations continue through the charrette or workshops to enable stakeholders to report on local character and conditions. Calibration information can be found at:

1. The Form-Based Codes Institute, www.formbasedcodes.org/
2. The Center for Applied Transect Studies (CATS), www.Transect.org/, SmartCode Central, under the direction of Andres Duany, Plater-Zyberk and Company, and the Codes Project http://codesproject.asu.edu/php/your_life.php

The calibration may include:

1. Vehicular lane dimensions (motor and bicycle)
2. Thoroughfare assemblies
3. Parking standards (motor and bicycle)
4. Parking calculations
5. Public frontages
6. Private frontages
7. Building configuration
8. Building disposition
9. Building function
10. Building types
11. Civic spaces
12. Public lighting
13. Public plantings

Prepare the People

The team engages and educates those directly or indirectly involved, impacted by, or who can impact the coding effort. The engagement process can include face-to-face meetings, interviews, and focus groups, workshops, and the public charrette. A random selection of citizens for participation in code-making permits a more diverse cross-section of community representation. By securing diverse participation, those who usually avoid public events, youngsters and minorities for example, can offer greater diversity of feedback to the coding team, and benefit from broader educational opportunities.

A thorough research should include the following tasks:

- Developing a stakeholder identification and analysis that describes the name, contact information, and specific stake or position relative to the project of people capable of supporting or resisting the coding process, in particular key residents, business, and property owners whom the coding will impact.

- Complete a stakeholder engagement plan for review by the jurisdiction and refine it into a strategic plan deployed and updated during the coding project.

- If deemed necessary or important, assist the jurisdiction in organizing an advisory committee composed of representative stakeholders to guide the coding process.

- Draft a promotional-quality project description and questionnaire for the Web and general distribution and collection to gather public input on the coding effort.

- Launch a project website with project description and questionnaire, and an introduction to the jurisdictional staff and consulting team, the process, and desired outcomes.

- Hold confidential interviews with key stakeholders, including city and agency officials, to explore code-relevant goals, ideas, issues, and concerns.

- Hold an educational workshop to gather feedback on preferred development patterns, and to introduce the public to the principles, practices, and the *tools of coding:*

  1. *Character*—coding tools for preserving and enhancing desirable neighborhood characteristics, and eliminating and preventing undesirable characteristics

  2. *Mobility*—coding tools for improving mobility and increasing choices, convenience, and safety

  3. *Patterns*—coding tools for "place-making," the physical patterns and timeless, practical principles that can create great places

  4. *Environment*—coding "best practice" tools for protecting and improving the built and natural resources

The tools will, in aggregate, comprise a "coding toolbox," text and images that define, describe, and detail how, why, when, and where to code

Develop Goals, Objectives, and Performance Measures

The coding process requires the development of goals, objectives, boundaries, and performance measures that provide the framework for assessing the efficacy of a range of coding principles, ideas, strategies, standards, and tools. The objectives should be defined as succinctly and precisely as possible, followed by the performance measures or metrics to evaluate each. Soliciting measurable goals and objectives should begin with the jurisdiction responsible for adopting and administering the code and then extend into the community. The coding team then attempts to establish common ground and resolve differences through private and public venues, discussions, and negotiations.

Questionnaires and surveys, distributed through the Web and print, with feedback from interviews and public events, provide opportunities for gathering public and private enterprises to discuss concerns, issues, and ideas to develop the strategies and tactics behind the codes. Walking tours and audits provide a way for citizens to understand the relationship of the buildings, streets, public and private spaces, historic resources, and communities that make up the place and the elements of the code.

Each method of research should refine the goals and objectives, and each can start by asking the jurisdiction and the community the following:

1. What are the goals, or desired outcomes of recoding the community? For example, a common coding goal might consist of developing a walkable community, redeveloping a decaying community with the new codes, or streamlining the plan application and approval process.

2. What are the **objectives**? A common coding objective of planning staffs, designers, and builders: creating an efficient and workable "bridge" between the existing and new code, or allowing taller building at significant intersections.

3. What are the **performance criteria** or **metrics** that will be employed to measure the qualitative and quantitative potential for proposed code? For example, the measure for achieving the goal of nondiscretionary code might warrant the exclusive use of prescriptive language throughout that details permitted materials, rather than describing a level of accepted performance.

Develop Code Strategies

The code strategies are best developed by engaging those identified in the people-preparation phase, or at minimum, a representative group of stakeholders. Their input, essential for "getting it right" or creating a code reflective of the needs of jurisdiction and the larger community, will garner support necessary for the code's eventual adoption.

The public charrette represents a preferred method of developing both the strategies and specific details, though a private version can be employed where public engagement is neither warranted nor desired, for example, when coding a secure military installation. The multiday event should open with a presentation of goals, expectations, and a detailed overview of the coding process. Since not all participants, whether public or private, will arrive properly prepared, continue education throughout the process. Commence several rounds of brainstorming, comparing, "design-testing," and evaluating the efficacy of code ideas. For those unable to participate in person, other forms of involvement such as Web and video can be incorporated into the charrette.

Develop a draft regulating plan quickly, since the map identifies the locations, size, boundaries, and basic features of each zone based in part on the site surveys or calibration completed during the place-research step. Professionals and nonprofessionals alike should propose strategies in a collaborative, workshop format. Each idea is design-tested against a set of agreed-upon metrics or evaluation criteria consistent with the goal and objectives. This method generates a sense of shared authorship and facilitates a consensus-built code. These activities can consume most or all of the charrette, at minimum the first day or two, depending on the coding complexities and the length of the event.

The actual coding strategies or the "rules" for achieving the jurisdiction and community's regulatory goals and objectives should include:

1. Introduction of the transect or T zones as a framework for organizing the physical place

2. Developing a conceptual regulating plan that describes the location, potential uses, the intensities of development areas (or T zones), with a focus on regulating the urban form instead of land use

3. Zoning for a mix of uses, considering use a secondary factor in regulating development

4. Coding for an increased development density where appropriate

5. Coding so that private buildings shape public space through the use of building form standards with specific requirements for building placement

6. Coding to require an interconnected, multi-use street network and pedestrian-scaled blocks

7. Coding the location and disposition of civic buildings and places like parks and plazas

8. Coding with graphic-based images or diagrams that are unambiguous, clearly labeled, and accurate in their presentation of spatial configurations

9. Coding standards that provide flexibility by permitting uses to change over time without regulatory approval

10. Coding building and blocks with predictable physical standards rather than numerical parameters

11. Coding standards keyed to specific locations on a regulating plan

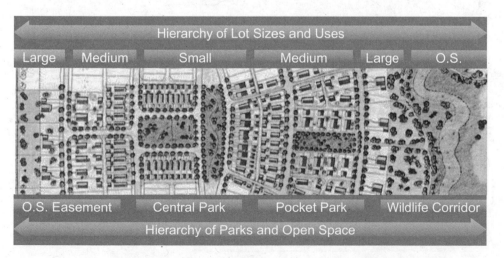

Figure 4-9
The form-based code should allocate development intensities and public space consistent with community design principles. *Lennertz, Coyle and Associates*

Upon completion of the code strategy development, the team commences drafting the physical, regulatory, and administrative elements, though an experienced team may undertake this concurrently.

Develop the Code

Develop the form-based code only after completing local customization or calibration by public and private planners and designers, gaining adequate jurisdictional and community input, and after establishing the coding strategies. The superior code incorporates precise and concise text, and clear, relevant, and readable supporting images. It should balance time-tested standards with technical sophistication, appropriate to the economical, social, aesthetic, and environmental context.

Subsequent to drafting coding strategies, the develop each of the elements or sections of the code. While this process can begin during the charrette, the scale and depth of design and technical efforts demand focused, iterative, and collaborative work by the coding team. The coded elements typically consist of the following:

1. *The regulating plan:* the graphic reference map that identifies and keys private lots and public rights-of-way to the transect zones and the building and lot standards, and describes the relationship of each lot to the public realm. The regulating plan describes the locations and boundaries of transect-based urban-to-rural zones, their centers, edges, and rights-of-way. The regulating plan may not be legally binding while the form-based code is legally binding and delineates

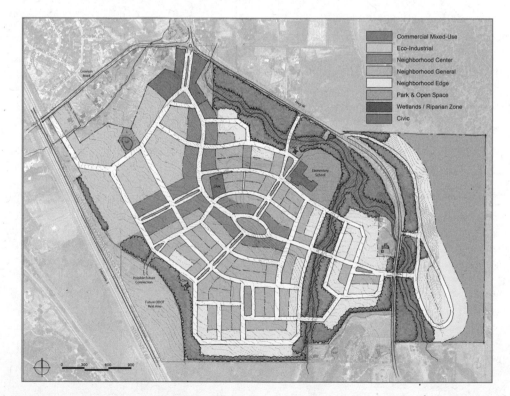

Figure 4-10
An example of a draft regulating plan that describes the form-based code zones that vary in intensity from edge to center. *Town-Green*

the laws that enable a regulating plan. The regulating plan revises or replaces the conventional zoning map.

2. *Zone standards:* the prescribed areas, from urban-to-rural that describe the permitted uses, forms, development intensities and character within each zone, and the ecotones between zones.

3. *Building and lot standards:* regulations that control the building and lot types, disposition, configuration, and functions that define and shape the public realm.

4. *Frontage standards:* regulations that describe the visual and functional physical conditions along the public and private interfaces.

5. *Public space standards:* regulations for the visual and functional elements within the public realm or right-of-way.

6. *Thoroughfare standards:* regulations for the design, functional classification, and configuration of public rights-of-way for public mobility.

7. *Parking standards:* regulations for parking design, type, locations, access, quantity, and configurations.

8. *Architectural standards:* regulations controlling external architectural materials, composition, and quality.

9. *Landscaping standards:* regulations controlling public and private landscape design and plant materials.

10. *Sustainability or environmental standards:* regulations that reduce the dependency on, or prevent the depletion or degradation of renewable resources, for example, controlling stormwater drainage and infiltration, development on slopes, tree protection, and solar access.

11. *Administration:* regulations clearly defining the application and project review process.

12. *Annotation:* text and illustrations explaining the intentions of specific code provisions.

13. *Definitions:* a glossary of precise technical terms.

The essential code elements consist of the regulating plan and zone standards and building and lot standards, though it may omit architectural and landscaping standards, or include signage requirements.

THE NEW
PLEASANT HILL BART
STATION PROPERTY CODE

PRINCIPLES AND REGULATIONS FOR
REDEVELOPMENT OF THE BART STATION PROPERTY

Figure 4-11
The Pleasant Hill BART Station Property Code describes the development standards for a transit village. *Lennertz, Coyle & Associates*

Refine and Adopt the Code

Form-based codes may be integrated into an established jurisdictional, regulatory framework or system such as a municipal code, or the code can function as an independent set of regulations. Since form-based codes may not initially provide consistency with existing general or comprehensive plan policies, the latter will require modification for consistency during an update or amendment. Communitywide regulating plans and general plan land use maps may contain entirely different zones and zone standards, necessitating incremental or wholesale revisions.

Ultimately, the adoption of a form-based code, a legislative act, requires a review and adoption process similar to plan or zoning regulations in California, Arizona, Florida, and states with similar statutes. This involves planning commission public hearings, recommendations to the local legislative body, and a city or county council or board of supervisors' public hearings, prior to adoption of the regulations, and the potential for environmental review and approval. The desired development outcomes and level of sustainability will be dependent on the quality of the vision, goals, and objectives rendered during the code-making process.

Implement the Code

The adopted FBC will either replace the existing, conventional regulations and zoning maps or require implementation through several approaches, such as the incremental application of the new code within the context of the conventional regulations and zoning maps. Each alternative presents benefits and drawbacks:

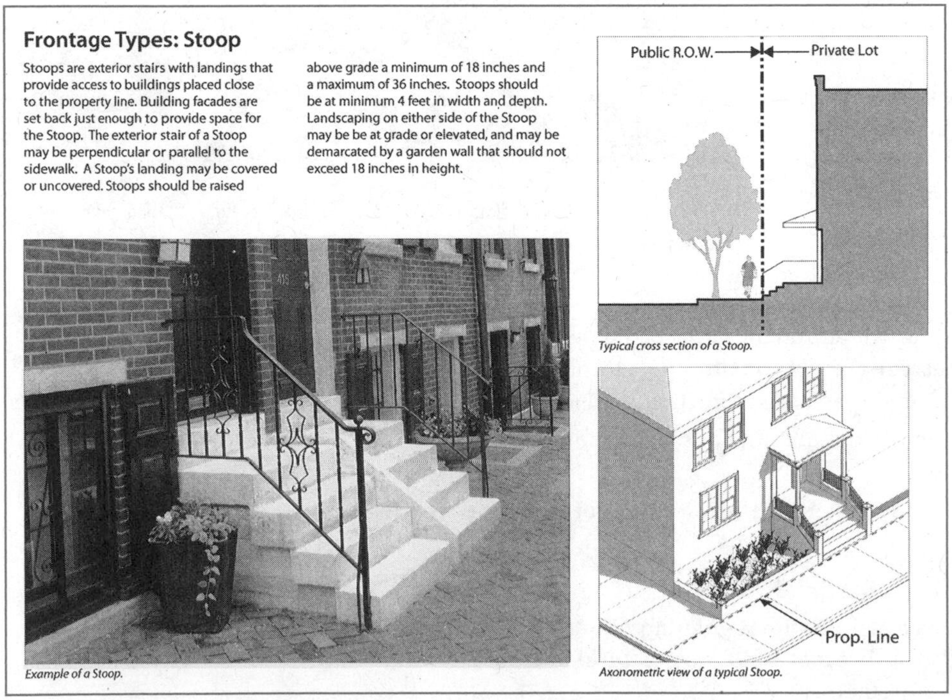

Frontage Types: Stoop

Stoops are exterior stairs with landings that provide access to buildings placed close to the property line. Building facades are set back just enough to provide space for the Stoop. The exterior stair of a Stoop may be perpendicular or parallel to the sidewalk. A Stoop's landing may be covered or uncovered. Stoops should be raised above grade a minimum of 18 inches and a maximum of 36 inches. Stoops should be at minimum 4 feet in width and depth. Landscaping on either side of the Stoop may be be at grade or elevated, and may be demarcated by a garden wall that should not exceed 18 inches in height.

Typical cross section of a Stoop.

Example of a Stoop.

Axonometric view of a typical Stoop.

Figure 4-12
Form-based codes regulate the physical forms that shape the public realm.

1. Replacing a conventional code with a form-based code creates the greatest range of opportunities for transforming targeted areas of a jurisdiction while maintaining an established character in others. This approach, similar to a conventional planning process, typically less expensive in smaller communities, offers the advantage of establishing overall consistency in both the regulatory vocabulary and procedures throughout the code. However, the risks include potential logistical, economic, and political complications in, essentially, starting over.

2. Implementing a form-based code while maintaining a conventional code and zoning map, a more typical situation, may cause several unintended consequences. It may create public uncertainty about the jurisdiction's commitment to better development. A set of codes with two different regulatory "vocabularies" can be technically confusing to applicants and more difficult to administer. However, this approach may offer a feasible option for those jurisdictions that wish to move into the field in phases or incrementally, or where political support may be tenuous. The use of the FBC should be incentivized, and made available only for large parcels, so that a hodge-podge of conventional and form-based standards does not occur in any one area.

Using the second alternative, the form-based code may be implemented through several approaches, and each option presents benefits and drawbacks:

1. Pilot projects that focus on a limited area that may include form-based codes executed in the form of specific or master plans, special-purpose zones, or "hybrid" codes.

2. Specific, precise, or master plans and other limited area codes that may include an FBC in states like California and others that allow a specific plan to include zoning regulations unique to its bounded or defined area, that supersede those in the citywide zoning code. However, unlike planned development ordinances that stipulate project-specific standards and densities, the superior form-based code facilitates flexibility and choice within a desired range of form and functional rules.

3. Special-purpose zones within conventional codes that provide a variation to the specific plan or limited area alternative. A jurisdiction may choose to adopt a new form-based zoning regulation by establishing and applying one or more new zones to specific limited areas within the jurisdiction through amendments to an existing conventional code text and property rezonings. The outcome, a "hybrid code," retains the "conventional" zones and related standards of the existing code in areas that are not rezoned. The integration of FBC provisions into a more extensive conventional code requires careful attention to the details of linkages or "bridges" to other standards and procedures in the code.

4. Alternative or "parallel optional codes" that consist of incentive-based FBCs that a development applicant may choose to apply under instead of the conventional jurisdiction-wide code. The incentives may include a more predictable and expedited development review process for the applicant under the FBC. The range of possible development types available to them can be both more cost-effective and more marketable than those allowed by the conventional

code. For the jurisdiction, the option can result in incrementally better development. However, given the complexity of planning and zoning in states like California, this approach increases the difficulty of administering two codes, and the potential for confusion over the requirements of two systems.

5. Floating codes or zones, used primarily in urbanized areas that apply the code without an underlying regulating plan and specific zone designations, leaving the existing code and zoning map in place. The form-based code standards "float" pending development applications for specific properties or parcels, or the planning of a multiple parcel area or corridor plan. The jurisdiction and developers can "field test" the code as applications and planning efforts emerge, in theory. However, the jurisdiction loses the ability to rationally organize or reform the urban pattern according to transect zones that graduate development intensities and forms with piecemeal results. These are similar to the conflicts that arise with "spot zoning": lack of coherent urban form.

Administering and Monitoring the Code

The form-based code requires administration and monitoring to assess or evaluate the efficacy of the code against the goals, objectives, and measures of success. Though an FBC differs from conventional codes, the jurisdiction will still review development and building applications for consistency and conformance with general or comprehensive plans, though applying the form-based code standards. Staff will require training on the underlying code principles and standards, and on the administration of the applications. A thorough training program is available through the Form-Based Codes Institute (FBCI), and more targeted training seminars in transect-based planning, coding, calibration, and administration are listed at www.transect.org.

Subsequent to the approval of a development or building application that incorporates the code, the jurisdiction should establish a methodology for assessing the performance of the built results. The Town Architect represents a time-tested approach. This position may be contracted through the jurisdiction, serving as an extension of staff or as a separate entity, compensated through development fees paid by the applicants.

The ultimate goal, to ensure the highest-quality projects by employing an experienced and qualified consultant or jurisdictional staff, requires a periodic review of applications that require a higher level of interpretation of or recommendations for consistency. The level of assessment of the quality of actual built results over time will depend on the decision-making authority authorized and the code employed. The Town Architect will help identify barriers in the code and the administration required while improving the quality of the process and the built products. Finally, they can educate and report back to the general public, staff, and elected officials on the benefits and drawbacks of the developments and the codes.

Through form-based codes, communities can plan and regulate higher-quality built environments that integrate rather than separate compatible uses. As a supplement to or replacement of conventional zoning and development ordinances, these codes help achieve the community's vision by designing and regulating desired outcomes appropriate to the people and place, from natural landscape to urban centers.

LEGAL IMPEDIMENTS SURVEY

Dan Slone
McGuireWoods, LLP

INTERVENTION TYPE: TOOL

Description

The legal impediments survey determines barriers that undermine sustainability programs and should be removed. Many jurisdictions have revised or replaced their zoning and subdivision codes only to find that other code requirements prevent optimization of construction of sustainable urban spaces. For example, resource protection ordinances which prioritize the protection of a single resource without regard to specific urban environments undermine sustainable urbanism. Thus, an ordinance that blocks roadway connectivity to protect the manmade wetlands of a drainage ditch may need adjustment to achieve sustainable urbanism.

SUPPORTS GOAL/OBJECTIVES

- Balance multiple objectives by carefully examining conflicting regulatory strategies to identify unifying goals and adjust the regulations to achieve the new goals.
- Eliminate situations where legal requirements to achieve one aspect of sustainable urbanism undermine efforts to achieve other aspects.

CONCEPTUAL STRATEGY

- Remove impediments by adjusting legal requirement—to sustainable urbanism.

POTENTIAL SYNERGISM

- This survey will allow localities to adjust codes to achieve the community vision. Future delays can be avoided by making simultaneous code adjustments in the multiple layers of a jurisdiction's regulations.

IMPLEMENTATION TIME

- The survey can be completed in one to three days, depending on local regulations and whether the review of the zoning and subdivision is required.

Figure 4-13
In most instances, fences cannot legally be located on top of parallel utility easements. The utility easement results in an unintended front setback.
Dan Slone

Benefits of Legal Impediment Surveys

Legal impediment surveys allow jurisdictions to:

- Work comprehensively on the legal requirements that can impede sustainable communities
- Avoid public and political disappointment when the results of development do not match public expectations
- Reduce or avoid criticism from developers when inconsistent portions of local codes reduce the viability of investment in urban spaces and result in delays

Drawbacks

- Surveys are best done by qualified experts and providers: The pool of experts is not extensive.
- Impediments, once identified, are used as indicators that the existing regulatory scheme is flawed, creating pressure to rectify it without proper funding.

Survey Topics

The following list assumes that form-based codes address problems that are identified at the zoning and subdivision level. Sources cited below provide more detail about impediments

Comprehensive Plans

- Describe appropriate densities
- Adapt to address retrofit issues and avoid single-use zones
- Have realistic projections of development areas
- Coordinate transportation and public works spending with timing for new development

Zoning Codes

- Address "planned densification," requiring low-density buildings to be designed so that density can be added later by expansion or retrofit without destroying buildings or infrastructure
- Allow banking of air rights expansion
- Provide more flexibility for the integration of high-quality, green modular homes
- Allow for "temporary uses" of buildings as interim steps to higher densities
- Transferable Development Rights (TDRs) need to focus on amount of land used per dwelling unit, not density
- Property right protections must be adjusted to eliminate risk to jurisdiction from shift to mixed-use
- Provide adjustments to accommodate green roofs, green walls, urban agriculture, wind turbines, and solar equipment

SUBDIVISION CODE

- Shift from FAR (floor-area ratio) regulation of commercial buildings which penalizes density
- Shift parking scheme to street parking and lower-ratio parking behind buildings
- Shift landscaping to sustainable trees and to canopy cover for parking areas
- Shift disconnected sidewalks to a connected scheme, with proper widths, on-sidewalk lanes for slower-wheeled vehicles, provide for street trees, and allow sidewalk encroachments
- Shift utilities from wide right-of-ways and no-shared trenches to minimum impact right-of-ways
- Address conflicts with Crime Prevention through Environmental Design (CPTED) officials who often oppose connectivity of streets and mixed-use districts and fire officials who often oppose narrow streets and tighter turning radii
- Building Code
- Recognize live-work and mixed-use buildings
- Code for green alternatives for materials and techniques
- Code for green roofs and walls, and address solar-shading while balancing desire for density
- Design "passive survivability" so buildings remain functional when power is interrupted
- Allow vernacular, passive approaches to energy efficiency

STREETS

- Adjust fire codes to allow safer streets (for example, in California safer street designs have been blocked by fire officials and fire code changes)
- Fire officials require overly wide alleys, overly wide streets and intersections, and suggest that some street trees be removed
- Roadways, often regulated locally and by the state, must be changed by both jurisdictions to allow sustainable urban streets.

UTILITIES

- Change private and public utility provider policies regarding street crossings, locations beneath pavement, proximity with other utilities, and minimum easement widths to avoid unnecessarily large setbacks
- Change utility regulatory schemes and local agencies to achieve the rethinking of water, stormwater, and wastewater utilization necessary to achieve efficiencies in retrofit, allowing increased density without replacement of utility infrastructure

SCHOOLS

- Eliminate required school size and configuration that mandate "big boxes"
- Require bus schemes consistent with walking protocols

- Enable safe school walk programs
- Locate schools for walking convenience, not vehicle convenience, and integrate school facilities into neighborhood programs

ENVIRONMENTAL ORDINANCES

- Adjust watershed protection and stormwater ordinances to allow urban forms while creating offset programs allowing flexible response to resource protection
- Adjust lighting ordinances to allow vigorous town-center lighting and subdued suburban lighting within "darksky" parameters
- Adjust tree preservation and landscaping ordinances to allow sustainable choices and urbanism

HOMEOWNER ASSOCIATIONS

- Eliminate bans and limits on wind turbines, solar cells, rain barrels, green roofs, photovoltaic, cool roofs, seasonal grasses, and front-yard gardening

INFORMATION AND REPORTS

- *A Legal Guide to Urban and Sustainable Development for Planners, Developers and Architects* by Daniel K. Slone and Doris S. Goldstein (2008, John Wiley & Sons) includes a chapter on impediments
- *New Urbanism: Best Practices Guide*, 4th edition (Steuteville, Langdon et al. (2009, New Urban News)
- "Code, Regulatory and Systemic Barriers Affecting Living Building Projects Report" by David Eisenberg and Sonja Persram (Cascadia Region Green Building Council) online at www.ilbi.org/resources/reports/Code Studies/codestudy3.

Figure 4-14
If the local vision is of an interactive public/private realm, then impediments to the location of private elements into the public right-of-way must be removed. Legitimate issues of maintenance and liability must be addressed in the process. *Dan Slone*

TRANSFER OF DEVELOPMENT RIGHTS

Rick Pruetz, FAICP
Planning and Implementation Strategies

INTERVENTION TYPE: STRATEGY, BEST PRACTICE

Description

Transfer of development rights (TDRs) works through a community's zoning to redirect urban growth away from natural and agricultural areas and toward places that are appropriate for sustainable development. The places the community wants to save are called "sending areas" and can include natural areas, farmland, historic landmarks, and open space. "Receiving areas," areas which are appropriate for sustainable development, are designated for growth by a community's general plan and are typically close to job sites, schools, shopping, transportation, and urban infrastructure. Sending area landowners receive compensation for preserving their land, receiving area developers experience greater profits, and the community implements its preservation goals using little or no tax money.

SUPPORT GOALS AND OBJECTIVES

The general plans of most communities include goals to protect environmentally sensitive areas, conserve open space, and preserve farmland. However, implementation of these goals can be difficult. Zoning, even when adequate, is temporary. Traditional land acquisition programs require repeated infusions of tax money, which is scarce even in a good economy. TDR provides a way for preservation to be financed, at least in part, by development.

PERFORMANCE CHARACTERISTICS

In receiving areas, developers are allowed to build up to baseline density with no TDR requirement. To exceed baseline density, they must purchase TDRs, or, in some programs, pay a density transfer charge that the community uses to preserve sending area land. The amount of land saved varies from community to community. Some jurisdictions are satisfied preserving 50 acres per year. At the other extreme, King County, Washington, has used TDR to preserve an average of over 9,000 acres per year.

POTENTIAL SYNERGISM

TDR can be combined with other programs to stretch limited preservation dollars. King County, Washington, dedicates a portion of its property tax revenue to open space preservation. When it uses money in that fund to buy land or traditional easements, the development potential of the protected land is simply retired. But when the money is used to buy TDRs, proceeds from these sales can be used to buy more TDRs, replenishing the original seed money and creating a perpetual revolving fund for preservation.

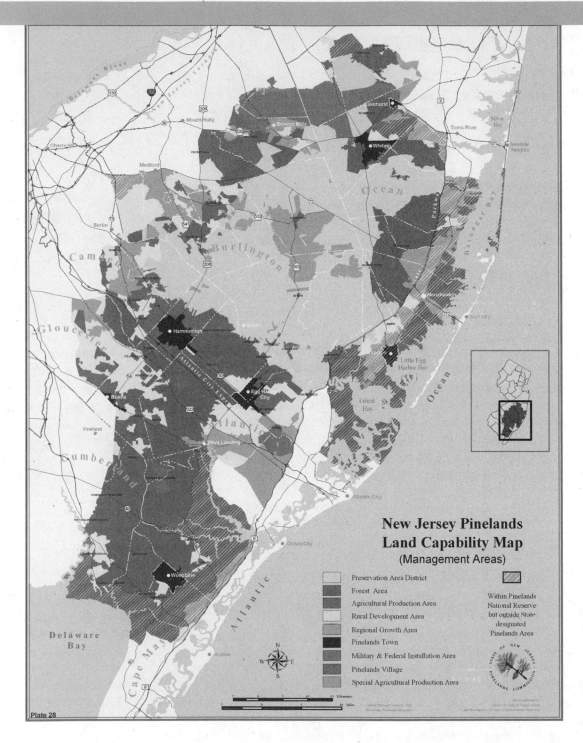

New Jersey Pinelands
Land Capability Map
(Management Areas)

Preservation Area District

Forest Area

Agricultural Production Area

Rural Development Area

Regional Growth Area

Pinelands Town

Military & Federal Installation Area

Pinelands Village

Special Agricultural Production Area

Within Pinelands
National Reserve
but outside State
designated
Pinelands Area

Plate 28

Figure 4-15
This map describes
management areas of
the New Jersey Pine-
lands, representing
enormous environ-
mental, economic, and
social assets saved
through a transfer of
development rights.
Richard Pruetz

IMPLEMENTATION TIME

In one year or less, a community with TDR-ready characteristics, as explained below, can adopt a TDR program by creating receiving areas from those places designated in its existing general plan as appropriate for up-zonings, meaning density-increasing zoning changes. Alternatively, if the creation of receiving areas requires a general plan amendment, the time frame could take up to three years because of the additional studies and public involvement needed to ensure that these proposed sites are suitable receiving areas.

BENEFITS

- Sending area property owners can continue to own their land and use it for non-development purposes consistent with a permanent easement. In addition, they receive compensation for development potential, which they might not have been able to actually use for decades.
- Receiving area developers are able to build at more profitable levels of development, and may be able to use a streamlined process that avoids the delay, unexpected costs, and uncertainty of traditional discretionary approval procedures.
- Communities facilitate compensation for those property owners who want to preserve their land. These communities implement their land preservation goals using a portion of development profits rather than tax revenue.

DRAWBACKS

- Adopting a TDR ordinance can be difficult because several stakeholder groups are involved, creating a great need for committed communication and collaboration. However, the ingredients for a workable TDR ordinance are often already contained in a community's general plan.
- Sometimes, residents fight TDR programs assuming that the receiving area development will negatively impact their community. In fact, receiving area development will always be consistent with a community's general plan.
- When there is a lack of community knowledge about the connection between the manmade and the natural environment, citizens do not perceive any personal benefit from preserving open space and farmland.

FIRST COST

Preparation of a TDR study and ordinance is likely to range from $20,000 to $30,000 if the community is TDR-ready and adopts a plan-consistent TDR program. "TDR-ready" means local developers regularly request up-zonings, the community's general plan designates areas appropriate for up-zoning, and the community's elected body is willing to require preservation for additional development potential resulting from up-zonings.

Alternatively, the cost will likely be greater for a plan-*amending* TDR program, one in which receiving areas require general plan amendments allowing higher development potential than the amounts depicted in the current general plan. A plan-amending TDR program could be completed for only $10,000 more than a plan-consistent TDR program. However, in communities with more demanding requirements for public involvement and infrastructure/environmental studies, the budget for a plan-amending TDR program could range from $30,000 to $50,000 per area requiring a general plan amendment.

LIFECYCLE COSTS

Ongoing TDR programs typically involve program marketing to potential participants, assistance with applications, record keeping of all TDR transactions, and maintenance of a list of landowners and developers who want to sell or buy TDRs. In most communities, these tasks can be accomplished using a portion of one employees' time. However, some programs have a full-time TDR manager, depending on program size and community dedication to the program.

Figure 4-16
King County, Washington, has used TDR to preserve 138,000 acres of open space to date, including the 90,000-acre Snoqualmie Forest pictured here.
Richard Pruetz

ESTIMATED QUANTITATIVE PERFORMANCE

TDR programs exist in 33 states and have preserved over 400,000 acres to date. The amount of land preserved varies greatly between jurisdictions. Some TDR programs preserve 1,000 acres, while King County, Washington, has preserved 138,000 acres.

IMPLEMENTATION SUPPORTS AND CONSTRAINTS

- Offer bonus development potential that developers want
- Customize the receiving areas to community characteristics
- Impose strict sending area development regulations to reinforce preservation
- Offer few or no alternatives to TDR for achieving additional development
- Promote TDR prices that attract both buyers and sellers

INFORMATIONAL SOURCES

- www.BeyondTakingsAndGivings.com
- www.farmlandinfo.org/documents/27746/FS_TDR_1-01.pdf

THE SMARTCODE

Sandy Sorlien
Center for Applied Transect Studies (CATS)

INTERVENTION TYPE: CODE

Description

The SmartCode is a model unified land development ordinance. It folds zoning, subdivision regulations, urban design, public works standards, and basic architectural controls into one compact document. It is a transect-based, form-based code that spans from the region to the community to the building. The base SmartCode and numerous plug-in modules are available open source, for use without charges or licensing fees. The code must be calibrated and assembled by professional planners, architects, and attorneys using the Base Modules (Articles) and desired Supplementary Modules, to suit the local character and needs of each municipality or project.

SUPPORT GOALS AND OBJECTIVES

The principal objective is zoning reform to allow the protection, creation, and completion of walkable, transit-ready neighborhoods, and in so doing, reduce VMT and improve quality of life. It allows for distinctly different approaches in the different transect zones within a town or neighborhood and integrates the processes of planning and zoning so they are not working at cross purposes.

PERFORMANCE CHARACTERISTICS

The SmartCode's rural-to-urban transect is divided at the community scale into a range of transect zones (T zones) each with its own complex character. Calibrating to the local transect ensures that a community offers a full diversity of building types, frontage types, thoroughfare types, and civic space types, and that they have location appropriate characteristics. The DNA for each zone comes from analyzing the best existing conditions in the local area, using an environmental method called the Synoptic Survey.

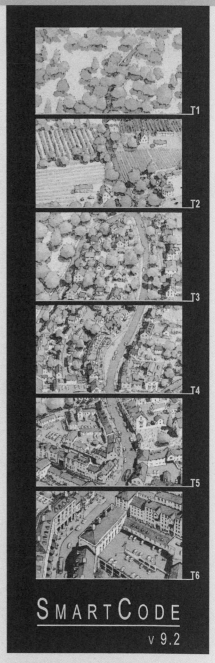

Figure 4-17
Version 9.2 shown; 10 of the model SmartCode was released in 2010, the first major upgrade to the "operating system" since 2007. *DPZ & Associates, Inc.*

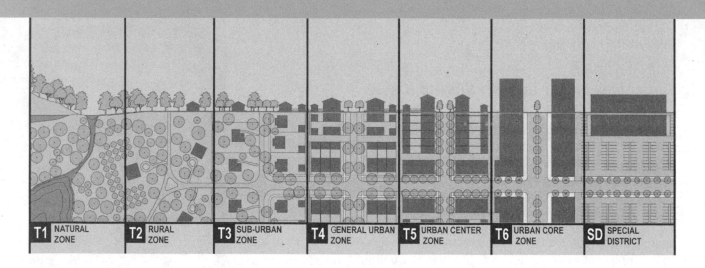

| T1 | NATURAL ZONE | T2 | RURAL ZONE | T3 | SUB-URBAN ZONE | T4 | GENERAL URBAN ZONE | T5 | URBAN CENTER ZONE | T6 | URBAN CORE ZONE | SD | SPECIAL DISTRICT |

POTENTIAL SYNERGISM

Using transect-based planning and coding allows supplementary modules to augment the base modules (articles) of the SmartCode or other transect-based codes. The modules represent numerous disciplines including hazard mitigation (flood and wildfire), sustainable urbanism, natural drainage, regional watersheds, affordable housing incentives, renewable energy, agricultural urbanism, architectural standards, sprawl repair, and more. Over 40 new urbanist firms have authored or peer reviewed one or more modules creating an investment and cooperation from many professional sources.

IMPLEMENTATION TIME

Implementation will take one to five years, depending on the size and complexity of the area to be coded and the political will. Most small to medium-sized towns take about two years from the initial visioning meetings and charrette to adoption by the legislative body, for targeted transect mapping and coding. The Miami 21 code took four years plus four months for comprehensive mapping and coding; Montgomery's took less than one year for the SmartCode's adoption as a floating zone.

BENEFITS

The SmartCode supports the outcomes of walkable and mixed-use neighborhoods, transportation options, proximity to parks and other civic spaces, conservation of open lands, preservation of local character, housing diversity, and vibrant downtowns. The Warrant system streamlines the permitting process, requiring far fewer variances to achieve the goals, saving developers commission and legislative bodies time and expense.

Figure 4-18
A generalized rural-to-urban transect was systemized in the 1990s by Andrés Duany for use in municipal zoning codes. *DPZ & Associates, Inc.*

DRAWBACKS

Besides the learning curve for planning staff to move from one kind of code to another, older planners and zoning officials may feel threatened and resist change. Others may find it difficult to think about zones as diverse, human habitats rather than single-use spaces.

FIRST COST

Though there's no cost to download the base code and modules, the annotated code and calibration handbook, *SmartCode Version 9 and Manual*, costs $79. The cost of outside consultants running a complete charrette, precharrette visioning meetings, code calibration, and a period of "code cleanup" edits will range from $60,000 to $300,000, depending on the size and experience of the team, and the size and complexity of the land area to be planned and coded. However, a motivated municipal planning staff that has gone through training can map an existing traditional pattern with transect zones and calibrate the SmartCode themselves.

LIFECYCLE COSTS

SmartCode is designed to save planning staff time in the long run or life cycle. Addition of new modules to the base code requires minimal adjustment in most cases. Amendments typically follow the same procedure as conventional code amendments, but the succession feature built into the model SmartCode makes future upzoning of an area a more integrated process.

ESTIMATED QUANTITATIVE PERFORMANCE

- Despite best intentions, in most jurisdictions it is still illegal to develop compact, mixed-use communities by right. By advancing zoning reform, the VMT of compact mixed-use development with transportation options may be reduced to nearly half of that produced by conventional auto-dominated development. Source: *Growing Cooler*, a review of numerous climate change studies by Smart Growth America and ULI. Projections for 2030 may be found at the SGA *Growing Cooler* page at: www.smartgrowthamerica.org/gcindex.html. The website states: "Depending on several factors, from mix of land uses to pedestrian-friendly design, compact development reduces driving from 20 to 40 percent, and more in some instances." The authors calculate that shifting 60 percent of new growth to compact patterns would save 79 million tons of CO_2 annually by 2030.

- A number of standards in the SmartCode and its modules support affordable housing options by prescribing smaller lots, accessory buildings, diversity in dwelling type, and a mix of useful destinations within walksheds so that car expenses decline. In addition, according to *New Urban News* (Oct/Nov 2009), "Infrastructure costs are 32 to 47 percent lower in traditional neighborhood development (TND) than in conventional suburban development."

IMPLEMENTATION SUPPORTS AND CONSTRAINTS

- Discuss adoption strategies early (replacement code, mapped parallel code, or unmapped floating zone). Consider incremental adoption of important mapped areas as neighborhoods become ready, with the SmartCode available and incentivized for new communities and sprawl repair on large parcels.

- Plan using pedestrian sheds (walksheds) and if possible map an area at least the size of one pedestrian shed, even if the project is smaller.

- Include zoning, building, and planning officials in initial meetings to allay their concerns early.

- Avoid "hybridizing" the code by forcing it into the old conventional format. If the transect-mapped area is only part of the municipality, name it and keep its standards separate from the rest of the ordinance.

INFORMATIONAL SOURCES

- www.smartcodecentral.org
- www.transect.org

REPORTS AND STUDIES

See the Resources page at www.smartcodecentral.org, and the Research page at www.transect.org. The Links page at the latter site includes links to Google maps presenting SmartCode calibrations and adoptions, with short reports for many of them, and a link to a list, within which are further links to municipal or project websites.

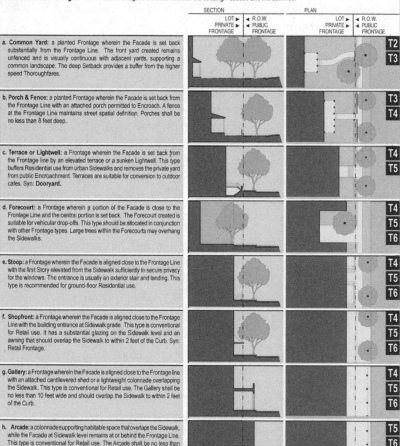

SMARTCODE
Municipality

TABLE 7. PRIVATE FRONTAGES

TABLE 7: Private Frontages. The Private Frontage is the area between the building Facades and the Lot lines.

a. **Common Yard:** a planted Frontage wherein the Facade is set back substantially from the Frontage Line. The front yard created remains unfenced and is visually continuous with adjacent yards, supporting a common landscape. The deep Setback provides a buffer from the higher speed Thoroughfares. — T2, T3

b. **Porch & Fence:** a planted Frontage wherein the Facade is set back from the Frontage Line with an attached porch permitted to Encroach. A fence at the Frontage Line maintains street spatial definition. Porches shall be no less than 8 feet deep. — T3, T4

c. **Terrace or Lightwell:** a Frontage wherein the Facade is set back from the Frontage line by an elevated terrace or a sunken Lightwell. This type buffers Residential use from urban Sidewalks and removes the private yard from public Encroachment. Terraces are suitable for conversion to outdoor cafes. Syn: Dooryard. — T4, T5

d. **Forecourt:** a Frontage wherein a portion of the Facade is close to the Frontage Line and the central portion is set back. The Forecourt created is suitable for vehicular drop-offs. This type should be allocated in conjunction with other Frontage types. Large trees within the Forecourts may overhang the Sidewalks. — T4, T5, T6

e. **Stoop:** a Frontage wherein the Facade is aligned close to the Frontage Line with the first Story elevated from the Sidewalk sufficiently to secure privacy for the windows. The entrance is usually an exterior stair and landing. This type is recommended for ground-floor Residential use. — T4, T5, T6

f. **Shopfront:** a Frontage wherein the Facade is aligned close to the Frontage Line with the building entrance at Sidewalk grade. This type is conventional for Retail use. It has a substantial glazing on the Sidewalk level and an awning that should overlap the Sidewalk to within 2 feet of the Curb. Syn: Retail Frontage. — T4, T5, T6

g. **Gallery:** a Frontage wherein the Facade is aligned close to the Frontage line with an attached cantilevered shed or a lightweight colonnade overlapping the Sidewalk. This type is conventional for Retail use. The Gallery shall be no less than 10 feet wide and should overlap the Sidewalk to within 2 feet of the Curb. — T4, T5, T6

h. **Arcade:** a colonnade supporting habitable space that overlaps the Sidewalk, while the Facade at Sidewalk level remains at or behind the Frontage Line. This type is conventional for Retail use. The Arcade shall be no less than 12 feet wide and should overlap the Sidewalk to within 2 feet of the Curb. See Table 8. — T5, T6

Figure 4-19
The form-based Private Frontage elements of Table 7 are correlated to transect zones, just as standards in conventional codes are associated with their zones.
DPZ & Associates, Inc.

GHG EMISSIONS INVENTORY AND FORECAST

Daniel Dunigan, AICP and Dana Perls
Town-Green

INTERVENTION TYPE: PROCEDURE

Description

A GHG emissions inventory estimates of the amount of greenhouse gas emitted by human activities within the jurisdictional boundaries, identified as either communitywide or municipal sources. It establishes a baseline year of data collection to calculate proposed reduction measures against current emissions and to better understand the sources and emission trends. The inventory combines emissions from multiple greenhouse gases into a single value of emissions, the amount of equivalent carbon dioxide, or CO_2e.

A GHG emissions forecast projects the inventory results into the future using several sources, including population and economic growth data, projections of changes in vehicle miles, electricity and other energy consumption, and other appropriate growth factors. Typical forecasts target emissions at year 2020, 2030, and 2050, sector-by-sector. The resulting estimates are compared to the baseline emissions to determine the total reductions desired.

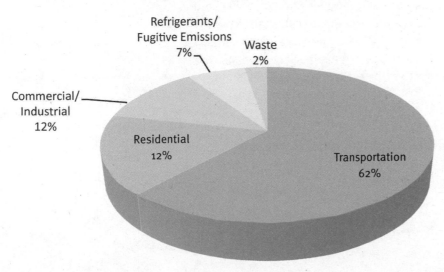

City-Wide GHG Emissions (including state highways)-2006 CO_2 equivalent

Refrigerants/ Fugitive Emissions 7%
Waste 2%
Commercial/ Industrial 12%
Residential 12%
Transportation 62%

Figure 4-20
Communitywide GHG emissions by sector. *Town-Green*

Support Goals and Objectives

Example of California GHG emissions reduction goals:

- Establish a baseline year for emissions data and calculate base year emissions and forecast "business as usual" emissions for the target years of 2020 or 2050.
- Set emission state reduction targets, reaching 1990 levels by 2020 or about a 20% decrease, and about 50 percent by 2050 below 1990 levels.

Performance Characteristics

The GHG inventory provides the data necessary to compare baseline emissions with the results of emission reduction programs and other measures, such as those that reduce vehicle miles traveled by motor vehicles that do not directly affect GHG reduction.

Potential Synergism

Greenhouse gas emissions represent a primary metric for measuring the efficacy of emission reduction actions, from facility energy retrofits to motor vehicle trip reductions strategies. GHG emissions inventories can provide the data necessary to establish the baseline for cap and trade programs.

Implementation Time

A GHG inventory may be completed within two or three months, though jurisdictions with less access to emissions data my take longer to complete. The time to complete a GHG emissions inventory and forecast depends on the size, complexity, and sophistication of the jurisdiction involved. Transportation emission sources often present data-gathering challenges for those jurisdictions that lack the sophisticated transportation-related information generated by traffic modeling and planning studies, more prevalent in larger metropolitan areas and regional transportation planning agencies. Communitywide data may require accessing multiple sources from power suppliers to landfill operators, with corresponding feedback time spans. The inventory and forecast can be adjusted to reflect the scale and complexity of the jurisdiction.

Benefits

- GHG inventories provide emissions information across multiple sectors of the jurisdiction and community, allowing each sector to assess and respond to their individual performance, relative to established regional or national standards, and create carbon reduction strategies.
- Forecasting is a good tool to show how much CO_2e reduction is needed to meet federal, state, and local targets, and what would happen if the city continued "business as usual."

- A GHG inventory may take much longer than necessary to collect the required data to provide an accurate analysis, depending on the level of detail and software being used to conduct the inventory. For example, if the off-road emissions data is difficult to find, it makes little sense to spend unnecessary budget and time on an emission source that has little impact on the overall GHG emissions of a community.

- Some of the emissions are difficult to quantify due to the complexity of the system they are a part of. For example, vehicular transportation emissions accredited to a city typically include trips completed within the city boundaries and one half of a round trip commute. Quantifying this data can be difficult if cities lack accurate trip data such as total number of trips generated, fuel and vehicle types, and trip lengths. Emissions from embodied water emissions, fugitive emissions, and the emissions from less-used fuels, such as propane and butane, can be difficult to quantify.

FIRST COST

Depending on the level of detail and complexity of the software used to perform the GHG inventory and forecast, costs can range from $5,000 to $30,000 or more. Several organizations have created emissions inventory software that helps streamline the calculation process, thus reducing costs. Each will require a degree of customization or "work around" to accommodate regional contexts and software shortcomings.

LIFECYCLE COSTS

Once a GHG inventory and forecast is completed, an update should be performed periodically (e.g., every five years) to determine the impacts of implemented CO_2e reduction strategies. The update costs will depend on the jurisdiction's ability to monitor and compile accurate data for each update. The more complete and distilled the data recorded, the less expensive the monitoring.

ESTIMATED QUANTITATIVE PERFORMANCE

The GHG inventory provides supporting data for cap and trade programs, and climate action and sustainability plans, so completing an accurate inventory and forecast is essential for creating the platform for calculating emission reductions and comparing performance against the targets.

IMPLEMENTATION SUPPORTS AND CONSTRAINTS

GHG inventories will be easier if jurisdictions track and record the emissions data for each emitting sector. Without ready access to accurate data, compiling GHG inventory will be time-consuming and without ready access to accurate data, conducting a GHG inventory will be more time-consuming and costly.

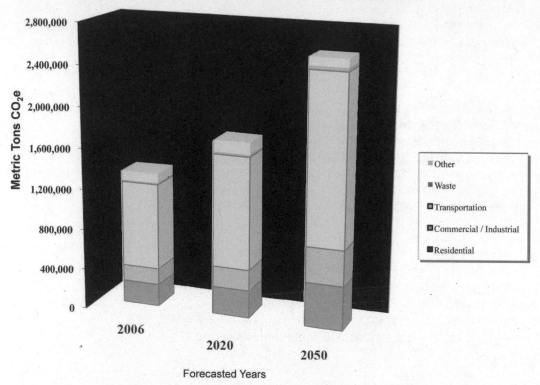

Community Emissions Forecast for 2020 and 2050

Metric Tons CO$_2$e

2,800,000	
2,400,000	
2,000,000	
1,600,000	
1,200,000	
800,000	
400,000	
0	

Legend:
- Other
- Waste
- Transportation
- Commercial / Industrial
- Residential

2006

2020

2050

Forecasted Years

Some emissions data (e.g., tailpipe) may be found through appropriate local and state agencies (e.g., departments of transportation). While governmental agencies usually keep accurate data, investigation from other sources (e.g., motor vehicle departments) may be required.

INFORMATIONAL SOURCES

- For information on GHG inventory training, please visit www.ghginstitute.org
- GHG Protocol Initiative, www.ghgprotocol.org/standard/ghg.pdf

REPORTS AND STUDIES

- U.S. GHG inventory information can be found at www.epa.gov/climatechange/ emissions/usinventoryreport.html
- Tufts Climate Initiative, Tufts Institute of the Environment, "Method for Conducting a Greenhouse Gas Emissions Inventory for Colleges and Universities," April 16, 2002

Figure 4-21
Community emissions forecast. *Town-Green*

Chapter 5

Transportation

Sustainable Transportation and Transit Planning— Strategies for Comprehensive Regional Transportation Plans and Transit-Oriented Development

Sam Zimbabwe, LEED
Director, Center for Transit-Oriented Development (CTOD)

The Transportation Challenge

In the United States, vehicle miles of travel (VMT), the primary driver of greenhouse gas (GHG) emissions from the transportation sector, have been growing faster than population in recent years. This growth is in large part a response to the auto-oriented transportation policies at the federal, state, and local levels. Auto-oriented transportation policies and investments lead to auto-oriented communities, in which households are left without transportation choices. Beyond the environmental impacts, auto-oriented transportation policies lead to higher household transportation costs, reduced physical activity, and increased public health costs, as well as more socially isolated communities.

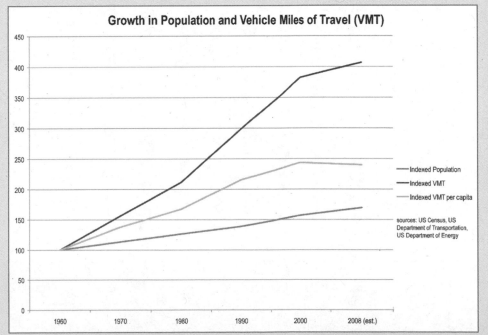

Figure 5-1
Since 1960, VMT have vastly exceeded population growth, and VMT per capita has more than doubled. *U.S. Census, U.S. Department of Transportation, U.S. Department of Energy*

In a sustainable place, households have easy transportation choices, with the option to walk, bike, take transit, or drive to meet their daily needs. Multimodal transportation networks linking to employment centers, schools, hospitals, and parks support a mix of uses and destinations that create demand for transit service beyond normal commute peaks, increasing the financial efficiency of transit investments. From higher-density communities with a greater mix of uses, to predominantly residential or employment-focused, the diversity of places builds demand for transit access and supports increased transit investment. In a sustainable place, transit is integrated into communities, with high-quality building materials, and low-impact and easily accessible alignments. While these choices can lead to higher up-front costs, they support the long-term benefits and patient approach of a sustainable place.

Transit ridership has grown substantially in the last 15 years as Americans have looked for ways to live more environmentally and economically responsible lifestyles. Investments in public transportation encourage a shift in regional and local development patterns that support the full range of transportation options.

Figure 5-2
Since 1998, transit ridership has grown quickly, with much of the gains resulting from rail-based transit systems. *American Public Transportation Association*

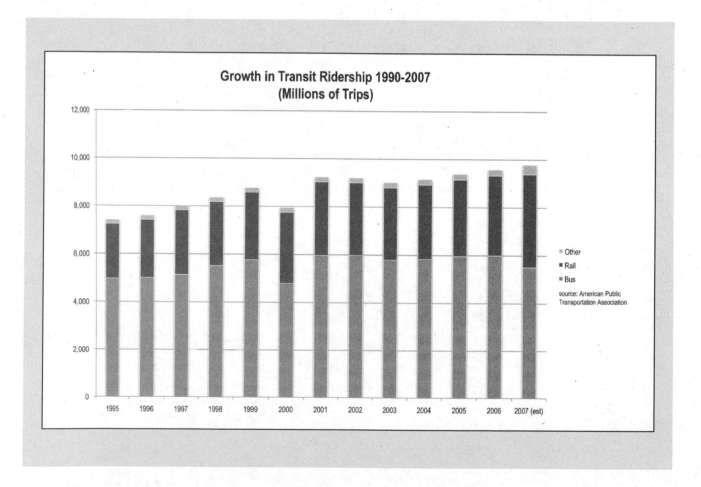

Regions and cities that have invested in transit have seen real estate investment follow, and are best positioned to capture demand from changing demographics and household preferences. Transit investments can include regional transit networks including commuter rail, subway, Light Rail Transit (LRT), and Bus Rapid Transit (BRT) lines, local-serving streetcars, bus circulator, or transit hubs. In many cases, improvements to walking and biking conditions are necessary to take full advantage of transit investments.

The following outlines strategies for assessing the state of your transit system and its ability to shape land use and real estate development, in addition to transit ridership, with the goal of creating a sustainable place. The strategies need to be evaluated in tandem with the federal, state, and local funding programs that guide transit investment in this country.

Principles for Creating a Sustainable Transportation Plan

There are three broad principles that guide the steps needed to create a sustainable transportation system.

- *Triple bottom line/full cost-benefit accounting*: All transportation investments are evaluated equally against the same long-term outcomes of environmental, economic, and social health.

- *Coordinated land use and transportation vision*: Transportation investments are made within the framework of a regional or local vision for long-term growth and development. Community impacts and opportunities from transit investments are assessed early in the planning process to maximize benefits.

- *Broad-based engagement and collaboration on the vision*: Transit investments alone cannot support sustainable communities, but rely on multiple stakeholders and investments to support the vision. Open and transparent communication and engagement on the planning and community development process are necessary to maximize the benefits.

The Process

In order to achieve the principles outlined above, a community should undertake a thorough process that incorporates all of the priorities inherent in these principles. This process is made up of four key steps, which may need to happen in a coordinated, rather than linear, timeline:

- *Develop a sustainable regional land use vision.* A transit system needs to take you somewhere. The land use vision should identify areas of growth and change and areas of stability and reinforcement. The land use vision can help communities understand how transit links destinations and helps people meet their daily needs. This vision can then be used to direct financial resources and shape policy decisions.

- *Develop a regional transit vision.* Transit should connect people to jobs and other activities, and should provide equitable access to all members of the community. Guided by existing conditions and ideally a regional land use plan, a regional transit vision provides the framework for the types of connections that can be made and prioritizes individual lines and corridors for investment.

Place Types

Places	Activity Mix	Housing Types	Commercial Employment Types	Proposed Scale	Connectivity	Local Examples	Color Code	Examples
Major Urban Center	Office Residential Retail Entertainment Civic Uses	Multi-Family/Loft	Employment Emphasis, with more than 250,000 sf office and 50,000 sf retail	5 Stories and above	Intermodal Facility/ Transit Hub. Major Regional Destination with quality feeder and circulator connections	Downtown Galleria District Medical Center		
Urban Center	Residential Retail Office	Multi-Family/ Townhome	Limited Office. Less than 250,000 sf office. More than 50,000 sf retail	3 Stories and above	Sub-Regional Destination. Some Park n Ride. Linked district circulator and feeder transit service	Areas of Montrose/ Museum District Allen Parkway		
Neighborhood	Residential/ Neighborhood Retail	Multi-Family/ Townhome/ Small Lot Single Family	Local-Serving Retail. No more than 50,000 sf	1-5 Stories	Walk up station. Very Small Park and Ride, if any. Local and express bus service.	Mid-Town West University Magnolia Park Montrose		
Retail Street	Residential/ Neighborhood Retail	Small Lot Single Family	Main Street Retail Infill	1-4 Stories	Bus or streetcar corridors. Feeder transit service. Walk up stops. No parking.	Rice Village 19th Street (Heights) Highland Village		
Campus/ Special Events Center	University/ Campus Sports Facilities	Limited Multi-Family	Limited Office/Retail	Varies	Large Commuter Destination	Rice University U of H TSU Reliant Park		

- *Fully evaluate investment alternatives.* In planning for an individual line or segment of the transit vision, the evaluation process should assess land use and development opportunities, transit alignment alternatives, and station locations. Competitive evaluation of potential projects, whether transit or roadway investments, should assess how well different alternatives support the land use vision, as well as meet a full cost/benefit evaluation.

- *Create lasting transportation investments that reflect community values.* Investments in transit lines and pedestrian and bicycle circulation incorporating high-quality materials, public art, and amenities for all users create valued community spaces that maximize benefits of transportation investment. Stations and stops should be accessible to all members of the population and be integrated with the surroundings to facilitate local circulation, rather than create access barriers.

Prepare the Team

Planning for the sustainable transit system is difficult. Conduct an interdisciplinary analysis and evaluation at every stage of the process, including multimodal transportation planning, engineering, real estate market analysis, land use planning, urban design, and potentially stormwater and other infrastructure planning and

Figure 5-3
These two examples of TOD typologies, used in Houston and Philadelphia, make clear that transit-oriented development is not a one-size-fits-all approach to communities. *Center for Transit-Oriented Development*

engineering. At the outset, focus on mapping, community outreach, surveying techniques, and transportation planning. As plans become more detailed and specific, engineering and construction feasibility take on increased importance, while stakeholder engagement remains an important component.

All stages of the planning and investment process require engaging multiple sectors and jurisdictions of public agencies. Planning, zoning, and transportation departments from all jurisdictions and regional agencies are needed to complete a plan. The Metropolitan Planning Organization (MPO) or another regional entity should lead regional scale planning. While corridor plans within a specific jurisdiction can be confined to that entity alone, involvement by regional agencies strengthens the overall process and outcome.

Budget constraints can vary widely based on the scale and level of detail. A basic rule of thumb is that each level of planning requires ten times the resources of the previous. Where a regional transit vision plan may require $1 million or more, detailed corridor evaluation and planning may require $10 million or more, engineering and design may run to $100 million, and construction of a segment or corridor may require $1 billion and above. Within this framework, however, costs can vary substantially based on the size, complexity, and physical requirements of a planning process.

Prepare the Tools

Many resources are available to develop and implement plans for sustainable transportation at all scales.

- *Advocacy organizations* provide research and technical resources, and advocate for policy changes. These organizations can be national in scale or can be regionally based. Reconnecting America and Smart Growth America are two examples of national advocacy organizations. Regional advocacy organizations develop place-based solutions and convene many stakeholders to come to consensus about regional and site-specific investments. San Francisco Planning and Urban Research (SPUR) in the San Francisco Bay Area, Envision Utah in the Salt Lake City region, and the Central Maryland Transportation Alliance in the Baltimore region are several examples of effective regional advocacy groups.

- *Public agencies* plan and implement infrastructure investments. Local and State Departments of Transportation, transit agencies, and MPOs develop transportation plans and finance infrastructure investments. These agencies are essential to implement sustainable transportation networks.

- *Practitioners and consultants* carry out the plans and designs for transportation infrastructure investments. Professional planners, designers, architects, and engineers are needed to design and build transportation networks. Consulting firms may be local or national, and are a key component of most transportation infrastructure investments.

- *Citizens* develop and articulate visions for their communities. Everyday citizens are the experts about their communities. Their views and visions for community change are needed for truly sustainable transportation networks. Knowing how people use transit networks or perceive the safety of walking and biking is important to know how improvements will be received and used.

Quantitative and Qualitative Tools

A number of tools, both quantitative and qualitative, can be used in the preparation of a regional transportation plan. Some of the most effective tools are outlined below.

- *United States Census.* This database provides basic demographic and housing data for every location in the country. While the full Census is updated only every ten years, the American Community Survey (ACS) provides some data on an annual basis. The Longitudinal Employment-Housing Dataset (LEHD) provides information about employment for most locations in the country. Budget implication: U.S. Census data is free and available online.

- *Center for Transit-Oriented Development National TOD Database.* This database includes Census information within a half-mile radius of every existing and planned fixed-guideway (rail and BRT) station in the country.[1] This information can help a community in understanding information about who lives and works near transit and compare stations or regional networks to those in other places. Budget implication: some aspects of the National TOD database are free; others are restricted and require membership dues.

- *The Housing + Transportation Affordability Index.* This site, at www.htaindex. org, provides information on housing and transportation costs in all 337 metropolitan regions in the United States. This site can be used to assess the impact of auto-oriented transportation policies and the impact of fluctuations in costs like gas prices and other components of transportation costs.

- *Direct Ridership Modeling.* This technique has been pioneered in the San Francisco Bay Area and several other regions by Fehr & Peers, a consulting firm. This technique models how various aspects of the built environment and transportation system influence transit ridership. This technique allows more fine-grained analysis than traditional ridership modeling. Budget implication: The Direct Ridership Model is a detailed tool that provides detailed modeling of behavior but requires more substantial financial investment.

- *County assessors data.* Parcel-by-parcel data about land values, uses, and building conditions are available from county governments. Some states (such as Maryland) aggregate data at the state level as well. This data provides fine-grained land use information. Assessor's data is the most generally available data for property values, but may not reflect current market realities. Budget implication: County assessor data is usually available for a nominal fee.

VISUAL MAPPING AND DATA-GATHERING TOOLS

In addition to the need to provide quantitative data and a qualitative framework using the tools outlined above, developing a transportation plan requires a visual perspective to pull the disparate elements together.

- *Geographic Information Systems (GIS).* ArcMap, made by ESRI, is the most common platform for GIS, combining mapping tools with powerful database layers. Other GIS systems provide similar tools for assimilating large amounts of data with geographic analysis.

- *Google Maps.* Google Maps provide a low-tech, freely available tool for multiple collaborators to edit maps. This is an effective technique for allowing residents to map community assets, opportunities, and issues.
- *Windshield surveys and community mapping.* Visual surveys, either on foot or by car (often called windshield surveys), are effective ways to gather detailed information about a place, especially to reconfirm other data sources. Asking residents to map their own communities can be a tool for building community engagement and gathering important information. Field data collection such as ridership counts or counts of the transportation modes riders are using to access stations are important in understanding the details of transit usage.

REGULATORY AND OTHER LEGAL TOOLS AND TECHNIQUES

Transit infrastructure is usually paid for through a combination of local and federal funding. Federal funding for new rail and bus rapid transit investments typically comes through the Federal Transit Administration's (FTA) New Starts Program. Smaller investments in transit may come through the FTA's Small Starts program. Both the New Starts and Small Starts programs require detailed documentation of costs and benefits, as well as a local funding match (typically 50 percent or more of the cost of the investment). Communities use a variety of sources to pay for the local match, most often through dedicated sales tax revenue.

Joint Development, a tool where publicly held land is developed in cooperation with the private sector, can be used effectively to support TOD, with the double benefits of ridership and revenue for the transit agency. Though success in implementing Joint Development around transit projects is mixed, the Washington Metropolitan Area Transit Authority (WMATA) in Washington, DC, boasts the most extensive program in the country that generates the most revenue from Joint Development (approximately $10 million per year). Revenues from Joint Development are used to pay for capital improvements and maintenance, while the ridership helps contribute to the overall system revenue as well. Other transit agencies have decided to use their properties more to generate ridership and supportive land uses around transit than to focus on the revenue potential.

Value capture tools include Tax Increment Financing (TIF), special assessment districts, or other techniques used to pay for transit infrastructure or transit-supportive development. These tools use the increased value of properties in close proximity to transit to fund capital improvements to streets or utility upgrades, or development projects. The tools vary in their application and the source of revenue. TIF is often an attractive source, because it does not add to the existing taxes paid by residents or property owners, but it can divert funding from other needs. Assessment districts directly link the benefits of transit access to property owners through special taxation.

Special development zones around transit are important to capture the benefits of transit service. Zoning modifications, such as reduced parking requirements and requirements for a mix of uses, can support increased transit ridership and transit-supportive development. The costs and revenue potential of all of these tools vary widely based on the application and local context.

COMMUNICATIONS TOOLS AND TECHNIQUES

Visualization tools such as photosimulations can show the transformative potential of transit and TOD for a specific site or street. This tool uses photorealistic images to communicate potential changes and phasing. Photosimulations typically cost $3,000 to $5,000, depending on the complexity of the site. Basic photosimulations can also be done for less.

Three-dimensional rendering and "fly-through" models use computer aided drafting and design (CADD) to illustrate future development and transportation scenarios. SketchUp is a tool that enables rapid 3D rendering. Basic SketchUp tools are provided free through Google.

VISSIM and other transportation modeling techniques can also provide visual models of transit and transportation improvements. These tools can model traffic levels for all modes and show how operations of an intersection or street will work in the future. These tools are more complex and expensive to use, and costs typically run from $3,000 to $5,000 per location.

PUBLIC EVALUATIVE AND DECISION-MAKING TOOLS

A TOD typology can be effective in communicating the differences among places around transit across a city or region. This tool is often based on existing conditions, such as residents and jobs or use mix and location. TOD typologies provide a framework for decisions about density and transit investments that can address issues of long-term land use change, needed uses, and approaches to station design and access.

Figure 5-4
Jameson Square, in Portland, Oregon, is an example of the type of public space that can be created through coordinated and comprehensive planning for transit-oriented development. *Reconnecting America*

Preparing the Place

The process of developing a transportation plan begs a number of questions: Where do people live? Where do people work? Where is there growth opportunity? What are the locally valued assets and opportunities? What are the regional and local market conditions? Where is congestion common? Are there existing rights-of-way that can be used to make transit connections? Where are populations that depend on public transit service (young, old, and low-income) located? The answers will help identify where transit investments can have the greatest benefits for shifting travel from cars to other modes and reducing VMT.

Researching the place requires quantitative and qualitative analysis of existing development using the tools identified above. Many regions have other local data sources that can be used to develop an understanding of existing conditions.

At this stage in the process, it is useful to develop a place typology to help categorize existing places and provide a framework for future planning. Place types can incorporate a number of different factors that are useful to the specific place and planning purpose.

Identify the Opportunities and Constraints

Opportunities for transit and TOD investment include:

- Areas of growing congestion that lead to support for local financing
- Existing programmed capital improvements and street repairs that can lead to easy pedestrian and bicycle improvements
- Federal funding, such as the Congestion Mitigation and Air Quality (CMAQ) program, that provide flexible resources to address multimodal transportation solutions
- Strong real estate markets that lead to redevelopment and infill pressures
- Available right-of-way that connects to regional employment centers and can be used for multimodal transportation connections
- Areas with excess street capacity that can be dedicated to exclusive transit rights-of-way
- Poor environmental conditions that require new approaches to transportation investments through enforcement of the Clean Air Act
- Existing successful transit investments
- Strong collaborative partnerships among the public and private sectors, particularly involving the business community and neighborhood groups

Constraints for transit and TOD investment include:

- Areas of disinvestment and concentrated poverty
- Local regulations that discourage intensification and new investment in existing communities

- Transit financing challenges for both operations and capital investments
- Lack of community understanding of the benefits of transit investments and transit-supportive development
- Fragmented local jurisdictions with weak regional planning and implementation frameworks

Produce Preliminary Reports, Studies, and Benchmarks

Regional transportation models outline the existing and future areas of growth and congestion, and can be used to generate greenhouse gas emissions estimates. The cost of regional transportation models varies, but its calculation is a time- and resource-intensive task.

A regional growth vision provides a framework for regional growth that can be agreed upon by many stakeholders and provide a framework for land use change over time. Building consensus around a regional growth vision can take significant time and resources in both outreach and technical analysis.

Existing travel and transportation conditions can be understood through direct surveys of transit riders and transit usage counts. The MTC in the San Francisco Bay Area undertakes a regional travel survey every two years to gather detailed information about travel and transportation patterns, and similar studies are performed by other regional agencies around the country. Many transit agencies do ridership surveys to understand how people are using the system, why they are riding, and how they access transit stops and stations. WMATA in the DC region also does surveys of development areas near metro stations to understand the ridership and usage patterns from different development locations.

Prepare the People

Building sustainable communities requires coalitions of different stakeholders. Identifying the key stakeholders may involve outreach and dialogue beyond the traditional environmental, smart growth, and multimodal transit advocates. Business and real estate interests, community-based housing and community development organizations, regional housing and affordable housing developers, ordinary citizens, "anchor institutions" (universities, hospitals, cultural institutions), labor unions, and philanthropic institutions (community foundations, corporate foundations, family foundations, and others) have been important "nontraditional" partners in regional and local initiatives around the country.

Constituencies outreach often requires translating the benefits of transit and TOD into new language that resonates with these partners. Highlighting the jobs created through transit investments helps with outreach to labor unions; reduced household transportation costs helps with affordable housing developers and community-based organizations; business opportunity and regional competitiveness helps with business and real estate interests. The specific partners will vary by region and subject matter.

ENGAGE AND EDUCATE

There are successful models of regional engagement and education:

- *Envision* processes are large-scale transportation and land use planning processes that identify a common vision for a region. The Salt Lake City, Utah, region and the Central Texas region around Austin are both successful models for this approach.

- *Blueprint* planning processes in places like Sacramento and Los Angeles have some of the same elements and incorporate more detailed implementation recommendations for both housing and transportation.

- *Reality check* processes, convened by the Urban Land Institute (ULI), provide a market-based approach to regional planning, with an evaluation of the market for different types of development and then apply those constraints to development visions.

There are also successful models of local engagement and education:

- *Station area plans* are successful ways of engaging local stakeholders in planning and visioning for a specific station and surrounding communities.

- *Community-based plans* and visions can be developed by local nonprofit organizations or advocacy groups. These nongovernment plans are a way to build consensus before an official planning process is underway.

The budgets for these regional and local planning efforts vary based on the scale and level of involvement and can range from the hundreds of thousands of dollars to millions of dollars.

BUILD LEADERSHIP

Part of a long-term strategy for working with the community stakeholders is to develop leaders with a knowledge base that allows them to fully participate in the process. There are several examples of resources available for leadership development.

- *Transportation "academies"* in Portland, Oregon, and New York City train elected and nonelected stakeholders in transportation planning processes. These "academies" are successful in building leadership at the local level to advocate for improved multimodal transportation and to broaden the technical understanding of tools and solutions.

- *The Great Communities Collaborative (GCC)* in the San Francisco Bay Area brings together regional advocacy organizations and community-based organizations to advocate for improved TOD plans and assist in implementation in communities around the region. The GCC is led by philanthropic foundations that supply funding and organizational resources.

- *The Mayors' Institute on City Design*, a 20+ year-old program run by the National Endowment for the Arts, the American Architectural Foundation, and the U.S. Conference of Mayors, works with local elected leaders to build their capacity to make good land use, transportation, and urban design decisions. This model has been successfully adapted by others and brought to the local level.

Developing Goals, Objectives, and Performance Metrics

In any planning process, determine the goals and objectives, and establish performance metrics that can be used to measure progress in meeting these goals and objectives. In transportation planning, some of the examples of goal and objectives set by various agencies or organizations include the following:

The GCC has set the following goal: "By 2030 all people in the Bay Area will live in complete communities, affordable across all incomes, with access to quality transit."

The MTC in the San Francisco Bay Area has set the following goals for their Transportation for Livable Communities (TLC) program:

- Improve the affordability of the region by allowing residents to own fewer autos and spend less on transportation

- Reduce greenhouse gas emissions from both housing and transportation

- Respond to the region's changing demographics by building the types of communities that will meet the needs of current and future residents

- Encourage walking, bicycling, and public transit by making these modes of travel safe, attractive, and convenient

The New York City Department of Transportation has established a number of benchmarks and targets related to the function and quality of the transportation system in the City. These include actions around the following topics:

- Safety

- Mobility

- World-class streets

- Infrastructure

- Greening

- Global leadership

Each topic includes specific short- and long-term actions that are communicated to a broad audience and set performance targets for the agency.

The Transportation for America Coalition, which brings together local and national organizations for the reform of federal transportation policy, has set ten performance metrics for federal transportation investments in the next federal surface transportation authorization:

- Reduce per capita vehicle miles traveled by 16 percent

- Triple walking, biking, and public transportation use

- Reduce transportation-generated carbon dioxide levels by 40 percent

- Reduce delay per capita by 10 percent

- Increase proportion of freight transportation provided by railroad and intermodal services by 20 percent

- Achieve zero percent population exposure to at-risk levels of air pollution

Figure 5-5
Charlotte's new South Corridor LRT
was planned in coordination with
development projects that revitalized
neighborhoods south of the CBD.
Reconnecting America

- Improve public safety and lower congestion costs by reducing traffic crashes by 50 percent

- Increase share of major highways, regional transit fleets and facilities, and bicycling/pedestrian infrastructure in good state of condition by 20 percent

- Reduce average household combined housing and transportation costs by 25 percent (use 2000 as base year)

- Increase by 50 percent essential destinations accessible within 30 minutes by public transit, or 15 minutes' walk for low-income, senior, and disabled populations

Methods and Examples of Moving Beyond Goal Setting

Incorporation of transportation affordability metrics and measures broadens the discussion of sustainability to include economic and equity outcomes in addition to environmental benefits.

Regional summits can bring together key stakeholders to start a conversation on specific topics. Summits can be convened by a range of stakeholders, but are usually initiated by the public sector or advocacy groups. Through a range of activities (tours, small group discussions, and speakers) these events can build consensus around specific topics and catalyze future actions. Summits are not expensive ways to build interaction and dialogue, and can be conducted for costs in the tens of thousands of dollars.

Awareness events, such as Critical Mass, Park(ing) Day, and car-free days build public awareness of the importance of multimodal transportation planning and investments. The Summer Streets events in New York City over the past two summers have closed down some streets on Sundays to encourage increased walking and biking citywide. By raising awareness and encouraging participation through "safety in numbers," these events can build momentum for changing the built environment.

Develop the Action Plan

When evaluating transit and TOD investments, compare and evaluate the regional and local benefits. Regional benefits include reduced congestion, reduced GHG emissions, and efficient infrastructure investments. Local benefits include community revitalization and investment, reduced household transportation costs, and improved access. Often, evaluation processes focus on the regional benefits, while overlooking the local benefits. Those investments that do the most for both sets of benefits should be prioritized over those that only benefit one or the other.

Methods for Finding and Securing Key Resources and Support

Finding support for transit investments often requires local funding measures, which usually must be levied through direct vote. Mobilizing support for these efforts through political campaigns is an essential element for passage. The FasTracks sales tax in the Denver region provides a good example of the type of coalition and actions necessary to implement a regional transit vision.

Sustained collaborative partnerships focused on transit and TOD are important in the ongoing success of these efforts. The GCC is an example of the type of partnerships between philanthropy, advocacy, and public-sector actors. Similar collaborative efforts existing in other regions and are successful ways to build momentum.

Implement the Action Plan

Demonstration projects can be critical for the success of transit investments. They often start small, but with a long-term vision of a full transit network. Demonstration projects should be located in places that make sense, even if they are not the easiest locations. Transit projects that fail to deliver on initial investments can set back progress on the regional vision. Starting with a streetcar segment or small-scale investment can be a challenge, though, since the benefits of transit and TOD start to accrue as the network grows. Without a clear timeframe for the regional network, individual pilot projects may not deliver on their potential.

An Incremental Approach: Developing a Long-Term Comprehensive Regional Transportation Plan

Trent Lethco, AICP
Associate Planner, Transportation Planning Group, Arup

The Vision and the Reality

To design a sustainable transportation system, the following high-level principles should underlie every transportation and land use decision being made:

- Humans first—plan for the pedestrian
- Supportive cycling and transit networks
- Transit-oriented development
- Connectivity—between modes and places
- Street design that supports activity and creates a vibrant public space
- Land use mix and density
- Parking—limit auto share
- Safety and security

Figure 5-6
No matter the size of a transit station catchment area, incremental increases in density and a movement toward a more multimodal, bicycle-, and pedestrian-centered station is possible. *Arup*

Catchment Area Typology

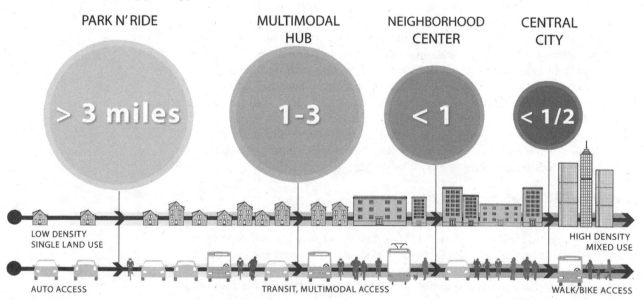

PARK N' RIDE — MULTIMODAL HUB — NEIGHBORHOOD CENTER — CENTRAL CITY

> 3 miles   1-3   < 1   < 1/2

LOW DENSITY SINGLE LAND USE — HIGH DENSITY MIXED USE

AUTO ACCESS — TRANSIT, MULTIMODAL ACCESS — WALK/BIKE ACCESS

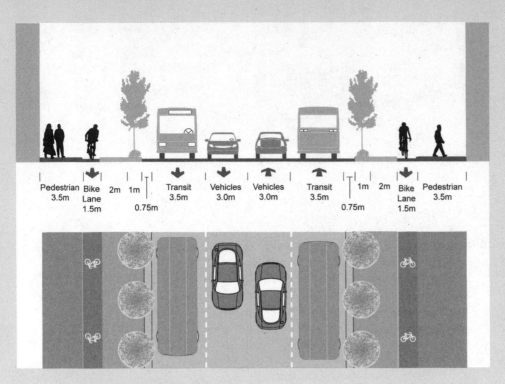

Pedestrian 3.5m | Bike Lane 1.5m | 2m | 1m 0.75m | Transit 3.5m | Vehicles 3.0m | Vehicles 3.0m | Transit 3.5m | 1m 0.75m | 2m | Bike Lane 1.5m | Pedestrian 3.5m

Figure 5-7
This cross-section and plan exemplifies a street type designed to prioritize pedestrians, cyclists, and mass transit. *Arup*

Long-range plans rarely translate into on-the-ground changes. Visions are often divorced from the day-to-day decisions and in the haste of the moment, the long-term goals are sacrificed to simplify or expedite an immediate decision. For example, a long-term vision may call for a community to densify and become more mixed use and transit-friendly. At the same time, with each new development proposal, the same amount of parking and the same traffic impact mitigation are required, so ultimately little change is realized. On day one of the new plan, it may not be appropriate to limit parking or reduce roadway capacity with the first project. However, reorientation of the buildings, introduction of pedestrian amenities, and the inclusion of transit facilities helps lay the foundation for a more sustainable mobility future. For the subsequent project, the fabric becomes more integrated, urban, and walkable, so less parking can be provided and more transit service deployed. As these virtuous and reinforcing cycles are created, additional ambitious travel demand management strategies can be employed.

Prepare the Team

In order to develop an integrated new transportation program, communities will need to move beyond their current auto-oriented land use patterns and restrictive planning codes and processes. Most important of all is to overcome the ingrained resistance to change at an agency and industry level. To bypass these obstacles, jurisdictions and organizations should set up a team of transportation planners and engineers skilled with the tools described below.

Prepare the Tools

The planning team should demonstrate expertise and experience with tools such as Geographic Information Systems (GIS) with Microsimulation Modeling in order to understand pedestrian, vehicular, and mass transit operations using such tools as VISSIM, MassMotion, and Syncro.

Trip generation spreadsheets, which require land use, density, and mode split data are essential in developing an integrated understanding of current usage patterns. ArcGIS is a useful tool in understanding and analyzing existing conditions by displaying data spatially, including demographics (household size, income, age, and so forth), transportation systems (roadways, railways, traffic and pedestrian volumes, bus stops, bus routes, and the like), and land use (retail, office, and open space).

A street management framework is a tool that allows cities to organize and maintain a street grid to accommodate all users and activities. A set of street types, such as major travel streets, pedestrian priority streets, and support streets for service vehicles, is established and mapped to the existing grid in the city. Key elements needed for each type are identified. This allows cities to effectively manage policies and prioritize street design improvements.

Street design guidelines can be used in conjunction with a street management framework, to provide a standard and streamlined method of improving various street types. Different designs are needed on different types of streets, and a design manual should include a list of design elements, approved materials, and a clearly defined process for making street improvements to prevent delay by numerous, lengthy review processes. The guidelines should be developed with heavy public involvement, and shared with the public to ensure their support of future street enhancements. The New York City Street Design Manual is a good example of this tool.

Figure 5-8
A human-centered transportation system puts people first and prioritizes planning for pedestrians, cyclists, and public transit over private vehicles. *Arup*

Figure 5-9
This VISSIM Model was developed as part of the planning process for a proposed transit neighborhood, and a 3D animation was created directly in VISSIM to use at public outreach meetings. *Arup*

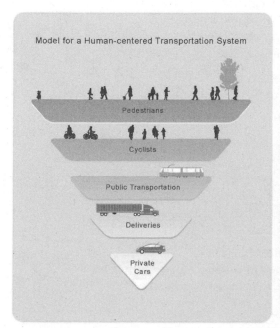

Case studies can provide examples that highlight programs and strategies a city or neighborhood may want to emulate. Case studies are powerful tools because they provide tangible information about costs, benefits, and lessons learned from actual projects. This approach often informs where more detailed quantitative investigations should be conducted. For example, a city's evolution toward a more sustainable transportation system can be guided by best practices and evidence from comparable cities around the world.

Prepare the Place

In understanding how a transportation network functions and what improvements might be needed, the following information is usually required to conduct a complete analysis:

- Complete road network including number of lanes, roadway widths, intersection spacing, signal timing, sidewalk width, presence of bike lanes, and the like
- Transit network data including all routes and stops for buses, streetcars, light rail, subways, commuter rail, and so forth
- Bicycle network data including on- and off-street bicycle lanes and paths and bicycle parking
- Traffic volumes including peak hour vehicle counts, pedestrian and bicycle counts, transit ridership volumes and so forth
- Accident report data—Pedestrian/cyclist/vehicle conflicts

An example of the type of report that should be incorporated into a transportation plan is an *Emissions Reduction Strategy Report.* To help make the case for transportation demand management (TDM) in cities and towns, an emissions reduction strategy report shows the degree to which certain transportation and land use strategies can reduce auto demand and, in turn, reduce emissions. The following elements are required:

- Analysis of current conditions
  - Demographics
  - Travel behavior (mode share, vehicle ownership, and so forth)
  - Pedestrian and bicycle counts and surveys
  - Transit routes, stops, frequency
  - Parking
  - Land use
- Calculate baseline carbon emissions based on transportation use
- Apply a reduction factor to estimate potential emission reductions for each proposed TDM strategy, such as improving the walking/cycling environment, increasing transit frequency, and so forth. These factors can be found in various academic studies that have measured the benefits of various improvements on lowering auto demand.

Prepare the People

Key stakeholders related to any comprehensive transportation plan include:

- Policy-makers
- City agencies including Departments of Transportation, Public Works, and Planning
- Community groups
- The public

To gain community support for transportation improvement projects, it is important to have a firm understanding of current travel behavior so that issues can be clearly articulated. A transportation agency can keep current on the state of the transportation network by creating and maintaining a robust model (using VISSIM, MassMotion, or other modeling tool) of the streets and transit systems in their jurisdiction. Frequent updates should be made to the model based on vehicle and pedestrian counts, surveys, and transit ridership information.

Figure 5-10
A street management plan such as the one shown here allows cities to effectively manage policies and prioritize street design improvements. *Arup*

Street typologies

- Access streets
- Community streets
- Living streets

Develop Goals, Objectives, and Performance Metrics

While each community or region will have its own specific issues and ideals, creating sustainability generally involves certain agreed-upon principles that guide planning efforts. Typical goals of a comprehensive transportation plan can include the following set of goals:

- Put pedestrians first
- Maximize pedestrian and bicycle connectivity
- Minimize local and regional transport footprint
- Capture trips on site by modes other than the car
- Optimize transit network, operations, and transit access
- Include well-designed, secure bicycle parking
- Provide and price appropriate levels of parking
- Plan for all ages and abilities

Strategic Planning

Three basic strategies can guide the strategic planning process by taking gradual steps to overcome current obstacles and realize the long-term vision:

- Develop new methods for planning and development
- Find case study examples of industry best practices
- Build relationships with other practitioners

Develop the Action Plan

An evaluation framework is a methodology to evaluate whether proposed measures or alternatives meet the transportation or sustainability goals set out at the beginning of a project. Based on the project objectives, a set of quantifiable, evaluation criteria is created (walking and cycling connectivity, access to new developments, preservation of natural environment, and so forth). Each criterion should have a clear rating scale as shown in Table 5.1. Proposed measures can be evaluated against this set of criteria, and can be compared to other measures, including a "do nothing," or existing conditions, case.

Table 5.1 Evaluation Criteria

	Rating		
	0	1	2
Walking and Cycling Provides interconnected and continuous pedestrian and cycling facilities that are safe, efficient, and convenient, and integrated with the citywide bicycle network	Disjointed network along corridor. Poor level of priority for pedestrians and cyclists in right-of-way.	Moderately connected. Moderate level of priority for pedestrians and cyclists in right-of-way.	Well connected, continuous along corridor. Good level of pedestrian and cyclist priority in right-of-way.

TRANSPORTATION FOR LIVABLE COMMUNITIES

Sam Zimbabwe, LEED
Reconnecting America

INTERVENTION TYPE: PROGRAM

Description: Regional Transportation for Livable Communities (TLC) Program

Regional programs can support the planning and implementation of multimodal streetscape improvements and transit-oriented development. The Metropolitan Planning Organization (MPO) using federal funds most often administers these programs. The programs give grants to local jurisdictions or other implementing agencies for both planning and capital funds. By setting regional priorities for TLC projects, these programs can implement sustainable community principles at the local level to the most deserving recipients.

SUPPORT GOALS AND OBJECTIVES
- Reduce VMT
- Increase transit ridership
- Increase infill and transit-oriented development
- Increase walking and biking

POTENTIAL SYNERGISM
The program should be coordinated with regional transportation investments and local transportation demand management programs and other multimodal programs.

IMPLEMENTATION TIME
TLC projects can typically be implemented in one year to 18 months.

Figure 5-11
The Livable Communities Demonstration Account in the Twin Cities region is a flexible fund to implement transit access and transit-oriented development projects throughout the region.
Reconnecting America

BENEFITS

- Addresses gaps in implementation of multimodal transportation improvements and TOD projects
- Encourages multi-agency and interjurisdictional coordination
- Makes tangible improvements that demonstrate the effectiveness of new strategies
- Reduces VMT by supporting multimodal transportation and increased transit ridership

DRAWBACKS

- Often created as a targeted funding source, rather than changing overall regional funding priorities
- Can be difficult logistically because there are no dedicated federal funding sources devoted to this purpose

FIRST COST

TLC programs range from relatively small (Washington, DC's is in the hundreds of thousands) to substantial (the San Francisco Bay Area's is now $30 million per year).

LIFECYCLE COSTS

TLC programs reduce lifecycle transportation costs by encouraging multimodal travel and reduced automobile use. TLC investments are also used to catalyze reinvestment in close-in locations that are "location efficient," meaning lower regional costs for a range of public services.

IMPLEMENTATION SUPPORTS AND CONSTRAINTS

- Can a regional agency create a flexible pool of funding for TLC programs that respond to the full range of needs?
- Are local jurisdictions willing and interested participants?
- Is the funding level sufficient to have a real impact?

INFORMATIONAL SOURCES—REPORTS AND STUDIES

- Metropolitan Transportation Commission (San Francisco) TLC Program: www.mtc. ca.gov/planning/smart_growth/tlc_grants.htm
- Metropolitan Council (Twin Cities) Livable Communities Grant Program: www. metrocouncil.org/services/livcomm.htm
- Metropolitan Washington Council of Governments Transportation and Land-Use Connections Program: www.mwcog.org/transportation/activities/tlc/
- Atlanta Regional Commission Livable Centers Initiative: www.atlantaregional. com/html/308.aspx

Figure 5-12
The Kedzie Station on the CTA Brown Line in Chicago, designed by Muller & Muller, Ltd., supports transit-oriented development. *Congress for the New Urbanism*

TRANSIT-ORIENTED DEVELOPMENT

Sam Zimbabwe, LEED
Reconnecting America

INTERVENTION TYPE: BEST PRACTICE

Description: Transit-Oriented Development Strategic Plan

TOD strategic plans define the strategies and actions necessary to make better connections between transit investments and development patterns at the neighborhood and regional scales. Taking into account the diversity of places around transit, TOD strategic plans identify additional investments in planning, infrastructure, and development, as well as policy reforms necessary to implement TOD. Because of their targeted nature, TOD strategic plans are able to bring together stakeholders and implementers from multiple disciplines.

SUPPORT GOALS AND OBJECTIVES
- Reduce VMT
- Increase transit ridership
- Reduce household transportation costs
- Increase walking and biking

POTENTIAL SYNERGISM
The program should be coordinated with transit investments, regional transportation plans, development incentive programs at the local and regional levels, and public-sector planning and implementation resources.

IMPLEMENTATION TIME
A TOD strategic plan can be developed in about a year, but implementation typically takes longer.

BENEFITS
- Targeting of public resources around implementation of transit-oriented development and an increased understanding of the needs and opportunities for TOD
- Long-term potential to reduce VMT and improve air quality, public health, and other outcomes by making better connections between the transit network and development patterns
- Opportunity to guide future transit investments to maximize community development and sustainability outcomes

Figure 5-13
In the Central Maryland region, a TOD strategy helps public and private stakeholders know where to prioritize their resources for implementing transit and TOD. *Center for Transit-Oriented Development*

Figure 5-14
In Denver, the City's TOD strategic plan outlines the different types of places along existing and future transit corridors, to facilitate land use planning and implementation. *City and County of Denver*

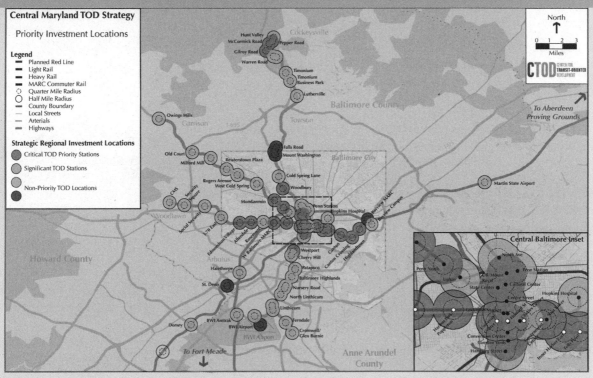

Central Maryland TOD Strategy

Priority Investment Locations

Legend
- Planned Red Line
- Light Rail
- Heavy Rail
- MARC Commuter Rail
- Quarter Mile Radius
- Half Mile Radius
- County Boundary
- Local Streets
- Arterials
- Highways

Strategic Regional Investment Locations
- Critical TOD Priority Stations
- Significant TOD Stations
- Non-Priority TOD Locations

North

0 1 2 3 Miles

CTOD CENTER FOR TRANSIT-ORIENTED DEVELOPMENT

To Aberdeen Proving Grounds

Central Baltimore Inset

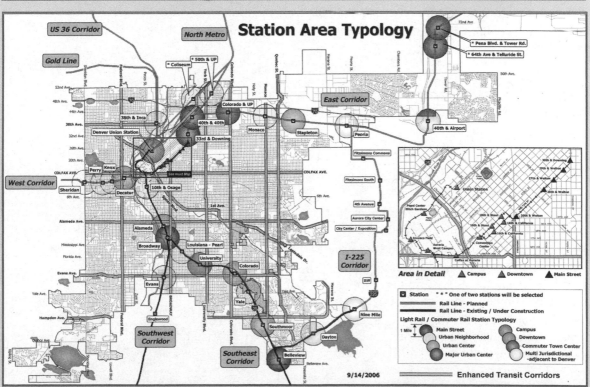

Station Area Typology

US 36 Corridor

Gold Line

North Metro

* Pena Blvd. & Tower Rd.

* 64th Ave & Telluride St.

East Corridor

40th & Airport

West Corridor

I-225 Corridor

Southwest Corridor

Southeast Corridor

Area in Detail ▲ Campus ◭ Downtown ▲ Main Street

☐ Station   " * " One of two stations will be selected
Rail Line - Planned
Rail Line - Existing / Under Construction
Light Rail / Commuter Rail Station Typology
- Main Street
- Urban Neighborhood
- Urban Center
- Major Urban Center
- Campus
- Downtown
- Commuter Town Center
- Multi Jurisdictional -adjacent to Denver

Enhanced Transit Corridors

9/14/2006

169

DRAWBACKS

- Requires up-front costs and coordination among multiple stakeholders
- Leads to targeting of implementation resources, and there is the potential for these not to lead to equitable outcomes

FIRST COST

Up-front costs for a TOD strategic plan typically are between $200,000 and $500,000, depending on the level of detail and analysis.

LIFECYCLE COSTS

Implementation of a plan has added costs, but also the potential for long-term benefits in reduced GHG emissions, higher transit ridership, and revenue from joint development or a broader tax base.

IMPLEMENTATION SUPPORTS AND CONSTRAINTS

- Does the transit agency understand the benefits of land use planning and development?
- Are there regional or local implementation entities that understand the value of transit?
- Is there enough existing or planned transit to influence regional development patterns?
- Are there advocacy groups that support transit and TOD investment?
- Is the development community engaged and do all parties understand the potential of TOD?

INFORMATIONAL SOURCES

Reconnecting America and the Center for Transit-Oriented Development have information on best practices in transit-oriented development available at www.reconnectingamerica.org.

REPORTS AND STUDIES

- Denver Transit-Oriented Development Strategic Plan: www.denvergov.org/Default. aspx?alias=www.denvergov.org/TOD
- Central Maryland Transit-Oriented Development Strategic Plan: www.cmtalliance. org/tabs_content/Central_Maryland_TOD_Strategy_FINAL_072009%5B1%5D.pdf
- Growing Cooler: www.smartgrowthamerica.org/gcindex.html
- Transit Cooperative Research Program (TCRP) Report 128: Effects of TOD on Housing, Parking, and Travel: www.trb.org/Publications/Public/Blurbs/Effects_of_TOD_on_Housing_Parking_and_Travel_160307.aspx
- Transit Cooperative Research Program (TCRP) Report 102: Transit-Oriented Development in the United States: Experiences, Challenges, and Prospects http://pubsindex.trb.org/view.aspx?type=MO&id=705110

SPECTRUM OF CHANGE TOOLS

Trent Lethco, AICP
Arup

INTERVENTION TYPE: TOOL/TECHNIQUE

Description

This tool informs cities about the sustainable transportation strategies, such as transit-oriented development, that other cities have adopted and how these strategies can be employed over time. These strategies can be phased in, so that a city or region may adopt them in an incremental way. This allows day-to-day decision-making to evolve so cities understand what steps to take in the near term that will help them achieve their long-term objectives. This planning tool will help inform cities of precedents and outcomes of similarly situated cities, laying a roadmap for change.

The Spectrum of Change tool organizes case studies into groups, or typologies, which describe a neighborhood's level of transportation sustainability. Case studies are powerful tools because they provide tangible information about costs, benefits, and lessons learned from actual projects. This framework provides a means of comparing cities that have different characteristics. An evolution toward a more sustainable transportation system can be guided by best practices and evidence from comparable cities around the world. The stages of change involve taking 30-year vision statements and breaking them down into smaller, incremental steps to ensure that day-to-day decision-making is aligned with the long-term vision of change and evolution over time.

Figure 5-15 is a graphical representation of the five typologies, moving from a low existing level of sustainability on the left, to the most sustainable on the right. Going from top to bottom, there are also notional ideas about what contributes to sustainable transportation: street network, land use and intensity, transportation options, and mode share. Inherent in this typology framework is the notion that each typology will suggest different opportunities and issues, and therefore different sustainable transportation strategies.

SUPPORT GOALS AND OBJECTIVES
The goals of the Spectrum of Change tool are the following:
- Create sustainable communities
- Create transit-supportive communities and environments
- Reduce activities that contribute to global warming
- Enable context-sensitive density and intensity of land uses
- Increase nonautomobile transportation mode share

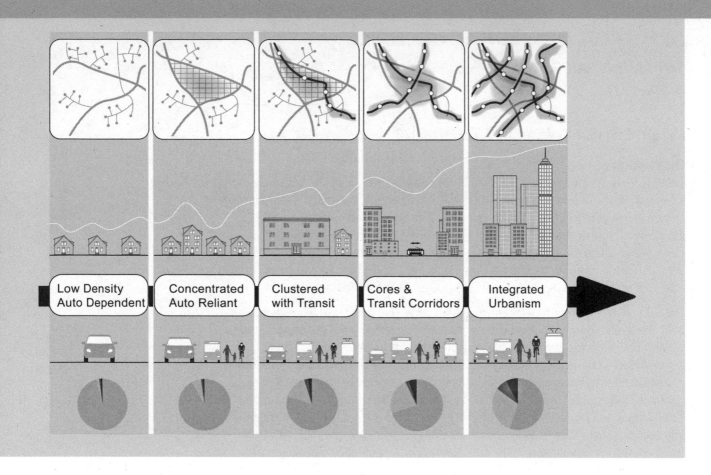

Low Density
Auto Dependent

Concentrated
Auto Reliant

Clustered
with Transit

Cores &
Transit Corridors

Integrated
Urbanism

PERFORMANCE CHARACTERISTICS

This is a tool to achieve different policy and design outcomes. Its performance is based on effective policy change over time.

Based on the notional ideas of sustainable transportation, the typologies are more specifically defined in terms of quantitative variables. The following five categories of variables guide the data-collection process:

1. Street pattern
2. Bicycle and pedestrian environment
3. Transit
4. Parking
5. Land Use

This tool is data-intensive and implementation is most effective when a comprehensive citywide GIS database and census data are available.

Figure 5-15
In Denver, the City's TOD strategic plan outlines the different types of places along existing and future transit corridors, to facilitate land use planning and implementation. *Arup*

This tool integrates several other planning activities that converge in the realm of transportation and land use planning. The tool is associated with travel demand management, encouraging the use of alternative modes of transportation, as well as land use planning focused on the integration of land use, urban design, sustainable mobility, street management frameworks, and street designs.

IMPLEMENTATION TIME

The Spectrum of Change tool can be implemented within six months of adoption of a long-range plan. However, it takes effect in a series of steps over the course of time. The recommended timeframe is 20 to 30 years, with five 5-year increments, creating a series of gradual steps toward the vision.

A neighborhood should also use the tool to monitor progress toward the vision, and its position along the sustainable spectrum, every five years.

BENEFITS

The benefits of a case-study-based, long-range planning tool include the following:

- Reduces up-front risk of major policy changes
- Articulates long-term planning goals and objectives in incremental steps over time
- Allows for incremental change to the plan
- Ensures delivery on the vision by protecting against vision erosion in the day-to-day decision-making, where immediate needs often take precedence over longer-term ideals
- Coordinates program elements at the right moment in time, place, and context
- Allows for a case-study approach supported by evidence that can be used to measure before and after performance

An example of the benefits of this incremental approach can be seen in the following scenario: demand management strategies may only be effective once a robust transit system is in place; communities can only afford robust transit service when transit-supportive land uses are widely present; transit-supportive land uses can only be widely present after urban design guidelines are developed and implemented, and building forms emerge as a result of these new guidelines. Only after the entire cycle is complete can the original goals be fully put into effect.

Perhaps the greatest benefit of a tool that facilitates movement toward a mass-transit, biking, and walking city are the quantifiable environmental benefits of

Table 5.1 Strategies that lower automobile mode share

Measure	Mode Shift Assumption	Source
Walkable environment	7–10% reduction in auto-trips for noncommuting trips	URBEMIS model baseline assumptions (7%); and Cervero, 1997. Travel Choices in Pedestrian versus Automobile-Oriented Neighborhoods. UCTC, No.281 Working Paper (10%)
Separated bike lanes	5–7% reduction in auto mode share	Petritsch, Landis, McLeod, Huang, and Scott. November 2007. "Energy savings resulting from the provision of bicycle facilities" TRB 2008 Annual General Meeting
Increased bus frequency	15–30% auto trip reduction	URBEMIS model assumption (15%), the City of Toronto Parking Standards Review (30%), Scarborough Meet-and-Greet Travel Survey
Increase in local serving retail	2% reduction VKT (vehicle kilometers traveled)	URBEMIS model baseline assumption
Discounted transit passes (e.g., CTP, free transit pass for newcomers)	8–25% reduction in auto-based drive-alone trips	Shoup, D. "Evaluation: The effects of cashing out employer-paid parking: Eight case studies" Transport Policy, Vol 4, No.4, pp. 201–216, 1997 (8%), URBEMIS standard baseline assumption (25%)
Car-sharing	45% of auto-drivers reduce VKT by 43%	Price, J. and C. Hamilton, "Arlington Pilot Car-Share Program: First-Year Report" Arlington: Arlington County.

reducing the automobile mode share and thus lowering GHG emissions. The following table shows studies that have quantified how street design, transit, and land use measures can reduce automobile mode share. While actual results depend on where a neighborhood falls on the sustainability spectrum, these factors can be used to gain support for implementing change to the transportation system.

DRAWBACKS
- Data-intensive
- Policy-based tool
- Requires a concrete, long-term vision
- Requires a strong commitment over the course of time
- Training of staff needed to understand how to implement and operate long-term vision

FIRST COST
To successfully implement the tool, a visioning study associated with a long-term planning strategy is needed. The cost of a complete evaluation of a neighborhood's sustainability, including an implementation plan and policy recommendations, varies based on the size of the community and complexity of the governance structure.

It would likely range from $150,000 to $2,000,000.

Lifecycle Costs

The costs over the life of the project are the ongoing staff time hours associated with the program implementation.

Estimated Quantitative Performance

The success of the tool should be measured in terms of both improvements in the planning process, as well as actual performance outcomes in moving toward a sustainable community.

Process based outcomes

- Phased implementation of sustainable transportation policy
- Actions of community will be in sync with approved policy program

Performance based outcomes

- Change in the type of developments approved by the planning department
- Mode shift, based on both the place type selected and timeframe in which the policy is developed. In the early days of implementation, no mode shift should be expected as policies and programs are being put into place, and behavioral change takes time. Development pattern and mode-share change should be phased over time.

Implementation Supports and Constraints

For the initial evaluation using the spectrum tool, data collection can be time intensive. Ensuring availability of data will facilitate this phase of the process.

Upon completion of the initial evaluation and recommended strategies, implementation will require:

- A proactive planning commission with a strong vision for the city
- Flexible zoning codes and incentives to encourage higher-density development that would support a public transit network
- Public outreach to gain community support for transit and land use intensification

Informational Sources

S. Zimmerman-Bergman, "Using Typologies to Simplify Complex Planning Decisions," Platform: Building the New Transit Town, *Reconnecting America*, Winter 2008

——. "Hidden in Plain Sight: Capturing the Demand for Housing Near Transit," *Reconnecting America*, September 2004

——. "Transit Connectivity Index," unpublished manuscript. Arup, Sustainable Cities Tool—Phase 1 Report, April 2009

PARKING—WHEN LESS IS MORE

Norman Garrick, PhD, P.E.
Associate Professor, University of Connecticut

Wesley Marshall, PhD, P.E.
Assistant Professor, University of Colorado, Denver

INTERVENTION TYPE: STRATEGY

Description

Parking and the provision of parking is an often overlooked aspect of the transportation system. But parking plays a key role in the economic and social vitality of American cities, towns, and commercial centers. The extent to which most towns address this issue is by ensuring that their zoning regulations mandate that an ample supply of parking accompanies any new development. There are sound reasons for this approach: the towns want to ensure that shoppers are not discouraged by a lack of parking and that spillover parking does not inundate neighborhoods. But when is enough parking too much of a good thing? In fact, can there be such a thing as too much parking?

SUPPORT GOALS AND OBJECTIVES

A growing number of cities and towns around the country are answering yes to this last question. They are beginning to recognize that too much parking can be as bad as too little and are taking steps to regulate the demand and the supply of parking. Some cities now mandate a parking maximum and not a minimum as is the norm. They point out that the detrimental effects of too much parking are insidious and hard to measure, but they are nonetheless quite real.

Too much parking wastes land and carries with it a sizable economic penalty, especially in terms of wasted opportunities. More importantly, too much parking often saps the vitality of an area by creating large dead zones where people do not want to be. Communities recognize that the arrangement of parking relative to the buildings, ownership, and operation is more important than the quantity factors that affect whether parking will have a positive or adverse effect on the surrounding land uses.

▲▲ Figure 5-16
Glastonbury Center, Connecticut, is dominated by underutilized surface parking and poor pedestrian amenities. *Norman Garrick and Wesley Marshall*

▲ Figure 5-17
Brattleboro, Vermont, has a downtown with managed, shared, and priced parking. *Norman Garrick and Wesley Marshall*

DATA GATHERING

In 2003, we started a two-year-long study, sponsored by the New England University Transportation Center, of parking at six centers around New England. Our primary goal was to compare parking at three traditional New England downtowns with mixed land uses supported by an organized system of parking with three more contemporary, automobile-oriented sites of similar size to the traditional sites. All three traditional sites had a significant number of on-street parking spaces while the contemporary sites had little or none.

PERFORMANCE CHARACTERISTICS

The analysis shows that the traditional sites use much less parking and use the parking more efficiently than did the contemporary sites. On average, peak parking usage (generally during the holiday shopping period) at the traditional centers was about 24 percent less than at the contemporary sites (1.8 cars per 1,000 square feet of building space compared to 2.3); the traditional sites attracted large numbers of people by foot, bicycle, and public transit.

BENEFITS AND COMPARATIVE ADVANTAGES

The contemporary sites contain more than twice the parking spaces required during peak shopping periods—a waste of land and impervious, asphalt paving, and a contributor to the "heat island"* effect. Less than 50 percent of the parking spaces at the contemporary sites were filled during the peak shopping period, versus 80 percent peak occupancy at the traditional sites.

Unused parking dampens the vibrancy of urban centers; traditional centers had more than five times the number of pedestrians on-site compared to the contemporary centers. Contemporary sites average just over 50 pedestrians; the traditional sites averaged over 250 pedestrians at any one time. Parking consumes land that could be more productively used and attract even more people.

Traditional sites have advantages that allow smooth operation at a much higher occupancy level. Although the automobile was the most prevalent mode of choice for all sites, almost 25 percent of users traveled to the traditional sites without cars compared to just 9 percent visiting the contemporary sites. Public transportation was used almost five times more at the traditional sites, noteworthy because all the sites had very similar levels of bus transit availability. Bike use reached 2.5 percent at the traditional sites compared to negligible use at the contemporary sites. Besides driving, walking was the next most popular travel mode. Our user survey found that almost 15 percent walked to the traditional sites while people at the contemporary sites walked at less than half that rate, or 7.4 percent. The traditional sites' better network of walkable streets accounted for a major difference in travel modes.

---

*"Heat island" effect describes undesirable urban temperature increases that arise from the absorption of solar radiation within low albedo or non-reflective materials such as asphalt and concrete paving.

POTENTIAL SYNERGISM

The paid municipal parking lots and garages at the traditional sites serve the whole center and not just individual businesses. This parking consolidation affords great efficiency and creates a "park once" district where people arrive, park, pay once, and then patronize numerous businesses. Most people at the contemporary sites drive from one business to another within the center, relying on multiple parking spaces for each visit—an inefficient use of parking.

The traditional sites are much easier and pleasant to walk around in. The contemporary centers' large, half-empty parking lots create a disconnected pedestrian path and generally unpleasant walking environment. The traditional sites contain more heterogeneous mix of land uses; each category of businesses' different demand cycle over the course of the day uses parking more efficiently, with consolidated parking in demand all day and evening. Each lot in the conventional style, dedicated to a specific type of business, is sometimes full during the day but empty in the evening; a large number for just a few hours each day.

IMPLEMENTATION: REGULATORY CONSTRAINTS

In spite of the six sites' differences in parking use, parking regulations for the five towns that host these sites all mandate about the same level of parking in their zoning regulations, about 5.5 spaces per 1,000 square feet of floor area. At more than 2.5 times the amount of parking actually used, even during peak shopping time, this standard illustrates the overly cautious approach adopted by many cities across the country. Other studies show similar results: Most towns demand far too much parking, thus waste land, increase development costs, deaden their urban centers, discourage walking and riding, and add to the runoff into streams and rivers.

ALTERNATIVE STRATEGIES

Based on this study, we suggest the following strategies for minimizing the negative impact of parking:

1. Reduce or eliminate minimum parking requirements: Most towns could significantly reduce the minimum parking requirements without noticeable adverse effect. Most developments could easily get by with from 2 to 3 spaces per 1,000 square feet of building, depending on the level of activity expected, with peak occupancy still only about 80 percent.

2. Encourage connected, mixed-use developments: Mixed-use centers use fewer parking spaces and use the parking they provide much more efficiently. A walkable network of streets to residential areas must connect these mixed-use places in order to accrue the full advantage in terms of reducing parking demand. However, so-called "life style" centers, though ostensibly mixed-use, often cannot be accessed without a car. Though unlikely to see reduced parking demand, they can use parking provided more efficiently because of the mix of businesses sharing the same lots.

3. Reinstigate on-street parking: Many towns eliminated on-street parking to increase the efficiency of traffic flow and do not provide on-street parking in new developments. Our study showed that on-street parking was most valued by customers and proved to be the most convenient. In comparison to surface parking, on-street parking typically uses less than 176 square feet per space compared to 513 square feet for surface lots, including access lanes and parking lot islands. A town center with approximately 2,000 parking spaces could save over 2.3 acres of land by providing 15 percent parking curbside instead of off-street.

4. On-street parking serves as a traffic-calming function. Our study found that low-speed streets with parking had by far the lowest rate per mile of fatal and severe crashes. On-street parking clearly marks the street as a place rather than just a conduit for traffic.

5. Consider shared municipal lots: Consolidated municipal parking promotes a park-once mindset, which benefits all the businesses in a center. Lots shared between different types of businesses are used more efficiently and are full more often. The parking revenue from municipal parking systems can be used to landscape, beautify, and maintain the streets and other public areas of the center—a number of studies suggest that customers are not resistant to paying a reasonable rate for parking.

Figure 5-18
Brattleboro, Vermont, provides streets with parking and desirable pedestrian amenities. *Norman Garrick and Wesley Marshall*

Summary

Though few U.S. cities and towns contain comprehensive commercial center parking plans, many town centers could benefit immeasurably from a coordinated approach to managing parking demand. Oversupplying parking is wasteful of land and resources, is environmentally unsound, and dampens the economic and social vitality of commercial centers. However, our study shows that relatively small changes (such as implementing shared parking) can significantly reduce the amount of resources devoted to parking while creating more vibrant centers in our cities and towns.

This research was sponsored by the New England University Transportation Center.

BIBLIOGRAPHY
W. Marshall and N. Garrick: "Parking at Mixed-Use Centers in Small Cities," *Transportation Research Record*, vol. 1977 (2006).
———. "Reassessing On-Street Parking," *Transportation Research Record*, vol. 2046 (2008).

GREEN STREETSCAPES FOR LOCAL STREETS

Paul Crabtree, P.E.
Crabtree Group, Inc.

INTERVENTION TYPE: PROGRAM

Description

Most American street systems have been built in the last 60 years. They were built as incomplete streets with a major emphasis on the automobile, wide pavement sections, and often missing sidewalks and street trees. A motor vehicle–focused street network of expensive, overly wide streets with unnecessary concrete storm drains is more costly to build and maintain. The reformation of the existing streetscape approach requires new standards, funding, and actions, in addition to a change in old attitudes.

A balanced street network, or complete streetscape, connects the community by providing safe, efficient, and attractive mobility for cars, pedestrians, and bicycles. It is also a green network, providing for rainwater infiltration. The street networks are an essential part of the public realm of a community, conveying the important infrastructure and mobility, and creating that sense of place.

Key stakeholders for the street network are the citizen users (pedestrians, bicyclists, drivers, property owners) public users (transit operators, fire and police departments, utility agencies), and those responsible for building and maintaining the system (state Department of Transportation, public works department, utility agencies, tree boards, developers).

In the following example, a community has a high percentage of local streets with 40 feet of paving within a 50-foot right-of-way, resulting in many streets without sidewalks and street trees. The consultant has analyzed this through GIS and field reviews, and has developed a possible pattern for streetscape repair that could be used as the basis for customized complete street programs in each neighborhood, to be developed in a public design charrette. The pattern includes a staged pattern for removing excess pavement; followed by installation of sidewalks, street trees, and bioswales.

A presentation of this analysis to stakeholders and the general public in an interactive workshop helps generate feedback and a future vision for the community's assets. The consultants and/or staff document the vision and develop the policy, coding language, and long- and short-term capital improvement plans, and get those documents adopted through the public hearing process. A complete and comprehensive capital improvements plan that is developed through integrated cross-disciplinary actions and public inputs can act as the control center for publicly integrated infrastructure to set sequences, priorities, and schedules, and to monitor performance.

Figure 5-19
A fine-grained network of streets and sidewalks maximizes mobility for pedestrians, bicyclists, and motor vehicles.
Stephen Coyle

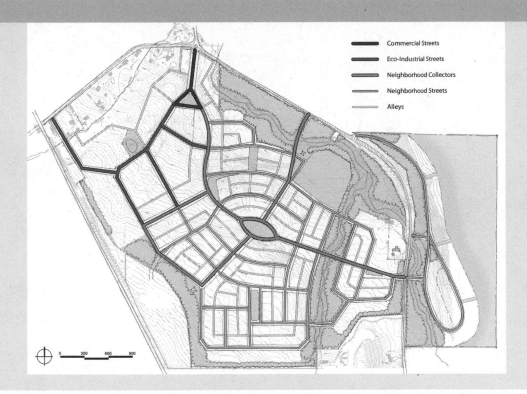

Commercial Streets
Eco-Industrial Streets
Neighborhood Collectors
Neighborhood Streets
Alleys

0   300   600   900

Support goals and objectives. Inventory all local streets within one year. Retrofit all local streets into complete green streetscapes within 20 years.

Performance characteristics. Increase mode share of pedestrians and bicycles by 20 percent within 20 years. Decrease rainfall runoff volume and pollution quantities from streets by 50 percent within 20 years.

Potential synergism. An in-depth review of existing policies, master plan studies, specialized studies, general or comprehensive plans, and land use ordinances will provide an indicator of how integrated (or not) the various special interests are, and how they may affect the particular planning or implementation of sustainable watershed or street network practices.

Street network analysis and repair is best done in conjunction with an overall community or regional land use planning process, and in coordination with an overall capital improvements plan. An analysis of the public infrastructure for the community both above and below ground by mapping, field reviews, stakeholder interviews, and analysis of various policies and records would reveal a complete picture of the community's infrastructure. This integrated mapping would include water, sewer, storm drainage and other utilities, street trees, sidewalks, paving, and curb and gutter.

Implementation time. The plan could be developed within a few months, while full implementation may take more than 20 years.

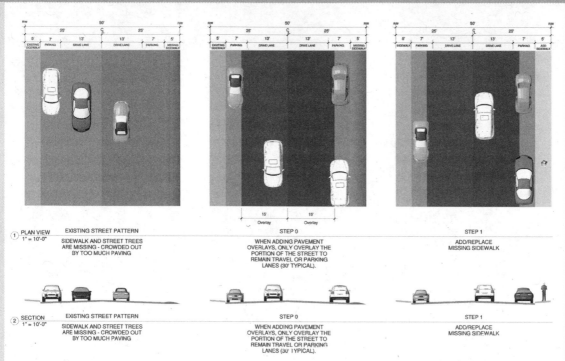

PLAN VIEW 1" = 10'-0"	EXISTING STREET PATTERN	STEP 0	STEP 1
	SIDEWALK AND STREET TREES ARE MISSING - CROWDED OUT BY TOO MUCH PAVING	WHEN ADDING PAVEMENT OVERLAYS, ONLY OVERLAY THE PORTION OF THE STREET TO REMAIN TRAVEL OR PARKING LANES (30' TYPICAL).	ADD/REPLACE MISSING SIDEWALK

SECTION 1" = 10'-0"	EXISTING STREET PATTERN	STEP 0	STEP 1
	SIDEWALK AND STREET TREES ARE MISSING - CROWDED OUT BY TOO MUCH PAVING	WHEN ADDING PAVEMENT OVERLAYS, ONLY OVERLAY THE PORTION OF THE STREET TO REMAIN TRAVEL OR PARKING LANES (30' TYPICAL).	ADD/REPLACE MISSING SIDEWALK

STEP 2	STEP 3	STEP 4 (OPTIONAL, FOR DENSER NEIGHBORHOODS)
PLANT TREES IN PAVEMENT CUT OUTS	REMOVE MORE PAVING, CREATING BIOSWALE	ADD CURB AND GUTTER

STEP 2	STEP 3	STEP 4 (OPTIONAL, FOR DENSER NEIGHBORHOODS)
PLANT TREES IN PAVEMENT CUT OUTS	REMOVE MORE PAVING, CREATING BIOSWALE	ADD CURB AND GUTTER

Figure 5-20
This streetscape retrofit pattern shows an example of how to convert a typical suburban street to a pedestrian-friendly green street. *Crabtree Group, Inc.*

BENEFITS

- Complete green streetscapes nurture a sense of community pride.
- Walkability and bikability increases, thus reducing vehicle miles traveled and increasing citizen health.
- Urban heat island effect is reduced.
- Quantity of rainfall runoff and pollution is reduced.

DRAWBACKS

- One of the biggest challenges in assembling a project team is to find and select highly trained and experienced specialists who are able to see the bigger picture and think and act holistically.
- Civil engineers require the technical equipment and analytical expertise of multimodal mobility, but they need to be holistic generalists and antisprawl practitioners who collaborate well with others. Specialists often have extensive experience in the design and implementation of suburban sprawl. A reeducation in "sprawl repair" coupled with the demonstration of the design and implementation of projects under a new Smart Growth paradigm helps develop a professional generalist who can be counted on to deliver sustainable solutions.
- The conventional process often involves a study done by a professional specialist (e.g., traffic engineer), adopted as a formal regulation to be implemented in a top-down structure. These numerous silos need to be pulled together and brought to the public through the charrette process to integrate them into bottom-up solutions that are implementable, with the process itself helping to instill community pride and ensuring successful implementation.
- Roberts Rules of Order, as practiced by planning commissions and city councils, their ad hoc committees, and independent professional consultants often create a climate of citizens versus the government and a stifling of open communication and collaboration.
- Existing street standards or public works manuals tend to support conventional, suburban street typologies. Their modification requires continual education, feedback, and consensus-building.

FIRST COST
The initial plan could be completed by city staff; or by a consultant team for $10,000 to $20,000.

LIFECYCLE COSTS
Once the community vision is obtained through the charrette process, the neighborhood complete green street plan is formalized and adopted through public hearings along with any necessary standards or details that would replace legacy systems. The plans are then incorporated into the capital improvement plan for the community. Some implementation will occur through the obtaining of grants, or the use of fees-in-lieu, through general funds, or through property owner participation.

Complete green streetscape successes can be measured through the CIP process and reporting system.

IMPLEMENTATION SUPPORTS AND CONSTRAINTS

The field of Geographic Information Services (GIS) is advancing rapidly, as witnessed by the continuing enhancements to Google Earth in terms of available databases and quality of information. Additionally, the National Map (http://nationalmap.gov/) is a free digital mapping service effort brought to the public through a partnership of several federal agencies. A local or regional GIS effort can be of significant cross-disciplinary value, largely dependent on the quality of informational inputs. Proper interpretation and use of GIS data involves the caveat that digital files do not replace direct observation of the physical environment.

Base maps consisting of all the necessary information including aerial photography, as-built infrastructure, natural topography, land use characteristics, and so forth, and the ability to view differing combinations of layers are essential. A good GIS system is often the first place to look for this information, or Google Earth, the National Map, old Sanborn Maps, or the local public works or utility companies. Often a new aerial photographic and topographic mapping will be necessary at a general cost of about $10,000 per square mile.

INFORMATIONAL SOURCES

- The City of Lawrence Kansas Capital Improvements Plan (CIP) www.scribd.com/doc/766652/20082013-Capital-Improvement-Plan is a good example of a comprehensive CIP. Nova Scotia, Canada provides a template for a CIP at www.nsinfrastructure.ca/pages/Capital-Investment-Plan.aspx.

- An excellent collection of complete streets and their performance characteristics can be found at http://transect.org/docs/CompleteStreets.pdf.

- The SmartCode model land use code provides an excellent framework for a sustainable, cross-disciplinary approach to regional and community planning that embraces watersheds, street networks, and several other important aspects of the built environment from the regional scale all the way down to the building scale. For more information, visit www.transect.org.

- Portland, Oregon is a leader in green street implementation; see www.portlandonline.com/BES/index.cfm?c=44407

- Reports and Studies. Green Street Initiatives Around the USA (EPA) www.epa.gov/owow/podcasts/greenstreetsusa.html; 22 Benefits of Urban Street Trees www.ufei.org/files/pubs/22BenefitsofUrbanStreetTrees.pdf .

MULTIMODAL NETWORK AND CONNECTIVITY PLANNING PROGRAM

Jim Daisa, P.E.
Kimley-Horn & Associates

INTERVENTION TYPE: PROGRAM

Description
The Multimodal Network and Connectivity Planning (MNCP) Program results in goals, objectives, policies, criteria, guidelines, and standards that communities integrate into their comprehensive and general plans, thoroughfare plans, zoning and form-based codes, and development standards. High levels of multimodal connectivity improve transportation choices and reduce automobile travel, traffic congestion, and associated GHG emissions.

Modern neo-traditional neighborhoods are developed around a dense grid of narrow streets and alleys. *James M. Daisa, P.E*

Supports Goals and Objectives

Reduce automobile VMT 40 to 50 percent when compared to conventional networks by 2030 in urbanized areas by shifting travel from the automobile to walking, bicycling, and public transportation, and by improving the directness of routes for local travel.

Performance Characteristics

GHG emissions reduction: From 30 to 40 percent of community transportation emissions from private vehicles.

Potential Synergism

This program should be coordinated with all other transportation programs as well as land use programs. MNCP supports compact, mixed-use, transit-supportive and walkable land use patterns. Further, community level network planning should be coordinated with network planning at the regional scale.

Implementation Time

The MNCP Program can be developed in a relatively short time period, usually in the form of policies and standards that are integrated into community regulatory documents. Implementation occurs with new projects or redevelopment. Significant improvement in communitywide connectivity, particularly with public streets, is a long-term effort. Public agencies can implement elements of connectivity in the short term in the form of new street connections, expansion of pedestrian, trail, and multi-use path systems, and completion of communitywide bicycle networks.

Benefits

- Higher street connectivity disperses traffic rather than concentrating it onto a limited number of large arterials, reducing the need to build larger streets and intersections.
- Multimodal connectivity generates more direct routes, which generate fewer VMT than conventional hierarchical networks.
- Multimodal connectivity increases route choice, improving convenience, variety, and ability to avoid blockages. This increases the reliability of the network.
- Encourages walking and biking through directness, route choice, and pedestrian-scaled development patterns
- Improved transit-friendliness with more direct walking routes to transit stops
- A smaller block structure where land use can evolve over time, providing development flexibility
- Benefits emergency service providers through increased access
- Regularly spaced traffic signals can be synchronized to provide a consistent speed and offer more frequent pedestrian crossings

- Multimodal connectivity offers more opportunity for physical exercise resulting in healthier communities.

DRAWBACKS
- Challenging to increase connectivity in built neighborhoods
- May increase local automobile traffic in some neighborhoods, increasing concerns of intrusive traffic and making it challenging to connect to existing neighborhoods
- Increase in streets can increase stormwater runoff though mitigated with implementation of green street and stormwater management best practices

FIRST COSTS
Initial costs are comprised of constructing streets and other multimodal facilities. The initial costs can be offset by a reduced cost in adding traffic capacity to existing arterial street system. Ongoing costs include maintenance of facilities.

LIFECYCLE COSTS
Estimated construction cost of new local and collector streets ranges from $700,000 to $1,200,000 per mile. Ongoing costs include maintenance and operations. Lifecycle costs offset by reduced VMT and associated fuel use, reduce the need to enlarge the existing arterial system, cost of environmental impacts related to automobile emissions, and reduce the health costs associated with the resultant increase in physical activity.

PROJECTED PERFORMANCE
There is a one-to-one relationship between VMT and CO_2 emissions. For every 1 percent reduction in VMT there is a corresponding 1 percent reduction in CO_2 emissions. Increases in residential density, land use mix, and street connectivity at household and employment locations reduce per capita levels of emissions.

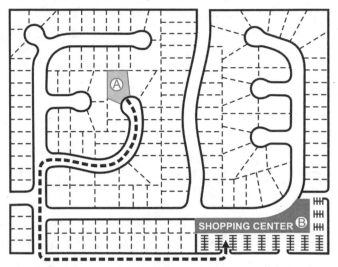

(A) Conventional suburban hierarchical network.

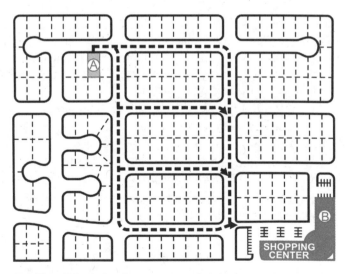

(B) Traditional urban connected network.

Figure 5-22
The conventional hierarchical network (A) channels traffic from local streets to the arterial street system. In a more traditional network, a system of parallel connectors (B) provides multiple and direct routes between origins and destinations. © 2009 Institute of Transportation Engineers, 1099 14th Street, NW, Suite 300 West, Washington, DC 20005-3438 USA, www.ite.org. Used by permission.

- Community education of the benefits of multimodal connectivity, key to acceptance of new connections and a change in the community's urban planning paradigm
- Multimodal connectivity begins with communitywide policy at the comprehensive, general, or specific plan level. Adoption of form-based code to replace older zoning codes provides a mechanism for integrating connectivity, urban form, and land use.
- As part of a connectivity plan, development of guidelines and standards should augment a community's thoroughfare plan, including connectivity guidance at the collector level, to ensure proper implementation.
- Adoption of a connectivity performance standard, a "connectivity index" for example, provides a means of assessing plans and development proposals.
- Pedestrian- and bicycle-only connections can offset lack of street connectivity.
- Coordinate with regional transportation planning to help communities meet legislated reductions in GHG emissions.

REPORTS AND STUDIES

- U.S. Environmental Protection Agency, Development, Community, and Environment Division. Our Built and Natural Environments: A Technical Review of the Interactions between Land Use, Transportation, and Environmental Quality. EPA 231-R-01-002, January 2001.
- Susan Handy, "Smart Growth and the Transportation-Land Use Connection: What Does the Research Tell Us?" *International Regional Science Review* 28(2) (2005) 146–167.
- Reid Ewing and Robert Cervero, "Travel and the Built Environment: A Synthesis," *Transportation Research Record*, vol. 1780 (2001), 87–114.
- Lawrence Frank and Co., Inc. *A Study of Land Use, Transportation, Air Quality and Health in King County, WA.* Final Report, December 2005.

Chapter 6

Energy

The Energy Shift

Jon Roberts
Director of Building Science, CTG Energetics

Energy Challenges and Opportunities Facing Our Communities

Cheap, abundant energy is the foundation of modern civilization and has fundamentally shaped and reshaped our communities over time. Understanding how energy molds and transforms the built environment is an essential starting point for making our communities more sustainable.

Fossil fuel dependence causes some of today's most pressing problems. Energy procurement disrupts societies and the environment (e.g., the vast mountain-top removal coal mining operations in the Southeast or oil production in the Gulf of Mexico). Dependence on imported oil presents significant energy security vulnerability and economic drain. Fossil fuel combustion causes air pollution, smog, acid rain, and mercury contamination of our waterways. Solid waste byproducts of coal combustion are very toxic and provide significant threats to communities (e.g., the December 22, 2008 TVA Kingston Fossil Plant ash spill which released 1.1 billion gallons of coal fly ash slurry into surrounding communities). The biggest challenge is the massive greenhouse gas emissions that are leading us on an irreversible experiment in global warming.

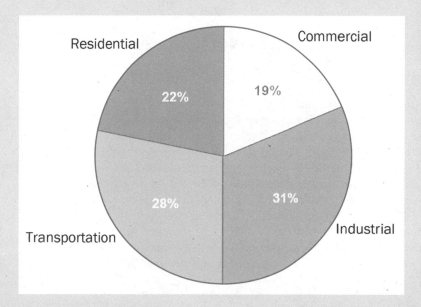

Figure 6-1
Energy consumed by commercial buildings, residential buildings, and transportation account for nearly 70 percent of the 2008 U.S. total end-use energy consumption. *U.S. Energy Information Agency, Annual Energy Review 2008 Report No. DOE/EIA-0384(2008). June 26, 2009.*

Buildings and transportation are two of the nation's largest energy consumers, as shown in the following figure. Nearly two-thirds of the nation's energy is consumed by buildings and transportation, and thus significantly influenced by the shape and structure of our communities.

Changes in the way we build, renovate, plan, and operate our communities can have tremendous impacts on local and national energy consumption. This is increasingly recognized in energy and community policy. There is a nascent shift toward more sustainable land use practices,[1] changes in community design and transportation infrastructure to promote walkable neighborhoods and mass-transportation, dramatic improvements in building efficiency,[2] a shift toward green buildings, and growing use of renewable energy and smart grids. With a strong collective effort, it is very possible that we will witness a significant change in our buildings, communities, and energy infrastructure that will once again transform our communities and help address our pressing environmental challenges.

This section examines opportunities to rethink our buildings, communities, and design processes to help achieve significantly more sustainable and less energy-intensive communities.

Prepare the Team

Developing a sustainable energy system is an inherently interdisciplinary task, reflecting the many users and uses of energy. There are six primary stakeholder groups that should be involved in the development of a sustainable energy plan:

1. personnel involved in the various stages of building design and operation
2. personnel involved in transportation planning and management
3. the planning community
4. energy utilities and providers
5. regulatory agencies
6. energy users

All major stakeholder groups need to be represented in the process.

Building Lifecycle Stakeholders

Buildings are one of the largest energy users and must be a key element of any sustainable energy plan. Building energy efficiency and renewable energy programs typically focus on the design phase of new buildings. While the design and technological features required to achieve high-performing building are important and merit significant attention, by the time a building reaches the design phase, many of the key building design features have already been made (or limited) during the planning, permitting, and entitlement processes. This is particularly relevant for larger development projects. Buildings endure for decades and sometimes centuries, and must adapt to ever-changing context (people, uses, policy, environment, and so forth), so it's critical to address the entire building lifecycle. Failure to do so presents a significant barrier to realizing energy-efficient buildings that perform over the long term.

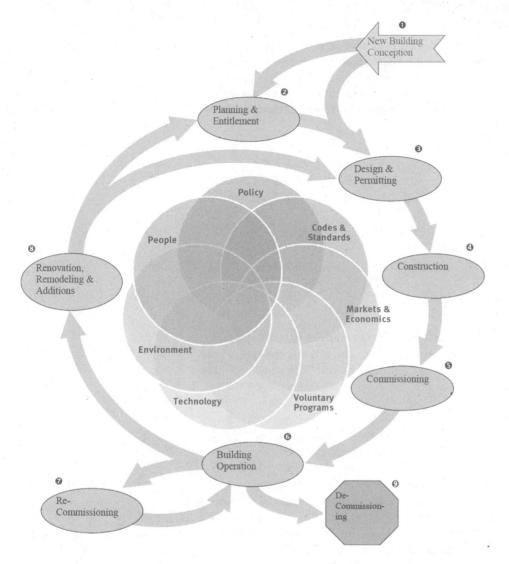

Figure 6-2
Buildings revolve through nine distinct lifecycle stages, with different stakeholders and decisions at each stage.
Jon Roberts, CTG Energetics, Inc.

Buildings revolve through nine distinct stages, as shown in Figure 6-2. Each stage of the building lifecycle involves different personnel and priorities. Furthermore, the policy, regulatory, market, technological, and environmental context is continuously changing.

Stakeholders from each phase of the building lifecycle should be engaged in the team. An important (but often overlooked) stakeholder is the building owner:

> Owners provide the main motivation for low-energy buildings. The owner was the driving force in each case. Each owner set the goals and made decisions to keep the project on track. The architects and engineers strived to meet the goals of the building owners, which resulted in the whole-building design process.[3]

TRANSPORTATION STAKEHOLDERS

Transportation represents nearly one-third of the nation's energy use. Preliminary data from the California Energy Commission indicates that for a typical office building, 50 percent more energy is spent transporting workers to and from the building than is consumed by the building. Any sustainable community energy plan must be closely integrated with a sustainable transportation plan and associated stakeholders.

PLANNING AND ENTITLEMENT

Planning decisions shape the character of communities and development. Many important decisions that fundamentally impact transportation and building energy use occur at the planning level. Planning is one area where cities and communities have significant leverage.

ENERGY UTILITIES AND PROVIDERS

Utilities are a key stakeholder and potential partner that can help the team tie into existing energy initiatives, funding sources, incentives, and other relevant programs.

POLICY-MAKERS AND REGULATORS

Policy-makers, government agencies, and regulatory bodies carry the "sticks" to drive high-performing building development. They set and enforce codes and policies that building developers and designers must comply with. Two energy-related policy-makers that should be engaged are the public utilities commission (PUC) and the state energy office.

The PUC is a state agency tasked with regulating utilities. It governs utility tariffs and rates, often administers "public goods charges" and other utility surcharges that are used for various projects (including energy efficiency and renewable energy), enables net metering, may run various energy efficiency, demand response, and other incentive programs. The PUC may not necessarily be a direct participant in local energy planning activities, but local energy planning will certainly need to be aware of and leverage existing PUC efforts.

State energy offices provide a variety of services, including helping develop statewide energy policy, conduct energy research, coordinate incentive programs, and so forth. Sustainable energy planning should coordinate with the state energy office and leverage statewide efforts to the greatest extent possible. In many cases, the state energy office can serve as an excellent resource.

ENERGY USERS

Sustainable energy use is ultimately in the hands of individual citizens and energy users who make thousands of day-to-day decisions on how energy is used. It is essential that this group be involved.

Prepare the Tools

Community-level energy planning typically uses a diverse range of tools, from simple spreadsheets to integrated energy master-planning tools. Due to the unique conditions and requirements of each community, spreadsheet tools in the hands of experienced energy planners and consultants are one of the most popular tools used to tabulate existing energy use across the community and project future energy use for different scenarios. A few of the more commonly used energy analysis tools/tool categories are summarized below. Refer to the DOE's Building Energy Software Tools Directory[4] for a comprehensive list of analysis tools.

SYSTEMS ENERGY AND SUSTAINABILITY ANALYSIS TOOLS

A "systems" model, a powerful tool for developing a sustainable energy plan, helps teams explore the complex and interdependent relationships between energy, sustainability, and the economy. Using a systems approach to sustainable energy planning can help identify and analyze savings and synergies

A number of holistic, systems-based analysis tools use integrated sustainability analysis emerging on the market. Each tool typically targets differing audiences and has differing levels of detail. Two examples of these types of tools are briefly described below.

One integrated systems-based analysis tool is CTG Energetic, Inc.'s Sustainable Communities Model (SCM),[5] which embodies a holistic, quantitative, systems-based analysis approach to sustainability auditing and analysis. The SCM quantifies total environmental impacts (including energy use, water use, greenhouse gas emissions, air pollution emissions, stormwater, transportation impacts, solid waste, and other factors) allowing communities to optimize planning and design decisions that result in the greatest environmental benefit for the least cost. This enables a project's design team to "connect" each specialty's detailed analyses together to explore and optimize environmental impacts that cross disciplinary boundaries. The SCM is scalable over a wide range of community sizes, and can been applied to "communities" ranging from municipalities, to large master-planned developments/redevelopments, to academic and corporate campuses, down to individual buildings.

PLACE³S[6] (**PLA**nning for **C**ommunity **E**nergy, **E**conomic and **E**nvironmental **S**ustainability) is a smart-growth planning tool jointly funded by the state energy offices of California, Oregon, and Washington. It integrates focused public participation, community development and design, and computer-assisted quantification tools (GIS) to help communities produce plans that retain dollars in the local economy, save energy, attract jobs and development, reduce pollution and traffic congestion, and conserve open space.

BUILDING ENERGY SIMULATION SOFTWARE

Buildings are complex, and estimating the energy impacts of different policy or design measures requires the use of detailed building energy simulation software. These programs perform detailed simulations of building energy performance throughout the year, accounting for hourly weather and climatic data, building envelope measures, occupancy and equipment schedules, thermostat set points, and equipment efficiencies. Utility incentive programs, energy code developers, and project designers all use building simulation software. The team may wish to use

Figure 6-3
The Subdivision Energy Analysis Tool
can analyze energy impacts for different neighborhood and street layouts.
Jon Roberts

building energy models that include: identifying the most effective energy-efficiency measures applicable to the local context; developing detailed savings estimates
for city- or community-owned buildings; and developing incentive programs. The
DOE's Building Energy Software Directory provides a comprehensive list of tools.[7]

SUBDIVISION ENERGY ANALYSIS TOOL

Another potentially useful tool for planning-level energy analysis is the Subdivision
Energy Analysis Tool (SEAT), which has been developed by the National Renewable Energy Laboratory with funding from the California Energy Commission. This
tool analyzes the energy impacts of street orientation and neighborhood pattern on
building energy use, solar energy generation, solar water heating potential, and a
variety of building energy-efficiency measures for single-family housing. This is a
relatively simple and easy-to-use program.

RENEWABLE ENERGY ANALYSIS TOOLS

There are numerous tools for analyzing renewable energy systems. The DOE's
Building Energy Software Directory provides a comprehensive list of tools.[7] Some of
the more popular tools include:

- PV Watts, an online tool for analyzing solar PV systems developed by the National Renewable Energy Lab (NREL) and Sandia National Lab

- NREL's online Renewable Energy Atlas, which provides renewable energy resource data for the United States
- RetScreen, a renewable energy and energy-efficiency screening tool

GREEN BUILDING RATING PROGRAMS

Another class of "tools" is the many green building rating programs on the market. These provide a structured framework for projects to implement best practices across a range of sustainability categories. The most widely used program in the United States is the U.S. Green Building Council's Leadership in Energy and Environmental Design (LEED).[8] Many communities provide incentives (e.g., tax credits, expedited permitting) for projects achieving a certain rating, requiring projects to achieve specific system ratings, or developing local green building programs.

POLICY AND REGULATORY TOOLS

In addition to analysis tools, there are a variety of regulatory, code, and legal tools that communities can use in their energy plans.

INCORPORATE ENERGY AND CLIMATE ISSUES INTO THE PLANNING AND ENTITLEMENT PROCESSES

California has taken the lead on incorporating energy and climate change issues into its planning processes. Municipalities, project designers, and others are using the California Environmental Quality Act (CEQA) to account for energy-related greenhouse gas emissions in general plan updates, specific plans, and related planning and entitlement processes.[9]

MUNICIPAL ENERGY-EFFICIENCY AND RENEWABLE ENERGY FUNDING PROGRAMS THROUGH TAX ASSESSMENTS (AB 811 FUNDING DISTRICTS)

In 2008, California enacted Assembly Bill 811, which:

> "authorizes the legislative body of any city, as defined, to determine that it would be convenient and advantageous to designate an area within which authorized city officials and free and willing property owners may enter into contractual assessments and make arrangements to finance public improvements to specified lots or parcels under certain circumstances."

Municipalities can create special funding districts in which property owners can finance energy-efficiency and renewable energy projects through land-secured loans that are paid back through assessments on tax bills. The assessment is passed on to subsequent property owners until the loan is paid off. This requires minimal local government investment.

BUILDING ENERGY CODES AND GREEN BUILDING CODES

Building energy codes are a very significant tool that cities and municipalities can use to assure a minimum standard for building efficiency. Energy codes are typically developed at the state level. For example, California's Title 24 Building Energy Code is one of the most stringent building codes in the United States. It is on a three-year update cycle, with the goal of continually increasing base energy efficiency. However, cities and other jurisdictions can implement more stringent energy codes. One example is San Francisco, which adopted its green building ordinance in 2008. One of the requirements includes more stringent building energy-efficiency standards than the State's energy code, which is permitted by California law. Cities across the nation are increasingly instituting green building codes. A detailed list of California green building ordinances can be found online.[10]

RENEWABLE ENERGY ORDINANCES

Municipalities can pass a variety of ordinances that can promote and enable various renewable energy systems. A few examples include:

- California Property Tax Exemption for Solar Energy Equipment

  Section 73 of the California Revenue and Taxation Code exempts from property taxes the value of solar energy equipment.

- California Solar Rights Act

  Section 714 of the California Civil Code was enacted in 1978 to ensure that any covenant, restriction, or condition contained in any deed or other contractual restriction, which affects the sale or value of real property, does not limit the installation or use of a solar energy system.

- Solar Easement Law

  California Civil Code Sections 801 and 801.5 provide for easements to ensure the right to receive sunlight for any solar energy system. Please note that an easement must be in place before a request can be made to address obstacles to sunlight.

- California Solar Shade Control Act

  California Public Resource Code Sections 25980-25986 provide limited protections against shading from vegetation on adjacent properties.

Prepare the Place

Creating a sustainable energy plan first necessitates the development of a detailed energy and/or greenhouse gas inventory. This establishes the community's baseline energy use and/or greenhouse gas emission data and should provide a comprehensive baseline of energy and emissions data for buildings, transportation, solid waste, and other sectors. Some communities collect data on urban forests (urban forests sequester carbon, and can help reduce urban heat island effects, with measured air-conditioning savings of up to 25 percent), embodied energy in water and wastewater, and so forth. This will form the foundation from which the strategic plan will be developed, and which performance toward meeting strategic plan updates can be tracked. Many municipal greenhouse gas inventories are online.[11] The inventory often represents a significant investment in time and money, requiring the gathering of significant amounts of data that have not typically been aggregated before. Many cities subcontract this to qualified consultants. The costs for greenhouse gas inventories vary significantly with community size, and the quality of data that a city has. Many resources are available to assist in the development of energy and greenhouse gas inventories, a few include:

- ICLEI—Local Governments for Sustainability www.iclei.org/
- Local Government Operations Protocol developed by the California Air Resources Board, the California Climate Action Registry, the Climate Registry, and ICLEI, www.arb.ca.gov/cc/protocols/localgov/pubs/pubs.htm

In addition to the basic energy/greenhouse gas inventory, communities may want to inventory and track other key energy metrics. For example, San Francisco has developed an interactive "Solar Map" which tracks PV installations.[12] This serves to document and track PV installations and progress toward annual renewable energy goals.

In addition to the consumption and emission data obtained from the inventory, communities should collect a variety of contextual data. This includes the sources of their electricity (e.g., percent of power derived from coal, natural gas, nuclear power, renewables, and so forth) and associated emission factors. This data is typically available from the energy utilities and/or state energy offices. The EPA's egrid database[13] also contains this data at various levels of aggregation. For example, power plant thermal losses typically represent up to 65 to 70 percent of the total initial input (primary) energy. Furthermore, significant amounts of water are often required for energy production, and fly ash must be landfilled or otherwise disposed of. Transmission and distribution losses are typically around 5 to 10 percent. Only a small fraction of the initial input energy makes it to the meter in the form of electricity.

Information on solid waste disposal facilities is needed to estimate solid waste energy use (transportation energy used to collect and dispose of solid waste), greenhouse gas emissions from the various disposal methods, and potentials for energy recovery from solid waste (options include landfill gas capture, traditional thermal waste-to-energy conversion systems, and a variety of newer small-scale waste-to-energy systems).

If the community desires to assess the embodied energy use in water, then the city will have to investigate the sources and energy contents of its water. This water-energy-carbon nexus is a focus of growing interest, and data is becoming increasingly available. However, some investigative work may be required.

Finally, normalization data such as population statistics, building area, and the like are useful for calculating energy use indices such as energy use per person, energy use per acre, energy intensity per building square footage, and so forth.

Prepare the People

Developers, financiers, architects, engineers, builders, operators, tenants, portfolio managers, and homeowners influence building energy use. Transportation stakeholders include commuters, transportation engineers, consultants, civil engineers, planners, transportation departments, and government agencies. Planners, utilities, policy-makers, regulators, and other government bodies all play a very important role in both buildings and transportation.

However, many of these people do not recognize how their roles, decisions, and actions influence community energy use. In order to inform stakeholders and develop participants in the sustainable energy planning process, first communicate some of the key energy use data obtained from the baseline inventory, why energy is important, and a vision for a sustainable energy future. Place into context and clearly communicate all three in terms that the general community can readily relate to.

One effective method for educating a community and developing local leadership, creating an energy/sustainability task force composed of citizens and experts within the community, helps in the development of recommendations for an energy/sustainability plan. The task force's recommendations, as well as grassroots interest and input that the task force engendered, can build a foundation for a follow-up committee to develop a more formal community energy policy, and other groups to help implement portions of the plan. This can be an effective way to increase grassroots support.

Develop Goals, Objectives, and Performance Metrics

Once the community energy and/or greenhouse gas inventory data is available, the city will want to *benchmark*, or compare its performance against other communities. Metrics include total energy use, energy use per person, energy use per acre, and sectoral energy use (e.g., residential commercial, industrial, transportation, and so forth). If the energy inventory data has sufficient spatial data, energy use versus average building vintage, single-family verses multifamily, and the like can be examined to help identify trends and opportunities. The Commercial Buildings Energy Consumption Survey,[14] The Energy Star Building Portfolio Manager,[15] the California Building Energy Reference Tool (CalArch),[16] and a growing number of publically available energy/climate/sustainability inventories all provide excellent benchmarking data.

Upon understanding a community's overall energy consumption, the community can begin developing realistic and actionable goals and objectives for its energy plan. There are three pathways that communities are taking to establish energy goals, each with strengths and weaknesses. Approaches include setting energy intensity goals (e.g., average communitywide energy use per person) and establishing absolute energy goals, such as reducing total communitywide energy use by 15 percent below current energy use. A third approach is setting sectoral energy goals (e.g., all new residential buildings should be zero-net energy, or vehicle miles traveled should be reduced by 10 percent). In many cases, communities select multiple types of goals.

Develop the Strategic Plan

The three approaches typically used for developing a strategic energy plan consist of developing the strategic plan using in-house personnel, hiring consultants to develop the plan, or using a community-based task force, committee, or similar group of stakeholders who are charged with generating the plan or developing recommendations for the plan. In many cases, a combination of approaches is taken. For example, the City of Claremont, California, used a series of citizen/stakeholder task forces to develop a sustainability action plan (a strategic plan) that was presented to the city council and voted on. The task forces included personnel from the utilities,

Figure 6-4
Developing a strategic plan requires
iterative input from key stakeholders.
Town-Green

local universities, schools, citizens, and practitioners. Although it is typically more time-consuming and can require significant guidance, using a stakeholder/citizen task force to develop a strategic energy plan can stimulate significant creativity and help generate the needed grassroots support and buy-in.

Develop the Action Plan

A sustainable energy action plan can be developed using similar approaches outlined for the strategic energy plan. The action plan typically requires more specific technical expertise and analysis to estimate the costs, savings, and environmental impacts of various energy-efficiency and renewable energy measures. Specific requirements for government and utility incentive programs require expert guidance, so energy action plans are often developed with input from experienced professionals who have a strong background in energy analysis and policy. These resources may be available in-house, or outsourced. Many larger cities create a position to coordinate energy and sustainability issues. This position often coordinates a group of consultants to help develop the action plan. The City of Claremont used citizen/stakeholder task forces to develop the strategic plan with components of an action plan, and then hired consultants to develop a more detailed energy action plan which included more specific technical analysis and data collection that were not feasible for a volunteer task force to accomplish.

The budgets for developing an energy action plan are highly variable, depending on the size of the community, depth and scope of the plan, and supporting data that the community already has available to feed the plan. At the lower end of the scale, a smaller city may be able to develop a reasonable energy action plan using partial planning staff time and an experienced, focused, well-guided citizen stakeholder task force doing most of the plan development. Outsourced energy action plans range anywhere from $50,000 to $300,000 or more, depending on the scope and size.

Implement the Action Plan

Typical energy action plans incorporate a wide range of measures. Some measures are quickly and easily implementable at minimal costs. Examples include establishing noncontroversial policies that promote energy efficiency and renewable energy (e.g., reducing or waiving permitting fees for efficiency and renewable energy projects; eliminating or rewriting ordinances that discourage solar energy). Other measures can be quickly implemented, but have costs. Still others are longer-term measures, or measures that require significant capital costs. Implementing an action plan requires grouping and prioritizing the measures, and then systematically pursuing the measures on a logical timeline.

Implementing the action plan and providing accountability for its fulfillment constitutes a critical personnel role. Some municipalities hire full-time staff to oversee energy and sustainability issues. Others establish a standing committee or board to implement the energy action plan. For example, the City of Claremont established a standing committee staffed by citizens to oversee and implement its sustainability action plan. They also established a nonprofit organization called "Go Green" that would take the lead on many of the action items that are important for the community at large, but are outside the normal purview of city operations. The nonprofit organization taps into different funding opportunities and leverages a greater amount of community involvement in its various programs than the city's formal sustainability committee would be able to generate.

Many innovative possibilities exist for implementing the energy action plan. For example, the City of Colorado Springs has implemented a citywide building energy auditing program as part of its energy action plan. The city is planning to use an energy consulting firm to train college students to conduct energy audits, and provide the necessary technical guidance, support, and quality control. This program is being implemented in conjunction with the municipal utility, a local college, and contracted consultant.

Ongoing monitoring, verifying, assessing, and evaluating the performance of the energy action plan are critical. For long-term effectiveness and durability, these activities should be "institutionalized" in the city's policy and practice, and sufficient time and budget provided. The American Recovery and Reinvestment Act has developed a detailed reporting protocol to track performance of stimulus money funding. This includes guidance on estimating job creation, energy savings reporting, and the like. Many municipalities will likely be familiar with this reporting template, which can be used for ongoing reporting for the entire energy action plan.

AWARENESS FOR COMMUNITIES ABOUT THE ENVIRONMENT

Cyane Dandridge
Executive Director, Strategic Energy Innovations

INTERVENTION TYPE: PROGRAM

Description

Strategic Energy Innovations' Awareness for Communities about the Environment (ACE) program educates participants about environmental issues and provides a comprehensive training in various energy-efficiency, alternative energy, and weatherization techniques. ACE-trained individuals have worked in small businesses, educational institutions, senior facilities, and residences to help reduce energy use and energy costs. Participants conduct building assessments and energy audits, develop reports with recommendations for energy savings, and assist clients in accessing no- to low-cost energy-efficiency retrofits. ACE brings information and enthusiasm to the community, initiating awareness and behavioral changes that help residents live more sustainable lives. Two separate initiatives encompassed by the ACE program are the Green Workforce Internship (GWI) program for Workforce Investment Act (WIA)-eligible individuals, contractors, and/or dislocated workers; and eco-auditing.

SUPPORT GOALS AND OBJECTIVES

The ACE program was devised to help today's young adults become tomorrow's environmental leaders. The program targets diverse ethnic and socioeconomic populations to provide them with the skills, experience, ethics, and vision to see themselves as innovators and stewards of their environment. ACE stimulates environmental education and awareness while increasing access to and procurement of jobs in the green workforce, linking participants to service-learning projects, internships, and long-term employment. ACE strives to create a community that is more energy efficient while promoting economic stability and environmental education.

PERFORMANCE CHARACTERISTICS

The ACE program believes that a comprehensive training program must include service learning:

- GWI participants are provided training in energy-efficiency, solar, and weatherization concepts, in addition to public speaking and communication through career coaching. Eco-audit participants are also taught auditing techniques, as well as sustainable living.

- GWI participants engage in hands-on experience through placement in internships with energy-efficiency and weatherization contractors. Those involved receive a stipend for participating. Eco-auditors share their knowledge with business owners, senior citizens, schools, parents, and community members through energy audits and sustainability fairs.

POTENTIAL SYNERGISM

ACE connects participants with college interns, local businesses, elders, contractors, utilities, and community and industry leaders. The program provides learning experience to participants, reduces greenhouse gas emissions in the surrounding area, and encourages an eco-friendly community. Through GWI and eco-audit initiatives, participants serve as energy-efficiency and weatherization contractors or auditors for the community at no or low cost.

IMPLEMENTATION TIME

It takes six to nine months to **plan** *for the following:*

- Acquire grants for GWI-only stipends
- Train participants as energy-efficiency contractors or eco-auditors
- Acquire service-learning/internship and placement for participants with industry partners
- Analyze and summarize report findings

BENEFITS

- Creates energy professionals with experience in energy efficiency and surveying
- Brings diverse voices to media by enlisting students in environmental journalism
- Decreases electricity expenses in senior affordable housing, businesses, and residences
- Strengthens community relationships by forming collaborative partnerships between students, senior citizens, homeowners, and small business owners; and provides the public with information about energy conservation and technologies
- Improves academic learning, environmental ethics, and civic responsibility
- Increases job readiness, marketable skills, critical communication skills, and professional skills gained by working with business owners

DRAWBACKS

- The GWI program's target population is low-income, unemployed, or at-risk individuals, all maintaining different levels of education and experience.
- Transportation must be arranged for participants who do not have personal transportation.

Figure 6-5
Green Workforce Internship Program:
An intern from the GWI program uses
safety precautions when cleaning out
and replacing old insulation from an
attic. *Cyane Dandridge*

FIRST COSTS

For GWI, the estimated cost is $3,000 per participant for a minimum of ten participants, not including a stipend. For eco-audit participants, the cost exists only for training purposes.

- Number of participants and infrastructure to set up placement in internships
- Stipends provided for those participating in the GWI program
- Administration costs to train, mentor, and oversee participants

LIFECYCLE COSTS

- Decrease in home retrofit and home utility costs
- Decrease in community unemployment rate

ESTIMATED QUANTITATIVE PERFORMANCE

Ten out of the fifteen youth participating in the GWI pilot program were offered long-term employment with energy-efficiency contractors, and all described the experience as "life-enriching." More than 500 students have been trained as eco-auditors.

IMPLEMENTATION SUPPORTS AND CONSTRAINTS

- Green workforce and environmental education are burgeoning industries in today's society.
- Acquiring placements and/or stipends might be difficult, depending on participants' and the community's interest.

INFORMATIONAL SOURCES

- Green Jobs, Clean Energy Workforce Training: www.energy.ca.gov/greenjobs/index.html
- Department of Labor's WIA webpage: www.doleta.gov/usworkforce/wia/
- Wallenstein, Sandy (Strategic Energy Innovations). Climate Protection Curriculum: Working with Teachers. 2009

REPORTS AND STUDIES

- Case studies can be found at www.seiinc.org/1175-summer-green-workforce-program.html.
- Evaluation report of ACE programs: Skumatz PhD, Lisa A., D'Sourza, Dana, Skumatz Economic Research Associated, Inc. *Evaluation of Indirect Effects of Four Student-Oriented "Green" GHG-Reductions Programs.* 2008.

Figure 6-6
Eco-auditors examine a private business's lighting for retrofits. *Annie Sexton*

HOUSING ENERGY PROGRAM

Cyane Dandridge
Executive Director, Strategic Energy Innovations

INTERVENTION TYPE: PROGRAM

Description

Strategic Energy Innovations' Housing Energy Program (HEP) was developed to address barriers to improving energy and environmental performance of existing multifamily housing in the affordable housing sector. Many owners of affordable homes are interested in increasing the energy and environmental performance of their homes, but find it difficult to secure the necessary financing and technical expertise. These difficulties—which are applicable to multifamily housing—include limited financial resources, staff capacity, housing regulatory issues, and budget cycles.

Figure 6-7
Green Demonstration Program: Harvey Mudd College students view a real-time energy monitor display. *Trevor Henley*

Support Goals and Objectives

The goals of HEP are to provide the necessary technical assistance to increase the energy efficiency and environmental performance of properties, improve property cash flow, and provide necessary physical improvements. These goals—combined with property owners' efforts to improve and preserve aging properties—link retrofit efforts with utilities and local government program offerings to leverage additional resources.

Conceptual Strategy

Improve access to technical and financial resources by providing comprehensive technical assistance and decision-making information to owners of affordable housing. Increasing the ability of property owners to manage energy-efficiency efforts, allows owners to benefit from innovative financing strategies—energy-performance contracting, bulk purchasing, and streamlined delivery of multiple utilities and local government programs.

Performance Characteristics

Electrical savings occur from lighting, appliances, plug-load measures, water and space heating and cooling retrofits. Gas savings occur from hot-water boilers. Water savings occur from high-efficiency toilets, faucets, and shower aerators. Energy efficiency can typically be increased by 20 percent.

Potential Synergism

The program can be coordinated with traditional utility low-/no-cost programs that provide typical weatherization measures, water utility district programs, and local government housing programs. This coordination allows multiple programs to be leveraged and delivered effectively. User-friendly service delivery increases participation of existing homeowners.

Implementation Time

HEP implementation takes three years. Improving the energy and environmental performance of existing affordable housing requires a long lead time. This allows properties to work around capacity issues, budget for long-term retrofit costs, and work through housing regulatory and bureaucratic processes.

Benefits

- Improves cash flow of properties and creates financial stability with energy and water savings
- Reduces utility costs and housing burdens of low-income residents of affordable housing
- Improves aging properties through retrofit and rehabilitation, replacing inefficient equipment with high-efficiency equipment, which in turn reduces maintenance demands

- Preserves aging properties, ensuring the continued existence of valuable communities

DRAWBACKS

- Minimal financial resources available for improving multifamily properties. Individual properties often have inadequate reserves to finance improvements internally.
- Property staff is limited, and technical assistance is often necessary to research, manage, and lead efforts to improve energy and environmental performance.

FIRST COST

- Up-front technical assistance and energy audit costs
- Coordinating multiple, disparate utility and local government programs
- Delivering ongoing, technical assistance throughout project
- Cost of actual energy and environmental saving improvements

There is an estimated cost of at least $50,000 for pilot properties, depending on local utility resources, identified property needs, and locally available energy service providers.

LIFECYCLE COSTS

Impacting an entire population of existing properties in a region could improve variable costs through economies of scale, and benefit the community through the ability to finance energy and environmental equipment and materials.

ESTIMATED QUANTITATIVE PERFORMANCE

Since 2006, the HEP program has made more than 3,000 affordable housing units in Southern California more energy efficient, saving 2.5 million kWh in electricity, more than 230,000 therms in gas, and almost 7 million gallons of water.

IMPLEMENTATION SUPPORTS AND CONSTRAINTS

- Existing homeowners need comprehensive technical assistance to research, manage, and lead energy and environmental improvement efforts.
- Coordinating existing no-/low-cost utility programs allows leverage of existing resources.
- Overextended property management leads to immediate priority issues; energy and environmental performance may be viewed as a lower priority.
- Individual properties have inadequate capital reserves to finance energy and environmental improvements, which leads to requiring outside technical assistance and implementation financing. However, there are a number of supporting programs and policies from utilities and local governments that incentivize affordable housing properties to move forward with efficiency improvements.

- Because multifamily property owners do not pay the bills for tenant units, they have no financial incentive to make energy-efficiency improvements.

- The Department of Housing and Urban Development (HUD) provides affordable housing properties with various programs to assist in financing and give technical support. Visit the HUD website for more information: www.HUD.gov.

INFORMATIONAL SOURCES

- Program information is available at: www.californiaenergyefficiency.com/calenergy_old/sce/2547.pdf

REPORTS AND STUDIES

- Stockton Williams, *Bringing Home the Benefits of Energy Efficiency to Low-Income Households: The Case for a National Commitment.* Columbia, MD: Enterprise Community Partners, Inc., 2008. Available at www.practitionerresources.org/cache/documents/663/66381.pdf (accessed September 2010).

- Matthew Brown and Mark Wolfe, *Energy Efficiency in Multi-family Housing: A Profile and Analysis.* Washington, DC: Energy Programs Consortium June 2007. Available at www.energyprograms.org/briefs/0706.pdf (accessed September 2010).

- Kimberly Vermeer, *Getting Started with Green Preservation: An Introduction to Issues and Resources for Greening Existing Affordable Housing.* New York: Low Income Support Corporation (LISC), June 18, 2009. Available at www.lisc.org/content/publications/detail/8298 (accessed September 2010).

- Green Rehabilitation of Multifamily Rental Properties: A Resource Guide. San Francisco: Bay Area LISC and Build It Green. Available at www.lisc.org/bay_area/resources/publications_8392/green_10365/index.shtml (accessed September 2010)

- Energy and Affordable Housing in California: Lessons Learned from the Field, San Francisco: Bay Area LISC, April 2006. Available at www.lisc.org/content/publications/detail/2181 (accessed September 2010).

ENERGY EFFICIENCY AND RENEWABLE ENERGY IN NEW BUILDING DESIGN

Jeannie Renne-Malone, LEED AP
Director, National Climate and Greenhouse Gas (GHG)
Management, HDR, Inc.

INTERVENTION TYPE: BEST PRACTICE

Description

Commercial and industrial buildings in the United States contribute 45 percent of our national greenhouse gas emissions. The U.S. Environmental Protection Agency estimates that over the next 25 years, GHG emissions from buildings are projected to grow faster than any other sector, with the largest amount of emissions from commercial buildings. Starting from the design phase, new buildings present a major opportunity to improve energy efficiency and reduce GHG emissions. Designing high-performance buildings results in significant economic, environmental, and social benefits. There are a number of best practices and

Figure 6-8
Architect Renzo Piano's design team achieved a LEED Platinum certification for the California Academy of Sciences building in San Francisco. *Daniel Dunigan*

resources available to create a high-performance building that integrate energy efficiency and renewable energy. One such resource is the USGBC's Leadership in Energy and Environmental Design (LEED) rating system, which has become a widely used tool for evaluating sustainable design in buildings. Another available best practice is the federal government's commitment to leadership in the design, construction, and operation of high-performance and sustainable buildings.

SUPPORT GOALS AND OBJECTIVES

Renewable energy dramatically lowers pollution emissions, reduces environmental health risks, and slows the depletion of finite natural resources. The ability to find out how, why, and where energy is being used in a building is fundamental to integrated design, and to meeting short- and long-term goals of reducing energy consumption, lowering costs, and the associated benefits to society in terms of improved public health, lowering air contaminants, and reducing GHG emissions.

PERFORMANCE CHARACTERISTICS

There are numerous opportunities to incorporate renewable energy and energy-efficiency technologies into building envelope and systems, including geothermal heat, photovoltaic solar panels, transpired solar collectors, passive solar, wind turbines, small hydro, biodiesel fuel for backup generators, underfloor air distribution, well-designed energy-saving mechanical and control systems, efficient lighting, and others. It is important to have access to renewable energy resource data in order to best design the building using the most feasible renewable energy technologies. Intensive commissioning is another important component of the high-performance building design process.

POTENTIAL SYNERGISM

Designing high-performance buildings and integrating renewable energy into the building design should be coordinated with sustainable community planning. Integrated planning and development can promote energy efficiency, water and energy conservation, alternative transportation, and renewable energy generation.

IMPLEMENTATION TIME

Designing a high-performance building can save time by ensuring close-knit team integration and can streamline the design and construction process.

BENEFITS

Designing high-performance buildings result in significant economic, environmental, and social benefits. High-performance buildings and integrating renewable energy technologies into building design can significantly reduce local air contaminants and GHG emissions by reducing the amount of energy consumed in buildings that is traditionally generated from the burning of fossil fuels. Other benefits

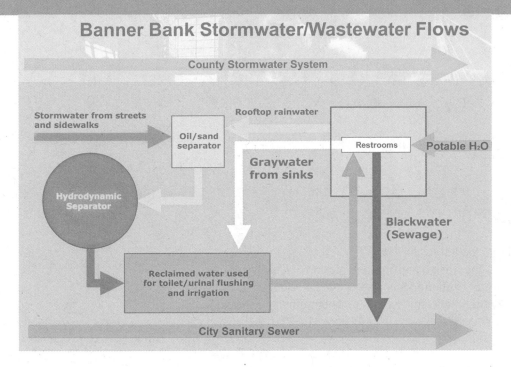

Banner Bank Stormwater/Wastewater Flows

County Stormwater System

Stormwater from streets and sidewalks

Oil/sand separator

Rooftop rainwater

Restrooms

Potable H₂O

Graywater from sinks

Hydrodynamic Separator

Blackwater (Sewage)

Reclaimed water used for toilet/urinal flushing and irrigation

City Sanitary Sewer

Figure 6-9
The 12-story Banner Bank building, designed by HDR, Inc. and certified as a LEED Core and Shell Platinum rating, uses 40 percent less energy than a typical mid-rise office building. The building recycles 100 percent of the graywater (water from lavatory sinks and showers) on-site, plus stormwater from 7 acres of adjoining streets and sidewalks, and recycles 100 percent of the graywater. *Jeannie Renne-Malone, HDR, Inc.*

include decreased capital and maintenance costs, reduced environmental impact, improved indoor air quality, increased occupancy comfort and health, and improved employee productivity.

DRAWBACKS
Initial support for designing a high-performance building may be difficult to obtain, unless the long-term benefits can be quantified, and if the up-front capital costs can be justified.

FIRST COST
Up-front capital costs may increase overall cost of building, but many energy-efficiency and renewable energy products pay for themselves quickly. In addition, it is important to incorporate not only the economic costs and benefits into the financial evaluation, but also the environmental and social costs and benefits, which may greatly improve the return on investment. Databases of federal, state, local, and utility incentives and policies for renewable energy and energy efficiency can be found at www.dsireusa.org.

LIFECYCLE COSTS
Given that high-performance buildings cost less to operate and maintain, the lifecycle costs are considerably lower than those of a traditional building.

ESTIMATED QUANTITATIVE PERFORMANCE

- GHG emissions
- Building energy use
- Building water use
- Solid sanitary waste
- Occupant turnover rate
- Building maintenance requests
- Recycled materials
- Total storm sewer output
- Renewable energy installed

IMPLEMENTATION SUPPORTS AND CONSTRAINTS

One of the primary challenges to the design and implementation of a high-performance building is the initial support obtained from the key stakeholders and project team. It is important to quantify the long-term benefits of a high-efficiency building as early as possible in the project cycle.

INFORMATIONAL SOURCES

- U.S. Department of Energy's Net Zero Energy Commercial Building Initiative www1. eere.energy.gov/buildings/commercial_initiative/design.html
- Lessons Learned from Case Studies of 6 High Performance Buildings www.nrel. gov/docs/fy06osti/37542.pdf
- Architecture 2030 www.architecture2030.org/news/news.php

REPORTS AND STUDIES

Architecture 2030 Case Studies:

- www.architecture2030.org/current_situation/case_studies.php
- HDR Banner Bank Building: www.hdrinc.com/13/38/1/default. aspx?projectID=406

Stormwater Management—Light Imprint Development

Thomas E. Low, AIA, AICP, CNU-A, LEED
Nora M. Black, Associate AIA, CNU-A
Guy Pearlman, RLA, CNU-A
Monica Carney-Holmes, AICP, CNU-A
DPZ Charlotte Architects and Town Planners

Challenges and Solutions for Sustainable Stormwater Management

Stormwater management is a challenge in any populated area. As land adjacent to cities, towns, and villages is developed, impervious surfaces contribute to the quantity and the rate of flow of runoff. Older developments with decaying infrastructure must be retrofitted to handle increasing amounts of stormwater without exceeding the budgets of municipalities for stormwater management. Much of what has been written on stormwater management is based on low-impact development, designed for conventional single-family, multifamily, and commercial developments as opposed to integrating natural drainage within compact, walkable, connected communities.

Manmade infrastructure and buildings may significantly change and cause stress to the equilibrium of the ecosystem by modifying the water balance and contaminating the water and soil. Impervious surfaces that receive precipitation affect the natural hydrological cycle by (a) reducing recharge of the aquifer by redirecting significant portions to stormwater management facilities, (b) increasing evaporation from impervious surfaces, and (c) polluting water that infiltrates the soil. Lawn nutrients, urban pesticides, rooftop runoff, first flush of stormwater, heavy metal contaminates, suspended sediments, and biological material contaminates are additional

Figure 7-1
These two plans compare the Griffin Park TND master plan before (left) and after (right) the application of light imprint engineering. On the light imprint TND master plan (right), note the added green space in the rain gardens and the reduction in the size of stormwater detention ponds.
Duany Plater-Zyberk and Company, Charlotte, NC

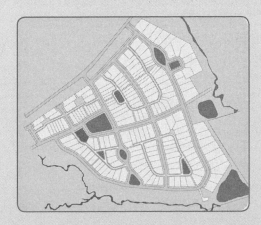
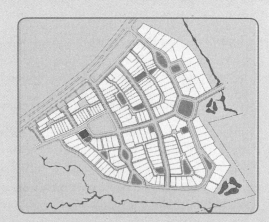

problems attributed to urbanization. The resulting impact is ecosystem deterioration and declining biodiversity.

The degree of impairment on a local scale (block and building) is proportional to the urbanization intensity and the built infrastructure. In general, rural areas may have less impact on watersheds compared to urban core areas. On both the neighborhood and regional scale, however, the impact on the entire watershed depends on the integral effect of the urban zones comprising a human settlement within the watershed boundaries. Thus, the effect will be cumulative, and while highly urbanized areas will have a greater impact on a local scale, on a regional scale the impact will be less severe compared to sprawl development patterns.

Conventional Stormwater Management Strategies

CONVENTIONAL GREEN URBANISM

Green Urbanism emphasizes an increased amount of open space within a site, usually 60 percent or more per project. In Green Urbanism, greenway fingers serve as organizing spines, and stormwater filtration mechanisms are placed outside of and around these green spaces. Green Urbanism developments often compromise social and community connectivity, and reserve significant open space that reduces developable land. The project may not be economically viable.

CONVENTIONAL LOW-IMPACT DEVELOPMENT

Low-impact development (LID), with origins in conventional auto-centric suburban development, attempts to manage stormwater quality by using both on-site design techniques and best management practices (see below). Well-intentioned municipalities adopt the approach without understanding the conflict between stormwater management tools and sustainable community design. Attempts to make conventional suburban developments environmentally friendly ignore the larger issues of exhaust pollution and congestion. Finally, many standards and practices of LID involve lot-based solutions, rather than block- or neighborhood-based, which increase the need for large lots.

CONVENTIONAL BEST MANAGEMENT PRACTICES

Best management practices (BMPs) focus on engineering rather than planning and design. Though the Environmental Protection Agency proposes using BMPs for stormwater management, their mechanical characteristics are not always successful. Furthermore, compact development suffers when BMPs result in detention areas in front of or beside buildings that interrupt social connectivity and interfere with the customers' access to goods, services, and public transit.

Light Imprint—A Model for Comprehensive Sustainability

Light imprint stormwater management can be used to:

- Form strategies for sustainability and pedestrian-oriented design in an economical way
- Change the mindset of a community from a conventional suburban development model to one of a New Urban and traditional neighborhood model

- Reduce costs associated with conventional engineering practices
- Provide an organizational framework to complement and expand the effectiveness of Leadership in Energy Efficient Design for Neighborhood Development (LEED-ND).

Light imprint complements other land planning approaches, including conventional suburban development, low-impact development, BMPs, the SmartCode,[1] sustainable sites, and the Environmental Protection Agency's Smart Growth and Choice Neighborhoods Initiatives.

When considering sustainable economic models, light imprint employs different tools in each transect zone (T zone) unlike other development strategies. Light imprint offers context-sensitive design solutions that work together at the community level. According to Georgio Tachiev, Ph.D., an environmental engineer at Florida International University, light imprint reduces infrastructure on the neighborhood scale in terms of roads, public works, and facilities. On the block scale, the implementation of light imprint methods results in reduced building footprint and stormwater runoff. The application of additional light imprint techniques at the individual lot and building scale increase the level of sustainability.

For example, light imprint strategies for the Griffin Park project include the introduction of tools for stormwater storage, channelization, filtration, and paving options including:

1. Introduction of an underground stormwater storage system
2. Reduction of the amount and length of pipe required
3. Reduction in the number of stormwater inlets
4. Use of pervious pavement in rear lanes
5. Reduction of the street widths
6. Introduction of small-scale, multiple-lot, communal bioretention swales
7. Elimination of curb and gutter in strategic edge areas
8. Replacement of the proposed large retention ponds with smaller natural filtration ponds
9. Introduction of vegetative surface filtration areas along the perimeter

Prepare the Team

Planners, architects, landscape architects, and engineers work in disciplines that require knowledge of stormwater management techniques, and would be compatible to work on a comprehensive team. Each discipline should be qualified or trained to use light imprint techniques to create stormwater management overlays that are appropriate for their part of a project.

Many governing bodies are not familiar with light imprint techniques. Numerous members of city councils and county commissions that must approve stormwater management solutions are only aware of conventional engineering techniques. Local stakeholders who have been trained in light imprint techniques, whether they are developers, investors, or ordinary citizens, will have to constantly monitor future stormwater management plans and educate elected officials and municipality staff members to the tax dollar savings and watershed protection realized by the use of light imprint techniques.

Prepare the Tools: The Light Imprint Toolbox

The four primary categories of light imprint tools are paving, channeling, storage, and filtration. The light imprint website allows users to select from these categories on an interactive basis. Light imprint can interface with GIS databases when creating the design and selecting the appropriate tools.

PAVING

Paving plays a large role in receiving, producing, and distributing stormwater runoff. The choices for paving materials include various degrees of permeability for any particular physical context or transect zone. For example, a very stable material that is less pervious would be used in the most urban zones; large amounts of commercial and vehicular traffic require greater stability and maintenance—a critical role in choosing an appropriate paving material.

Mixed-use development and mass transit reduce vehicular volumes, which can affect paving material selections. Less durable materials are more appropriate for transect zones with light traffic volume. The best features of each paving tool can be maximized by selection based on mode and volume of traffic.

The Environmental Protection Agency (EPA) found in a recent study that a traditional neighborhood design yields 634 square feet of pavement per dwelling unit. In contrast, a conventional suburban design on the same site requires 2,018 square feet per dwelling unit. Eliminating that extra 1,384 square feet of paving per dwelling unit highlights one of the many advantages of traditional neighborhood development.

CHANNELING

For thousands of years, human settlements have used various techniques for channeling stormwater. Whether an aqueduct rushing water to an ancient city or a canal directing water out of a city, channeling tools have been developed and perfected throughout history. The ability to direct and control the flow of water offered flexibility for locating settlements, provided expanded agricultural opportunities, and mitigated flooding. The gardens of the Alhambra in Grenada, Spain, are an exemplary model of channeling that provides beauty and functionality. When selecting channeling tools, the designer must consider pedestrian movement and impervious surfaces. Along with the other three toolbox categories, the channeling tools are often combined with other tools to maximize the functions of storage and filtration.

STORAGE

Water is collected and stored using tools ranging from collection pools to rooftop barrels. In many eras, storing a large volume of water was necessary for the survival of a society, especially in areas that did not receive consistent rainfall. Today, in the United States, both the quality and quantity of water available is a strong determinant of the quality of life in a community. Storage of water remains as important today as it has throughout history.

Retention and detention ponds are the utilitarian tools of choice used for development over the past several decades. Often these become unsightly, weed-filled depressions that require fencing for safety. Such ponds consume acres of potentially developable land. Overly large ponds limit traditional neighborhood development because of size, volume, and flow regulations. Higher-density development calls for tools more appropriate in urban conditions such as underground storage, pools, and grated tree wells. Light imprint supplies a range of sophisticated storage tools that are calibrated for a wide variety of developments.

Storage tools can make beautiful amenities in public spaces such as parks, plazas, and greenways. The costs cover two purposes. Public spaces with a storage device as a main component should be located in low areas to allow water to drain naturally and to minimize the grading costs. Storage tools are available in different sizes, but several used together can attain the capacity required by most developments.

FILTRATION

Private citizens, municipalities, and government agencies want runoff filtered by techniques that will produce pure, unpolluted water. Many current stormwater filtration processes use expensive, highly technological methods to accomplish the same results that natural processes have throughout history. Light imprint filtration tools mimic the natural system with its general simplicity, while finding a place for new innovations that may be appropriate choices. For example, expensive filtration tools are economically feasible in more urban zones of the transect where the cost can be justified by higher-density development.

Like tools in the other categories, filtration tools can also serve as civic amenities when well integrated into a design. Rain gardens can be attractive public features; green fingers can be very active parks; and waterscapes are beautiful in urban plazas.

Using paving, channeling, storage, and filtration tools, light imprint presents actual tools that can be calibrated across all the determinant factors found on any given site. Over time, it is more cost effective than established, conventional practices. The tools are especially effective for protecting water resources while encouraging higher-density development.

GIS DATABASES

For specific sites, light imprint can interface with GIS databases when creating the design and analyzing the appropriate tools. Currently, many agencies already map data giving the specifics of the soil, climate, and slope of many sites. A form-based code regulating plan can be converted into GIS data on a parcel and block basis, with mapping as the only variable cost. This provides a list of light imprint tools that would allow developers to calibrate their stormwater infrastructure budget at the earliest stage of planning.

Since light imprint supplements conventional stormwater management systems, it can be applied to developments designed using Green Urbanism, low-impact development, best management practices, suburban retrofits, LEED-ND, the Sustainable Sites guidelines, and the EPA Smart Growth Initiative.

LIGHT IMPRINT WEBSITE

One effective communication tool is the light imprint website at www.lightimprint. org. The website allows one to interactively calibrate a project, whereas the handbook organizes light imprint tools on the Transect Matrix and Classification Matrix. Presentations and workshops also effectively communicate the light imprint strategy to government officials, community leaders, planners, engineers, architects, and developers.

Prepare the Place

ORGANIZATION

To create a simple framework, light imprint tools are classified into four main categories: paving, channeling, storage, and filtration. Some tools can be used for more than one function. The team classifies most tools by their principal function and refers to their benefits in other categories. For example, some tools in storage may also be useful for filtration.

Part of the process of creating a living system is to conduct sufficient research about the place and framework into which the living machine will be formed. That includes research about the slope, climate, and soil type.

THE TRANSECT

The Transect Matrix serves as an organizational framework. It is by its nature somewhat subjective. The Transect Matrix shows where each tool is most useful from the rural to urban zones. Depending on the transect location, each project will need a specific set of tools.

SLOPE

Typically, slope is analyzed to determine appropriate locations for drainage, roads, buildings, and infrastructure. The classification of slope as flat (up to 8 percent), moderate, or steep (over 15 percent) allows the selection of light imprint tools that avoid significant grading and landscape disturbance. The tools complement natural features, including ridges, valleys, drainage corridors, natural ecologies, and habitats.

CLIMATE

For light imprint, the following six variables define different climatic conditions:

- Cold—Average low below 32°F (0°C) for more than three months per year
- Temperate—Average low below 32°F (0°C) for one to three months per year
- Hot—Average low never drops below 32°F (0°C)
- Dry—Average precipitation less than 10 inches (254 mm) per year
- Moderately Wet—Average precipitation between 11 and 60 inches (255–1,524 mm) per year
- Wet—Average precipitation more than 60 inches (1,524 mm) per year

SOILS

Soils have been generalized into broader types based on particulate size and soil composition for light imprint. This is useful in determining the drainage capabilities of soil. It does not take into consideration the nutrient makeup of the soil. The classifications include poor drainage consisting of rock and clay, medium drainage consisting of silt and loam, and good drainage consisting of loam and sand.

ACCESSIBILITY

Accessibility is an important factor in tool selection, especially in the paving category. It must be considered when calibrating each specific project. Life safety and fire codes shall always take precedence over the use of any tools.

Even with the complete toolkit, constraints still emerge in stormwater management. Light imprint requires the use of stormwater management techniques that initially may seem at odds with conventional wisdom. For example, some locations might ordinarily have a paved sidewalk, but a shallow channel footpath could provide a walking surface that also channels stormwater during heavy rainfall.

Another example is the paving material used for parking areas. The usual approach is to use one type of impervious surface for the entire parking lot, but other pervious surface materials can be considered. A constraint that is often mentioned is rutting of the surface caused by heavy vehicles and the necessity of a solid pad for handicap parking and dumpster sites. By specifically addressing each of these special conditions, the overall design can be more flexible.

Studies critical to the success of light imprint include the following: stormwater runoff quality, quantity discharge volume rates, and percolation rates for aquifer recharge. With the use of light imprint, studies found measurable positive progress in all these categories. The planning principles of regional scale, context-sensitive design using transect-based and light imprint techniques, when combined with standard hydrology practices including source control principles, result in simple and inexpensive short-, mid-, and long-term solutions.

Prepare the People

One crucial factor in the creation of a successful stormwater management system is community buy-in through stakeholder involvement. One key group of stakeholders is the general public. Whether they are community activists, environmentalists, or simply taxpaying citizens, the general public is aware of problems caused by stormwater runoff. By demanding that waterways be preserved and cleaned up if necessary, they have gotten the attention of local government officials and the EPA. As an environmentally friendly solution, light imprint can offer choices for paving, channeling, storing, and filtering stormwater that may be appropriate and inexpensive while also serving as civic amenities when well integrated into a design.

A second group of key stakeholders are town founders or developers. Light imprint stormwater management techniques provide significant infrastructure reduction and cost savings over conventional or gold-plated engineering used in the past. Investors and bankers working with town founders and developers can calculate savings realized with light imprint techniques when making decisions on funding requests. Other stakeholders include elected officials and the staff members who advise them on the selection of stormwater management techniques. When staff members share all the research, elected officials can make better choices that save citizens tax dollars.

A charrette provides an excellent forum for ideas and offers the unique advantage of giving immediate feedback to the designers while giving mutual authorship of the plan to all who participate. The charrette can help the transformation from old, heavily engineered infrastructure into the more natural drainage, channeling, and storage systems of light imprint treatment trains.

The second educational method is a training workshop that can train developers, public officials, planners, architects, landscape architects, engineers, investors, bankers, environmentalists, and community activists in the methodologies of designing and managing stormwater systems. Through this interactive process, they study actual field performance, costs, and lessons learned developing cutting edge methods for successful stormwater management.

Develop Goals, Objectives, and Performance Metrics

The stormwater management goals include:

1. Achieve a higher quality and lower quantity of stormwater reaching natural waterways

2. Allow for evaluation of the success of various tools by measuring water quality and quantity before and after implementation

3. Reduce infrastructure cost, and analyze savings by comparing conventional construction costs to light imprint infrastructure costs.

4. Increase walkability and connectivity between public and private spaces after light imprint techniques have been established.

While some aspects of light imprint reflect quality of life issues that can be difficult to measure, most aspects are measurable quantities such as linear feet and percent of savings. Developers and elected officials usually prefer to have financial data to support decisions.

The stormwater management infrastructure objectives should:

- Be compatible with successful urban design that emphasizes compact, mixed-use, pedestrian-oriented design, and environmental efficiency

- Be designed to reduce the anticipated infrastructure costs of a community

- Use paving, channeling, storage, and filtration tools collectively at the sector, neighborhood, and block scale

- Organize natural drainage on a rural-to-urban transect[2]

- Complement and expand the effectiveness of LEED-ND and other environmental initiatives

- Complement other land planning approaches, including conventional suburban development, low-impact development, and best management practices

- Allow for adjustments to be made, based on the location of the site (climate), the character of the soil (soil type), the intensity of the development (transect), the topographical conditions (slope), the initial budget of the project (cost), and the plan for upkeep (maintenance cost)
- Recognize the importance of public civic spaces and connectivity

Develop the Strategic Plan

Examples of preliminary strategies, policies, regulations, programs, tools, techniques, and actions from private, public, and government sources include the following:

- Developers and town founders can jumpstart a project by using light imprint
- Planners, architects, landscape architects, engineers, and other professional designers can incorporate light imprint during the master planning stage of development
- Public governing bodies can adopt the light imprint module of the SmartCode as part of the local stormwater management plan
- If other regulations and standards are already allowed in a community (such as LID standards or BMPs), light imprint could be included for smart growth developments with New Urbanist plans that provide compact, multimodal, and pedestrian-friendly neighborhoods
- Anyone can calibrate a specific project using the interactive tool search found at www.lightimprint.org or by using the Light Imprint Handbook.

Figure 7-2
Habersham's constructed wetland filters stormwater before it drains to creeks and marshes. *Duany Plater-Zyberk and Company, Charlotte, NC*

Stormwater management strategies from a regulatory and legal perspective include the Supplementary Free Modules to *SmartCode v9.2*. Since light imprint supplements conventional stormwater management systems, it can be applied strategically to developments designed using Green Urbanism, LID, BMPs, suburban retrofits, LEED-ND, sustainable sites, and the EPA Smart Growth Initiative.

Develop the Action Plan

Duany Plater-Zyberk and Company created the master plan for the new town of Habersham in 1997. Habersham is used as an example of how to select measures for the action plan, and as a case study for DPZ's light imprint initiative, which provides a framework for the design of sustainable neighborhoods based on New Urbanism planning principles.

Figure 7-3
The town center median in Habersham is a light imprint stormwater management tool that stores and filters rainwater. *Duany Plater-Zyberk and Company, Charlotte, NC*

The first step to selecting measures to be included in the action plan and master plan was to analyze the history, climate, natural environment, and culture of the site. Located on Port Royal Island in Beaufort County, South Carolina, Habersham is less than a mile from the intercoastal waterway. In all, it has over 13,000 linear feet of marsh frontage. Habersham has a climate ranging from temperate to semitropical. That environment makes the site notable for its ancient live oaks draped with Spanish moss and resurrection fern, magnolia trees, and palmettos.

The DPZ master plan for Habersham prioritizes preservation of the natural environment, while still creating an urban center for surrounding villages. The architecture respects the local Low Country vernacular. It employs methods used in traditional designs for ventilation and cooling.

Select the Most Effective Stormwater Management Techniques

The selection of light imprint stormwater management measures for Habersham's action plan began early in the planning and development phases. Since the 283-acre site is crossed by a number of small creeks that drain to the Broad River marshes, the development team had to safeguard the quality of water draining to the marshes. For that reason, 73 acres of parks, common areas, and natural drainage basins within Habersham incorporate low technology techniques to channel, store, and filter runoff.

Because of the site's proximity to the Atlantic Ocean, heavy squalls can produce a large amount of rain in Habersham in a short time. The region is prone to excessive rainfall accumulations from tropical storms and hurricanes. To handle the quantity of runoff, the development team selected a number of stormwater management techniques that could be combined into a light imprint treatment train. The effectiveness of the system has been proven by its performance through at least five years of storm events with minimal maintenance.

Refine and Finalize the Action Plan

Planning for Habersham began with a rezoning process that designated the parcel as a Planned Unit Development (PUD). As a PUD, the project was able to create its own urban, architectural, and landscape standards that permitted much higher-quality urbanism than standard zoning. At the beginning, an Architectural Review Board (ARB) was established to ensure the rigorous standards were followed and the design intent upheld. The ARB also approves qualified architects and builders. These two early decisions, accompanied by the development team's decision to manage the neighborhood association in-house, have proven to be three key reasons the development has been successful in fulfilling the original design intent.

The town founders worked with environmental groups and government agencies to meet residents' needs while preserving the inherent beauty of the site as part of the implementation of the action plan. Extensive tree surveys were conducted early in the planning process; wetland preservation and marsh buffers were important features of the master plan. As part of their commitment to excellence, the town founders remain active in the local political arena.

Implement the Action Plan

When Habersham was conceived, it was viewed as one part of a larger regional light imprint plan called the Burton Area Conceptual Sector Plan. That plan connects natural systems to human habitats by forming continuous networks throughout the region. To facilitate alternative routes for storm evacuations, emergencies, and accidents, the road infrastructure was conceived as a north-south and east-west network to connect the mixed-use centers of neighborhoods throughout the region. The same neighborhoods would serve as nodes for intermodal transit stations. Larger village centers throughout the Burton area could be connected by transit that would originate at Beaufort. The town center of Habersham would serve as the western terminus of the transit line.

SHORT- AND LONG-TERM ACTIONS

As construction proceeded, the development team used a number of techniques to manage stormwater on the site. Habersham uses innovative engineering and traditional planning techniques instead of gold-plated engineering standards.

The multimodal street design safely accommodates pedestrians and bicycles as well as automobiles and transit vehicles. The street widths vary based on the vehicular traffic load. While some streets have sidewalks on only one side, the development team eliminated some sidewalks in the neighborhood edge in favor of shared walking and driving lanes. All of the town center, neighborhood center, neighborhood general, and portions of the neighborhood edge are served by rear lanes using economical pervious stone for paving.

Most all the street paving in Habersham is asphalt, a cost-effective and readily available material. Since the street widths vary from very narrow to multiple lanes, the traffic load determines the width of pavement. Using narrow paved streets allows more vegetation to absorb runoff and to filter impurities from the runoff.

Figure 7-4
As a light imprint technique, this gravel swale channels runoff during a storm at Habersham. *Duany Plater-Zyberk and Company, Charlotte, NC*

Figure 7-5
During fair weather at Habersham, the same gravel swale is still an attractive feature with charming wooden footbridges. *Duany Plater-Zyberk and Company, Charlotte, NC*

Some streets have sidewalks on only one side, further reducing the amount of paved surfaces. Wood planks are used to pave one of the bridges in Habersham. Natural creeks crossing the site channel runoff to the marshes. This mitigates the need for catch basins and underground piping across the site.

GRAVEL SWALE

Gravel swale, during a rain event, combines vegetation and gravel that channel water away from the tennis courts, recreation areas, and parking lots, naturally filtering runoff before it enters the aquifer or the Broad River.

Figure 7-6
As a light imprint technique, the pervious parking plaza at Habersham reduces pavement required while it stores and filters stormwater. *Duany Plater-Zyberk and Company, Charlotte, NC*

Figure 7-7
A beautiful allee of live oaks in a grassed median adds community value as it serves as a light imprint tool to store and filter stormwater. *Duany Plater-Zyberk and Company, Charlotte, NC*

Green fingers of land (narrow strips of vegetation) between structures provide another means of filtering runoff. In the most urban zone, paver blocks with gravel and planted joints were used in the formal interior courtyards of many of the live-work units and townhouses.

Sheet flow runoff from some roads goes to pervious areas, grass and stone swales, and to a series of filtration ponds.

Habersham Allée of Live Oaks, where the green space along the allée doubles as a light imprint tool to absorb runoff, and where mature trees give Habersham its beauty, provide a return on the money invested in tree surveys and protection fences during construction.

Conventional TND Stormwater Plan

Light Imprint TND Stormwater Plan

KEY

☐ Stormwater Inlet	► Storm Water Discharge
● Manhole	⊟ Underground Stormwater Storage
— Stormwater Pipe	▩ Rain Garden

Figure 7-8
The chart shows the savings realized at Griffin Park using light imprint engineering (right) instead of conventional engineering (left). *Duany Plater-Zyberk and Company, Charlotte, NC*

Implementation Costs and Benefits

The strategic action plan can save costs over time. For example, to achieve light imprint goals within the Griffin Park plan, tree protection fences used in the erosion control phase protect existing natural areas including mature trees. That strategy results in a 27 percent cost increase compared to the conventional method. Yet, using light imprint, there is a 50 percent cost savings in the stormwater management phase. Bioretention swales, rain gardens, and vegetative surface filtration areas add aesthetically pleasing natural areas and neighborhood recreation areas. Rain gardens filter runoff to remove pollutants before they reach the adjacent creeks and river.

Two road pavement techniques reduce costs. First, building roads 24 feet wide instead of 26 feet wide results in a significant reduction of paving costs. Second, substituting crushed stone for asphalt for rear lane surfacing saves significantly on material and labor costs. For the Griffin Park project, the savings of over 30 percent equates to almost a half-million dollar savings in the first 37-acre phase. Pearlman summarizes, "Implementing the Light Imprint engineering method results in over thirty percent engineering cost savings in actual construction dollars. That savings is in addition to the added community value realized by the preservation of mature trees and communal rain gardens."

In conclusion, light imprint techniques have life spans that exceed that of many of the highly technological stormwater management techniques. The simplicity of installation and maintenance makes them a natural choice for developers and municipalities working to construct new and retrofitted developments that function, flourish, and endure as successful, sustainable communities for the twenty-first century.

Decentralized Wastewater Management

Eric Lohan with Will Kirksey
Worrell Water Technologies, LLC

Wastewater Infrastructure

Water, along with energy, is coming to be widely recognized as one of the key resources for sustainability. Conventional centralized water and wastewater infrastructure is expensive, energy inefficient, and substitutes technology for nature. The emerging ecological model of wastewater infrastructure is decentralized and uses ecological treatment technologies. To be successful this model requires new standards, new regulations, new tools, new partnerships, and new technologies but has the potential to fundamentally transform our relationship with water. From the "once-through" centralized approach is emerging a decentralized fractal network of wastewater treatment and reuse that saves water, energy, and money, supporting sustainable community development.

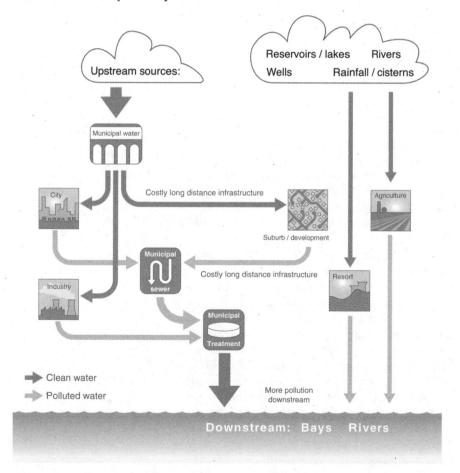

Figure 7-9
The conventional centralized wastewater treatment and disposal model wastes water and energy. *Worrell Water Technologies/Interface Multimedia*

The current model, outlined in Figure 7–9 is complex, energy-intensive, and wastes water. This approach is focused on large-scale, centralized systems, using water once before sending it downstream, and treating all water to drinking standards regardless of intended use. It requires moving water long distances, with obvious high consumption of energy, and using treatment technologies that also are large energy consumers. Limits to this approach to water treatment are becoming evident. For example:

- resources are declining in quality and quantity.
- The capacity of receiving waters to safely assimilate wastes is being exceeded.
- Maintenance and new construction costs are becoming intolerable. The EPA Office of Water estimates that if capital investment and operations and maintenance costs remain at current levels, the gap in funding for 2010–2019 will be almost $600 billion for water and wastewater infrastructure.

Our centralized water system is reaching the point of diminishing returns; resources have become constrained, and we can't safely dispose of the harmful by-products. We need to think about creating smarter, more natural wastewater treatment approaches.

The Ecological Model—Decentralized Infrastructure Systems

An alternative approach for wastewater treatment is to apply an ecological model to wastewater infrastructure. This model can be used to apply ecological concepts to both the design of the infrastructure and the design of the treatment processes. The ecological model is based on more decentralization, integration with local economic and ecosystem needs, local water reuse, and adaptation of ecological water treatment processes. A broader recognition and application of this new approach requires improving awareness of the possibilities among the major stakeholders.

A new decentralized wastewater strategy must be put in place that is cost-effective, technically sound, and sustainable economically and ecologically. Such a strategy will include and maintain the best of the current systems and existing tactics, such as water conservation. In addition, continued, reliable access to water requires the new approach to be resilient in the face of changing conditions and help deal with ongoing drought and water scarcity challenges.

Beyond being a well-conceived approach to providing water, the new water strategy must also contribute to addressing other interrelated issues such as energy, climate change, and economic strength. An ecologically based model of wastewater treatment infrastructure has the potential to meet all of these goals.

Natural streams and rivers display a decentralized structure of repeating patterns at different scales. Small streams or brooks may transport entrained sediments or nutrients to wetland areas scattered throughout the upper reaches of the watershed, which help improve water quality. At other points in the watershed, when seasonal rains raise water levels, riparian floodplains slow the flow rate of the river and intercept large amounts of sediment and nutrients. If one component of this process is impaired there are numerous back-up components at the same scale or different scales that can rebuild the lost capacity. Integrated strategies for decentralized wastewater treatment and water reuse at multiple scales can mimic this approach, improving the overall effectiveness of our water infrastructure (Figure 7–10).

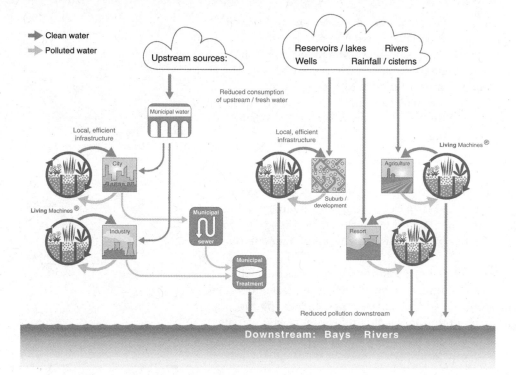

Clean water

Polluted water

Upstream sources:

Reservoirs / lakes   Rivers

Wells   Rainfall / cisterns

Reduced consumption
of upstream / fresh water

Municipal water

Local, efficient
infrastructure

Local, efficient
infrastructure

Living Machines ®

City

Agriculture

Living Machines ®

Suburb /
development

Industry

Municipal
sewer

Resort

Municipal
Treatment

Reduced pollution downstream

Downstream: Bays   Rivers

Figure 7-10
The ecological decentralized wastewater treatment and reuse model saves energy and water, mimicking the natural process. *Worrell Water Technologies/Interface Multimedia*

The Ecological Model—Treatment Technologies

The ecological model can be applied not only to the design of infrastructure but also to the design of wastewater treatment technologies that play a pivotal role in these larger systems. Most centralized or municipal treatment facilities use an activated sludge approach to wastewater treatment. This technology uses diffused air to accelerate the growth of bacteria and the removal of nutrients. It requires a very small footprint but uses a large amount of energy. The process is most stable at larger scales. Smaller decentralized applications require much greater operational attention and may not be able to consistently meet the water quality standards required for wastewater reuse.

The development of new technologies over the last two decades has allowed decentralized treatment systems to be much more widely applicable. The activated sludge process has been modified with the addition of membrane filtration technology to create Membrane Bioreactors (MBRs). These membrane filters help polish effluent from the activated sludge treatment process creating consistent high-quality effluent required for reuse and further shrink the footprint of activated sludge systems but they also increase the energy requirements of an already energy-intensive process.

Another approach has been adopted in the development of advanced wetland treatment systems. Wetland treatment systems mimic natural treatment processes in nature using more complex communities of bacteria, other microorganisms, and plants living on rock aggregate to remove nutrients. Early systems were energy efficient but required a very large footprint and hence were not appropriate for suburban or urban applications. A new generation of advanced wetland treatment processes have been developed which turbo-charge wetland processes with the use of high-efficiency pumps. Tidal wetlands (see Living Machine® STEP sheet) are a very efficient process that reduce the footprint of early wetland designs by 80 percent but yet require only 25 percent of the energy of MBRs. These systems can be readily incorporated into urban and suburban sites due to the compact footprint. Because they are also beautiful in addition to being functional they have been incorporated into site design or even into building architecture as atria.

Prepare the Team

Water issues are among the most complex facing our communities right now. In particular, we need to reexamine and update policies, design standards, engineering models and analysis tools, monitoring and control technologies, funding programs, and management structures to support decision-making and maintain quality and public health standards.

These efforts require the support of a diverse group of professionals who need to be educated on the current limitations of centralized systems and both the strengths and limitations of a decentralized ecological approach. New partnerships are required to develop and implement this approach. Professionals who will play a key role in this process include municipal water and wastewater officials, regulators, engineers, planners, architects and landscape architects, contractors, operators, and civic leaders.

Prepare the Tools

The complexity of natural water systems, the intricacies of existing water infrastructure and the complicated existing legal and regulatory requirements for water use, disposal, and reuse prohibit simple prescriptive qualitative or quantitative standards for sustainable water use and reuse. Despite these challenges a few standards have been developed or are under development that attempt to provide a template for sustainable water infrastructure.

1. **LEED**—The U.S. Green Building Council (USGBC) Leadership in Energy and Environmental Design (LEED) standards are the most widely adopted and most well-developed standards for green building. LEED standards promote water-efficient fixtures, xeriscaping, and water reuse for irrigation, toilet flushing, and other water reuse requirements. Although these standards have played a key role in launching the green building movement in the United States, they have been criticized by water advocates as water credits are more difficult to achieve than others and are frequently passed over.

2. **Living Building Challenge**—The Cascadia regional group of the USGBC has recently developed a new standard the Living Building Challenge (LBC). LBC does not have elective credits but only prerequisites. The water prerequisites include:

   Prerequisite Ten—Net-Zero Water

   > 100 percent of occupants' water use must come from captured precipitation or reused water that is appropriately purified without the use of chemicals.

Prerequisite Eleven—Sustainable Water Discharge

> 100 percent of stormwater and building water discharge must be handled on-site.

These standards set a much higher bar for water reuse but may place unrealistic expectations on small buildings. They are trying to solve watershed problems by focusing only on the building scale that may not be the optimum approach.

3. **Water Neutral**—The LEED and LBC approaches address the building industry but many other industries and development practices affect the water cycles in our communities. A UNESCO working group is developing criteria that reflect a more comprehensive approach to "Water Neutral" development and industries. They define three criteria:

   1. Defining, measuring, and reporting one's water footprint

   2. Taking all action that is reasonably possible to reduce the existing operational water footprint

   3. Reconciling the residual water footprint by making a reasonable investment in establishing or supporting projects that focus on the sustainable and equitable use of water

4. **Alliance for Water Stewardship**—While the approach developed by the UNESCO group provides a general template, there are no binding requirements to give the language credibility. New water standards are under development by the Alliance for Water Stewardship, an umbrella organization that represents key water and environment NGOs including the Pacific Institute, The Water Environment Federation, World Wildlife Foundation, the Nature Conservancy, and the European Water Partnership. The goal of these standards is to apply the LEED-type framework exclusively to water infrastructure from a holistic and global perspective. It could become a very important tool.

Communities will need to draw from the approaches elucidated above to develop standards that fit with their specific requirements. There is no "one size fits all" solution but it is hoped that tools developed by the Alliance for Water Stewardship and others will be flexible enough to become widely applicable.

Prepare the Place

The implementation of useful water standards requires detailed knowledge of water flows between community infrastructure and the environment. This information needs to be developed from a number of sources depending on scale. Regional GIS databases often contain a wealth of important information about soil conditions, land use, and development. Utilities are increasingly using information management systems to streamline utility operations. A variety of government agencies maintain important information about water and environmental quality including the USGS, EPA, and the NRCS. Significant work is generally required though to integrate the various sources into an effective analysis framework.

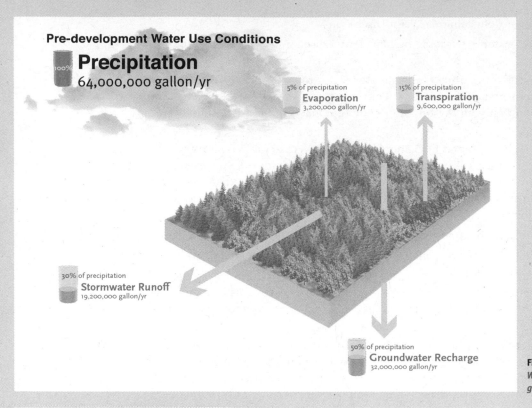

Pre-development Water Use Conditions

100% **Precipitation**
64,000,000 gallon/yr

5% of precipitation
Evaporation
3,200,000 gallon/yr

15% of precipitation
Transpiration
9,600,000 gallon/yr

30% of precipitation
Stormwater Runoff
19,200,000 gallon/yr

50% of precipitation
Groundwater Recharge
32,000,000 gallon/yr

Figure 7-11
Worrell Water Technologies/Interface Multimedia

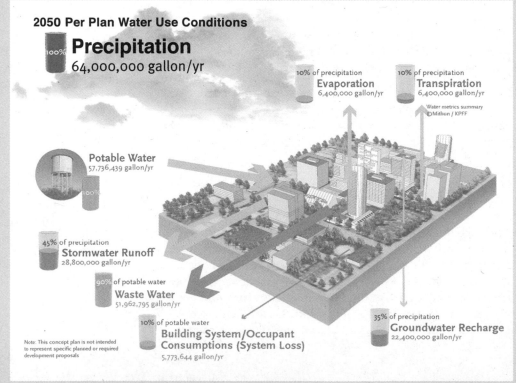

2050 Per Plan Water Use Conditions

100% **Precipitation**
64,000,000 gallon/yr

10% of precipitation
Evaporation
6,400,000 gallon/yr

10% of precipitation
Transpiration
6,400,000 gallon/yr

Water metrics summary
©Mithun / KPFF

Potable Water
57,736,439 gallon/yr
100%

45% of precipitation
Stormwater Runoff
28,800,000 gallon/yr

90% of potable water
Waste Water
51,962,795 gallon/yr

10% of potable water
Building System/Occupant Consumptions (System Loss)
5,773,644 gallon/yr

35% of precipitation
Groundwater Recharge
22,400,000 gallon/yr

Note: This concept plan is not intended to represent specific planned or required development proposals

Figure 7-12
Worrell Water Technologies/Interface Multimedia

Develop Goals, Objectives, and Performance Metrics

The LEED and water neutral standards described above require an accurate knowledge of water sources and uses. The first step in implementing a sustainable water reuse plan is to develop a water budget or water footprint. This should detail the sources of water used in a community, including potential nontraditional sources such as rainwater or stormwater, and potential water reuse as well as a detailed view of water uses. By identifying water sources and sinks we can qualitatively match high-quality sources with uses such as municipal water for potable applications and lower-quality water sources such as reclaimed water with uses such as toilet flushing or cooling towers. The second goal of the water budget is quantitative and requires detailed calculations or estimations of water sources and sinks and allows the development of water efficiency and reuse strategies which accurately match water availability with water requirements.

Water budgets are necessarily linked to design standards or goals. There are two common interpretations of how to balance a water budget, with respect to "developed conditions" or "predeveloped conditions." Using the developed conditions interpretation, the Thames Gateway Project, a 40-mile redevelopment project along the Thames Estuary from the London Docklands to Essex, is proposing to increase density by 10 percent without increasing the total water use of the area by implementing efficiency upgrades in new and existing buildings. This interpretation has been criticized because in many cases developed conditions are grossly unsustainable and should not be used as a baseline, even if new development doesn't make it worse.

Building Scale

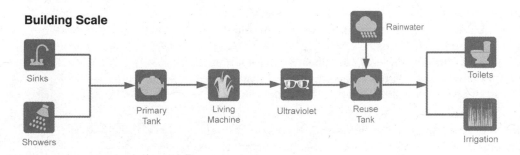

Community Scale

Municipal Scale

Figure 7-13
The above example illustrates development of a site water analysis in three scenarios from the Lloyd Crossing Sustainable Urban Design Plan; a 35-square-block, mixed-use area of Portland, Oregon, developed by Mithun; and a team of green design experts. The first scenario shows predeveloped water flows and quality that would occur on a similar area of undeveloped Oregon forest providing a truly sustainable reference point. The second and third illustrations describe current conditions and proposed postdevelopment water impacts, respectively. *Worrell Water Technologies/Interface Multimedia*

Develop the Strategic Plan

The water use provides the framework for designing sustainable water infrastructure. This process entails designing systems and selecting technologies that achieve the required flows and quality for each use. At present there is no systematic process for achieving this goal. As discussed above, this process will entail a variety of stakeholders and design professionals working closely together. Only a few communities have begun to address these questions so models are limited and what may be ideal in one community may be inappropriate in another. A few key considerations should drive the design of sustainable infrastructure systems.

1. Infrastructure systems should be designed to optimize their interrelation with the natural hydrologic cycle. Using low-impact development practices such as bioswales and other natural stormwater retention or detention strategies is one example.

2. Sustainable infrastructure systems should be developed at multiple scales and should be mutually self-reinforcing across all scales.

3. Sustainable water infrastructure systems should use technologies that are also energy-efficient and cost-effective from a capital and lifecycle perspective. A number of technologies such as desalination sacrifice energy efficiency for water efficiency and thus are not likely to be successful long-term solutions in many areas.

4. Innovative technologies and systems must protect public health as well as or better than existing systems. These systems must also foster public acceptance of recycled or reclaimed water by eliminating all odor and color from water before reuse even for nonpotable applications.

The lack of unified national or, in many areas, even state standards for water reuse has hampered development and implementation of new technologies and systems. A recent report commissioned by the Cascadia USGBC, *Code regulation and systemic barriers affecting Living Building Projects,* identifies seven important steps for modifying the regulatory environment to foster the adoption of sustainable systems and technologies. These steps are particularly relevant for supporting water reuse projects.

1. *Identify and address regulatory impediments.* Byzantine and, in some cases, outdated standards for water reuse are hampering the adoption of new technologies and stifling innovation.

2. *Create incentives matched with goals.* Water savings that accrue from water reuse should result in direct economic savings similar to net metering approaches for solar energy. Unfortunately this is not always the case.

3. *Develop education and advocacy programs.* With proper training and support the regulatory community can become the strongest allies of appropriate sustainable water reuse technologies. Community leaders, developers, and design professionals would all benefit from understanding more about successful new technologies or applications.

4. *Accelerate research, testing, development, deployment, and monitoring.* States, and particularly the federal government, need to develop appropriate incentives to certify new technologies to assure their performance but also foster the devel-

opment of new technologies. This should include appropriate consistency and reciprocity among jurisdictions. Every new cell phone does not have to undergo unique performance and safety evaluations in every U.S. city in which it is sold.

5. *Create Green Zones—designated sustainable development districts.* There are always risks associated with the implementation of new technologies and systems. The Green Zone model allows new technologies to be demonstrated on a provisional basis with adequate regulatory oversight.

6. *Facilitate the creation of a holistic integrated regulatory process.* For water system approval there are frequently overlapping and conflicting water regulations for public health, environmental protection, and resource allocation. A holistic integrated regulatory process would allow social and environmental goals to be met most effectively.

7. *Ensure social equity in policies that safeguard public health, safety, and welfare.* Frequently, water reuse practices are targeted at addressing the needs of the wealthy (irrigation of golf courses) while parks in working-class neighborhoods do not have access to reuse water for irrigation. In the United States and globally, the poor have disproportionately borne the cost of environmental pollution.

Develop the Action Plan

At the core of sustainable water infrastructure systems are decentralized wastewater treatment systems. These systems are generally composed of six discrete steps as represented in Figure 7-15. Wastewater conveyance systems collect and transport wastewater from a variety of sources. Treatment processes include physical treatment such as filtration, screening, and clarification, and which can remove inorganic materials or larger organic constituents. Biological treatment processes, such as MBRs and advanced wetland systems, remove suspended solids and dissolved organic constituents such as carbonaceous materials, and nutrients such as nitrogen, and phosphorus. After biological treatment, final filtration, and disinfection may be required to remove any remaining viruses, bacteria, or other harmful microorganisms.

Implement the Action Plan

Opportunities to implement sustainable infrastructure development and water reuse will be different in each community but will generally be easy to identify since we collectively waste a lot of water. Three different examples are described below to illustrate projects in urban, suburban, and rural areas from the Southeast to the Southwest and the Rocky Mountains to the Northwest.

Implementation of these technologies requires selecting applications that are appropriate for a given scale. Figure 7.14 provides examples of water reuse process diagrams at three different scales: building scale, institutional or community scale, and municipal scale. Different technologies and water reuse goals are appropriate at different scales. The optimum overall performance from a cost and water-efficiency perspective is achieved by developing appropriate projects at a variety of scales.

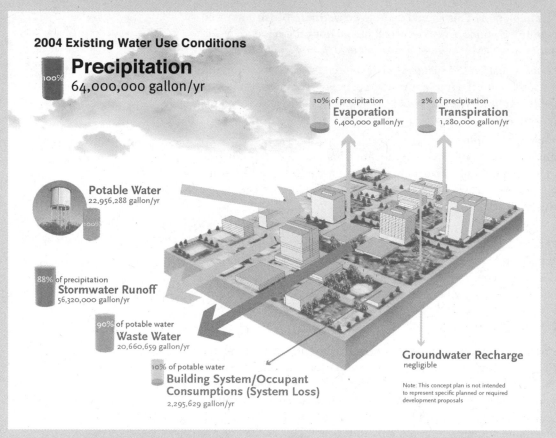

2004 Existing Water Use Conditions

Precipitation
64,000,000 gallon/yr

100%

10% of precipitation
Evaporation
6,400,000 gallon/yr

2% of precipitation
Transpiration
1,280,000 gallon/yr

Potable Water
22,956,288 gallon/yr

100%

88% of precipitation
Stormwater Runoff
56,320,000 gallon/yr

90% of potable water
Waste Water
20,660,659 gallon/yr

10% of potable water
Building System/Occupant Consumptions (System Loss)
2,295,629 gallon/yr

Groundwater Recharge
negligible

Note: This concept plan is not intended to represent specific planned or required development proposals

◀ **Figure 7-14**
The water reuse designs can be applied at three different scales: building scale, community or institutional scale, and municipal scale. *Worrell Water Technologies/Interface Multimedia*

▼ **Figure 7-15**
The six steps of a sustainable water infrastructure system begin with the wastewater source, continue through four treatment steps, and end at the reuse discharge points. *Worrell Water Technologies/Interface Multimedia*

Wastewater Sources + Conveyance
Showers · Sinks · Toilets · Wastewater Conveyance · Dog Kennel

Physical Treatment
Filtration/Screening · Settling/Clarification

Biological Treatment
Living Machine · Membrane Bioreactor

Chemical Treatment or Disinfection
Ozone Gas · Ultraviolet · Chlorine

Water Reuse
Irrigation · Washwater · Cooling Tower

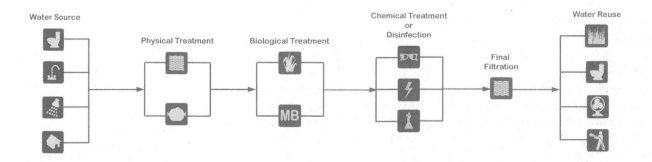

Water Source

Physical Treatment

Biological Treatment

Chemical Treatment or Disinfection

Final Filtration

Water Reuse

For maximum effectiveness, implementing new technologies must be appropriately targeted. The application of new decentralized treatment and reuse systems should be focused in areas of rapid growth or failing existing treatment (e.g., septic systems or package plants), in regional networks as a means of avoiding expansion of a centralized plant and the interconnecting infrastructure, and as standalone applications to serve specific needs. In this way they help rehabilitate and extend the life of existing critical infrastructure by reducing the load on these systems.

These decentralized systems should be constructed as part of a regional natural and human ecosystem, so that the design of the wastewater treatment can help integrate natural water cycles with human and environmental needs. In some cases, it may be appropriate to undo or modify some of the existing infrastructure such as sewer mining to reuse water, removing water control structures, or restoring natural water channels. Environmental and infrastructure benefits can also enhance the local economy. The design of wastewater treatment can be coupled with the creation of business opportunities and new jobs by involving community interests in planning of water reuse opportunities to optimize the creation and maintenance of livelihoods and locally productive economic activity.

Figure 7-16
This example of a building scale sustainable wastewater treatment process treats and reuses the effluent for equipment, gardens, and other building and site functions. *Worrell Water Technologies/Interface Multimedia*

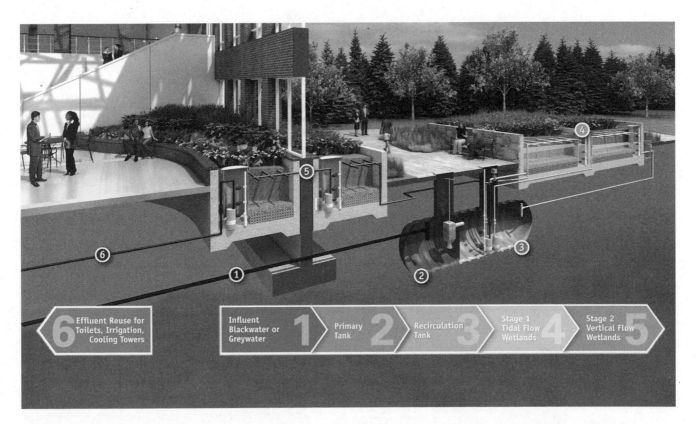

6 Effluent Reuse for Toilets, Irrigation, Cooling Towers

Influent Blackwater or Greywater

1

Primary Tank

2

Recirculation Tank

3

Stage 1 Tidal Flow Wetlands

4

Stage 2 Vertical Flow Wetlands

5

Implementation Project Examples

OREGON HEALTH AND SCIENCE UNIVERSITY, PORTLAND, OREGON

The Center for Health and Healing at the Oregon Health and Science University along the Willamette River in Portland is 16 stories tall and totals about 400,000 square feet. This building uses a series of interconnected water systems designed by Interface Engineering to reduce municipal water use and to eliminate surges of stormwater. While all potable water comes from municipal supply, highly efficient sinks, showers, and toilets are used throughout the building, and rainwater is captured and stored in a 22,000-gallon cistern for fire suppression, HVAC (heating/ventilation/air-conditioning) cooling towers, as well as radiant cooling.

Collected rainwater is also used for a portion of the toilet flushing demand and building wastewater is treated on-site with an MBR in the basement. Treated and disinfected water is reused for toilet flushing as well as irrigation. All wastewater is disposed on-site through the irrigation system. A green roof on the building collects a portion of the rainfall and reduces stormwater runoff. With these design changes, the building's potable water demand is reduced by over 60 percent—saving an estimated 5 million gallons of water per year.

GUILFORD COUNTY SCHOOLS, NORTH CAROLINA

When a suburban school district outside of Greensboro, North Carolina, wanted to build a new middle school and high school campus they estimated that sewer connection fees would be over $4 million. They opted for a decentralized approach to water reuse at less than one quarter of that price. A 365,000-gallon concrete rainwater cistern was constructed to collect runoff from the roofs of both buildings. All toilet flushing on campus is provided with rainwater. The roof of the tank is used as a regulation-size basketball court. All wastewater is treated by a Living Machine advanced wetland treatment system. This treatment system is located between the two buildings and provides aesthetic and educational benefits in addition to supplying irrigation water for all of the school's athletic facilities.

BP, CASPER, WYOMING

Significant water reuse potential exists in industrial applications and in environmental remediation. BP of Casper, Wyoming is spending the next 100 years or more cleaning up petrochemicals that have leached into the soil and contaminated groundwater. They are using an advanced wetland system designed by North American Wetland Engineers that reclaims almost 1 billion gallons of water per year that is then used for irrigation of an adjacent golf course. This energy-efficient process was also cost effective, saving BP at least $12 million over other alternatives.

REGIONAL WATERSHED MANAGEMENT PLANNING

Paul Crabtree, P.E.
Crabtree Group, Inc.

INTERVENTION TYPE: BEST PRACTICES

Description

Regional Watershed Management Plans (RWMP) shall integrate with regional land use plans, and integrate the largest practical geographic area, overlapping property lines as necessary and municipal boundaries if possible, and encompassing the regional watersheds. RWMPs shall conform to the following general sequence:

1. Adequate and appropriate base maps shall be compiled for the region showing topography, soil types, cover types, rainfall gradients, parcel configurations, development patterns, combined sewer overflows, and known stormwater hazard areas.

2. The existing conditions for the regional watersheds shall be modeled using standardized hydrological methods such as the USDA's Technical Release 55. At a minimum, the 2-, 25-, and 100-year storm events shall be modeled.

3. The natural conditions for the regional watersheds shall be modeled. Natural conditions shall be defined as those cover conditions that existed prior to significant alterations by humans.

4. Watershed failure mechanisms shall be identified through the analyses of the above three points and historical records. These stormwater hazard symptoms shall be ranked by severity of potential damages to health, safety, and urban and environmental welfare.

5. Appropriate community-based remediations for the highest ranked stormwater hazards shall be developed. This may require hydrological analysis and value engineering of alternatives; and may involve short-, medium-, and long-term solutions involving both private and public entities. The hydrological analysis for these remediations should show significant hydrograph improvements as

Figure 7-17
Manhattan wetland showing a small rain garden (wetland) at Teardrop Park, inside Battery Park City. *Payton Chung*

compared to the existing condition for the watersheds, and show progress in the direction of the natural condition hydrograph in terms of time of concentration, runoff rate, runoff volume, and water quality.

6. Recommendations shall be made for the Regional Land Use Plan based on the RWMP results, especially as regards lands recommended for Preserved Open Space, Reserved Open Space, and Infill Growth.

7. A detailed stormwater analysis shall be conducted for New Community Plans and Infill Community Plans and the RWMP shall be revised and updated to incorporate those analyses.

The RWMP shall provide incentives for compact urban patterns, infill, redevelopment, and sprawl repair and shall balance those incentives through stricter requirements for lower-density areas. Site regulations shall not be uniform across the region, but will be context sensitive; downtown property characteristics are immensely different from large-lot, detached single-family properties and the regulations should reflect these contextual differences. The RWMP shall provide methods for achieving overall improvements to the watershed character and avoiding cumulative regional watershed hydromodification by development.

The RWMP shall emphasize the retrofit of conventional sprawl land use patterns and conventional pipe-and-dump stormwater systems, and advocate the implementation of source-control best management practices. Light imprint exemplifies these source-control methods such as porous pavement materials, infiltration of rainwater near where it falls, and green streets. Rainwater shall be treated as a resource and not a waste product.

A system for the gradual Transfer of Stormwater Mitigation (TSM) shall be established and administered for the purpose of transferring stormwater mitigation activities from intended growth areas to intended open space, or from higher-density zones to lower-intensity zones; in order to help incentivize infill, redevelopment, sprawl repair, and higher-density development.

SUPPORTS GOALS AND OBJECTIVES
- Supports groundwater recharge
- Supports rainwater capture and reuse
- Supports compact, walkable, diverse neighborhoods
- Supports sprawl repair, infill, and redevelopment

PERFORMANCE CHARACTERISTICS
Reduce stormwater runoff rate, volume, and pollution characteristics in the watershed by up to 50 percent or more, while increasing rainwater infiltration by 50 percent in a 20-year period.

Potential Synergism

The program should be integrated with regional land use planning, complete green street standards, landscaping standards, and community water conservation programs.

Implementation Time

The program can be implemented within 6 to 12 months as it is best done in conjunction with a regional land use planning process, which will add time to the implementation.

Benefits

- The RWMP will address NPDES stormwater regulation concerns, and actually put the community ahead of that program.
- The RWMP will help to encourage and incentivize downtown redevelopment, infill, and sprawl repair.
- The RWMP will address flooding concerns by pinpointing the underlying causes and addressing them through leveraged opportunities available only when addressed on the regional watershed scale.
- The RWMP will help to replenish the groundwater aquifers, thus enhancing the water supply, and natural base stream flows.

Drawbacks

- The RWMP may not achieve all its goals without the joint participation of multiple jurisdictions, since the natural regional watershed likely does not follow political boundaries.
- A substantial amount of conventional urban pattern in the form of sprawl, overly wide pavements on streets, large parking lots, and pipe-and-dump stormwater systems needs to be retrofitted. This is a challenge, but also a great opportunity to make substantial urban and watershed improvements.

First Cost

- The cost of developing an RWMP can vary significantly ($10,000 to $100,000 or more) depending on the size of the watershed, the availability of existing base map materials, and the severity of existing conditions.

Lifecycle Costs

- A sustainable RWMP should pay for itself many times over in, even, a 10- or 20-year horizon; through aquifer replenishment, flood mitigation, and receiving water body enhancements.
- Because the RWMP largely redirects funds from conventional measures to more sustainable measures, the costs of the program would not need to increase while the benefits would.

ESTIMATED QUANTITATIVE PERFORMANCE

The hydrograph illustrates that implementation of an RWMP can significantly improve the existing hydrologic characteristics for the watershed, sometimes even approaching natural cover conditions.

IMPLEMENTATION SUPPORTS AND CONSTRAINTS

A key to success is to diagnose and address the health of the watershed in a holistic fashion that integrates with other key disciplines such as land planning and public works. Once the key regional watershed issues are determined, then laser-precise context-sensitive site solutions can be regulated and attained.

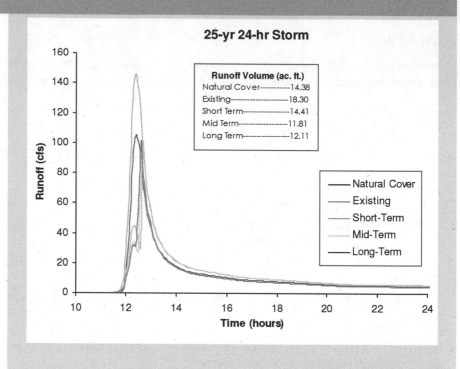

INFORMATIONAL SOURCES

- U.S. EPA Watershed Academy Web: www.epa.gov/watertrain/smartgrowth/
- SmartCode Regional Watersheds Module: www.transect.org
- 3. For context-sensitive, low-impact practices: www.lightimprint.org

REPORTS AND STUDIES

- U.S. EPA Protecting Water Resources with Higher-Density Development. www.epa.gov/dced/pdf/protect_water_higher_density.pdf
- U.S. EPA Growing Toward More Efficient Water Use: Linking Development, Infrastructure, and Drinking Water Policies www.epa.gov/dced/pdf/growing_water_use_efficiency.pdf
- wing_water_use_efficiency.pdf
- U.S. EPA Reducing Stormwater Costs through Low Impact Development (LID) Strategies and Practices www.epa.gov/owow/nps/lid/costs07/
- Westcliffe and Silver Cliff Regional Watershed Management Plan: www.crabtreegroup.net

Sustainable Landscaping

John Harris
Landscape Economist, Earth Advisors, Inc.

Conventional Landscape Systems

Many communities and individual property owners today treat their landscapes and natural areas as second-class citizens. They expend most investments and maintenance efforts on new buildings and paved areas, allocating the remaining funds for the development or protection of green spaces. During times of decreasing tax and development-generated revenues, parks, landscape maintenance, and property maintenance are often targeted first for budget reductions or even elimination of services. We find our green spaces and blue spaces (waterways and water bodies) filled with debris, overgrown with invasive species (both plants and animals), and undesirable. The costs to rejuvenate these community assets increase the longer protection and maintenance is underfunded or unfunded.

Figure 8-1
Here is a children's play area in a park nestled with shade trees and accent landscaping.
Stephen Coyle

The Sustainable Landscape

The sustainable community vision must include green spaces and blue spaces. These natural environments are necessities in any community. The Earth is a worldwide ecosystem that has successfully operated through the natural systems for millennia. Replacing the preexisting natural systems (considering that many areas of the Earth have been impacted by humans for thousands of years) with the current development model for cities and communities continues to damage our shared environment. Local air quality, ambient air temperatures, stormwater management, and energy use are all improved by healthy natural environments, for example, those that provide tree canopy with the appropriate understory plant communities.

Most communities exhibit a mix of native plants, exotic noninvasive plants, and exotic invasive plants. By cooperating in the removal of the invasive plants, control of the use of exotic noninvasive plants, and promotion of the use of native plants, we improve the ecosystem and habitat values in our communities for open spaces, such as parks and wild lands, and for developed spaces in residential, commercial, industrial, and public properties. Even cities such as New York City or Los Angeles require a balance of both built and natural elements since both contribute to the health of their surrounding region.

Prepare the Team

Sustainable landscapes will be protected and created in direct proportion to the value placed upon them by those who understand their importance and are responsible for their design, development, and management: foresters, arborists, horticulturists, hydrologists, landscape architects, biologists, landscape maintenance professionals, planners, nursery owners, economists, and others involved in the development of ecological environments. Sustainable landscapes should be considered concurrent with the design of buildings and site improvements, including the utilization of green spaces for water management systems and air purification. With surveys showing the importance of green spaces and woodlands as key elements in community planning, communities have multiple reasons to include sustainable landscapes into development efforts.

A community embarking on a sustainable landscape program should verify the professional qualifications of the proposed team, and review their completed projects in person, preferably. The review should extend to the landscape design or plan used for the project, and those components or elements that make the work sustainable as opposed to another pretty landscape.

Sustainable landscape training is available through green industry best management practices, waterwise or xeriscape landscape principles, energy-saving landscape principles, and sustainable landscape principles education programs. Experts in sustainable landscaping require a working knowledge of local native plants, local soils and conditions, best management practices, and municipal regulations for landscaping.

Prepare the Tools

The best measuring tool for evaluating existing landscapes, the Annual Maintenance Contract and Specifications, evaluates the performance of professional maintenance providers. Assessing the sustainability of a new landscape, the Landscape Design or Landscape Plan and Specifications, is a tool for evaluating species choices, site preparation, installation and establishment care practices. Each contract requires performance-based specifications for each work area to assure that landscapes begin and continue to grow and remain healthy. The specifications should cover the desired community values: air cleansing, water filtration, water retention, wildlife habitat, property aesthetics, and other natural environmental attributes.

One example, the standard for mulch placed over soils in landscape beds, assists with soil moisture retention, weed suppression, and organic matter. Mulch may be specified as two to three inches deep, and kept at least two to three inches away from any plant stems to reduce the opportunity for rot and disease to enter plant stems and trunks. This performance-based specification allows for judging the performance of contractors doing maintenance work, and provides for the best management practices in sustainable landscapes for the mulch element. References and information sources for sustainable landscapes include:

- Local Cooperative Extension Office, the Horticultural Agent
- Soil and Water Conservation District Office
- City, County, and/or State Department of Environmental Regulations, Protection, or Management
- Water Management or Conservation Districts
- American Society of Landscape Architects
- Society of American Foresters
- International Society of Arboriculture
- Tree Care Industry Association
- Audubon Society
- National Arbor Day Foundation
- USDA Forest Service
- United States Department of Agriculture
- Home Depot Foundation
- Hands On Network
- Habitat for Humanity

VISUAL MAPPING TOOLS

In order to evaluate and improve natural environments, the team should visually illustrate the subject area and depict it on paper or in other media. The standard visual tools include design drawings, plans, and renderings as 2D line depictions.

Figure 8-2

Using an aerial photo as background along with full-color drawings helps make maps more interesting for reviewers, and more impactful. *Produced and copyrighted by Earth Advisors, Inc.* ©2010.

Computer programs allow the use of site photographs and photo editing to show the old landscape, and then to render in sustainable changes to show the proposed landscape concept. This "reality view" helps promote the value of the new landscape.

Geographic Information System (GIS) programs can map natural environments and sustainable landscape relative to properties and larger-scale projects, and place location points of landscape. Using a recent aerial photograph as the base layer, the interactive GIS program allows the layering of different site information and construction plan elements (soils, elevations, drainage plans, pavement plans, site plans, building plans, landscape plans, and so forth). Importing the total development project into a GIS program greatly improves the opportunity for interaction and the successful implementation of sustainable practices for a development site.

Costs for GIS programs range from $500 to $25,000 or more. The cost depends on the add-on modules, desired compatibility with other design programs, and the amount of data to be used in the program. Entire city information systems, across departments and with public access sections, are operated through GIS programs.

MANAGEMENT TOOLS

Computer-based management programs can better manage and budget maintenance. The recommended maintenance practices, equipment inventory, staffing, and budgets can be included to allow for a holistic management of the maintenance department. Management programs range from $1,000 to $15,000 or more, depending on the modules included and the depth of the database to include everything from personnel to tools to vehicles to work plans to financial records keeping.

REGULATORY AND LEGAL TOOLS

Regulations are required to move sustainable landscape principles into sustainable development and property maintenance practices. Minimum Landscape Standards, one code section or regulation enacted by municipalities and counties, require better design and maintenance of the natural environment. Other examples of progressive regulations include:

1. Standards of practice for choosing sustainable plant species
2. Better spacing of individual plants to achieve overstory and understory in landscapes
3. Minimum plant quality standards to improve the health and structural integrity of the nursery stock used
4. Installation practices that follow current best management practices (BMPs) for better plant health
5. Ongoing maintenance practices that meet current knowledge of integrated pest management, pruning practices, and water management

Other regulations contain incentives to attract more sustainable design choices and help increase their acceptance. Incentives include the reduction of the overall green space requirements, allowances for greater choice of plant species, and the reduction of mitigation requirements for plants removed. Violations of these codes include fines and requirements for replacing landscapes, increasing landscapes, or restoration maintenance to bring landscapes back to health. The fines are usually placed in a trust fund (at least partially) to be used for funding public property sustainable landscape improvements and restoration projects.

Examples of regulations found on the Internet under Minimum Landscape Codes, or Landscape Codes, or Tree Protection Codes can be found through websites for the City of Miami, Florida; Broward County, Florida; and Albemarle County, Virginia. Upgrading or writing new codes involves staff time, outside consulting experts, public hearings, and board or commission votes. Cost estimates for new codes range from $50,000 to $300,000, depending on the complexity of the regulatory process and the length of the timeline from initial meetings through final approval. Regulatory changes can take multiple years to complete in most jurisdictions.

COMMUNICATION TOOLS

On-the-ground examples represent the best sustainable landscape communication tool. Slide shows, discussions, and brochures provide informational sources, but real-life examples, especially those in community focal points, best motivate others to proceed with their own improvements, and demonstrate the leadership and investment in sustainable landscapes on public and private properties. Because we

Figure 8-3
The form, type, and scale of sustainable landscape should be responsive to the surrounding urban context. *Produced and copyrighted by Earth Advisors, Inc. ©2010.*

live and/or spend time in shared environments, we need to act, not just discuss, the development of green spaces.

The charrette, a communication process for developing and completing a sustainable community or sustainable landscape design and plan elements, integrates the input of design professionals with community stakeholders. Through the generation and testing of ideas and issues from each discipline and diverse, interested parties, the best outcomes will emerge and gain the buy-in of all parties.

Prepare the Place

Preparing the place begins with the evaluation of the current site or property conditions at the start of a design process. Essential site data to obtain and use include: elevations, water conditions, soil types, existing vegetation inventory with health conditions, and the new site plan for a property. Since much of this information is also required for engineering purposes, obtaining and sharing it early is most economical. Costs for obtaining this information will vary depending on the complexity of the existing property, ease of access, and requirements for inventory and mapping work.

We recommend gathering an inventory that describes the types of plants, size, and health condition, desirability for preservation or removal, and each location. The required reports should include:

- Tree Surveys
- Wildlife Surveys
- Elevation Plans

- Drainage Plans
- Vegetation Management Plans
- Conservation Easements
- Annual Landscape Maintenance Plans
- Monitoring Reports

Costs for the inventory and mapping for the property are within the same $500 per acre to $20,000 per acre or more for intensely vegetated or environmentally disturbed properties.

The Environmental Site Assessment (ESA) for development sites, requested for new development and financing, generally focuses on the observed existence of any pollution or site contamination. However, the ESA should be expanded to include an assessment of the natural environmental conditions: soils, vegetation, water, and wildlife. An ESA that includes these additional environmental conditions can provide the basis for determining the best parts of the property for locating the water detention areas, wetlands vegetation for water cleansing, and uplands vegetation. The design will be more sustainable when it is based on the total natural environment; not just the development design parameters.

Agencies and municipalities should require that any ESA done for site development include natural environmental elements. This provides a better starting point and will improve the chances for preserving beneficial habitats and will direct development toward the less valuable property sections. One measure of success requires calculating the degree of improvement to the predevelopment wildlife use, water flows, and water quality.

Figure 8-4

Including all the uses and all the sections of a property in the site plans improves understanding of the elements and their relationships for better decisions. *Produced and copyrighted by Earth Advisors, Inc. ©2010.*

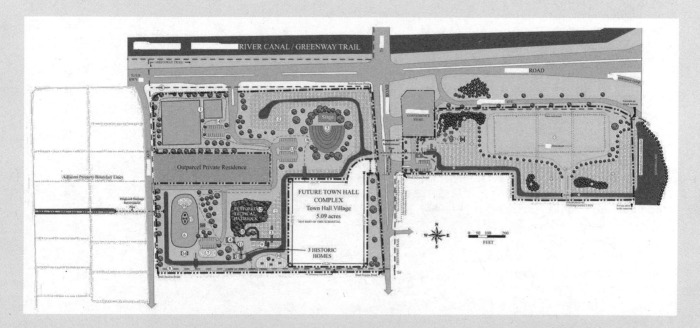

Opportunities and Constraints

The effort to protect and develop or improve the natural environment and landscapes is most constrained by conventional jurisdictional regulations and comprehensive plans. Budgets for development projects, especially the specific percentage dedicated to the natural environment, currently in the range of 0.5 to 2 percent in many community-scale projects, are inadequate. Both constraints stem in part from 60 years of developing single-use, conventional suburbia that consumes land and paves over natural environments for commercial arterials, housing pods, shopping centers, and office parks.

The best opportunities for inculcating the value of sustainable, natural environments are tangible examples. Immersing people in these places allows them to understand their *necessity* in enhancing community health and quality of life, and helps gain support for better natural environments. Sustainable landscapes become part of the required infrastructure when citizens, jurisdictional staffs, and politicians appreciate their value in providing stormwater detention and cleansing, graywater reuse, air pollution filtration, and shading hardscapes and buildings.

Prepare the People

Natural environments and sustainable landscapes are often subject to the dictates of politicians and lobbyists who decide and influence the fate of properties in their jurisdiction. Citizens will gain or lose the quality of their natural environments to the extent that they treasure or ignore these assets, and act upon those values. Though public interest in landscapes remains high in most communities, educational programs, sustainable landscape projects, and field trips to showcase best practices all help maintain support and increase awareness and encourage citizens to improve their properties. From purely volunteer efforts to professional programs and tours of sustainable landscapes, first-hand examples represent a faster and more lasting way to gain supporters for good planning and practitioners for their implementation.

Many regional and local environmental fairs, symposiums on landscape issues, botanical gardens, and community events provide local leadership oppor-

Figure 8-5
A commercial site, developed as a model sustainable landscape to reduce costs of ownership and provide habitat values. *Produced and copyrighted by Earth Advisors, Inc. ©2010.*

Figure 8-6
This swale area demonstrates water balancing including reuse and biotreatment. It is providing landscape irrigation, wildlife habitat, and community values. *Produced and copyrighted by Earth Advisors, Inc. ©2010.*

tunities and venues for setting up exhibits to solicit input and ideas for improving natural environments. These provide places and times to obtain survey information of public interest in natural environments. Educational programs offer the chance to recommend new policies and priorities for natural environments and obtain feedback on sustainability efforts

Set Goals and Objectives

Setting goals and objectives for the natural sections or landscaped sections of properties begins with the identification of nonhuman biological communities native to that region, city, or climate zones. The initial environmental assessment provided in the Place Preparation step included the soil types, elevations, water bodies, plant communities, and wildlife, with recommendations for their preservation in the proposed plan. Based on these site and environmental conditions and recommendations, goals and objectives can be developed, refined, and codified. The long-term goals and interim objectives should articulate the desired general and specific outcomes, including a plan that will deliver the highest environmental benefits to the development and to a community.

Since numerous past and current development standards negatively affect water quality and quantity, as the limiting factor for human development, we recommend setting rigorous goals and measurable objectives for water use, reuse, and release. For example, communities should strive to release water in natural areas and landscapes instead of discharging into the rivers, lakes, and oceans.

Figure 8-7
Sustainable landscapes can be highly aesthetic, have high-end visual impacts, and still reduce costs of ownership for properties. *Produced and copyrighted by Earth Advisors, Inc.* ©2010.

Since the goal of comprehensive sustainability requires establishing planning and development objectives for both constructed and natural areas, requirements for greenways and blueways, for example, allow human and wildlife mobility. Accurate maps and databases help set quantifiable performance measures for inter- and intraconnectivity, for sufficiency of vegetation and adequacy of waterways.

Develop the Strategic Plan

A strategic plan begins with the development of a spatial framework for the protection and enhancement of the natural environment. This effort requires coordination with and accommodation of the existing and proposed development to make a plan that balances both. However, protecting the natural environment, ensuring that irreplaceable resources are neither damaged nor destroyed, requires a set of strategic planning guidelines, principles, policies, and/or standards for the protection and enhancement of the natural environment:

1. Sustain and enhance biodiversity, from wildlife and plant habitats to domesticated species.

2. Protect the nonrenewable resources, from lakes, rivers, and aquifers to natural habitats and wildlife corridors, and distinctive and attractive landscape features.

3. Promote best planning and management practices that result in the highest stewardship of land, woodland, water, and wetland resources, as well as distinctive natural heritage resources, and need to conserve biodiversity.

4. Protect and manage areas set aside or otherwise designated for scientific and conservational importance.

5. Identify areas that help protect environmental assets within or adjoining settlements, such as distinctive landscape views, settings, landscape buffers, and prominent ridge lines.

6. Encourage sustainable patterns of development that place a strong emphasis on the sensible use of resources and care for the whole environment—built and natural.

The USDA Forest Research Stations publish urban forest values that provide strategies for improving the natural environment and gaining public investment. Their research results quantify the qualitative benefits from sustainable and healthy landscapes. The National Arbor Day Foundation, International Society of Arboriculture, Society of American Foresters, American Society of Landscape Architects, and state departments of environmental protection or environmental management can all provide information and research results for the benefit of the natural environment—and many are free.

Develop the Action Plan

Transforming a strategic plan into a set of actions requires the support of decision-makers and funding sources, after gaining citizen interest and involvement. These actions can include:

1. The use of the transfer of development rights, or TDR, to encourage the voluntary redirection of growth away from natural areas and other environmental assets that the community wants to save and toward areas that a community wants to grow

2. State, regional, and local policies the enable the goals and objectives by codifying the implementing regulations and ordinances

3. Regulatory standards that mandate rather than merely encourage the protection and enhancement of the natural environment while permitting the rational development of compact, walkable, and diverse human habitats

4. Developing and adopting regulating plans or replanning regions and communities to clearly define the boundaries between existing and proposed urbanization, and areas desired or designated as permanent natural environments. This can be accomplished in part by replacing a conventional use-based land development system with a form-based code.

5. Policies and standards created or rewritten to regulate utility systems, such as water and energy, to minimize the depletion of renewable resources and maximize the long-term sustainability of those resources

6. Best practices that separate or integrate, as appropriate, sustainable agriculture and other land-intensive industries

7. Educational venues that describe the necessary balance between natural and built environments, their multiple roles and values to the entire ecology

The action plan should identify the specific tasks, timelines, and resources necessary for its implementation. It will activate the community's vision by enabling the desired outcomes appropriate to the people and place, including the protection of natural landscapes.

Implement the Action Plan

For successful implementation, action plans require the right people, both short- and long-term projects, sufficient funding, adequate time, and plenty of energy.

1. People and projects: Gather green industry professionals and businesses as volunteers in changing conventional residential and public landscapes into sustainable spaces. Such projects gain media attention, community leadership attention, and demonstrate commitment from the business community for sustainable community efforts. A public landscape project specified to meet the sustainable landscape principles provides a good and quick start-up project.

2. A college, cooperative extension office, and private nonprofit organizations can help launch and continue sustainable landscape endeavors.

3. Government agencies and officials can provide the needed information and energy to motivate community politicians to activate sustainable community policies and programs.

4. Identify good locations for pilot or model projects, submit this to the community leadership, and continue to push for the launch of worthy projects.

5. Advocate for a revision to the jurisdictional zoning or landscape codes to meet sustainable landscape principles.

6. Address the more long-term actions that require sustained attention as you begin to build momentum with on-the-ground examples of sustainable landscapes.

Figure 8-8
Demonstration sustainable landscapes are best done in public areas where people can see and learn about them for their own properties. *Produced and copyrighted by Earth Advisors, Inc. ©2010.*

Monitor and Evaluation

The efficacy of sustainable landscapes should be evaluated quantitatively and quantitatively. Assess changes in public attitudes toward the value of green spaces, frequency of use, demand for upgrades or additional space, and improvements in air, water, and soil quality. Measuring methods include public surveys, inspections of the green spaces, and measuring environmental indicators according to established, jurisdictional monitoring and reporting standards, and against timelines, budgets, and established goals for the projects. Monitoring techniques can include drive-by or walk-through inspections by maintenance supervisors, staff biologists, staff arborists, or other natural science professionals, and trained volunteers. Monitoring operations should employ checklists of landscape and site elements with both qualitative and quantitative measurements for each. Include monitoring costs in normal budgets for property management and property maintenance or include special staff or consultants. Reasonable budgets range from $5,000 to $50,000.

SUSTAINABLE LANDSCAPING: BUILDING GREEN ASSETS

Katie O'Reilly Rogers, ASLA
The Offices of Katie O'Reilly Rogers, Inc.

INTERVENTION TYPE: BEST PRACTICE

Description

Sustainable landscapes encompass a holistic approach to design, construction, and maintenance of the built environment, and respond to local conditions with the following principles:

- Design a low requirement for supplemental irrigation
- Use efficient and appropriate irrigation systems
- Minimize turf and locate turf only in usable areas
- Design low greenwaste-producing designs
- Minimize pruning requirements
- Recover yard trimmings for compost and mulch
- Mulch deeply with organic mulch for water conservation, weed abatement, and to nurture healthy soils
- Use integrated pest management to minimize chemical use
- Incorporate stormwater cleansing practices into the garden
- Consider rainwater harvesting
- Use permeable paving to the greatest extent possible
- Consider the use of edible plants

SUPPORT GOALS AND OBJECTIVES

A well-designed and thought-out landscape costs less to maintain, protects the local environment, and provides aesthetic appeal. These spaces:

- Absorb CO_2 and air pollution contaminants, functioning as carbon sinks or sequestration
- Decrease stormwater runoff and detain, retain, filter, recycle, and/or infiltrate stormwater

Figure 8-9
Native and Mediterranean plants complement a local sandstone cobble at the edge of a permeable gravel pathway. *Katie O'Reily Rogers*

- Provide a balancing environment for communities by providing nature in proximity to urbanism
- Protect or enhance the habitat for flora and fauna

PERFORMANCE CHARACTERISTICS AND BEST PRACTICES

- Use appropriate plant material, native or native-in-character, to ensure the best results in a sustainable landscape. In most parts of California, drought tolerance is a major factor in plant selection; however, in the Pacific Northwest, drought tolerance (or moisture intolerance) would be a negative.
- Condition the soil with organic amendments such as compost or mulch. Mycorrhizal fungi, the foundation of ecosystem function, can be beneficial in more sterile soil to improve soil structure, increase root systems, and increase plant survivability. In healthy landscapes, rainwater percolates through soil that is rich in organic matter and living organisms. Living soils absorb and retain water while filtering out pollutants.
- Install progressive, efficient irrigation systems to avoid water waste and excessive soil moisture problems. The use of drip irrigation, and the use of low-volume spray or rotor heads can be connected to rain shut-off devices and soil moisture sensors.
- Use natural color and textured paving materials, permeable to the greatest extent feasible. Permeable paving allows stormwater to infiltrate, and helps keep runoff on-site and in the garden. The use of local materials, such as stone pavers or decomposed granite, can reduce the carbon load of hauling these heavy materials long distances.
- Employ progressive maintenance practices. However, gardeners and maintenance personnel are typically taught to use the quickest and least expensive practices, and are often reluctant to change from the chemical tried and true.

POTENTIAL SYNERGISM

The opportunities for landscape synergy include the use of appropriate plant material, efficient irrigation systems, permeable paving/stormwater management, and progressive maintenance practices. Water quality studies can help pinpoint pollutants, some of which may be treated on a given project site. Anticipated on-site source pollutants, such as runoff from streets and parking lots, can be treated using landscape BMPs.

IMPLEMENTATION TIME

The process of developing base plan, site inventory and analysis, construction documents, and the implementation of a sustainable landscaping may require more time and care because of the need to create a relatively self-sufficient ecology. However, the time and expense required for maintenance should be less.

Figure 8-10
Durable stone steps hewn from local sandstone boulders work nicely with native Mediterranean plantings. *Katie O'Reily Rogers*

BENEFITS

Sustainable landscapes remedy most of the environmental problems of so many contemporary landscapes. These include:

- Reduce or eliminate common installation and maintenance practices that rely on chemical fertilizers, herbicides, pesticides, and fossil fuel requiring landscape tools such as soil tillers, leaf blowers, and mowers.

- Protect and attract beneficial insects typically killed through the use of pesticides. Reduce or eliminate herbicides usually used to control or destroy weedy plants.

- Protect and/or add native plants that, when removed or absent, provide more ground space for tenacious weedy invasives to recover.

- Reduce or eliminate the use of mechanical gardening tools that create noise and air pollution, and further remove us from our natural environment.

DRAWBACKS/CONSTRAINTS

- Insufficient education of designers, contractors, and maintenance personnel in the creation of sustainable spaces

- Educating the general public about the benefits of a well-designed sustainable garden, i.e., a native meadow in lieu of a standard mown lawn, can be challenging. Traditional and European garden standards are rarely the best design choice when attempting a sustainable landscape, so public expectations for ornamental solutions must be tempered early and with appropriate alternatives.

- Although LEED is a useful tool for building design, the site and landscape rating components are not yet developed to the point where they have a meaningful impact on sustainable site or landscape design.

First Costs

Many jurisdictions have created "Green Gardener" programs and certifications for designers and maintenance personnel offered at low or no cost to the participant. Local community colleges and adult education programs frequently offer similar classes for the home gardener.

- $100 to $200 per acre budget provides a base value for evaluation of conditions
- $0.25 to $1.00 per square foot of landscape area for the design for new sites
- $2 to $5 per square foot of landscape area for site preparation, procurement of materials, and installation
- Reduce costs by improving existing natural environments or landscape areas, instead of installing a new landscape into bare soil

LifeCycle Costs

The best measurement of sustainable practices in the garden is a lower cost of maintenance, the sounds of wildlife and birds, and the easy, natural beauty of the place. Budgetary benefits include no/low cost of chemical treatments relative to organic or holistic approaches, and no/low time/labor costs for motorized maintenance in lieu of sweeping, tilling, or using push mowers.

Figure 8-11
Lawns can be limited to areas of active recreation, and the area can cleanse stormwater. *Katie O'Reily Rogers*

ESTIMATED QUANTITATIVE PERFORMANCE

The design and subsequent assessment of a sustainable landscape requires current and accurate data regarding soils, hydrology, the rain cycle, climate/winds, and other environmental factors. Accurate existing topography in the form of a current survey offers critical information in terms of grading and drainage, and the potential for solar orientation and wind attenuation.

IMPLEMENTATION SUPPORTS AND CONSTRAINTS

To move forward with sustainable landscapes as a common reality, local staff and decision-makers need to embrace holistic landscape practices as part of local building codes. Landscape designers and landscape architects need to think in terms of environmental protection and progressive stormwater management as an integral part of design solutions. Landscape contractors and installers need to be educated about the critical role they play in creating environmentally sound gardens. Maintenance personnel need to take a leading role in creating and sustaining environmentally superior landscapes.

INFORMATIONAL SOURCES

Local jurisdictions typically have landscape guidelines for both residential and project-scale proposals. These guidelines address critical issues on a regional basis: water consumption, irrigation practices, energy efficiency in the garden, solar shading and cooling through the use of trees, stormwater BMPs and a site design to incorporate them, greenwaste requirements, and so on.

Local colleges, adult education, or local botanic gardens offer green gardener classes and certificates that can be used for marketing purposes in more progressive-minded neighborhoods and communities. The green gardener principles are aligned with local planning and development requirements; lists of those who have passed the courses are given to developers and landowners.

REPORTS AND STUDIES

The University of California Cooperative Extension, California Department of Water Resources has developed WUCOLS (Water Use Classification of Landscape Species). WUCOLS offers a clear understanding of the potential evapotranspiration rates for various plant communities, helping to shape an appropriate plant palette for the site. This guide to estimating irrigation needs of landscape plantings in California uses a Landscape Coefficient Method to calculate supplemental irrigation needs of various plants. Selecting species with minimal calculated supplemental irrigation requirements will create a regionally appropriate plant palette. Other states and jurisdictions have developed similar tools on a regional basis.

PLANT *SF

Jane Martin, AIA
Shift Design Studio

INTERVENTION TYPE: PROGRAM, BEST PRACTICE

Description

The acronym "Plant*SF" stands for: Permeable Landscape as Neighborhood Treasure in San Francisco. Its mission combines sustainability of stormwater diversion with beautification of neighborhood gardens to reduce the volume of rain entering the City's combined sewer system by converting excess areas of pavement to neighborhood gardens. When strategically placed, these modest localized efforts can add up to considerable contribution, reducing the number of overflows of contaminated water into receiving waterways. This is most urgent with combined sewer systems; however, there are environmental benefits for separated systems as well, including natural filtration and replenishing aquifers.

Founded in 2004, Plant*SF pioneered sidewalk landscaping by initiating a permit process with the City and has since worked to reform public space policy in support of citywide de-paving of excess surfaces, especially on public land. The organization designs and implements pilot projects to challenge notions of "dry" gardens, using native and drought-tolerant species leading the way for creativity in public space gardening. Its website provides a supporting "How-To" guide.

In its first three years, the work of Plant*SF has resulted in more than 700 locations being converted from excess pavement into sidewalk gardens, in every district of the City, sparking grassroots neighborhood investment and bringing back nature to the doorstep.

Plant*SF is a "Parks Partner" of the nonprofit San Francisco Parks Trust.

SUPPORT GOALS AND OBJECTIVES
The major goal of the project is to reduce a significant volume of stormwater runoff through Low Impact Development (LID) while providing many benefits of community-oriented diversified landscaping.

PERFORMANCE CHARACTERISTICS
The conversion of every square foot of impervious surface to permeable landscaping is an immediate reduction to overall runoff volume. Locating landscaping on the curb side of the sidewalk captures water shedding from the overall

▶ Figure 8-12
BEFORE: The existing condition of San Francisco city sidewalks included street trees in small basins and wide expanses of excess concrete. *Photo © Jane Martin; Courtesy Plant*SF*

▶▶ Figure 8-13
AFTER: Flowering native and climate-adapted plants grace both sides of an improved walkway that meets permitting guidelines. *Photo © Jane Martin; Courtesy Plant*SF*

area. Further efficiencies are gained with strategic placement in regard to topography and soil type. The San Francisco Public Utilities Commission is currently funding demonstration projects and integrating LID strategies into the Clean Water Master Plan for systemic benefit.

POTENTIAL SYNERGISM
The project works alone or in tandem with other LID approaches and complements a wide array of physical and social enhancements to every street type. These range from traffic calming, neighborhood group building, and crime deterrence, to recreation for youth and seniors, support for local species, and encouraging small businesses.

IMPLEMENTATION TIME
While times for internal decision-making, permitting, and securing funding are highly variable, with these in place, actual project development and implementation are achievable within a matter of days. Ideally, this process culminates during appropriate seasons for planting to conserve water.

BENEFITS
• Works in tandem with street trees
• Appropriate for locations where trees are not possible

- Beautifies the neighborhood
- Reduces sewer backups and combined sewer overflows
- Deters crime
- Creates habitat
- Increases property values
- Encourages walking
- Calms traffic
- Recharges aquifer
- Makes a place to garden
- Reduces sidewalk parking
- Creates community interactions
- Publicly available to economically, socially, and age-diverse demographic
- Conserves water

DRAWBACKS
- Maintenance depends on and varies with property owner involvement
- Not yet an integral part of the formal citywide sewer system plan
- Is an option rather than an expectation
- Ad-hoc implementation limits effectiveness and cost efficiency

FIRST COST
Initial cost is equal to replacement of concrete, an important consideration for sidewalks already in disrepair. Assuming volunteer planting and prudent plant choices, approximately half of initial cost is for professional concrete removal. Costs vary depending on number, species, and size of plants. In San Francisco it can be achieved for $10 per square foot. Professional plant installation increases price but is generally not required. Permit can be achieved without professional design or documentation. San Francisco offers price break for multiple neighboring properties to promote economies of scale.

LIFECYCLE COSTS
Maintenance is generally done by property owner at negligible cost. ROI is achieved in one cycle of repair/replacement of existing concrete. Perennial, self-propagating, and edible plants are most economical and can result in net benefit.

ESTIMATED QUANTITATIVE PERFORMANCE
Accurate quantification of benefits depends on: soil type, topography, rainfall rate, up-slope catchment area, and canopy coverage.

IMPLEMENTATION SUPPORTS AND CONSTRAINTS

Behind-the-scenes advocacy was focused on identifying opportunities and reducing obstacles. Outreach and education are focused on a simple message of "sustainability plus beautification" to capture the more complex interworking of numerous aspects. Providing clarity in the permit process and accessible physical pilot projects enable citizens to visualize the final product and investigate how it may be adapted for their location.

INFORMATIONAL SOURCES

- www.PlantSF.org
- www.SFwater.org
- www.lid-stormwater.net/
- www.coastal.ca.gov/nps/lid_workshops.html
- http://cfpub.epa.gov/npdes/home.cfm?program_id=298
- www.lowimpactdevelopment.org/

REPORTS AND STUDIES

- www.nrdc.org/water/lid/
- http://epa.gov/owow/nps/lid/costs07/
- www.thompson.com/public/newsbrief.jsp?cat=ENVIRONMENT&id=1953
- www.toolbase.org/Technology-Inventory/Sitework/low-impact-development

DIVERSIFIED CARBON SEQUESTRATION, CELLULOSIC BIOFUELS, AND OILSEED BIODIESEL PROGRAMS

Daniel Dunigan and Stephen Coyle
Town-Green

INTERVENTION TYPE: PROGRAM

Description

The Diversified Agricultural Carbon Sequestration (DACS), Cellulosic Biofuels, and Oilseed Biodiesel[1] (CBOB) programs are administered by municipalities, counties, townships, state, or other government agencies, and/or by private industry for the purpose of sequestering carbon and/or for producing biofuel (e.g., ethanol) or biodiesel production on public or private land. The programs enhance the value of marginal pasture and/or low-value cropland through the cultivation and maintenance of:

- Urban, suburban, and rural tree farms and/or productive fruit and nut orchards that sequester carbon for the natural life of the planting
- Cellulosic biofuel farming of dedicated energy wood, grasses, or nonfood plants such as switchgrass that meet or exceed the CSBP Provisional Standards of the Council on Sustainable Biomass Production.
- Oilseed farming of dedicated nonfood plants such as Camelina sativa for the production of biodiesel, or grown in conjunction with food crops.
- Both cellulosic biofuels and biodiesel crops require processing to extract the ethanol, a more energy-intensive process, and biodiesel.

Carbon sequestration is a geoengineering technique for the long-term storage of carbon dioxide or other forms of carbon. Carbon dioxide is usually captured from the atmosphere through biological, chemical, or physical processes.

Cellulosic biofuel is an energy fuel, primarily ethanol, produced from wood, grasses, or the nonedible parts of plants.

Biodiesel is a renewable fuel for diesel engines derived from natural plant oils, and from fats and oils from food processing and food waste, which meet the specifications of ASTM D 6751.

SUPPORT GOALS AND OBJECTIVES

- Carbon sequestration removes and stores CO_2e in trees and other types of plants and soils.

Figure 8-14
Planting orchards provides additional benefit to the landowner and to the environment. *Steve Coyle*

- Cellulosic biofuels and biodiesel provide a replacement for or supplement to fossil fuels that reduce their carbon content and demand.

Each transaction benefits the landowner/farmer as follows:

- DACS's economic value is based on the monetized carbon market value of the carbon sequestration total in metric tons of CO_2e; and

- CBOB economic value is based on the market value of the biofuel, or biodiesel crop yields that will rise with the cost of petroleum fuels.

- Additional benefits derived from sequestration and/or biofuel crops include potential increases in the ecological value of the land, and enhanced protection from development.

Performance Characteristics

The DACS consists of an agreement between the jurisdiction and, if necessary, an independent management entity that represents the interests of the jurisdiction, and individual private or public property owners. Each agreement requires that the landowner/farmer develop and maintain sequestration on the designated parcel(s) approved by the jurisdiction for, typically, a minimum of 99 years.

The CBOB requires conventional market transactions between growers and ethanol and biodiesel producers based on supply and demand. Camelina Sativa and similar biodiesel crops that thrive on marginal farm land may be grown with wheat and other food crops on prime soils.

POTENTIAL SYNERGISM

Both programs result in the development and sustainment of multifunction, biologically diverse greenbelts, croplands, orchards, and forests surrounding or proximate to cities, and incentivize the reclamation, enhancement, and protection of natural and cultivated lands. Besides sequestration, plants tend to reduce the albedo effect or reflect sunlight.

IMPLEMENTATION

The process requires quantification and qualification of lands both suitable and available for sequestration or crop cultivation; each landowner's participation, ability, and commitment to fulfill the program or production agreements; and the jurisdiction or business organization's capacity and willingness to set up, administer, and manage the sequestration program and/or biofuel/biodiesel business.

For sequestration, each agreement should include verification and reporting protocols for periodically assessing the health and growth of each sequestration site, and for determining current sequestration values.

BENEFITS

- Trees and other plants "sequester" carbon by removing it from the atmosphere and storing it in their fibrous tissue and in the soil. Planting or replanting of trees on marginal crop and pasturelands transfers CO_2 from the atmosphere to new biomass.
- Sustainably farmed biofuel and biodiesel crops, such as native perennial grasses capable of producing high yields, and crops such as Camelina, can be planted and sustainably managed on marginal or retired land without irrigation or chemical fertilizers or pesticides.

DRAWBACKS

- Carbon sequestration requires the maintenance of the plantings—trees, shrubs, grasslands—through their natural life, lest they prematurely release their stored carbon.
- Cellulosic biofuels and biodiesel crops should only be extracted from nonfood sources that meet or exceed the CSBP Provisional Standards of the Council on Sustainable Biomass Production.

FIRST COST

- Order of magnitude cost of $250 to $300 per tree for roughly 35 to 40 trees per acre.
- Cellulosic biofuels and biodiesel planting and harvest costs vary with the crop types, soil and climate conditions, and market supply and demand.

Lifecycle Costs

- Order of magnitude cost: $15 to $40 in maintenance per tree per year.
- Cellulosic biofuels: The Department of Energy hopes to reduce the cost of switchgrass CB to $1.07 per gallon by 2012. This compares to the current cost of $1.20 to $1.50 per gallon for ethanol from corn and the current retail price of about $3 per gallon for regular gasoline which is subsidized and taxed.
- Biodiesel from crops: Current production costs, about $0000 per gallon; current price at the pump, $1.50 to $1.60/gallon, and the current retail price of about $3 per gallon for diesel which is subsidized and taxed.

Estimated Quantitative Performance

Depending on species, condition, and location, carbon sequestration, based on metric tons per acre per year unit is approximately:[2]

- Vineyard/orchard: .59 to 1.68* per acre
- Oak woodlands: 3.71* per acre
- Coniferous forest: 8.89* per acre
- Grasslands and shrubs: .389 per acre
- No-Till Cropland: .223 per acre
- Urban: calculated at .007 per tree per acre.

Figure 8-15
Cellulosic biofuels can be grown in closer proximity to development than the typical crops that require pesticides. *Daniel Dunigan*

Cellulosic biofuels reduce CO_2e by up to 85 percent over reformulated gasoline; biodiesel, up 99 percent if unblended. The EPA finalized new regulations for the National Renewable Fuel Standard Program for 2010 and beyond on February 3, 2010. The Renewable Fuel Standard program will increase the required volumes of renewable fuel to 36 billion gallons by 2022.

IMPLEMENTATION SUPPORTS AND CONSTRAINTS

Both oilseeds and native perennial grasses are capable of producing high biodiesel and respectively, ethanol yields, and both can be planted and sustainably managed on marginal land, without irrigation and fertilizer.

INFORMATIONAL SOURCES

- The Department of Energy: Fossil Energy: DOE's Carbon Sequestration Research Program helps develop affordable and safe ways to capture and permanently dispose of carbon gases from coal and other sources. http://fossil.energy.gov/sequestration/

- The Carbon Sequestration Leadership Forum (CSLF) is a ministerial-level international climate change initiative that is focused on the development of improved cost-effective technologies for the separation and capture of carbon dioxide for its transport and long-term safe storage. www.cslforum.org/

- The Council on Sustainable Biomass Production is a multi-stakeholder organization established in 2007 to develop comprehensive voluntary sustainability standards for the production of biomass and its conversion to bioenergy. www.csbp.org/

- The National Biodiesel Board (NBB) is the national trade association representing the biodiesel industry in the United States. Biodiesel is a domestic, renewable fuel for diesel engines derived from natural oils like soybean oil, and which meets the specifications of ASTM D 6751. www.biodiesel.org/

REPORTS AND STUDIES

- Co_2 Tree Capture: How much carbon dioxide do trees really capture? (April 19, 2007) www.abc.net.au/catalyst/stories/s1901661.htm

- Carbon Sequestration in Dryland Soils, The Food and Agriculture Organization of the United Nations, Rome, 2004 www.fao.org/docrep/007/y5738e/y5738e00.htm

- The Council on Sustainable Biomass Production's Draft Standard: www.csbp.org/?q=node/215

- The National Biodiesel Board (NBB): Biodiesel Basics www.biodiesel.org/resources/biodiesel_basics/

Chapter 9
Food Production/Agriculture

Sustainable Food Systems

Lynn Peemoeller
Consultant, Food Systems Planning

The Conventional Food System Conundrum

Despite significant progress in the conventional food system over the last half-century to become a model of streamlined economic elegance, many have begun to question its long-term sustainability. This is especially true in light of climate change, loss of arable land, shifting population and demographic concentrations, food safety, insecure global markets, and reliance on non-renewable resources. While we blithely accept abundance today, the question of how will we feed ourselves in the future still starkly remains.

As consumers in the conventional food system, we navigate through a false reality where food prices do not reflect the entire cost of production. In the developed world, we are taught that food should be cheap and abundant. For better or worse, the entire conventional food system has been built around this premise. However, like with most cheap things, they do not come without a cost.

Figure 9-1
The annual Chicago Food Policy Advisory Council Summit is an opportunity for community-based participation in food systems planning.
Lynn Peemoeller

Today, the world population is approaching 7 billion people. Despite the fact that food is not distributed equally throughout the world, feeding that many people creates a huge stress on the environment. Meat production alone is one of the biggest environmental problems from the local level to the global level. The United Nations produced a report called *Livestock's Long Shadow* (2006),[1] which stated "the livestock sector is one of the top two or three most significant contributors to the most serious environmental problems, at every scale from local to global. The findings of this report suggest that it should be a major policy focus when dealing with problems of land degradation, climate change and air pollution, water shortage and water pollution, and loss of biodiversity."

Few people realize that eating is an environmental act. Every choice we make as consumers has an effect on the food system. If we want to continue to feed ourselves, and the world, we have no choice but to try to look our food system straight in the eyes and figure out what we can do to put it on a path toward sustainability. This is true for individuals and planners alike.

A Sustainable Food Production Vision

It is unlikely that any place will be able to feed itself 100 percent through local resources in the near or distant future. What is needed is an approach that takes into account the strengths and opportunities of the community and regional role in the global food system and develop priorities and recommendations in order to support the growth and development of a more robust and localized system.

A sustainable food system will recognize the environment, the economy, social, cultural systems, and social justice conditions under which food is produced, prepared, and consumed. A food system will only be sustainable as long as it can maintain its ability to feed people without depleting natural resources. In order to move toward this, strategies in the following areas need to be developed to help steer development:

- Infrastructure investment in new and old systems
- Education at all levels from elementary through workforce training
- Localized investment and asset development in regional economies
- Renewable resources in agriculture
- Technology for increased productivity
- Land protection mechanisms
- Community owned or "bottom-up" solutions
- Indicators for progress

Conventional and Sustainable Economic Models

Economics are a major driving force in the food system. They set the stage for the entire industry that we rely on to keep us fed. Because of the globalized food system and supply chains, the economics of the food system are complex. The smallest gap between farm and fork represents an elegant system that can be sustainable on a localized level. An example of this may be a freshly harvested salad from a backyard garden or a subscription to a community supported agriculture program (CSA) —a popular model where the consumer invests in a farm share at the beginning of the season and receives weekly boxes of produce straight from the farm.

Local food has gained a following in recent years. In fact, *locavore*, defined as one who attempts to eat only foods grown locally, was the 2007 Oxford dictionary word of the year. Recent advocacy around food systems and healthy eating has also led to increased awareness of local food issues. This demonstrates a growing movement that is reaching people around the world.

Nonetheless, it is too easy to say that local food is the universal answer to sustainability. We must not fall into the "local trap,"[2] which suggests that local food systems are preferable to systems at larger scales. A sustainable and balanced food system must be diversified in order to keep us fed in the long term. Large and small, global and local, organic and nonorganic systems are part of the sustainable economic model. The contexts in which decisions are made both individually and systemically need to allow for flexibility. There are a range of scales and decisions appropriate for each social and ecologic system in which food is produced and consumed.

Planners have the unique advantage of working with systems that interweave the built environment with social and political systems. This can happen at any scale. Food systems planning requires the involvement and collaboration of multiple stakeholders. The more diverse the participants, the more robust the plan.

Basic principles for a healthy and sustainable food system include the following but are not limited to:

- Develop green technology in food and agriculture systems
- Encourage local and regional food systems
- Develop supportive land use policies
- Encourage green procurement policies
- Create green-collar jobs
- Strive for LEED compliance
- Prioritize energy efficiency
- Mitigate climate change

One desired outcome of food systems planning is "food security" or the idea that all residents should have access to healthful, affordable, and culturally appropriate foods. A food-secure community is a resilient community.

▼ **Figure 9-2**
Mobile Electronic Benefit Transfer (EBT) machines enable USDA Supplemental Nutrition Assistance Program (SNAP) benefits to be redeemed at farmers' markets. *Lynn Peemoeller*

▼▼ **Figure 9-3**
Farmers' markets are a popular way for people to get to know where their food comes from and to support local farmers. *Lynn Peemoeller*

Prepare the Team

As a component of urban planning and design, food systems are becoming recognized as part of plans that integrate sustainability, quality of life, and public health. Several municipalities are doing this by incorporating food systems into the comprehensive planning process, and working in public and private partnerships to develop programs to address food systems issues. While support to integrate the issue is generally high, food systems still remain a low priority for planners.

The American Planning Association asked members to identify barriers to its involvement in promoting access to healthful foods. Lack of resources, trained staff, and support were the top results. This indicates that a good deal of education and training will need to happen to prepare planners to become more active in food systems.

A large amount of funding for our food system has traditionally come from the government. Public policies that support food systems originate in a wide range of government departments at all levels. Federal funding allocations like the Farm Bill and the Child Nutrition and WIC Reauthorization Act are examples of multi-billion-dollar government investments in the food system that trickles down to the local level through programs administered by local agencies. The challenge with federal program funding is that it often comes with a comprehensive set of rules and regulations that are often inflexible. This can make it difficult to make sustainable decisions at the most local level.

For example, the school lunch program by the federal government funds two meals and a snack each day for all public school students. This ensures that even children who are most vulnerable to hunger can get fed a hot meal on a daily basis. However, the different levels of bureaucracy needed to administer this program leaves very little left over for food cost. In most cases, food quality suffers and the ability to purchase local and organic food for the school lunch program is nearly inaccessible. The farm-to-school movement is one example of an effort that advocates for better public policy and helps to leverage private partnerships to find creative solutions to the school lunch problem. This example demonstrates how public and private partnerships are needed to make systems change.

Connecting the dots for professionals offers a big challenge in creating partnerships in food systems. Food policy councils have sprung up as a part of the movement as an effort to convene citizens and government officials for the purpose of providing a comprehensive examination of a state or local food system. This unique, nonpartisan form of civic engagement brings together a diverse array of food system stakeholders to develop food and agriculture policy recommendations.[3]

Food systems work is interdisciplinary; people from many backgrounds have built the field—professionals, from farmers to chefs to moms, have found a voice in this work. Universities today offer courses in food systems from public health, to agro-ecology, to environmental policy. The field of food systems is growing in the discipline of urban planning. The American Planning Association (APA) recently adopted a policy guide on community and regional planning and offers a food systems track at the annual APA conference.

Figure 9-4
American farmland. *Lynn Peemoeller*

Prepare the Tools

Sustainability indicators of the food system are a way to assess, understand, and measure the progress toward our goals. Desired indicators consist of data that are valid, reliable, consistent, available at appropriate scale, accessible, and simple. Because indicators are used to help manage and compare complicated systems, a good data-collection and management agency is essential.

Gathering and organizing data necessitates different approaches depending on the context of the desired outcome. For example, if the goal is sustainability of the food system, indicators can be sought and organized by the principles of sustainability. To generate comparisons of the food system at different scales, data must reflect those scales. If the goal is to achieve a vision or mission statement like "the food system should provide food for all that is good, clean and fair,"[4] then data must be organized under those categories.

One example of a food system indicator is *the number of farms engaged in direct market and value of product sold.* This data is available through the USDA National Agricultural Statistics Service. Direct marketing refers to sales made directly between the farmer and the consumer. This category encompasses most activities that we associate with local food, including farmers' markets, community-supported agriculture businesses, farm-to-restaurant sales, agritourism, U-Pick, and so forth. While we cannot quantify the amount of local food being produced from this data, we can interpolate the amount of farmland in production, which is a useful measure for potential food production.

Other food system indicators include food security, data on land use, water use and water quality, energy use, workforce in agriculture and food manufacturing, public health, and consumer habits and spending.

VISUAL MAPPING TOOLS

Mapping is a powerful tool to help visualize the food system. Multidimensional maps generated by GIS can turn data into a spatial application. Data from indicators go hand-in-hand with mapping and can provide layers of information, including demographics of a community, including food security index values like income, ethnicity, employment, and education.

Maps are often a component of community food assessments (also known as community food security assessments), which help us understand the landscape of localized food systems by illustrating both assets and deficits at the community level. They can include everything from farms producing food, to processors, distributors, retail food outlets, farmers' markets, and institutions like schools and hospitals. They are useful tools to link to specific policy actions.

Maps are also useful for consumers to find local food. A number of interactive websites have emerged from maps of city fruit trees to maps of farmers' markets, U-Pick farms, and other sources that help to identify where local farm products are being sold.

Examples of maps generated in food systems planning follow:

Food security: These maps can include many combinations of information from an inventory of where people get access to food, to the food transportation network, to food security index values. By defining a community or region, it can help to give us information to measure the food security of a population.

Farms by type: This can be useful in a number of ways and is especially helpful to visualize the landscape of food production in relation to population. It is also helpful for determining a foodshed for a region.

Community gardens: The ability to grow food in the urban environment is one strategy for food security. Community gardens in a metropolitan area give us information about urban land use that is potentially available for growing food. Although not all community gardens are used for food production, the number and distribution of community gardens can give us information about where people have access to this resource.

Farmers' markets: Although not all farmers' markets run year-round, they are an important part of the local food chain. The distribution of farmers' markets in a community or region can tell us where local food is being bought and sold.

Urban fruit trees: As urban food production becomes a more integrated form of land use, mapping fruit trees can be a useful resource for the entire community. Urban fruit is another resource of local food that can be sold, shared, and eaten.

REGULATORY OR LEGAL TOOLS

Policy is an effective partner in food systems planning. Several cities use a systemic policy approach

Figure 9-5
A variety of greens at the farmers's market. *Lynn Peemoeller*

to inform and create a framework for food systems within city government. In 2009, San Francisco released an executive directive from the Mayor on "Healthy and Sustainable Food for San Francisco." This charter declared a commitment to increasing the amount of healthy and sustainable food in the City and directed city agencies to take action and formally decreed a food policy council to inform decisions made by city government.

Food policy councils are active throughout the United States and range in scale from state to county to local city. They convene citizens and government officials to study local food systems and develop recommendations and goals for food policy. Food policy councils are sometimes appointed or are open to all, providing opportunities for citizen engagement in food systems development. Some food policy councils employ pilot projects that work closely with government, like the Portland Multnomah Food Policy Council, which operates several programs related to local food planning and policy.

LEED-ND, another useful tool for developing sustainable food systems, has integrated several credits related to building healthy communities that are useful for food systems planning. The "Local Food Production credit" is given to promote community-based and local food production to minimize the environmental impacts from transporting food long distance and increase direct access to foods. This may include everything from implementing a farmers' market to setting aside space for community gardens.

Land use policies can help to support and protect land use for food production, and can encourage the type of development patterns in the built environment. Planners can use their toolbox of traditional planning methods like zoning to help encourage sustainable food systems. For example, zoning can help designate permitted areas where community gardens and commercial urban agriculture are encouraged, including small livestock. Many urban areas have discouraged food production in their local ordinances that today are often permitted under regulatory programs. Zoning can also help with food access by designating priority areas for grocery development in underserved areas.

Public financing, another way to attract healthy food retail in underserved communities, the Food Trust in Philadelphia has led the way in by establishing "Fresh Food Funds" using public funding and public-private partnerships to encourage supermarket development in underserved areas. Illinois recently passed a recommendation to appropriate $10 million in its capital budget for a business financing program that provides grants and loans to local supermarket and grocery store development projects in underserved communities for two to three years.[5]

COMMUNICATION TOOLS

There are many competitive Web-based resources that are closing the gap between consumer and producer. The website www.LocalHarvest.org is a national database and open-source website that helps consumers find farmers' markets, family farms, and other sources of sustainably grown food. Other examples are more regional in scale and range from websites like Food Routes (www.foodroutes.org) which promotes the Buy Fresh, Buy Local program, to Farm Fresh in Rhode Island and the *Eat Well Guide.*

Prepare the Place

The food system relies heavily on land use. Agriculture is the foundational architecture of space from which it is built. It occupies the space around which the built environment of the food system orients itself. Spatially, the food system occupies the entire transect of land from its most wild areas (wild mushroom networks) to the urban core (corner liquor stores). It is impossible to avoid, although it is often hidden. Planners can start to get involved in food systems work by identifying its role in the built environment.

Understanding the role of the built environment in the food system requires an assessment and inventory of existing infrastructure. Defining key infrastructure and its role in the food system is a good starting point. It includes a wide scope from land use assessments, transportation networks, to grain silos, to intermodal storage facilities, food manufacturing plants, grocery retail, and even walking paths to and from stores. The approach can be tailored to fit the needs of the study in terms of geography and scope.

For example, a comprehensive study may require a comprehensive inventory of food-related infrastructure at the regional scale. This may include everything in the food system from production to waste handling. Planners may ask what resources farmers have and need to further the development of postharvest handling, storage, and transportation to local markets.

Existing data sources for food system infrastructure are not uniformly developed. They often exist as both public and private resources. To understand the existing conditions of the place, helpful starting points are land use indexes, transportation network assessments, business and retail indexes, and other tax records. Alternatively, or in addition to, an inventory format, a case study of how food moves through a supply chain spatially, may be an effective way to illustrate the food systems in the built environment.

Supporting Systems

The supporting systems of the food system are less tangible than the built environment. They reflect the diversity of the food system and can range in scale from the global to the local. Operationally they range from corporate, to cooperative, public, social venture, and nonprofit business models. In all cases they require management, promotion, and resource development.

Supporting systems produce the "food product" and get it on grocery shelves as well as social and economic capital for the food system. This may include jobs, funding, programs, services, networks, research, education, and knowledge related to food. Quantifying these support systems is difficult because data is not consistent in every area, and requires a systemic weaving together of pieces of information that currently exist in isolation. When studying these systems in the big-picture context, clear goals and objectives will help clarify and focus the plan.

Comprehensive research requires a good deal of investment in time to identify all supporting systems at play, and organizing them. A community food assessment, a place-based planning strategy that emphasizes a bottom-up approach, focuses on strengthening and making relationships between consumers and the food system. A community food assessment may prioritize food access as a key goal. Although part of a larger context, the supporting systems needed to increase grocery retail, farmers' markets, nutrition assistance programs, and other ways to get food to people become prioritized.

Opportunities and Constraints

While best practices for food systems planning are still under development, some prevailing constraints will remain. For example, extracting the local food system from the global food system is nearly impossible as the two are so closely intertwined. This makes it difficult to extrapolate the ability of a region to feed itself using its own resources. Metrics for these kinds of equations are still being developed.

Defining "local" and "foodshed" are similar challenges in food systems planning. Although the "100-mile diet"[6] has been popularized and widely adopted as a measure for what defines local food, this may not be relevant depending on the community or region being studied. Foodshed refers to *a desired system or desired elements, usually within a defined geographic area, which is an alternative to the existing food system.*[7] Each community or region will need to define its own parameters for a foodshed. Larger regions will have more sophisticated political and geographic boundaries that need to be taken into account.

Data is another constraint on food systems planning. In some cases formalized data sets do not exist for some parts of the food system, such as urban agriculture sites in a city, where local food is available, or the food waste chain. Identifying what data needs to be collected, and the appropriate agency to do so, is one step in the food systems plan.

RESOURCES

Policy Guide on Community and Regional Food Planning. Chicago, IL: American Planning Association, May 2007. Available at www.planning.org/policy/guides/adopted/food.htm.

Barbara Cohen, *Community Food Security Assessment Toolkit.* Washington, DC: USDA Economic Research Service, July 2002. Available at http://www.ers. usda.gov/Publications/EFAN02013/.

Jack Kloppenburg Jr., John Hendrickson, and G. W. Stevenson. 1996, "Coming in to the Foodshed." *Agriculture and Human Values,* vol. 13, no. 3, 33–42. Available at www.springerlink.com/content/u1pn44q884603t70/

Hannah Burton, Andy Fisher, Hugh Joseph, and Kami Pothukuchi. 2002, *What's Cooking in Your Food System: A Guide to Community Food Assessment.* Venice, CA: Community Food Security Coalition, 2002. Available at http://foodsecurity.org/pub/whats_cooking.pdf.

Prepare the People

Food systems planning is most effective through multistakeholder input. Because food systems are systemic and highly participatory, there is a strong grassroots and advocacy movement to support this kind of work. Both communities of place and communities of purpose have come together over these issues. At the same time, a comprehensive plan requires that an effort be made to bring in specific stakeholders in certain areas. Examples of representatives that can play an important role in the research, planning, and advocacy of food systems are:

- Elected officials
- Government departments: planning, public health, environment, workforce development, public schools, parks, economic development, youth and seniors, procurement, and so on
- Farmers
- Business owners
- Grocery retail
- Health practitioners
- Chefs
- Community and economic development agencies
- Educators
- Citizens from diverse ethnic backgrounds and ages
- Funders
- Planners
- Gardeners
- Architects

ENGAGE AND EDUCATE THE PUBLIC

Remember home economics? Ongoing educational campaigns are a key strategy for engaging the public in food systems. From elementary education through adult learning, food systems planning should include ongoing education programming about healthy and sustainable food systems.

Networking events and conferences play a big role in education and building the "movement" around food systems. Organizations like the Community Food Security Coalition host national gatherings annually and cover a wide range of food systems topics. Additionally, other organizations host conferences on more specific food systems issues like Farm to School, the American Planning Association, and the Growing Food and Justice for All Initiative. Regional and citywide meetings or summits, often hosted by food policy councils, universities, or other stakeholders, are other opportunities for education and can even be somewhat more purpose-driven and action-oriented. Derived outcomes like policy platforms and reports are used to define work moving forward.

In order to move forward with food systems planning, strategic outreach by cultivating a network of community leadership is essential. Planners should invest the time in getting to know the people, organizations, businesses, and institutions that encompass the local food system and their concerns. In order to become stakeholders in a vision for the future, people need to understand the relevance of food in their personal and professional lives. Other methods of outreach and education involve programming with community partners, and developing partnerships with specific leaders at the community level.

A wider range of stakeholders makes a stronger plan. Food systems efforts must recognize the strength of diversity, and engage elders, youth, and people of marginalized income and ethnicity. Developing partnerships with these stakeholders and cultivating leadership among people with diverse backgrounds and points of view is critical to adding diversity to the process. Because we all eat, we are all stakeholders in the food system and we need to recognize the inequities of the system and the barriers that some people have. Not everyone has equal access to high-quality food. By engaging leaders who can share knowledge about this, the food system plan will be more robust and sustainable.

▼Figure 9-6
Healthy eating and cooking awareness are part of the education component of food systems planning. *Lynn Peemoeller*

▲Figure 9-7
Many new farmers in the United States come from other countries, such as these Hmong farmers in Milwaukee, Wisconsin. *Lynn Peemoeller*

Develop Goals, Objectives, and Performance Metrics

Goal setting is an important starting place for sustainable food systems work. The nature of multiple stakeholders in food systems work benefits from an integrated learning process. This process uses a participatory approach to develop goals, using both bottom-up or community-based expertise, and top-down or professional expertise.

A visioning process is useful in setting goals, core values, and objectives for food systems. This process-driven approach allows multiple stakeholders to come together to establish a collaborative and systemic way of defining and taking ownership of the future of the food system. Goals should be simple and defined by a timeline.

Often food systems planners act as conveners or coordinators of the stakeholders in the food system as they go through the process of identifying goals and objectives. They can also provide resources to the process. In some cases, goals will be predetermined or predirected by funding sources, community groups, or prescient needs. The scope of the project will vary based on timeline, funding, geography of the community, or purpose of the plan.

The *Food Systems Report for the Chicago Metropolitan Region (2009)* is an example of a comprehensive approach to the regional food system that was commissioned by the Chicago Community Trust to support the GO TO 2040 comprehensive regional planning effort led by the Chicago Metropolitan Agency for Planning (CMAP).

Several factors were predetermined before the work began: the timeline of the project was just under one year, there was limited funding for the work, the report needed to reflect geographic and ethnic diversity of the seven-county region, and a collective vision for the food system in the year 2040 needed to be defined.

The process began by identifying diverse stakeholders in the regional food system. From educators to farmers, to community activists, program directors, and retail operators, over 30 people were identified to participate in the process. A facilitator led a community visioning process, which involved an interactive forum in which people shared personal and professional values and goals for the future of the food system. They were then organized by type and prioritized and eventually developed into a short statement:

In 2040 we will have a regional food system that nourishes our people and the land. The food system will:

- Achieve economic vitality by balancing profitability with diversification in all sectors
- Preserve farmland and enhance water and soil quality in closed-loop systems
- Contribute to social justice through equal access to affordable, nutritious food
- Support vibrant local food cultures based on seasonality and availability

Subsequently, the vision was shared in a number of community-based forums and received feedback. This helped to inform the process of setting objectives for the plan. Writing, researching, and developing the methodology for the plan was completed largely by a core group of stakeholders. The stakeholder feedback provided satellite feedback and reinforcement throughout the process. A final report was generated over the course of several months and is now included in the comprehensive plan for the region.

Develop the Strategic Plan

Plans are often developed in phases and may seek to accomplish different things depending on the defined region and the scope of the project. Food

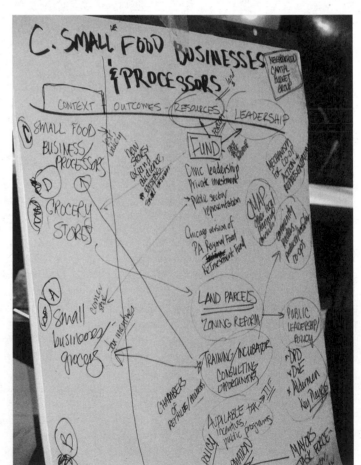

Figure 9-8
Community-based input is an important part of food systems planning.
Lynn Peemoeller

systems plans can stand alone to address specific issues, they can be inclusive in a larger planning process, they can be community generated, or they can be comprehensive.

An example of a community-based plan called *Food, Fitness & Health* was produced by the Englewood Community on Chicago's south side. It was part of a Quality of Life Strategy to promote healthy lifestyles including physical fitness, good nutrition, and better use of health-care resources. The main elements to this plan included a background on the history and context of the successes and challenges in the community; a community-generated vision; and a work plan including strategies, recommendations, and next steps.

When approaching food systems from the planning discipline, the American Planning Association recommends five broad strategies that planners can use to help develop sustainable and healthy food systems. They include: information generation, program implementation, facilitation and coordination, plan-making and design, and zoning and regulatory reform.

While there is no one way to proceed with food systems planning, the following outline will help planners and conveners to map out the steps needed in the planning process.

- Define the goal or rationale for the process
- Identify partners to participate
- Define the approach to fit the goal
- Engage stakeholders in a visioning process
- Research, analyze, and organize data
- Prepare recommendations
- Solicit and review and stakeholder feedback
- Identify measures of success and timeframe for assessment
- Identify how the plan will be implemented and proceed

Develop the Action Plan

In developing the action plan for food systems, priorities can be organized according to different factors, from the environmental to economic, to social or cultural. Often priorities are determined by the low-hanging fruit, projects that are either easy to implement, or that are extremely ripe and need to be addressed immediately. For example, to build nutritional knowledge and cooking skills, classes can be arranged in a short timeframe with relatively little financial overhead. In other cases, for more comprehensive recommendations, priorities should be organized chronologically. If the goal of an institutional food procurement agency requires purchasing a certain percentage of locally grown food, the supply must be there in order to reach that goal. The priorities of the recommendation then shift to farmer development and increasing local supply chains to provide enough volume for institutional purchases. The progress of the goal may have to be monitored over time.

Figure 9-9
Urban land is converted into productive farmland in cities all over the United States. *Lynn Peemoeller*

Advancing the outcomes of the planning process depends on identifying agencies that have realistic capacity in time, funding, and human resources to carry out the work. It also requires the buy-in of stakeholders. In many cases, once the stakeholders have come together for the planning process they will continue formal and informal relationships beyond the project. Education, learning, and stakeholder involvement are all important outcomes of the process.

Who comes to the table will largely determine who will carry out the next steps. As part of the process, recommendations need to be prioritized and an acting agency needs to be identified to carry them out. In food systems planning there are roles for both the public and private sector to implement programs and policies. Appropriate governing bodies like a food policy council, or a community council, should be identified or created to monitor the efficacy of proposed measures.

Securing Resources

There is increasing awareness of the need for funding for food systems work. One good way to ensure that funding sources will understand the value of plans and recommendations is to engage them as stakeholders in the process. Since 2010 there is an increasing amount of federal funding for food systems work, especially under the USDA Community Food Security Grants and the Know Your Farmer,

Know Your Food Program. But barriers to funding do exist in marginalized communities. As part of the planning process, resource allocation is one area that needs to be addressed in order to make sure that communities have resources needed to proceed with recommendations and action plans.

Political capital is also important to carry out the action plan in food systems work. The same way that funding sources need to be engaged as stakeholders in the planning process, so do government agencies and elected officials. The support of an elected official or city council can go a long way toward implementing a plan.

When developing and finalizing a report, take sufficient time and use a review committee for thorough vetting. An attractive, easy-to-read layout that is not text heavy or language dense is the best way to communicate the plan. A distribution plan is also essential for getting publicity and buy-in to the plan. In some cases a press release, gathering, or organized activity to announce the plan will help to publicize it.

It is important to recognize at the outset that evaluation is a critical part of the planning process. It allows us to understand if we are meeting our goal and objective. One way to help stay on track is to set a timeline with the action plan. Prioritizing indicators and monitoring them over time will also help to evaluate progress. Interviews at the community level and with those most affected by the food system plan will also help in the evaluation process. A review committee or evaluation agency should be set up ahead of time to keep track of the progress. This is a good role for a food policy council if one has been established.

Implement the Action Plan

Once the action plan has been publicized, it is time to be implemented. Implementation strategies are useful to help achieve short-term goals as well as lay the groundwork for long-term goals. An example is as follows.

Launching action plans in the short term requires a quick assembly of participation through personnel, and funding. If it is a program, a timeline is useful for helping to keep it on track. If it is a policy, an advisory committee may be set up to monitor its progress over time. Long-term plans can integrate more stakeholder development in the area of policy and funding.

URBAN ORCHARDS

Lynn Peemoeller
Food Systems Planning

INTERVENTION TYPE: PROGRAM

Description: Establish an Urban Fruit and Nut Tree Network

A number of efforts to connect urban people with fresh fruit and nuts are being cultivated by urban orchard projects nationally. Projects range from identifying and mapping fruit trees in the urban environment; to fruit rescue and harvest; distribution of fruit and nut trees in low-income communities; and the establishment of urban orchards. Fruit- and nut-bearing trees can vitally change the way people interact with the urban environment. By cultivating and preserving urban space for fruit and nut production it brings people closer to understanding where food comes from. It creates more beautiful and sustainable communities, and creates healthy physical opportunities for residents to interact.

SUPPORT GOALS AND OBJECTIVES

- Use urban land for food production
- Make fresh, nutritious local food available to urban residents
- Encourage alternative urban land use and community beautification
- Connect people to where their food comes from
- Create opportunities for community food security and stewardship of the land

PERFORMANCE CHARACTERISTICS

- Increased inventory of fruit trees growing in the urban environment
- Production capacity of fruit trees
- Organization of harvest and distribution
- Create credible and reliable partnerships
- Stable partnerships with landowners

POTENTIAL SYNERGISM

The program can work with a number of different partners:
- Private residences
- Public housing
- Schools

▶ Figure 9-10
There are a wide variety of apple species. Some have place-based history. *Lynn Peemoeller*

▶▶ Figure 9-11
The fruit harvest can bring people together for fun and learning. *Lynn Peemoeller*

- Parks
- Food banks
- Community-based organizations

IMPLEMENTATION TIME

In the short term the program should establish its mission or goal. Short-term work can include an inventory of preexisting fruit trees in a community, including those that are on public or private property and their condition and potential for production. Harvest parties can be organized to get fruit from trees to people. Longer-term plans should include identifying sites and partners for permanent orchards, including partnerships with different landowners and programs to establish orchards and promote home growing to residents. The time it takes for fruit and nut trees to produce varies by variety and care—it can range from 2 to 6 years. Education and outreach throughout the process should be ongoing.

BENEFITS

There are many benefits to urban orchard networks including education about food production, community development and beautification, contact with nature, stewardship of the environment, and promoting healthy eating habits.

DRAWBACKS

- Maintaining fruit trees requires a specific knowledge base.
- Harvest time is restricted to a limited time of year.
- It takes some trees a long time to bear fruit.
- Squirrels and other urban foragers may compete for harvest.
- Trees may require chemical applications from time to time to keep production viable.

FIRST COST

Initial costs include the purchase of tree or scion wood and rootstock.

LIFECYCLE COSTS

- Tree maintenance including nontoxic fertilizers, mulch, tools, water, and fencing
- Land maintenance costs

ESTIMATED QUANTITATIVE PERFORMANCE

The performance of this program can be evaluated in one way by the quantity of fruit harvested. Other indicators for performance vary from the amount of trees in the network, to the number of members in the network, to the number of workshops and participants in workshops and other support programming.

IMPLEMENTATION SUPPORTS AND CONSTRAINTS

Land use plays a big role in the long-term viability of urban orchards. There are models for private property, public property, and community-owned property. Support will be required at the community level. The best way to support the efficacy of this kind of work is for one or more organizations to partner and invest operationally in the program.

INFORMATIONAL SOURCES

- Treefolks, Austin, Texas
- Chicago Rarities Orchard Project (CROP), Chicago, Illinois
- City Fruit, Seattle, Washington
- Earthworks, Boston, Massachusetts
- Treepeople, Los Angeles, California

URBAN AGRICULTURE

Raoul Adamchak
Student Farm Manager, University of California, Davis

INTERVENTION TYPE: PROGRAM: AGRICULTURE/FOOD

Description

Urban agriculture includes private farmers growing for profit within city limits, farms funded by nonprofit organizations, city employees or residents farming city-owned land, and residents growing in their backyards or in community gardens. In a few cases, an urban farm has been included in a housing development planned outside the city limits, which is then incorporated by a city. Urban farms can provide fresh, local food for urban dwellers, help educate children and adults about where food comes from and how it is grown, provide work for urban youths and seniors, help recycle urban green waste back to urban land, promote community economic development, and help beautify and remediate urban landscapes.

SUPPORT GOALS AND OBJECTIVES
- Reduce imports of food and associated energy use
- Educate citizens about agriculture and food
- Recycle urban green waste
- Build community
- Beautify landscape
- Improve nutrition and health for urban residents

PERFORMANCE CHARACTERISTICS
Each acre of urban land can provide fruits and vegetables for approximately 40 people a year (as part of a community-supported agriculture type operation, for example), and if intensively farmed, produce from $20,000 to $35,000 a year, gross, depending on the

Figure 9-12
Community gardens are a source of both food and serenity. *Raoul Adamchak*

Figure 9-13
Urban farms provide fresh, local food.
Raoul Adamchak

length of season. A plot in a community garden can provide $200 to $500 worth of vegetables and fruits per year. Urban youth can be employed and educated by urban farming. School children can improve their understanding of agriculture, food, and nutrition.

POTENTIAL SYNERGISM
Urban farming can be integrated with green waste recycling, farmers' markets, food banks, nonprofit food and nutrition education, and city parks programs.

IMPLEMENTATION TIME
Private or city-run farms may require infrastructure improvements and zoning changes. These changes may take up to a year to implement. Turning empty lots into community gardens may require environmental remediation, infrastructure improvement, and community organization. These processes could take a year or more to implement. Backyards can be transformed in a couple of weeks.

BENEFITS
- Fresh and local food is being produced in hundreds of cities around the United States.
- Urban environments are improved.
- Local hunger and malnutrition is reduced.

- Urban green waste is recycled to grow food.
- Children and adults are educated on food and farming issues.
- Jobs are created by urban farming enterprises.
- Food transport energy is reduced.
- Community investment and development is enhanced.

DRAWBACKS

- High-value urban real estate is used for agriculture.
- Legal and zoning restrictions can be barriers to urban agriculture.
- Pollution from urban environments may contaminate crops.
- Vandalism and theft can be problems.
- Land tenure issues may limit long-term establishment.
- Reasonably priced water may not be available.
- Community gardening often requires community organization.

FIRST COSTS

Costs for the city for urban farming projects are a function of the type of project. Leasing land to private farmers or to a non-profit organization is the lowest cost option. In most cases, water and utility access costs would be all that is required. There would be additional costs if zoning changes are required. Costs for city-owned and operated farms would be much higher. Initial infrastructure and machinery capitalization could be as much as $250,000. Salaries of employee(s) add another substantial cost. Costs for community gardens would be modest as most inputs, (except a water system) would come from the plot holders. Promoting backyard gardens would be the lowest cost option. If a farm was included as part of a housing project, the developer would pay the costs of needed infrastructure.

LIFECYCLE COSTS

Urban land leased to private farmers or nonprofit organizations could generate some income for the city. A city-owned farm would generate income from produce sold and educational activities, and could operate at a break-even level. Community garden fees should cover lifecycle costs, except for water and utility maintenance. A farm in a housing development would be supported by sales or by the homeowners.

Estimated Quantitative Performance

Every acre of urban farmland can meet the vegetable and fruit needs for approximately 40 people during the growing season. Measures might include: pounds of food produced and/or consumed; number of people served; and income per acre. Hundreds of school children can participate in urban farm education programs. Measures might include: number of children who participate in education programs; and changes in knowledge, attitudes, and eating behavior as a result. Urban farms can employ young people. Measures might include: number of new jobs. Other measures: number of youth who go on to higher education as a result of participation in these community ventures; total sales of food from farms/gardens; changes in eating patterns in participating residents; dollars saved by growing one's own food; pounds/tons of urban green waste used.

IMPLEMENTATION SUPPORTS AND CONSTRAINTS

The city must make land available to farm for farmers, nonprofits, or the general public, and may have to provide infrastructure and make zoning changes. Farmers, nonprofits, and community gardeners must be available and organized to implement urban farms. For private farms, the location must be profitable.

INFORMATIONAL SOURCES

- Foundations: W. K. Kellogg Foundation www.wkkf.org/Default. aspx?tabid=90&CID=4&lte
- The Geraldine R. Dodge Foundation http://grdodge.org/environment/index.htm
- Organizations: Urban Farming www.urbanfarming.org/
- American Community Gardening Association
- National Gardening Association
- Resource Centres on Urban Agriculture and Food Security www.ruaf.org/
- Community Food Security Urban Agriculture Committee www.foodsecurity.org/ua_home.html

REPORTS AND STUDIES

- Feenstra, Gail, Sharyl McGrew, and David Campbell. 1999. *Entrepreneurial Community Gardens: Growing Food, Skills, Jobs and Communities*. DANR Publication No. 21578. Davis, CA: University of California Agriculture and Natural Resources.

URBAN EDGE AGRICULTURAL PARKS

Sibella Kraus
Director, Sustainable Agriculture
Education (SAGE)

INTERVENTION TYPE: PROGRAM

Description

Urban Edge Agricultural Parks (or AgParks)
—part working agriculture and part public
parkland amenity—are designed to accommodate multiple uses that include small
farms, public areas, and natural habitat.
AgParks support farmers with opportunities
for affordable land, shared infrastructure,
and direct marketing of agricultural products.
AgParks provide fresh food, and offer educational, environmental, and aesthetic benefits
for nearby communities. The combination of
a cultivated and natural context can attract a
diversity of people, flora, and fauna.

The nonprofit organization Sustainable
Agriculture Education (SAGE) developed
the AgParks model with background
research and real-world implementation and
consultation. The AgParks concept draws
from existing models on both public and
private land including educational farms,
collective farming, farmer-incubator projects,
eco-villages, and urban-edge allotments and
market gardens. The naming of the concept
as a "park" is intended to convey the role an
AgPark plays in open-space preservation and
public engagement. The term also evokes the
traditional model of a business park, where
multiple tenants operate under a common
management structure.

 Urban Edge Agricultural Parks Toolkit

Produced by:
SAGE: Sustainable Agriculture Education

In Partnership With:
The USDA Risk Management Agency
Community Outreach and Assistance Partnership Program

Additional Partners:
Agriculture and Land-Based Training Association
Bay Area Economics
Wallace, Roberts & Todd, LLC

December 2005

Figure 9-14
The Urban Edge Agricultural Parks Toolkit provides a
guidebook for creating these important community
elements. *Sustainable Agriculture Education*

SUPPORT GOALS AND OBJECTIVES

AgParks help sustain and contain urban areas. Within an AgPark, the combinations of nature trails, food production, jobs, and agricultural learning—all addressing economic, health-related, educational, and recreational needs—yields a multifunctional setting, mutually beneficial to urban residents and farmers.

SUITABLE SITES AND JURISDICTIONS

AgParks are for metropolitan regions that want:

- Activated and permanently protected edges that contain cities and provide a "sense of place"
- Viable agriculture as an intrinsic element of sustainable communities' access to fresh food, parks, and green spaces

AgParks are suitable/adaptable for public lands that:

- Have existing mandates for agriculture, agricultural education, passive recreation, natural resource protection, curation of cultural and historical artifacts, and community linkages
- Can contract with public and private partners to help fulfill this mandate

AgParks are suitable/adaptable for private lands that:

- Are permanently preserved for agriculture or reserved for the future preservation as farmland
- Can provide development and operational financial support through mechanisms such as Home Owner Association (HOA) assessments or real estate transfer fees
- Are viable for aggregated, small- to medium-scale agriculture
- Have potential for discrete home sites affordable by farm families
- Are located within a place-based agricultural marketing initiative area
- Have regulations that permit farmers to operate value-added types of enterprises

IMPLEMENTATION TIME

Implementation time can depend on factors such as the duration of a planning process (e.g., master plan, specific plan, and area plan), negotiation for a master lease, establishment of infrastructure and improvements, approval and permitting processes, and fundraising efforts.

BENEFITS

Working Agriculture: AgParks are "farm-ready" for small farmers seeking:

- Affordable land near affordable, healthy places to live
- Conducive agronomic conditions
- Management services and technical assistance for production, marketing, and business planning

- Capitalized infrastructure
- Potential for shared-use equipment and facilities
- Opportunities for on-site marketing and "place-branded" direct marketing
- Opportunities to create value-added products and to offer value-added services
- Multiple opportunities for collaboration with public education, recreation, and natural resources stewardship organizations

Parkland: AgParks provide for nearby communities:
- Locally grown fresh food
- Educational activities
- Passive recreation, including trails linked with regional and city trails
- Environmental services and benefits
- Natural and landscaped areas and buffers for habitat
- Community involvement, partnerships, and celebrations

DRAWBACKS

As a hybrid that combines farm business incubation with public amenities, the AgParks model requires planning and capital-intensive start-up. Ideally, a management plan would outline clear goals, strategies, and policies and would also have flexibility to allow for adaptation of the model. An experienced management team and sufficient capitalization will help ensure success. Engagement of multiple types of partnerships also can significantly affect successful implementation.

FIRST COST

Provision of irrigation infrastructure often represents a major development cost, especially when factors such as multiple separate meters and pressure regulators, filter systems for drip irrigation, water storage capacity, and drainage systems are required. Other major costs range from fencing and construction of multifunctional buffers, to the establishment of facilities such as barns, corporation yards, repair shops, and processing and marketing facilities. Less obvious costs include the development of documents such as lease and sublease agreements, share-equipment use agreements, and policies governing required, allowed, and disallowed activities.

LIFECYCLE COSTS

The AgPark should remain self-sustaining once it is established. However, achieving this stabilized model depends on many factors such as the overall complexity and scale of the operation, the level of experience of the farmers and their needs for technical assistance, base costs and expenses, and availability of ongoing revenue and in-kind support. Education programs require ongoing support.

Figure 9-15
The 18-acre Sunol AgPark has
four tenant farmers. *Sustainable
Agriculture Education*

ESTIMATED QUANTITATIVE PERFORMANCE

Performance can be measured by the following factors: viability of the farm enterprises over time; level of public and partner engagement; and the flexibility of the project to meet challenges and realize new opportunities.

IMPLEMENTATION SUPPORTS AND CONSTRAINTS

The most critical implementation support emerges from the same compelling reasons that generated the AgPark in the first place: demand from new farmers, location and scale of land well-suited to the model, and partners with a strong interest in participation.

INFORMATIONAL SOURCES

Existing models include Intervale in Vermont; AgParks, operated by the Hawaii Department of Agriculture; and the Sunol AgPark and Martial Cottle Park (in development), both in California.

REPORTS AND STUDIES

- The website of Sustainable Agriculture Education (SAGE) www.sagecenter.org
- *Urban Edge Agricultural Parks Feasibility Study* (Available at www.sagecenter.org/wp-content/uploads/2009/07/agparks-bw-22105_complete.pdf; accessed October 2010.)
- Urban Edge Agricultural Parks Toolkit (Available at www.sagecenter.org/wp-content/uploads/2009/07/toolkit-121405.pdf; accessed October 2010.)

Chapter 10

Solid Waste

Sustainable Materials Management

Daniel T. Sicular, PhD
Principal, Environmental Science Associates (ESA)

Concept

The transition to a sustainable community, and to a Resilient/Low-Carbon Built Environment (RLC) will naturally lead to lower consumption levels and a simpler waste stream, as people adopt—and the built environment enables—practices and behavior that use less energy and materials. A parallel shift in attitude may be expected, away from acquisition and accumulation of material goods as key components of personal satisfaction and fulfillment, to greater emphasis on community, family, and society as the sources of personal growth and accomplishment. This shift will have an even greater and more substantive effect on reducing energy and materials consumption.

Figure 10-1
Conventional solid waste management relies on landfilling for final disposal of materials. *Daniel T. Sicular*

Consequently, the size and complexity of the "problem" of managing solid waste both decline as a community becomes more sustainable. With a reduction in the use of energy and materials, and with the shift to a more sustainable economy, less waste is produced, and the waste that is produced is simpler and more easily used for beneficial purposes. Consider, for example, the different waste outcomes of two different modes of acquiring food for the household dinner table: shopping at the supermarket or at the farmers' market. The trip to the supermarket from a suburban neighborhood likely requires a car, and the selection of food is limited mostly to packaged, preportioned, processed items that may originate from all over the world. The waste produced in the household related to this meal may consist of paper, plastic, metal, and glass packaging. Because packaged food is preportioned, there may be more leftovers than can be used, and a portion of the prepared food itself may become waste. In addition, there will be waste associated with the production, processing, and transport of the food items and packaging materials.[1] Outside of the home, largely unseen and unconsidered, and spread literally across the globe, this meal is responsible for its small portion of the vast quantities of waste associated with mining, timber harvest, extraction and refining of fossil fuels, food processing, manufacturing of packaging products, transportation, and construction and operation of the infrastructure necessary to bring the packaging and the food to market.

On the other hand, consider a walking or bicycling trip to a local farmers' market. Food is unprocessed or minimally processed, locally produced, and unpackaged, and one may purchase just the amount needed for the meal. The solid waste produced will be limited to food trimmings and scraps, which may be composted, and bags, which may be reused.

The decades since the conclusion of World War II have seen the proliferation of consumer goods and the packaging in which they are marketed. At the end of their useful life, these items become waste. Over this time period, the sheer quantity of wastes produced, the per capita rate of waste generation, and the types of materials making up the waste, have all increased dramatically.[2] Since the advent of municipal recycling systems in the 1970s, the growing complexity of the waste stream has complicated efforts to redirect the great river of waste out of landfills and back into the economic mainstream. The recycling movement has largely been a game of catching up to a moving target.

Avoid the challenge of a future in which technological fixes allow us to continue on the same trajectory of unchecked consumerism, only with incrementally lighter ecological footprints. This only delays, but does not prevent ecological catastrophe. Instead, transition to a future in which our relationship to the material world itself shifts, where we understand and acknowledge the limits of the Earth's ability to sustain us.

A transition to a more sustainable materials management system will require a reduction in consumption by homes, businesses, and communities. Much of our economy, however, has come to depend on retail sales, and therefore, sustainable materials management is at odds with our consumer economy. One goal of sustainable materials management should be to encourage and enable members of the community to consume less. This would have to be reconciled with an acceptance that our happiness and fulfillment are not defined by the material goods we acquire and hold. In short, the goal should be to nurture an attitude of "buy less, live more."

SOLID WASTE MANAGEMENT, DEFINED

Solid waste management may be defined as a set of institutions, practices, and technologies that prevent the accumulation of waste in the built environment. The type and quantity of waste that we produce is directly related to the material goods we acquire, use, and discard. Because we constantly process materials through the cycle of production, consumption, use, and discard, the generation of waste at the community scale never ceases, and solid waste management consisting of periodic removal is a necessity.

Conventional solid waste management systems consist of periodic collection of wastes at the point of generation using diesel-powered equipment and disposal in sanitary landfills, which are engineered, regulated facilities in which waste is isolated from the environment, and where the byproducts of decomposition (liquid and gaseous) are collected and managed. A variation on landfill disposal is incineration, generally with recovery of energy from the heat of combustion, in combination with landfilling of the resultant ash.

Recycling and centralized composting are variations on the conventional disposal-based system. In recycling, select materials are collected separately, or separated after collection, graded, processed for shipment, then sold as commodities. Centralized composting involves the separate collection of organic materials, especially yard waste, but in some communities now including food waste, and its controlled biological decomposition in an aerobic or anaerobic (digester) system. The end product may be used as a soil amendment or mulch. Anaerobic digestion allows for the recovery of methane and its use in generating power.

The solid waste management system currently in place in most North American communities effectively prevents the accumulation of waste in the built environment. Secondarily, the system has become a source for recycled commodities (most of which are exported) that are used in the manufacture of a variety of products and packaging. Centralized composting effectively keeps putrescible materials out of the landfill, thereby reducing methane generation; it also produces a valuable soil amendment.

Recycling and composting programs are generally regarded as key steps toward greater sustainability. However, even the most ardent efforts at reorienting the conventional system to recycling and composting, and away from dis-

Figure 10-2
At a materials recovery facility, sorted paper is prepared for market. *ESA, Inc.*

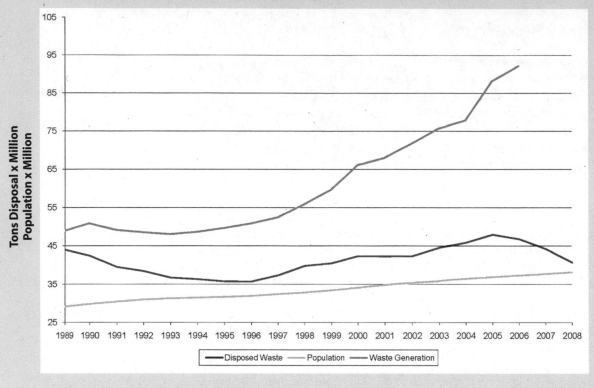

Statewide Solid Waste Disposal and Population in California, 1988–2008

Disposed Waste — Population — Waste Generation

posal, are doomed to fail as a sustainable materials management strategy. For example, in 1989, California enacted Assembly Bill 939, a landmark piece of legislation that required all cities and counties in the state to plan and implement comprehensive waste reduction, recycling, and composting programs with a goal to reduce the amount of waste sent to landfill by half by the year 2000. Programs enacted at the local level in California since the passage of this law have in fact reduced the per capita level of waste disposal and have greatly increased the supply of recycled commodities and compost products. The law has done little, however, to reduce the volume of waste disposed. As shown in Figure 10-3, Californians disposed of more waste in landfills in 2005 (47.9 million tons) than they did when the law was enacted in 1989 (44 million tons), despite 15 years of intensive planning and program development. An even more telling statistic, the estimated amount of waste generated (i.e., disposed plus diverted) nearly doubled from 1989 to 2006, and far outstripped population growth: Population grew by 28 percent over this time period, while waste generation increased by 88 percent.

The current conventional system is unsustainable because it only addresses waste after production, and fails to consider the underlying issue of our relationship with material resources and material goods. This relationship has resulted in an ever-increasing volume of waste, and an ever-increasing variety and combination of materials making up the waste stream.

Figure 10-3
From 1989 to 2008, California's rate of waste generation grew more quickly than its population. Disposed waste decreased with the implementation of recycling programs in the early 1990s, but began to increase from about 1995-2005. *Daniel T. Sicular*

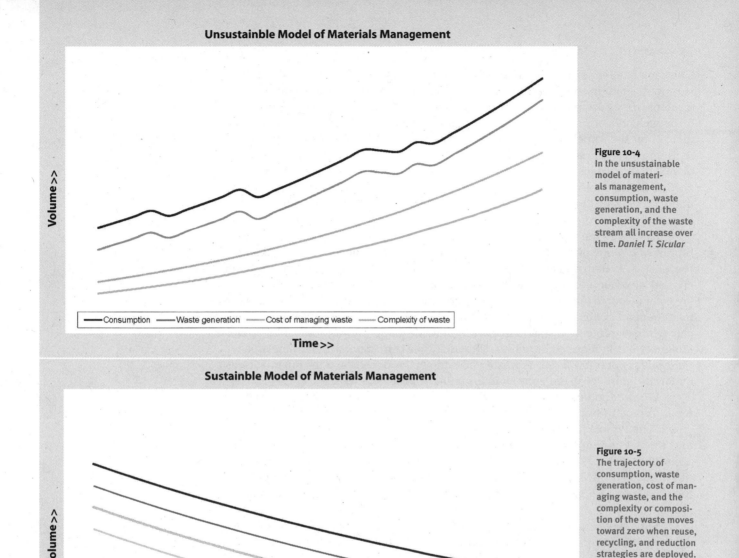

Unsustainble Model of Materials Management

Volume >>

Time >>

—— Consumption —— Waste generation —— Cost of managing waste —— Complexity of waste

Figure 10-4
In the unsustainable model of materials management, consumption, waste generation, and the complexity of the waste stream all increase over time. *Daniel T. Sicular*

Sustainble Model of Materials Management

Volume >>

Time >>

—— Consumption —— Waste generation —— Cost of managing waste —— Complexity of waste

Figure 10-5
The trajectory of consumption, waste generation, cost of managing waste, and the complexity or composition of the waste moves toward zero when reuse, recycling, and reduction strategies are deployed. *Daniel T. Sicular*

In a sustainable community, this relationship must be reexamined and redefined. Effect a transition from solid waste management to sustainable materials management, where the rate of consumption of goods, and the resultant waste production, decreases over time. The waste stream will become simpler, as the afterlife of materials is considered in their design and manufacture.

Preparing the Team

Complex challenges face the reformation of existing systems of solid waste management. Though some are due to scarcity of resources or environmental considerations, many are political. In most communities, waste is collected through long-term exclusive or nonexclusive franchise agreements that usually guarantee a profit margin for the franchisee. These agreements also include franchise fees that accrue to the government agency that franchises the service. For some city and county governments, franchise fees, collection fees, and tip fees represent a substantial portion of the general fund. Powerful interests benefit monetarily from a continuation and expansion of the existing system, and thus resist a transition to a less wasteful society.

To modify the waste management system, a particularly strong team should represent a range of expertise. Most of all, the necessary political will must change the existing system and challenge entrenched interests. The system reinforces trends created by other elements of resilience and sustainability that tend to result in lower levels of resource and energy use. The emphasis should shift from a back-end waste management system to a front-end materials management system. Over time, per capita waste generation should decline, and waste that is produced should be simpler and more easily recycled or reused. Ultimately, the management team should put themselves out of business, as waste generation rates decline and the quality of waste materials improves to the point that less management is necessary.

Working in favor of change is the cyclical nature of waste management systems. Typically, franchise agreements are written for set periods, such as 10 or 15 years. The typical lifespan of collection equipment is on the order to 7 to 10 years, and waste handling facilities typically require major refurbishing or replacement after 20 or 25 years. Since the procurement of new equipment, services, and facilities takes several years, the planning team should look forward to the completion of the next franchise or equipment replacement cycle as an opportunity to reform the system.

Such a reformation will require a broad knowledge of municipal government services and finances, and more specific knowledge of materials management methods. Some of the specific areas of technical expertise include:

- Knowledge of commodities markets and trends in manufacturing and marketing of consumer goods
- Municipal finance and administration, particularly rates and rate setting, services procurement, and franchise agreements
- Understanding of legal authority and limits of local governments to control waste streams and regulate sale and use of consumer goods
- Civil and environmental engineering
- Truck fleet management, facilities management, material handling (for recycling collection and processing)
- Biology, horticulture, agriculture (for composting)
- Effective public outreach

Preparing the Tools

At the beginning of any sustainable materials management plan is a waste characterization study. The waste characterization study provides a snapshot of the current situation, and answers the questions: How much waste is produced? By whom? What does it consist of? These studies are often based on hand-sorting of representative samples of discarded materials, and compilation and statistical extrapolation of the data, which is a labor-intensive and costly process. It is, however, possible to conduct a "desktop" waste characterization study using published sources and Internet databases, including those produced by the Environmental Protection Agency (EPA) and the California Department of Resources and Recycling. Desktop studies may lack specificity, and can be expected to be less accurate, but may nonetheless serve the purpose for the initial planning process.

The waste characterization study forms the basis of the sustainable materials management planning effort: It contains the crucial data that allows for targeting materials, prioritizing programs, and monitoring progress.

Figure 10-6
A conceptual budget for a sustainable materials management planning process for communities of various sizes.
Daniel T. Sicular

Conceptual Budget for Sustainable Community Guidebook:
Sustainable Materials Management Plan

	Small Community (5,000–25,000)	Medium Community (25–75,000)	Large Community (75,000–125,000)	Very Large Community (Over 125,000)
Data Gathering and Analysis				
Waste Characterization Study: Desktop	$ 1,000	$ 1,500	$ 2,500	$ 3,500
Waste Characterization Study: Empirical	$ 20,000	$ 30,000	$ 50,000	$ 100,000
Waste Stream Analysis	$ 2,000	$ 3,000	$ 5,000	$ 10,000
Existing Conditions Report	$ 2,000	S 5,000	$ 10,000	$ 20,000
Action Plan Preparation				
Set Goals and Objectives (includes public workshop)	$ 2,000	$ 3,000	$ 5,000	$ 10,000
Develop Program and Policy Options	$ 3,000	$ 6,000	$ 9,000	$ 20,000
Evaluate, Compare, Select Options	$ 2,000	$ 3,000	$ 5,000	$ 9,000
Public Participation, including Review, Revise Plan	$ 5,000	$ 8,000	$ 15,000	$ 25,000
Action Plan Implementation and Monitoring				
Pilot and Demonstration Projects	$ 4,000	$ 10,000	$ 25,000	$ 50,000
Service Acquisition (RFP process)	$ 30,000	$ 60,000	$ 90,000	$ 200,000
Public Outreach and Education (start-up and annual budget)	$ 7,000	$ 15,000	$ 40,000	$ 100,000
Ongoing Oversight, Monitoring, and Reporting	$ 15,000	$ 30,000	$ 45,000	$ 100,000

Conceptual Budget

By using data generated in the waste characterization study, a series of graphs and charts can be developed to provide a quick visual map of waste types, origins, and volumes. Two examples are shown in Figures 10-7 and 10-8.

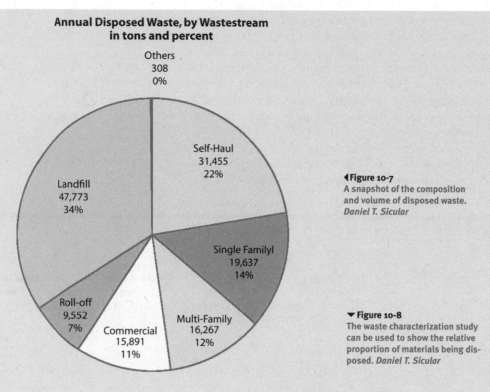

Annual Disposed Waste, by Wastestream
in tons and percent

Others
308
0%

Self-Haul
31,455
22%

Landfill
47,773
34%

Single Familyl
19,637
14%

Roll-off
9,552
7%

Commercial
15,891
11%

Multi-Family
16,267
12%

◀ **Figure 10-7**
A snapshot of the composition and volume of disposed waste.
Daniel T. Sicular

▼ **Figure 10-8**
The waste characterization study can be used to show the relative proportion of materials being disposed. *Daniel T. Sicular*

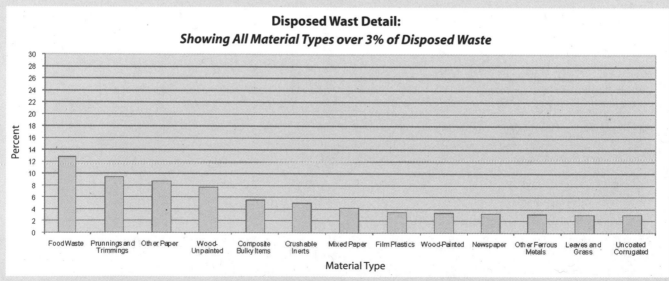

Disposed Wast Detail:
Showing All Material Types over 3% of Disposed Waste

Several key legal/regulatory tools are being employed in communities that are transitioning to systems that discourage waste generation and enhance recovery of materials and energy from waste. These include volume-based rates, which provide a price signal to residents and businesses to waste less; contract incentives that increase profitability for franchisees if the level of waste disposal declines and the level of recycling and composting increase; and ordinances requiring sufficient space in new and remodeled development to accommodate containers for separate collection of materials for recycling and composting.

For wastes from the building industry, an important legal/regulatory tool being employed is the construction and demolition (C&D) recycling ordinance. This often takes the form of a mandatory requirement for contractors to plan and implement construction site waste reduction and recycling programs. A number of mechanisms are being employed to ensure and report compliance, such as posting a bond or filing a final report prior to final inspection. Often, these programs can be started, with relatively little expenditure, using existing building and planning department staff, and existing facilities.

It is important to consider the current limitations on local governments for reforming waste management systems. Waste is produced locally, but the goods that become wastes are not. Local governments have limited control over how materials are extracted, manufactured, packaged, and shipped. Product bans and fees may be considered tools for local control of the sale or distribution of problematic consumer goods. Examples of products that have been banned or controlled through fees include expanded polystyrene foam (Styrofoam) fast-food packaging, and plastic shopping bags. Product bans tend to come in waves, with a few communities first deliberating on and establishing ordinances, which are then emulated by others.

Flow control—the ability of a local government to direct waste materials produced within its boundaries to a particular facility—is fraught with legal difficulties as it may run afoul of the Commerce Clause of the U.S. Constitution. Flow control is the subject of several Supreme Court cases (e.g., *C & A Carbone, Inc. v. Clarkstown*, 511 U.S. 383 (1994)). Without flow control, the financing of solid waste infrastructure, including facilities for recovery of materials, may be difficult, as it may be impossible to guarantee a reliable revenue stream from tip fees. Flow control generally can be achieved through contractual means, but in communities where collection of waste, especially commercial waste, is open to free market competition, flow control may be impossible.

Preparing the Place

In addition to the waste characterization study described above, required data and information for formulation of the sustainable community waste and materials management plan include the following:

- Existing system components, including municipal contracts and franchise agreements
- Existing rate structure for refuse, recycling, and composting collection services

Generator Sector	Disposed		Diverted		Generated		Diversion Rate
	Tons	% of Whole	Tons	% of Whole	Tons	% of Whole	Rate
Self-haul and roll-off	42,397	40%	22,057	22%	64,453	32%	34%
Commercial	21,605	21%	22,419	22%	44,024	22%	51%
Single-Family residential	15,699	15%	29,780	30%	45,479	22%	65%
Multifamily residential	19,377	18%	16,300	16%	35,678	17%	46%
University of California	5,680	5%	9,284	9%	14,964	7%	62%
Total	**104,758**	**100%**	**99,840**	**100%**	**204,598**	**100%**	**49%**

Sources: ESA, City of Berkeley

- Existing processing facilities (transfer stations, landfills, composting facilities, materials recovery facilities) capacities, and processing capabilities, and current conditions

- Role of local community and nonprofit organizations in promoting and operating recycling, composting, and waste reduction

Figure 10-9
A comprehensive waste characterization study allows for a complete profile of waste generated, disposed, and diverted.

Intimate knowledge of the existing local landscape of materials production, handling, and disposition is required. Plan for a two- to three-week period of information-gathering. It is useful to produce an existing conditions report to serve as a basis for the sustainable community planning effort.

As noted above, a waste characterization study provides the basic information for planning a sustainable materials management program, and an existing conditions report is highly recommended. The EPA's WARM model can be used to estimate current GHG emissions associated with waste material handling, and emissions reductions associated with alternative management methods (e.g., a comparison of composting versus landfilling).

Preparing the People

The reformation of the waste management process, from the creation of the product to its disposal, requires the involvement of several stakeholders, including:

- Community leaders and visionaries
- Local waste haulers and facility owners/operators (landfills, transfer stations, materials recovery facilities, composting facilities)
- Salvaged and second-hand goods merchants and organizations (Goodwill, Salvation Army)
- Agricultural extension agents, horticulturalists, nurseries
- Local chamber of commerce, building owners/managers associations, restaurant associations
- Nonprofit and advocacy environmental organizations

Developing Goals, Objectives, and Performance Metrics

Many states and some local governments have established goals for reducing landfilled waste, usually with a target amount expressed as a percentage of generated waste (e.g., California's 1989 law, which required diversion of 50 percent of generated waste from landfills by the year 2000). These laws and policies provide an overall framework for local government actions, and many have specific planning and program requirements. Some also provide funding mechanisms or incentives.

A sustainable materials management strategy should be based on a set of principles that places greatest emphasis on reducing wastes, then using wastes that are produced for beneficial purposes. Following are two example strategies:

The **Zero Waste Principles,** *as espoused by the Grass Roots Recycling Network:*

- Flow of resources viewed as a cycle with minimized input and output
- Responsibility by producers for the lifecycle impacts of products and packaging, creating incentive to design more benign products
- Focus on increasing benefits to communities and optimizing productive uses of resources
- Focus on locally owned, independent industries
- Accounting for environmental costs and benefits

The *Integrated Waste Management Hierarchy.* Variations of the hierarchy are embodied in California's landmark Integrated Waste Management Act of 1989, and also in the EPA's 1989 Agenda for Action. The EPA version follows:

- Source reduction (or waste prevention), including reuse of products and on-site (or backyard) composting of yard trimmings
- Recycling, including off-site (or community) composting
- Combustion with energy recovery
- Disposal through landfilling or combustion without energy recovery

Specific objectives may target particular material types (such as reducing or recovering food waste or beverage containers), or groups (such as commercial establishments or single-family households). The waste characterization study is a key tool in establishing objectives, since it facilitates targeting of priority materials for the goals of reducing waste at the source, recycling, and composting. This can be accomplished with a spreadsheet exercise similar to developing priorities and targets for GHG emissions reductions.

Expected performance may also be measured against a waste characterization study; for example, Figure 10-10 shows the projected disposal reduction associated with the program and policy options considered in the same City of Berkeley plan. Note that the table relates disposal reduction to the particular component of the waste stream (e.g., single-family residential) and to the whole city waste stream.

Diversion Potential for Program and Policy Options

Waste Stream	Program Option	Diversion Potential: Specific Waste Stream Disposed Waste		Diversion Potential: Specific Waste Stream Generated Waste		Diversion Potential: Whole City Generated Waste	
		Low	High	Low	High	Low	High
Single family	1. Mandatory 3-way separation (organics, recyclables, rubbish)	50%	60%	17%	21%	4%	5%
	2. Nonmandatory 3-way separation	25%	40%	9%	14%	2%	3%
	3. Increased outreach and public education	10%	20%	3%	7%	1%	2%
	4. Revisions to rates and billing	n.a.	n.a.	n.a.	n.a.	n.a.	n.a.
Multifamily	1. Small buildings included in residential 3-way separation	15%	30%	8%	16%	1%	3%
	2. Increased outreach and public education	10%	20%	5%	11%	1%	2%
Commercial-industrial-institutional	1. Increased franchisee reporting requirements	n.a.	n.a.	n.a.	n.a.	n.a.	n.a.
	2. Increased outreach and education	10%	20%	5%	10%	1%	2%
	3. Space allocation and mandatory source separation ordinance	25%	50%	15%	30%	4%	7%
Self-haul and roll-off	1. Sorting facility at Second and Gilman	20%	30%	13%	20%	4%	6%
	2. Transfer unsorted C&D	20%	30%	13%	20%	4%	6%
	3. Minor facility modifications	15%	20%	10%	13%	3%	4%
	4. C&D ordinance	30%	35%	20%	23%	6%	7%

Source: City of Berkeley Solid Waste Management Plan Update, 2005

Developing the Strategic Plan

Strategy development should proceed from the establishment of goals and objectives. For example, if a community places the highest priority on reducing waste at the source, the programs that follow from this might include product bans, educational and training programs to manage organic wastes on-site, and public outreach programs to encourage residents and businesses to make purchasing decisions that result in less waste.

New recycling and composting programs require large expenditures of capital and ongoing operating costs for collection, processing, and transportation. These programs are also limited (and enabled) by the local availability of processing facilities and markets for secondary goods. If, however, some programs and their supporting infrastructure are already in place, incremental improvements may be made relatively inexpensively, such as adding materials to a recycling collection program, or expanding a residential program to serve small businesses and apartment buildings. The strategic plan should retain and build on the useful aspects of the current system, but should envision the transition to a more sustainable one.

Figure 10-10
A table such as this, developed for the City of Berkeley, can be used to project waste diversion by sector.

Even incremental changes may have major implications for collection equipment and processing facilities. Furthermore, incremental improvements may lead to inefficiencies, if equipment and facilities are retrofitted or adapted for purposes for which they were not originally designed. If sufficient resources are available, the management team may consider a complete system changeover, in which all aspects of the system are reexamined and an integral action plan is developed. This may, in the long run, allow for substantial savings of resources and better system performance. For example, the addition of food waste to a weekly yard debris collection program and a comprehensive recycling collection program might enable a switch from weekly to bi-weekly collection of the remaining, dry fraction of waste, termed "rubbish." This would reduce the number of collection vehicles and routes. Such a changeover is usually only possible if the separation of the organic putrescible fraction is mandatory, to avoid public health and nuisance problems.

Developing the Action Plan

Upon developing the strategic plan, distill the program options and compile them into an action plan. Use a combination of quantitative and qualitative criteria or metrics to prioritize strategy options. These should flow from the waste characterization study. For example, does the strategy target high-priority waste stream sectors and materials, and what is the potential for diversion both as a percentage of the specific waste stream and the entire waste stream? The evaluation should consider the consistency of the program being considered with plan goals and objectives (e.g., does a strategy have the potential to increase awareness of our relationship with the natural world; can it facilitate more sustainable consumption and self-management of waste materials; does it support local businesses and community institutions?).

Reforming a material management system can be fiscally prohibitive for some jurisdictions. However, there are a myriad of techniques for securing funding resources. An entire sustainable materials management system can be financed from refuse rates, at least until it puts itself out of business (by reducing disposed waste, which could be considered one goal of a sustainable materials management plan). Refuse rates are usually under the control of municipal governments, though they may be established in existing long-term collection contracts and franchise agreements.

Communities that own their own landfill, or that control land use at landfills, may be able to impose tip fee surcharges, such as those imposed at Alameda County, California, landfills where proceeds from these surcharges (about $12 million per year, initially) are mandated to be used for the development and operation of recycling, composting, and waste reduction programs.

Sustainable materials management plans generally consist of a combination of the following:

- Regulatory programs that place the burden of altering materials management on producers of waste. These include product bans and fees, construction and demolition debris recycling programs, and extended producer responsibility programs that require manufacturers or retailers to "take back" items or packaging materials at the end of their life. These programs are usually launched through the passage of an ordinance or policy that requires or encourages the action. Launching the program therefore involves research and drafting of the ordinance or policy, and then subjecting it to the local agency approval process, prior to establishment of the institutional structure to implement the program.

- Collection and processing services provided through contract or franchise or directly by the local government agency as a municipal service. Launching a new collection program may involve a cycle of budgeting, equipment acquisition, and hiring for a municipality, or competitive or noncompetitive bids for a private service provider. More and more, communities are using the bidding and contracting process to build-in incentives and performance standards to maximize the effectiveness of a program.

- Public education, outreach, and informational and training programs require development of a message as well as outreach materials and strategies. Training programs may require physical facilities, such as a backyard composting demonstration garden, and the development of a curriculum.

Implementing the Action Plan

The action plan is an important guide for implementing the projects that will reform materials management. Short-term demonstration projects are good ways to exemplify how the implementation looks. Two examples include:

- Work with a local retailer to promote durable, low packaging, and easily recycled or reused items.

- Establish a home composting demonstration within a community garden (see Action Sheet).

Each program should be monitored and assessed for efficacy of meeting the goals and objectives. Contracts and franchise agreements should be written to include internal monitoring mechanisms, which may serve as the basis for evaluating program effectiveness. Programs that collect and handle materials, including recycling and composting programs, are generally easy to track, since most truckloads are weighed and recorded. Contracts for these services should include a periodic reporting requirement.

Programs and policies that reduce waste, on the other hand, are notoriously difficult to track. These programs may be tracked using periodic surveys, or by tallying attendance at training or informational events. Public education and outreach programs may best be monitored and assessed through surveys and written evaluations, for example, at the conclusion of a training workshop.

HOME COMPOSTING

Daniel T. Sicular, PhD
Environmental Science Associates (ESA)

INTERVENTION TYPE: PROGRAM

Description

Home composting programs encourage residents to manage their organic wastes at home, and in so doing, to create a valuable soil amendment that can be used in home gardens. Home composting reduces the amount of organic wastes that are disposed of in landfills, thereby reducing methane generation. Managing wastes at home also has the advantage of reducing the weight and volume of wastes needing collection and transport, which may result in reduced municipal waste collection service cost and use of fossil fuels.

Home composting programs usually have several components, including education, training of "master composters," and provision of free or discounted composting bins. Involving local health departments and vector control agencies in the design and initial operation of the program will help overcome possible objections that the program could result in a nuisance or public health hazard. A wide variety of techniques and technologies are readily available, and may be adopted by a substantial portion of the community population.

SUPPORTS GOALS AND OBJECTIVES

- Reduce organic wastes sent to landfills or other disposal facilities, and associated GHG emissions
- Create closed-loop home systems (use of waste as soil amendment for home gardens)

PERFORMANCE CHARACTERISTICS

Household waste typically consists of 20 to 30 percent compostable material. Participating households may be able to reduce their waste generation and the level of waste collection service. They may also increase the soil fertility and productivity of their home gardens, and reduce use of water, fertilizers, and pesticides.

Figure 10-11
Home composters can use conventional composting methods or earthworms.
Larry Kass

POTENTIAL SYNERGISM

Home composting is synergistic with many other sustainable community programs and policies, including local food production, improvement in diet and nutrition, and reduction of vehicle miles traveled (VMT).

IMPLEMENTATION TIME

Home composting programs typically require six months to one year to plan and start-up. Implementation may be phased in over two to three years. The program may be expanded to include schools, parks and recreation areas, and other facilities.

BENEFITS

Several communities have long-established home composting programs. Benefits include the following:

- Communitywide reduction in the amount of organic waste sent to the landfill or other disposal facilities.
- Participating residents manage a substantial portion of their own wastes at home, reducing their need for waste collection services.
- Participants turn organic wastes into valuable compost, which can be used in home gardens as a soil amendment or mulch. Compost increases soil fertility and tilth (the improved suitability for promoting plant growth), and reduces the need for water, fertilizer, and pesticides.
- Produce from home vegetable gardens and fruit trees provides nutritious food at low cost, and without the need for transportation.

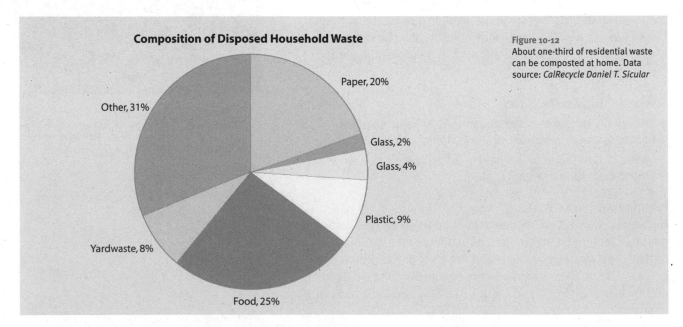

Composition of Disposed Household Waste

Paper, 20%
Glass, 2%
Glass, 4%
Plastic, 9%
Food, 25%
Yardwaste, 8%
Other, 31%

Figure 10-12
About one-third of residential waste can be composted at home. Data source: *CalRecycle Daniel T. Sicular*

DRAWBACKS

Home composting requires space. While composting is possible indoors, it is best done outside, and is therefore more suitable for residential areas with yards.

Poorly managed home composting bins are subject to problems including odors and attraction of flies and rodents. With a strong educational program and technical support, these problems can be avoided and minimized.

FIRST COST

Initial costs include staff time for a project coordinator. This position may be within a municipal or county government, or within a nonprofit agency, community college, or other entity. A program can be started in one year with a half-time coordinator. Additional costs may be incurred for design and production of customized educational materials, for construction of demonstration gardens, and so forth. The estimated cost is $40,000 to $80,000 for the first-year planning and start-up.

LIFECYCLE COSTS

Ongoing costs depend on the scale of the program. They include staff time, cost of outreach efforts, and possibly subsidies for composting bins sold through the program.

ESTIMATED QUANTITATIVE PERFORMANCE

Performance metrics may include the following:

- Number of participating households and percentage of eligible households participating
- Rate of continued participation over time
- Amount of waste reduced
- GHG emissions reduction based on waste reduced

Since compostable organics typically make up about 25 percent of household waste, participation in a program by 40 percent of households in a community would result in a 10 percent reduction in residential waste. This will also result in a disproportionately greater reduction in methane generation at landfills.

IMPLEMENTATION SUPPORTS AND CONSTRAINTS

It is advisable to involve local environmental health and vector control agencies in program design, implementation, and monitoring, in order to ensure that their legitimate concerns regarding the potential for odors and vector attraction are addressed. Properly managed compost piles produce minimal objectionable odors, and do not attract flies or rodents.

Support for home composting programs may be garnered from farm advisors and agricultural extension agents; local nurseries and garden suppliers (who may be interested in selling subsidized or discounted compost bins); garden clubs and master gardener programs; nonprofit recycling organizations, and existing home composting programs of neighboring communities.

INFORMATIONAL SOURCES

- Master Composter website: www.mastercomposter.com/
- "A hub for all composting information:" www.Howtocompost.org
- Los Angeles County Department of Public Works Smartgardening website: http://ladpw.org/epd/sg/
- Santa Cruz County Department of Public Works composting program website: www.compostsantacruzcounty.org/Home_Composting/Backyard_Composting/library_resources.html
- www.ci.santa-cruz.ca.us/pw/homecomposting.html
  Cornell University Waste Management Institute Composting Program website: http://compost.css.cornell.edu/Composting_homepage.html
- Texas A&M Horticulture Program Composting Guide. Includes Chapter 7: You Can Start a Home Composting Education Program:
- http://aggie-horticulture.tamu.edu/extension/compost/compost.html

REPORTS AND STUDIES

- Campbell, Stu, *Let It Rot!: The Gardener's Guide to Composting*, 3rd ed. Pownal, VT: Storey Communications, 1998.
- Clarence G. Golueke, *Composting: A Study of the Process and Its Principles*. Emmaus, PA: Rodale Press, 1972.

COMMERCIAL AND INSTITUTIONAL RECYCLING: TARGETING THE TOP WASTE PRODUCERS

Daniel T. Sicular, PhD
Environmental Science Associates (ESA)

INTERVENTION TYPE: PROGRAM

Description

This program involves targeting and conducting direct outreach to the largest producers of waste in a community. The intended outcome of the program is to increase participation in programs to reduce, reuse, recycle, and compost wastes.

The program requires the close cooperation of the public or private entity responsible for collecting commercial, industrial, and institutional waste. The program may be initiated by having the waste collector create a list of their customers who produce the most waste, for example, the top 30, or all those producing over five cubic yards of waste per week. The program then works with individual large waste producers one-on-one to develop a set of strategies to reduce waste and increase their participation in existing collection programs.

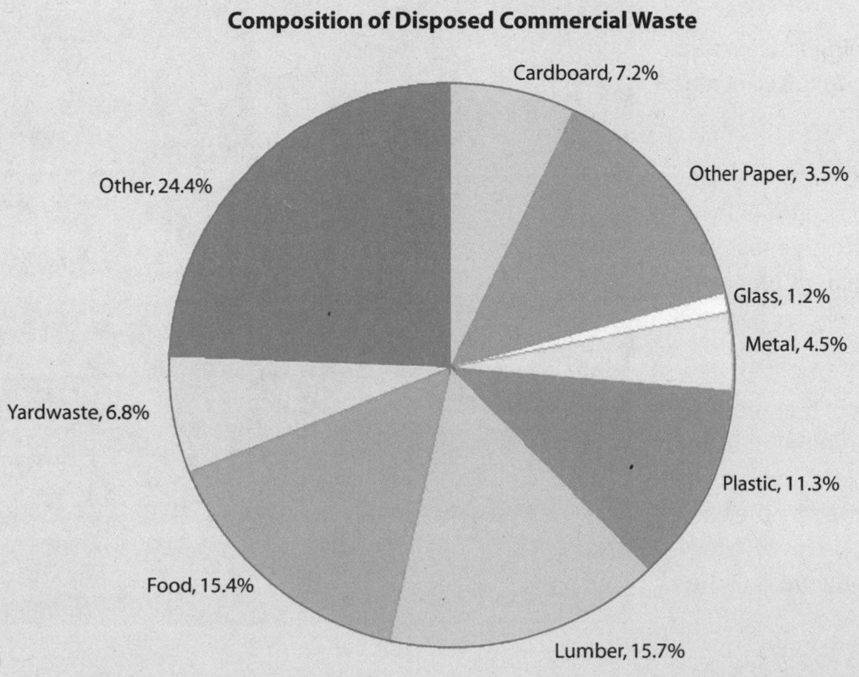

Composition of Disposed Commercial Waste

- Cardboard, 7.2%
- Other Paper, 3.5%
- Glass, 1.2%
- Metal, 4.5%
- Plastic, 11.3%
- Lumber, 15.7%
- Food, 15.4%
- Yardwaste, 6.8%
- Other, 24.4%

Figure 10-13
Major recyclable materials in commercial waste include cardboard, beverage containers, and compostable food scraps. Data source: *CalRecycle Daniel T. Sicular*

SUPPORT GOALS AND OBJECTIVES

This program supports the goals of waste reduction, beneficial use of waste materials, and leveraging existing programs and efforts.

Strategies may include changes to purchasing and processing to reduce residuals and byproducts; changes to internal waste handling methods; and changes to the configuration of loading docks or refuse enclosures. The program may include technical assistance for implementing recommendations, researching materials and processes, and working with the waste collector to change the size of refuse and recycling containers and the frequency of collection. The program manager follows up at intervals to monitor effectiveness, trouble-shoot, and fine-tune strategies.

PERFORMANCE CHARACTERISTICS

Typically, about 20 percent of businesses and institutions in a community produce about 80 percent of the commercial solid waste. Targeting the largest producers therefore has the potential to achieve significant reductions in this waste stream, with associated reduction in greenhouse gas emissions.

POTENTIAL SYNERGISM

The program is synergistic with existing recycling and composting collection programs, and also with programs to encourage and assist businesses and institutions to reduce energy and water use.

IMPLEMENTATION TIME

This program requires minimal planning and start-up. Implementation period is generally two to six months.

BENEFITS

The program provides direct outreach and assistance to the largest producers of waste in a community. Its chief benefit is to increase the effectiveness of other sustainable materials management programs already in place.

DRAWBACKS

The program requires a high degree of technical knowledge on the part of those conducting the outreach. Over time, participation and effectiveness of strategies that have been implemented by the targeted waste producers tend to slip; periodic follow-up is essential to maintain the effectiveness of the program.

Figure 10-14
Successful commercial recycling programs depend on the involvement of employees. *Larry Kass*

First Cost

For a mid-size community, initial costs may be:

- $2,000 to $5,000 in staff time for data-gathering and planning
- $5,000 to $15,000 for development and production of outreach materials (information sheets, labels, and the like)

Lifecycle Costs

Lifecycle cost considerations include ongoing staff time to continue outreach, training, and follow-up, local transportation costs for site visits, and a budget for producing outreach materials. The program will result in a reduction in refuse collection costs for participating businesses and institutions.

Estimated Quantitative Performance

The program has the potential to reduce the commercial and institutional waste stream by 15 to 20 percent, through waste reduction and increasing participation in recycling and composting collection programs. Greenhouse gas reduction can be calculated using the EPA's WARM model.

Implementation Supports and Constraints

The program depends on a close relationship with the waste collector. This is more complicated in communities where there are multiple companies providing commercial waste collection services. The program may be facilitated by the establishment of contract terms that require waste collectors to provide recycling and composting collection services along with refuse collection service, and that establish rates that cover collection costs even with a decrease in collected waste and a shift from disposal to recycling and composting.

Informational Sources

There are many Internet-based sources of information on commercial and institutional waste reduction, recycling, and composting. Some of these may be tailored for local use. See, for example, the California Department of Resources Recycling and Recovery's business and school waste reduction pages:

- www.calrecycle.ca.gov/ReduceWaste/Business/
- www.calrecycle.ca.gov/ReduceWaste/Schools/

Several cities and counties have very active programs of this kind, including:

- San Francisco Department of the Environment: www.sfenvironment.org/our_programs/topics.html?ti=5
- Alameda County Waste Management Authority and Recycling Board: www.stopwaste.org
- EPA Warm Model: www.epa.gov/climatechange/wycd/waste/calculators/Warm_home.html

GHG EMISSIONS BENEFITS OF RECYCLING AND ORGANICS MANAGEMENT

Jeff Caton, PE, LEED AP
Environmental Science Associates (ESA)

INTERVENTION TYPE: BEST PRACTICE

Description

Generally, there are significant greenhouse gas emissions reductions associated with recycling and composting municipal solid waste (MSW). Recycling reduces the demand for raw or virgin materials while remanufacturing with recycled materials generally reduces overall energy use. Recycling also leaves more carbon sequestered in forests since fewer trees need to be harvested for wood and paper products.

Composting keeps organics out of landfills, where anaerobic decomposition releases methane—a powerful GHG. Carbon dioxide released through composting is considered biogenic and carbon neutral, as it originates from decomposition of recently living plant sources, not fossil fuels, and will presumably be sequestered by new plant growth. Well-managed composting operations minimize the release of methane and nitrous oxide (more powerful GHGs than carbon dioxide), while compost application increases soil carbon uptake and lowers the demand for water, fertilizer, and other soil inputs. However, composting is a process dependent on many variables, including local methods and site conditions, making it difficult to predict the precise fraction of organic material that is successfully converted into CO_2 through aerobic degradation. Also, organic material that is high in nitrogen, such as food scraps and grass clippings, can produce significant nitrous oxide under wet and oxygen-limited conditions.

Many cities use the International Council for Local and Environmental Initiatives (ICLEI)'s Clean Air and Climate Protection (CACP) software, or the recently released Local Government Operations (LGO) protocol,[3] to estimate the GHG emissions

Figure 10-15
GHG emissions associated with municipal solid waste can be reduced significantly through recycling and composting. *Jeff Caton*

associated with disposal of solid waste. However, neither of these approaches includes methodologies for estimating lifecycle GHG emissions reductions associated
with recycling or composting.

Despite the uncertainties associated with quantifying the GHG benefits of recycling
and composting, there are several models available. The EPA's Waste Reduction
Model is probably the most widely used. WARM calculates the full lifecycle emissions
impacts of a baseline situation (e.g., 100 percent landfilling) and compares that to the
alternative management options for 34 separate categories of waste material. WARM
takes into account the upstream benefits of recycling, the carbon sequestration benefits from composting, and the grid energy offsets from combusting solid waste or
landfill gas. To compare alternatives, the model includes inputs for transportation distances, landfill gas (LFG) capture percentage, and LFG energy recovery.

More accurate and site-specific methods are being developed to quantify GHG
emissions associated with composting. A current project by the California Department of Resources Recycling and Recovery (CalRecycle) is developing data, methods, and tools for quantifying the full lifecycle costs and GHG impacts of various
alternatives to landfilling, including recycling, composting, biomass-to-energy, and
anaerobic digestion. The study should address some known shortcomings of the
WARM tool. Ongoing research by others should also prove to be useful in quantifying the GHG benefits associated with the end use of compost, including increased
soil carbon sequestration, decreased water demand, and improved soil health.

SUPPORT GOALS AND OBJECTIVES
Estimate the GHG emissions reduction benefits of waste recycling and composting. For
municipalities that have ownership or operational control over waste management and
disposal, the associated emissions count toward their municipal operations inventory
of GHG emissions (Scope 1). For other municipalities, emissions associated with waste
management generally count toward their communitywide inventory (Scope 3).

PERFORMANCE CHARACTERISTICS
Quantify and compare the GHG emissions reduction benefit of recycling, composting, and landfilling of municipal solid waste.

POTENTIAL SYNERGISM
Analysis should be coordinated with planning and implementation of residential
and commercial waste collection and management programs, and with development of municipal or communitywide GHG emissions inventories.

IMPLEMENTATION TIME
With good data or valid assumptions on amount of waste material generated, recycled, and composted, meaningful analysis using WARM takes just a few hours. Use
of more sophisticated tools will add to implementation time.

BENEFITS

- Knowing the GHG emissions impacts associated with different municipal solid waste management options provide planners with valuable information for evaluating climate impacts and comparing the carbon footprint of management alternatives for specific waste materials.

- As carbon markets develop and mature, such reductions may qualify for carbon credits that can be sold or traded. In 2009, the Chicago Climate Exchange (CCX) released an offset project protocol for Avoided Emissions from Organic Waste Disposal.

- The co-benefits of composting are many, including increased soil carbon uptake and lower demand for water, fertilizer, and other soil inputs (synthetic fertilizers are a big source of nitrous oxide emissions).

DRAWBACKS

WARM is probably the most widely used model for estimating GHG emissions associated with waste management practices, but like all models it has inherent uncertainties, embedded simplifications, and boundary conditions that limit its accuracy and applicability to all situations. WARM's recognized shortcomings include reliance on nationwide rather than site-specific data, and the model likely overestimates methane capture resulting from landfill capping because most landfills do not install LFG recovery systems until several years after waste has been deposited into a cell, while wet organic wastes like food and grass clippings decompose in a much shorter timeframe. Some suggest that users of WARM should assume no recovery of landfill methane to get a better estimate of GHG emissions associated with food and grass waste. Also, many believe WARM incorrectly assumes there are no methane or nitrous oxide emissions associated with composting, while others believe there should be more credit for the full lifecycle benefits of composting after it is applied to soil, including displacement of synthetic fertilizers, fungicides, and pesticides. Those who use WARM for estimating composting emissions should consult additional research in these areas, including the ongoing 2009 CalRecycle study and a 2007 study by Brown and Subler.

FIRST COST

Labor cost is the primary determinant. The WARM tool is available free from the EPA. There are costs associated with measuring material flows at the detail appropriate for WARM analysis (34 possible categories).

LIFECYCLE COSTS

There are no lifecycle costs.

ESTIMATED QUANTITATIVE PERFORMANCE

Material reuse, recycling, and composting can have a dramatic impact on climate preservation. Composting keeps organics out of landfills, which are commonly thought to contribute from 2 to 3 percent of global GHG emissions. However, this figure grossly underestimates the total impact of waste on climate change because it does not account for the full lifecycle impacts of discarded materials, including energy used to extract, manufacture, and transport those materials to the marketplace. Every ton of discarded material sent to landfills or incinerators represents approximately 71 tons of discards associated with mining, manufacturing, oil and gas exploration, agriculture, coal combustion, and other processes (Pratt et al., 2008). The EPA released a report in 2009 that estimates 42 percent of total U.S. GHG emissions are associated with provision of material goods and food, from extraction or harvest of materials and crops, production and transport of goods, and ultimate disposal. Material reuse, recycling, and composting are important stages in the overall materials management process that provide significant opportunities for GHG emissions reduction.

Figure 10-16 depicts the steps in the material lifecycle, from raw materials to products to final disposition, showing associated GHG emissions, carbon sequestration, and/or grid energy displacement (avoided fossil fuel use). (From EPA report *Solid Waste Management and Greenhouse Gases*, Executive Summary, page ES-11, www.epa.gov/climatechange/wycd/waste/SWMGHGreport.htm)

Figure 10-16
Greenhouse gas-producing materials should move through a lifecycle process that results in carbon offsets, sinks, sequestering, or reuse. ***Source:*** *Environmental Protection Agency*

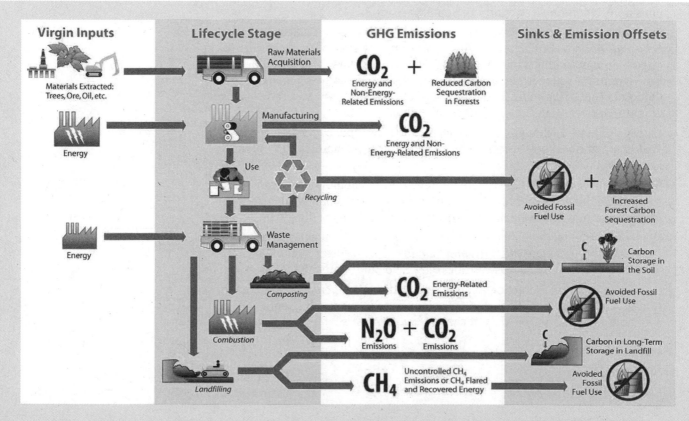

IMPLEMENTATION SUPPORTS AND CONSTRAINTS

GHG emissions estimates developed with the WARM tool, or any other model, will only be as accurate as the available data on material types and weights. Consult WARM instructions to obtain the list of material categories included in the model.

INFORMATIONAL SOURCES

- Download the WARM tool and associated guidance at: www.epa.gov/climatechange/wycd/waste/calculators/Warm_home.html.
- For an evaluation of existing lifecycle assessment tools used to analyze municipal solid waste, including WARM, see a report by RTI International to CalRecycle, available at: www.calrecycle.ca.gov/Climate/Organics/LifeCycle/default.htm#Scope

REPORTS AND STUDIES

- Sally Brown and Scott Subler, "Composting and Greenhouse Gas Emissions," *Biocycle*, March 2007, Vol. 48, No. 3, pp. 37–38.
- California Air Resources Board (CARB), CCAR, ICLEI, and TCR, Local Government Operations Protocol for the quantification and reporting of greenhouse gas emissions inventories, Version 1.0, September 2008.
- California Department of Resources Recycling and Recovery (CalRecycle), *Economic Analysis and Life Cycle Assessment of Diversion Alternatives,* an ongoing project with RTI International, R.W. Beck, Matthew Cotton, and Dr. Sally Brown perform a lifecycle assessment of diversion alternatives in support of the California Global Warming Solutions Act of 2006 (AB 32). www.calrecycle.ca.gov/Climate/Organics/LifeCycle/default.htm#Scope
- Chicago Climate Exchange (CCX), *Avoided Emissions from Organic Disposal Offset Projects,* a 2009 Offset Project Protocol. www.chicagoclimatex.com/content.jsf?id=1814
- Brenda Pratt and David Ciplet, Kate M. Bailey, Eric Lombardi, *Stop Trashing the Climate,* Institute for Local Self-Reliance with Global Alliance for Incinerator Alternatives and Eco-Cycle, June 2008. www.stoptrashingtheclimate.org/
- U.S. Environmental Protection Agency, *Opportunities to Reduce Greenhouse Gas Emissions through Materials and Land Management Practices,* September 2009, available at: www.epa.gov/oswer/docs/ghg_land_and_materials_management.pdf
- U.S. Environmental Protection Agency, *Solid Waste Management and Greenhouse Gases, A Life-Cycle Assessment of Emissions and Sinks,* 3rd ed., September 2006, available at www.epa.gov/climatechange/wycd/waste/SWMGHGreport.html

Sustainable Economic Development: The Longer View

Dave Leland, CRE
Leland Consulting Group

Chris Zahas, AICP
Leland Consulting Group

Introduction

For the past 50 years, urban development has not been built to last. Disposable practices have extended to the real estate industry, resulting in a dramatic reduction in the economic life span of buildings. Irresponsible lending practices and access to cheap capital drove the economic recession and resulted in too many ill-conceived developments. Unstable financing—coupled with inexperienced development, weak design, undercapitalized tenants, and poor tenant mix—has driven many of these centers out of business. This creates areas of blight and disinvestment, but it also represents a significant waste of building energy and infrastructure. Considerations of economic value should be addressed at all stages of a sustainability planning process by asking questions such as: Will this action create short- or long-term value for the community, owner, or both? Can the long-term value be capitalized to make it financially attractive today? If not, what tools need to be brought to bear to close the gap? This longer view of sustainable economic development is not a stand-alone step or plan, but rather a philosophy and approach that adds to and improves other planning models.

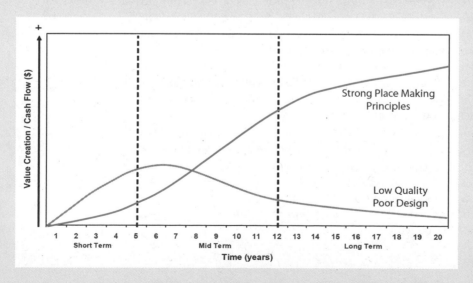

Figure 11-1
Sustainable development provides economic benefits over the long term, in contrast to traditional development which often reaps short-term profits at the expense of long-term value. *Leland Consulting Group*

Guiding Principles for a Longer View of Sustainable Economic Development

- *Comprehensiveness:* Systems that allocate costs and capture benefits from all components of a city must be put in place—incorporating natural resources, the built environment, transportation, economic development, social justice, and more.

- *Patience:* Change takes time. A core measure of a sustainable system is the rejection of short-term, quick-fix models that have led to our current urban problems. Thus, long-range physical and economic plans are needed to adequately implement the goals of sustainability and capture long-term benefits.

- *Public-private partnerships:* While the public sector establishes policies, goals, and objectives to encourage sustainable planning practices, implementation is largely the responsibility of the private sector. Sustainability is good for business. Establishing strong partnerships with the private sector and other public agencies can help municipalities win grants, attract business and political support, and identify and implement successful strategies that match public regulatory tools with private-sector implementation needs.

- *Flexibility and adaptability:* Economic sustainability means that citizens will have economic opportunity. Pinning a community's hopes on a narrowly defined economic development strategy or industry can leave a community behind if market, economic, or technological conditions change.

- *Leadership:* Strong leadership is the hallmark of any successful initiative. A sustainability program must have meaningful and broad support from civic, community, and business leaders.

Key Challenges Moving Forward

While there is general awareness and support for more sustainable planning and development methods, in practice, achieving sustainability goals and objectives is difficult. Some key challenges include:

- *Restrictive lending practices:* The loose lending practices of the recent past are history. Even when capital does become available, the conditions for development will be considerably tighter. Yet these new lending practices may not address the issues of quality, acceptance, and the community and design considerations that make the difference between an asset that ages well and poorly designed assets with limited lifecycles. A significant collaboration between the lending and development industries is necessary to ensure that decision-making processes balance design, market, and financial needs.

- *Unfamiliarity with business principles:* Implementation of community plans is largely the role of the private sector through housing, commercial, industrial, and mixed-use development. However, public policy-makers often lack a basic understanding of the financial and economic processes that drive business decisions. Without an understanding of the role that risk, certainty, investment, and profit makes in business decisions, public policy often inhibits the desired type of investment rather than encourages it.

- *Overly prescriptive planning:* It is common for planning and development ordinances to be overly prescriptive. Markets change, and plans that don't allow for change can leave cities flat-footed. To ensure the visual and physical diversity that makes cities interesting places, plans must balance a developer's need for flexibility with a municipality's need for assurance.

- *Political cycles:* A recurring theme of economic sustainability is that it is a long-term proposition. However, public policy is implemented by elected leaders who often make decisions based on short-term political cycles and events. This conflict can lead to decisions that are based on short-term goals of expediency or public opinion and not the long-term benefit of sustainability.

- *"Pay as you go" financing:* In fast-growing regions of the country, municipal financing systems have become increasingly reliant on development impact fees to fund ongoing services. This pay-as-you-go funding structure encourages sprawl development. Likewise, when cities retain sales taxes generated within their boundaries, there is an incentive to expand commercial zoning whether or not there is a demonstrated need for additional inventory. The recession that began in 2008 has shown that growth alone cannot sustain a community's economy, but *can* encourage sprawling developments that become the blighted areas of the future.

- *Lack of holistic planning:* Cities are measured and seen as a whole, rather than the sum of their parts. New development has become very costly due to impact fees assessed for infrastructure, making many projects unaffordable. More flexibility is needed to reflect the positive impact that smart-growth projects can have on the greater community. Expanding the "balance sheet" to incorporate positive economic and noneconomic impacts can help to quantify fee structures for new development and levels of public participation in these projects.

Figure 11-2
Compartmentalized decision-making processes limit the information available at any given stage and prevent integrated, sustainable analysis from taking place. *Leland Consulting Group*

- *Compartmentalized decision-making:* Many municipal management structures compartmentalize technical divisions with the intent of focusing on narrow issues and creating efficiencies. Such models often create "silos" and encourage compartmentalized decision-making that results in incomplete solutions or solutions that conflict with decisions made from another silo. A strategic development plan should inform the details of all departments.

Preparing the Team

Some of the professional qualifications that are necessary to create and pursue new sustainable models include:

- *Strategists:* While every plan must have a solid technical foundation, every plan also needs a strategic and holistic leader to bring together technical elements, and to ensure that silo-based thinking doesn't control the development. The strategist should have experience working in a wide range of communities, and should also be a visionary who understands the long-term trends that will shape communities and is capable of communicating that vision to technical disciplines participating in the plan.
- *One-stop liaison:* A sustainability initiative will require participation from all City Hall departments. To outsiders, it can be difficult to navigate this complex and interrelated system. A dedicated person should be chosen to serve as a liaison between the community (citizens and businesses) and the various City Hall departments. This will help ensure the initiative is a priority on every department's radar and will help avoid the "silo effect" of singular department leadership.
- *Economist:* A sustainability program needs to strike the proper balance between strategic and technical thinking. Therefore, access to technical experts fluent in economic forecasting, statistical analysis, and financial analysis is needed to ensure that programs and actions are supported by sound data and realistic projections.

Preparing the Tools

Many performance measurement tools are useful in creating a baseline to track sustainable economic progress. The U.S. Census publishes demographic and socioeconomic data needed to assess existing conditions and long-term performance. Employment data, typically published by state employment departments, may be used to track workforce characteristics, industry composition, and unemployment. Examples of key performance measures that municipalities can track with such data include:

- Unemployment and poverty rates
- Education rates
- Population and household income growth
- Industry mix and average wages

Visual mapping tools such as GIS are useful for identifying geographic concentrations of industries, job-housing ratios, and other key economic and demographic data. Regulatory and legal tools, such as those described below, can help ensure balanced economic development.

DATA TYPES

Types of data that municipalities should collect and update regularly include:

- Demographic data: population, households, education, ethnicity, income
- Employment data: unemployment rate, size of workforce
- Industry makeup: total businesses, employment by NAICS industry classification
- Recent building permit data can help highlight the locations of new investment and areas of disinvestment.
- Research on emerging technologies, demographic shifts, consumer preferences, and other broad influences can help to better understand how global conditions will shape local opportunities.

TYPES OF ECONOMIC ANALYSIS

Cities can use a variety of economic analysis tools to gauge their economic strengths and weaknesses, opportunities, and progress toward long-term goals:

- *Market reconnaissance (baseline economic study):* A market reconnaissance identifies baseline demographic, economic, and real estate conditions and trends in order to understand the current composition of a community, evaluate its opportunities and constraints, and inform a variety of subsequent analyses.
- *Employment and population forecasts:* While the future is uncertain, it is important to base plans on future assessments of where a community is headed. In collaboration with regional or statewide agencies, cities should establish forecasts for population and employment.
- *Economic opportunity analysis (EOA):* An EOA is a technical study that compares projected demand for land for industrial and other employment uses to the existing supply of such land. Information from the EOA can be used to develop policies and programs that respond to existing conditions and strategically target new or emerging industries.
- *Retail leakage analysis:* A leakage analysis helps identify the strengths and weaknesses of specific retail sectors within a community by illustrating where consumers are spending their money within the region and identifying specific categories that are over- or underserved.
- *Economic impact analysis:* Economic impact analyses evaluate the direct and indirect economic activity that is generated by a project, proposal, or action. Ranging from jobs created, direct spending, and multiplier effects, economic impact analyses are vital to understanding the value of proposals and particularly in comparing options.

- *Fiscal impact analysis:* The purpose of fiscal impact analysis is to estimate the impact of a development or a land use change on the costs and revenues of government units serving the development. The analysis enables local governments to estimate the difference between the costs of providing services to a new development and the revenues—taxes and user fees, for example—that will be generated by the development.

- *Vacant and underutilized land analysis:* A vacant and underutilized land analysis can identify infill and redevelopment opportunities. The analysis, which identifies where improvement values are low compared to the underlying value of the land, can be used to guide public policy and planning related to redevelopment incentives, zoning densities, and strategic property acquisitions.

OPPORTUNITIES AND CONSTRAINTS

While there are a myriad of opportunities to support the creation of an economically just and sustainable community, there are also constraints that will make the process more challenging.

Figure 11-3
Mixed-use urban neighborhoods such as the Pearl District in Portland, Oregon, are likely to thrive based on long-term demographic and economic trends. *Leland Consulting Group*

Opportunities

- *Demographic trends:* Nationwide demographic trends are increasingly support-ive of more sustainable communities. For example, up to two-thirds of most cities are comprised of one- or two-person households; people who delay marriage and children, and the Baby Boom generation, which is now reaching retirement age. These demographic groups are ideal candidates for urban housing, where homes are smaller and community amenities are within walking distance.

- *Rising gas and energy prices:* As the long-term trend of rising energy prices con-tinues, the cost of living in auto-dependent neighborhoods far from employment will increase. This will increase the demand for environments that support hous-ing and employment centers, alternative modes of transportation, and smaller homes.

- *Diversified economic bases:* As the viability of resource-based economies con-tinues to decline, there is a growing national trend toward economic diversifica-tion. Diversification can benefit the overall economy by providing opportunities for displaced workers to retrain and find new jobs, thereby reducing the adverse economic impacts of a single industry's downturn.

Constraints

- *Lack of economic or population growth:* When competing with places with better opportunities (e.g., better schools, public facilities and community amenities, and so on), it is difficult for communities and regions with little or no growth to attract new investment.

- *Fixed infrastructure that is costly and difficult to modify:* Suburban America is poorly designed to adapt to a future sustainable model. Transportation and land use patterns are fixed through zoning codes, property titles, covenants, and other legal mechanisms, which make them difficult and costly to change.

- *Lack of data:* There is often a lack of good economic data with which to analyze impacts and measure success, particularly in smaller communities. Where de-tailed data does exist, it often varies in format, frequency of update, and regional accuracy.

Preparing the People

KEY STAKEHOLDERS

For a plan to be truly economically sustainable, its development must include meaningful input, responsibility, and ownership from all sectors of industry and society. Examples of key stakeholders likely to be involved in a sustainability plan-ning process include:

- Property and business owners
- Bank/lending executives
- Real estate brokers (commercial and residential)
- Elected leaders
- Trade groups (chamber, business association)

- Residents
- Community groups (nonprofit, neighborhoods, cultural, religious)
- Educational institutions
- Ports and railroads

STAKEHOLDER EDUCATION

Educating policy-makers and community members is a critical part of every planning process and helps ensure that informed decisions are made. Stakeholder education can take a variety of formats, including the following:

- *Work sessions:* City council work sessions can provide valuable background information about a specific issue. They can also educate council members and the general public on complex issues, such as the economics of development.

- *Developer and broker educational lunches:* In many communities, the lack of sustainable development is a supply problem rather than a demand problem. While there is a market for more innovative development, the pool of experienced local developers and the diversity of existing products in the marketplace are limited. In this environment, it is important to reach out to the development and brokerage community, introducing new concepts, demonstrating how success has been achieved elsewhere, and getting feedback on potential barriers.

- *Success audits:* Without acknowledgment of progress toward sustainability goals, it is easy to lose momentum. A success audit is a tool (e.g., website, hard-copy brochure, or multimedia presentation) that catalogs projects, actions, and initiatives that already have taken place, in order to accurately describe progress that is being made and provide a sense of continuity.

Downtown *Vancouver*

CIVIC IMPROVEMENTS

Esther Short Park Redevelopment

Location: Columbia Street to the east, 8th Street to the north, Esther to the west, 6th to the south.

Timeline: 1997 - June 2002

Description: Esther Short Park is Washington's oldest public square. It was bequeathed to the City of Vancouver in 1862 by one of Vancouver's original landowners, Esther Short, whose sole condition was that the 5.2 acres be used as a community square. By the mid-1990's, the park had deteriorated to become a place where people felt unsafe and therefore, didn't visit. The current transformation has taken place with the help of a $2.7 million donation from long-time parks and recreation supporters, George and Carolyn Propstra. The most recent phase of improvements have resulted in a 33,000 square foot brick and concrete community square with a bell tower, and an additional 9,200 square feet of planting beds, and a 3,000 square-foot water feature.

A Community Resource Team made up of parks and recreation commission members, residents and community leaders developed the design objectives for the park's redevelopment. The playground equipment, donated by the Angelo family, is constructed in a Victorian theme that reflects the history of the park. The other amenities, including benches, planters, lighting, signage and bike racks are designed in the Stickley furniture style of the early 1900's. Other amenities include an oval walkway with radiating walks connecting perimeter sidewalks to the surrounding development and streetscape, a gazebo, bronze sculpture, restrooms, rose gardens, a brick civic plaza, an interactive stone water feature,

Developing Goals, Objectives, and Performance Metrics

Participatory workshops are ideal for developing goals and objectives that the entire community will support, as demonstrated by a recent international sustainability conference co-chaired by a principal of Leland Consulting Group. The conference explored the topic of sustainability in a holistic way for the community of San Miguel de Allende, Mexico. At the outset of the workshop, the definition of "sustainability" was expanded to include the physical, economic, social, cultural, and other miscellaneous facets of society. Throughout the course of the workshop, illustrative examples in each of the sectors were explored and debated. Recommendations were made for specific problems, and portable principles were identified that could be applied elsewhere.

Including "target-based" performance metrics—whether a specific reduction in carbon emissions, the number of units of affordable housing to be built, or jobs to be created in an industry—is one of the most effective methods to measure a plan's progress toward economic goals and objectives. Terms such as "more," or "increase," or "reduce" are ambiguous and difficult to quantify. Targets should be evaluated annually—as a part of an annual report, success audit, or business plan—and modified and updated based on new information.

Developing the Strategic Plan

Workshops are an effective format for any type of strategic planning process, particularly where many different disciplines and stakeholders are involved. Workshops can follow a variety of proven models, ranging from NCI charrettes to Urban Land Institute Advisory Service Panels. Common workshop elements include:

- Three- to five-day duration with timelines that are strictly adhered to
- Focus on multidisciplinary collaboration and provide multiple points of stakeholder involvement
- Decisions are made quickly through the involvement of experienced advisors
- Public- and private-sector decision-makers are engaged
- Led by a dynamic and effective manager and facilitator
- Outcome-based, not a design exercise

Conceptual budget: While budgets can vary widely, most strategic planning workshops can be carried out for $50,000 to $150,000.

Developing the Action Plan

Once a strategic plan has been completed, the next step in the process is to assess proposed projects and measures, and prioritize projects in the action plan. Project evaluation and selection criteria give an agency the power to be proactive moving an initiative forward, rather than simply reacting to spontaneous ideas. They can be used to identify good ideas, and explain to decision-makers why certain initiatives should move forward. Criteria should be tailored to a community's unique needs, but should include variations on the following principles:

- *Public-private leverage:* How will the initiative help attract investment, and how does it build on past investments? Is there a private element to the project? Is the private sector ready to match the public's initiative?

- *Community support:* Has the project been developed through a process that involved community input? Will the community support it?

- *Sustainability goals:* Does the project meet vehicle miles traveled (VMT) and carbon emissions targets?

- *Economic opportunity:* Does the initiative support a community's economic development strategy? Will it help attract desired employment?

Implementing the Action Plan

Action plans should have early successes. While a successful project will sustain momentum for a few months, a failed project can delay implementation for many years. Thus, targeting projects that are relatively easy to achieve early on is one strategy to get the ball rolling. Early successes can include the following:

- Communicating the plan's progress and the accomplishments completed

- Forming partnerships—formal or informal—between public and private stakeholder groups

- Concurrency policy: A concurrency policy requires that there be a committed plan and funding in place to pay for the infrastructure required by new development at the time that development occurs. This prevents the unsustainable policy of building something new without a plan to adequately provide critical infrastructure (e.g., roads, utilities, schools, parks, and so forth) and ensures that the cost of new development is not kept artificially low by excluding the cost of basic needs or pushing those costs onto future generations. Consequently, infill and redevelopment sites become more attractive since it is more likely that adequate infrastructure is in place.

- Intergovernmental agreements: Since economic trends, issues, and influences spread well beyond the boundaries of any individual jurisdiction, the solution to economic challenges is often beyond the means of any particular entity. Intergovernmental agreements are used to clarify the goals, roles, and responsibilities of a partnership.

Launching an action plan requires a combination of implementing short-term tasks in the context of a long-term vision. To be effective, the goals and actions of the plan must be fully embedded within the departmental work plans of the various agencies that will implement each task. Part of the work plan should be an assessment of the following year's plan so that adjustments to future years can be made that reflect projects completed; changing economic cycles; and new community priorities. As work is completed, projects from future year work plans are rolled forward into the immediate timeframe and subsequent years are advanced. In this way, the action plan becomes a living document where projects are continually moved forward incrementally.

A Sustainable Return on Investment

John Williams
HDR Engineering, Inc.

Securing Support for Sustainable Strategies

A significant challenge in creating sustainable communities is that "green"—first and foremost—is a local issue that must be supported by the community and impacted stakeholders; implementation is dependent on this support. Stakeholders need to know the costs and benefits expected, who will pay, and

Figure 11-6
John Williams made a Commitment to Action to the Clinton Global Initiative to test and push the SROI framework into the public domain to encourage broader application of efforts to measure "green." The framework was introduced to the public at CGI's 2009 annual meeting. *Clinton Global Initiative*

how action will contribute to creating a sustainable community. The application of the Sustainable Return on Investment (SROI) methodology answers these questions and provides objective and transparent information needed to craft a Green Business Case (a compilation of objective, transparent costs, benefits, risks, and probable outcomes that include the value of a wide range of triple-bottom-line implications).

To secure support for investments in specific sustainable strategies, planners and policy-makers need to articulate the reasons for spending money on initiatives that result in energy or water conservation, development of high-performance buildings, creation of bike trails, or preservation of urban forests. They need to explain the value the community can expect from the use of local, state, and federal tax dollars. The explanation will be stronger if it includes the objective measurement of costs and benefits developed from SROI methodology.

Planners and policy-makers need to take account of traditional lifecycle costs associated with a given initiative, including capital invested as well as operations and maintenance, commissioning and decommissioning costs. Financial Return on Investment, or FROI, projections drive investment decisions today, with some qualitative considerations for environmental and social impacts. Given the goal of creating sustainable communities, there are costs and benefits not captured by FROI that are critical and should be accounted for to fully inform decision-making.

The SROI approach, however, calculates the costs and benefits associated with the social, environmental, and economic attributes of specific initiatives. Planners and policy-makers who are equipped to articulate the value of this entire "triple bottom line" will be positioned to help stakeholders contribute through informed decisions and with the establishment of priorities aimed at creating sustainable communities. As planning activities are organized and stakeholders activated, goals and objectives can be aligned with performance metrics that drive alternative evaluations to dollar-to-dollar comparisons of projected outcomes. Actions can be prioritized to achieve the maximum sustainable benefit. Objective, transparent alternatives and performance analysis can be pursued to enhance the odds of securing funding.

Conventional planning or engineering estimates are often used to guide investment decisions, but unfortunately, these often do not support sustainable outcomes. These estimates are known to have varying degrees of accuracy depending on the level of detail available and the relevancy of comparisons made to establish values. They often include only capital costs and projected operations and maintenance costs.

More sophisticated estimates involve the use of Life Cycle Cost Analysis (LCCA) to evaluate specific alternatives. LCCA takes into account capital investment, operations and maintenance, commissioning and decommissioning costs. LCCA also factors in the future value of money used to state a projected outcome in terms of Net Present Value (NPV) for FROI. Often that value is presented as a single number without taking into account the degree of risk and probability of a range of outcomes.

The engineering estimates and LCCA approaches do not account for nonfinancial or external risk and benefits for the triple bottom line. They typically understate the full range of sustainable benefits, such as worker productivity, community health, and safety considerations that are legitimate concerns when using taxpayer dollars. They fail to account for the risks and benefits associated with external factors including implications related to GHG, criteria air contaminants, and fugitive emissions; energy, water, and vehicle miles saved, water saved; reduced energy consumptions and waste generated. Actions that address these risks and benefits are the foundation for sustainable communities. The failure to account for externalities has significantly contributed to the environmental challenges we face today.

Full accounting for SROI is essential to achieving this goal of sustainable communities.

Conventional engineering estimates and LCCA projections that fail to address noncash and external benefits result in community sustainability plans that lack the depth, clarity, and objective metrics needed to secure public support. By not counting the value of external benefits, many common practices including use of fossil fuels, leave a false impression regarding the full costs associated with their use. Guidance provided in the following section includes a description of the methodology that can be used to measure and assign monetary values to the full range of costs and benefits associated with the triple bottom line. The methodology includes four steps:

1. Development of structure and logic to guide and assure transparency in the analysis
2. Quantification and validation (including source credibility) of input data assumptions
3. Risk assessment process
4. Quantification of ranges of risks and benefits of potential outcomes

Figure 11-7
The four-step SROI process provides a standard way to measure financial, social (noncash), and environmental variables by assigning dollar amounts. *HDR, Inc*

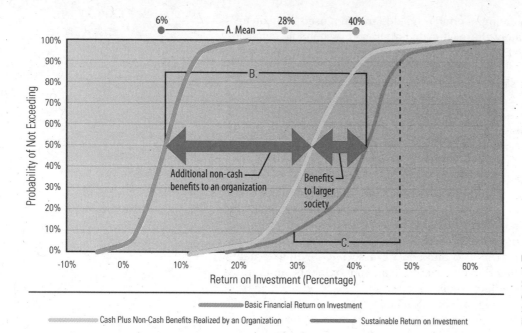

Figure 11-8
The SROI process is summarized in the SROI curve on the diagram. The difference between the values shown for the SROI curve and the financial ROI curve is the value of "green." *HDR, Inc.*

While a number of outputs can be produced as part of the SROI methodology, the sustainability "S" curve (Figure 11-8) is perhaps the most significant, as it allows for a comparison of the attributes of a given project, program, or initiative including FROI, value of noncash benefits, and value of external costs and benefits stated in either percentage terms or dollar values.

Eight principles should be considered when comparing sustainable strategies:

1. Implemented strategies make the difference
2. Stakeholder support is a prerequisite to approval for implementation
3. Stakeholders should be equipped to make informed decisions
4. The information available should account for the full monetary value of costs and benefits associated with a given initiative across the triple bottom line
5. Single number projections are always wrong—use probability-based projections to provide a more precise description of potential outcomes
6. Objective measures are superior to subjective when setting public priorities
7. Transparency is mandatory to maintain credibility
8. Performance measurement, monitoring, and reporting are important for long-term credibility

The use of sustainability "S" curves to evaluate and articulate a Green Business Case will be invaluable in addressing the principles listed above. Guiding decisions without the benefit of this information can be difficult, frustrating, and often leads to choices that abandon sustainable objectives.

Preparing the Team

SROI-based economic valuations are challenging to introduce into public decision-making. Examples of how these challenges manifest are as follows:

- Many public entities make investment decisions based upon planning/engineering estimates and/or LCCA that fail to value the entire triple bottom line. A major transit organization in the Northeast declined to support sustainable strategies, because they appeared more costly on the basis of FROI, and lacked knowledge that would reveal sufficient sustainable benefits to warrant support.

- A large county in central Florida declined to apply the SROI methodology because it is viewed as a new framework that reaches beyond traditional decision tools.

- A regional planning organization in California declined to use the SROI methodology, because a broader analysis would be more costly (marginally) than traditional approaches, which discouraged communities from conducting the analysis to help prioritize energy-related investments.

- Preexisting budgetary priorities that were established on the basis of political objectives or obligations can run counter to a desire to present comprehensive, transparent analysis of alternative priorities.

Figure 11-9
EECBG and SROI analysis was provided to the City of Boston, Massachusetts.
© *Barry Howe/Corbis*

- Many communities see access to certain grant programs as a means of supplementing their general funds to support activity that would otherwise be addressed with local tax dollars. These expenditures are aimed at closing budget gaps as opposed to producing sustainable results; the communities see no need for additional analysis or the potential downside of increased transparency.

To apply the SROI methodology, there are several qualifications needed on the team. Expertise required to pursue the SROI methodology includes:

- Research skills in science, technology, planning, and economics
- Economics skills including statistics, cost/benefit, probability, and budget analysis and modeling
- Knowledge of built and natural environments, the regulatory climate, and community
- Facilitation skills and mastery of collaborative, consensus-building, and evidence-based processes
- Written, spoken, and graphics skills to aid in soliciting input and conveying conclusions

▼Figure 11-10
SROI was provided for an analysis of carbon trading for Enbridge Gas Distribution in Toronto, Canada. © *Barry Howe/Corbis*

▲Figure 11-11
SROI was used for campus programming at Johns Hopkins University in Baltimore, Maryland. © *Alan Karchmer*

Preparing the Tools

Several types of quantitative, qualitative, visual, and participatory tools are applicable for the SROI methodology. It relies on a series of available risk/benefit, probability, Monte Carlo analysis, and spreadsheet software programs, including Excel, @Risk, and energy-modeling tools.

In addition to software, the methodology is informed through a large collection of data inputs sourced through Meta review, industry-sector research, and applied knowledge of planning, design, scientific, and economics professionals. Regulatory agency input, business groups, and outside expert opinions are sought to help in assembling data input.

SROI is *not a proprietary product,* although knowledge of the proper application is required, as is a skilled facilitator.

When applying SROI, project scale will matter when justifying the cost of the analysis. Additionally, SROI includes the LCCA and FROI that are usually applied in traditional feasibility analysis. The incremental cost associated with SROI inclusion and monetary metrics begins at around $25,000. For projects valued at $1 million or more, there is sufficient scale and benefit to warrant an SROI analysis.

While practices like LCCA follow accepted steps to produce results, there is no regulatory framework to guide the measurement of sustainable benefits. This lack of a regulatory or standardized approach to performance rating has been a common challenge in the sustainability field. The resulting vacuum has led to the development of solutions by organizations (including individual companies) that are active in the marketplace. One of the best examples can be found in the emergence of LEED via the U.S. Green Buildings Council. LEED-based rating systems are expanding across a variety of applications yet still do not offer a standardized approach to assigning monetary values to "green" project attributes.

Credibility associated with SROI-based projections is related to the effectiveness of communication and transparency of the analytical process. Charrette-based facilitation tools are used to present the analytical parameters, inputs, and alternatives under consideration, and to facilitate input and the building of consensus for the process. The analysis occurs and results are presented and adjustments to reflect regional or market considerations are made within the charrette setting.

The risk assessment process associated with SROI methodology relies on a decision-making tool, an automated form of charrette development that speeds analysis through software and available databases. Scenarios can be run in real time to shorten effort spent in debate. The analytical tools help sort a wide range of alternatives based on their contribution of risk or benefits, which helps prioritize tactics that matter most to achieving desired outcomes.

Preparing the Place

To conduct a credible SROI analysis, clearly organized research methods and the use of data inputs—that closely relate to the strategy—are essential. Most projects will begin with a meta-review (screening of existing related research), which will focus on published peer-reviewed data from credible sources, including federal agencies, professional associations, market or industry indices, actuarial tables, and public surveys. SROI methodology will identify values drawn from research. Those values will be validated through risk assessment and charrette-based consensus-building process.

With regard to the specific categories of analysis for a sustainability initiative, in addition to the normal LCCA- and FROI-based inputs, SROI will typically take into consideration the following variables:

- Energy consumption/conservation
- GHG savings or production
- Criteria air contaminants
- Fugitive air emissions
- Traditional jobs saved or lost
- Green jobs created
- Water used or saved
- Solid waste produced, recovered, reduced, or disposed of in landfills
- Vehicle miles traveled
- Development density
- Worker productivity
- Employee and community health
- Injuries and deaths avoided
- Barrels of oil saved
- Resiliency, the ability to mitigate implications of a manmade or natural disaster

As SROI methodology is applied more frequently, it is easier to understand the opportunities and constraints with the approach.

Opportunities that are emerging as a result of the application of the SROI methodology include the ability to:

- Move sustainable strategies into implementation as a result of better understanding their benefits
- Reprioritize capital improvement programs on a basis of total SROI as opposed to strict FROI or political considerations
- Anticipate the implications of development in a carbon-regulated environment and use that information to influence decisions and priorities
- Help stakeholder groups understand a broader range of costs and benefits associated with given actions
- Help public policy-makers balance tradeoffs;
- Help communities craft green business cases to articulate the benefits associated with funding applications required to participate in competitive funding programs
- Help communities ease the performance measurement, monitoring, and reporting effort required when using state and federal funding

- Help federal funding agencies screen, select, and justify decisions for grant awards

- Attract private-sector capital to public sustainability initiatives through better understanding, balancing, and management of project development costs and benefits

- Better manage negotiations with private partners engaged in large-scale and/or long-term development initiatives that promise sustainable outcomes

Constraints that will slow the adaptation of SROI include:

- Financial constraints that reinforce decision-making focused on immediate/essential needs instead of long-term sustainability

- Dependence on federal funding and a need to frame sustainability strategies around policy priorities (Recent developments, including the October 5, 2009, issuance of Executive Order 13514, mandating a full accounting of social and economic costs and benefits associated with federal agency environmental initiatives, are reversing the potential for constraint to the use of the SROI framework and are providing incentive for adoption of the practice.)

While SROI assessments may be used as standalone findings, there is significant added value to be derived from using SROI outputs to better inform a range of traditional studies, plans, and reporting including:

- Feasibility studies
- Real estate market demand analysis
- Green jobs analysis
- Bond feasibility opinions
- Performance baseline studies
- Performance measurement, monitoring, and reporting

Preparing the People

Key stakeholders who are relevant to the SROI methodology include:

- Elected officials/policy-makers
- Agency/department heads and project managers
- Senior financial managers
- Funding agency representatives
- Impacted community group and NGO leaders
- Rating agency representatives
- Representatives of local academic institutions
- Representatives of regional planning organizations

These stakeholders should be involved throughout the planning and implementation of any project. Following is an illustration of how SROI was used to engage the public in discussion.

A county in Florida planned to redevelop a prime real estate parcel it owned in the center of a densely populated city. Cooperation among the county, city, and local development community was essential to move the redevelopment forward. Each party had different and conflicting visions. Given the need to strike a balance among these interests to agree to a feasible development program, SROI was used to measure the cost and benefits of different development alternatives so that the diverse collection of stakeholders would more fully understand each scenario. The transparent process featuring open charrette sessions and analytical runs enabled community members to understand the tradeoffs. The process provided credibility for the final plan and its potential to address the long-term interests of all parties. The budget involved hundreds of millions in development investments through a public-private partnership and the SROI process cost less than $50,000.

SROI enables community leadership to understand and articulate the risks and benefits associated with an action. Leaders are more likely to lend support to initiatives that they fully understand and can convey to their constituents.

Developing Goals, Objectives, and Performance Metrics

When conducting economic and SROI analysis, we begin by defining scope, schedule, limits or boundaries of evaluation, available and required information, responsibilities for collecting information, and description of deliverables, as well as assumptions (this work can often be done in two to four weeks depending upon availability of data and stakeholder participants). Beyond these steps, implementing the SROI methodology proceeds along lines of other planning studies, albeit with a new level of emphasis on performance metrics and getting to the value of the triple bottom line.

Developing the Strategic Plan

Mentioned above, the optimal use of the SROI methodology occurs as early in planning as possible. It is appropriate to use SROI when evaluating planning and implementation alternatives. Strategic plans that are informed with SROI-based performance metrics will be enhanced from objectivity and transparency perspectives.

Developing the Action Plan

Once the strategic plan has been developed, it's important to assess the efficacy of the proposed measures and prioritize which ones should be included in an action plan. The SROI methodology provides a well-informed review of the costs and benefits of a given initiative and related alternatives. Communities will want to set priorities on a basis of FROI and SROI. Given federal and state policy priorities, employment projections (traditional and green jobs) and other relevant nonfinancial metrics—equivalent barrels of oil saved, gallons of fresh water saved, or number of injuries avoided—will influence prioritization. As priorities are set based on SROI the logic and data behind the rankings can be used to secure political resources and support.

Implementing the Action Plan

Implementation would follow traditional steps, however, SROI-based plans will influence priorities and establish performance monitoring and reporting based on SROI performance metrics.

The programming needed to integrate SROI into a broader planning framework for short- and long-term actions would involve the following:

- *Footprint:* establish a starting point and boundaries for the analysis
- *Metrics:* identify the most important data and confirm its coverage in the structure and logic map
- *Risk and Opportunity:* quantify input and data assumptions related to the risks and potential opportunities that could impact or enhance the community's triple bottom line
- *Plan and Test:* conduct cost and benefit analyses based on FROI and SROI
- *Adapt:* select a short list of strategies that work best for the community's circumstances
- *Implement:* refine planning, design, and delivery details to assure smooth execution
- *Report:* measure and monitor results associated with the initiative and create periodic reports that build upon SROI baseline projections
- *Adjust:* as operating results accumulate, use the information to guide modifications that will enhance outcomes

While SROI is used to form the basis of a Green Business Case, it can facilitate performance measurement, monitoring and reporting feedback, and documentation as required by federal and state funding programs. Given current and emerging policy direction, community planners and policy-makers should insist on development of performance baselines for community-owned and controlled assets that incorporate current consumption/performance levels related to:

- Energy and fuel
- GHG emissions
- Water
- Solid waste
- Vehicle miles traveled

As initiatives move to implementation, specific performance should be measured against the baselines and results recorded. This information will be helpful in complying with the reporting requirements associated with funding programs. For programs built on an SROI foundation, performance data should be incorporated with the original inputs so that periodic (quarterly, annual, and five-year projections) updates can be made available to show more precise readings on projected versus actual outcomes.

DOWNTOWN REVITALIZATION

Dave Leland and Chris Zahas
Leland Consulting Group

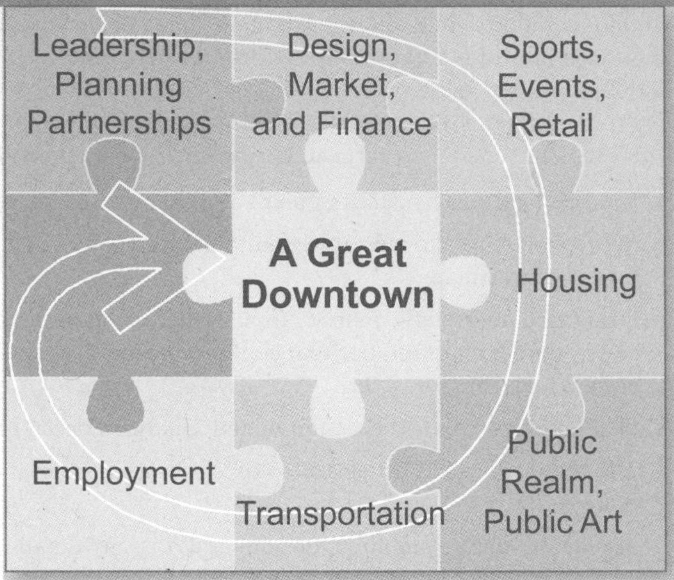

INTERVENTION TYPE: STRATEGY

Description

A downtown is more than just the city's central district—it is the commercial, civic, and cultural "heart" of a community. The health of a downtown often indicates a community's overall health. Downtown revitalization and reinvestment is an integral part of a sustainable economic development strategy for the city. Reinvestment in a downtown supports locally owned businesses and helps reduce sprawl by creating livable environments in pedestrian, bicycle, and transit-accessible locations. A healthy downtown helps to instill pride and often becomes a great marketing tool for attracting and growing business. Reuse of existing infrastructure reduces the pressures of sprawl and better leverages investments in infrastructure, parks, and buildings.

Leadership, Planning Partnerships — Design, Market, and Finance — Sports, Events, Retail — **A Great Downtown** — Housing — Employment — Transportation — Public Realm, Public Art

Figure 11-12
Many important elements combine strategically to make downtown economic development strategies successful. © *Barry Howe/Corbis*

SUPPORT GOALS AND OBJECTIVES

- Reuse underutilized and vacant land
- Reduce vehicle miles traveled (VMT)

PERFORMANCE CHARACTERISTICS

- Increase housing units within the downtown
- Increase employment in the downtown
- Increase assessed values on underutilized and vacant properties

POTENTIAL SYNERGISM

A downtown revitalization strategy is a comprehensive economic development program that will involve housing, job creation and retention, open space, infrastructure, and transit planning.

IMPLEMENTATION TIME

A revitalization initiative begins with a downtown planning process that includes significant public involvement. Typical downtown plans take from 6 to 12 months to complete. Implementation of the various initiatives in the plan is an ongoing process.

BENEFITS

- Broad public and political support for downtown revitalization efforts
- Downtown development has low carbon footprints compared to suburban development
- Infrastructure is already in place
- Public-private partnerships are an established model for implementation
- Downtowns are well-served by transit

DRAWBACKS

- It is more expensive to redevelop infill sites than to build on green-field sites
- Inadequate funding tools to support revitalization
- Stronger regulations, design standards, and site constraints makes development in a downtown the hardest place to do business
- High cost of structured parking
- Public misperception that public-private partnerships represent an unfair subsidy to developers

FIRST COST

Downtown strategy plans cost from $50,000 to $500,000 for a large city. Variables include the following:

- Amount of public outreach required
- Strength of private organizations to support the planning effort

- Amount of time any prior plans were completed
- Ease or difficulty in accessing select stakeholder groups
- Specific technical challenges in the downtown

LIFECYCLE COSTS

A downtown strategy is a living document that should be updated annually as economic conditions evolve, action items are completed, and new actions are needed. A downtown "manager" position should be established within a city to oversee implementation. This may be at a dedicated redevelopment agency or within the planning department of the city.

ESTIMATED QUANTITATIVE PERFORMANCE

The introduction of more housing in a downtown will be the strongest catalyst for revitalization. Set appropriate targets for the community that reflect market conditions but achieve a critical mass of development.

IMPLEMENTATION SUPPORTS AND CONSTRAINTS

- Leadership: Downtown revitalization must be a true public-private initiative. Strong leadership from elected officials, community members, and business and property owners will accelerate implementation.
- Market demand for new uses: It is difficult to attract investment without underlying demand from economic and demographic trends.
- Cost: Redevelopment can be expensive—a robust toolkit of financial resources is necessary.
- Vision: A bold, realistic vision is the foundation of any downtown strategy. A vision creates the interest and excitement that motivates stakeholders and attracts investment.

INFORMATIONAL SOURCES

- National Trust for Historic Preservation Main Streets Program
- Urban Land Institute
- State, regional, and local economic development agencies

Creating and Managing Sustainability for a Municipality

Using Vision and Leadership to Achieve Results in Sustainability

Susan J. Daluddung, Ph.D.
Deputy City Manager, City of Peoria, Arizona

Concept

To truly embrace sustainability, a local government—a city, county, town, tribe, or school district—must gain the active support of its people: political leaders, management, employees, and constituents. Orchestrating such a wide-ranging coalition takes leadership, vision, and ultimately, a comprehensive plan that includes involvement of all the relevant stakeholders yet remains realistic enough to produce measurable results.

Who Should Be Involved?

Sustainability is about conserving resources, delivering smarter service, and saving money. But it's mostly about people—people to coalesce around a vision of a sustainable community, people to turn that vision into a plan, and people to take green concepts from the drawing board to the industrial parks and neighborhoods where they can have a measurable impact on a community's long-term quality of life.

Among the first steps of any successful sustainability plan is identifying the people who can sketch its outline and give it life. So where do these people come from? There is no single answer to that question. In some communities, elected officials have campaigned and won elections on platforms of sustainable growth, making themselves leaders of the cause. Sometimes the right people will be less obvious, as in the case of a reluctant yet effective neighborhood leader whose actions speak louder than words, or the small-business owner who does business the right way because it's the right thing to do.

When a community sets out on the path to sustainability, chances are individuals who feel passionately about the topic—either for or against—have, or will, make themselves known. But simple tools can aid in the process of identifying those who can help, as well as people who will attempt to derail the effort. Strong leadership and inclusive communication are crucial to keeping the effort on track, and even can turn foes into supporters.

Surveys can be an important element in measuring the opinions of those most passionate about the subject. Statistical validity is not the most important thing here; identifying people who are willing to personally engage in the effort is. One of the most significant challenges is to select people for the team who will pursue the "green" mantra and work diligently to deliver results.

Exchange information on all levels:

- Ask elected officials for names of concerned, motivated constituents from whom they've heard.

- Solicit members for an *ad hoc* committee on the subject—only those who are interested will apply to serve, and the final group can be screened for additional qualifications.

- Contact existing citizen boards and commissions (particularly those that deal with planning and parks) are fertile ground for selecting informed advocates who already have demonstrated a willingness to be involved.

- Conduct a simple content analysis of local newspapers, websites, blogs, and other online social spaces which may reveal activists on both sides of the issue.

The goal is to get the right people on board: passionate, informed, and active individuals. Members of this group need to understand and believe in the vision, and be willing to roll up their sleeves and work to achieve it. With the players identified, there are four key elements in successfully creating and managing a municipal sustainability effort.

1. Leadership and Vision
2. Action Plan
3. Results that Matter
4. Recognizing Accomplishments

Leadership and Vision

In almost every community, a drive toward sustainability means change—change in the way business is conducted, in delivering services, and in the way government and citizens interact. Without a high-ranking champion—without inspired and visionary leadership—there is no impetus for change. The champion may be a mayor, a city councilmember, or an official in the city manager's office. The champion also could be a community activist or a business leader. But there must be an energetic leader at the front of the effort.

Figure 12-1
Achieving sustainability starts with empowering people. *Susan J. Daluddung*

One of leadership's first tasks is to paint a picture of the desired destination, and then inspire the government, and ultimately the community, to align efforts and organizations with that vision. A meaningful vision is simply a tool that focuses energy and motivates people. And it will be especially compelling and most successful when it is purpose-driven—when people can understand desired outcomes. Whether the purpose of the sustainability effort is to improve the environment by changing behavior, save dollars through reducing material and energy consumption, or create quality jobs through renewable industries, the result is much stronger when the purpose is clear. The vision must be meaningful and attainable.

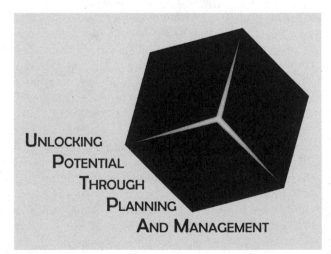

UNLOCKING
POTENTIAL
THROUGH
PLANNING
AND MANAGEMENT

Ultimately, elected leaders must adopt the vision as official policy. This sets the stage, invokes key standards, and creates a sense of history that makes the vision lasting and inclusive. An official policy lays the foundation for a variety of plans, activities, strategies, and ideas. With the vision in place, leadership can marshal the forces necessary to work toward its realization. For a government organization, support from the professional management team is a must for success—because that group holds sway on budget allocations, and staff deployment and development of policies and procedures. Staff must understand and support the leadership's vision, and then themselves lead by example— "walking the talk" —to earn the support of other stakeholders in the community. When leadership has painted an inspiring vision that is supported in this way, a groundswell of support can occur at all ranks of an organization and in each corner of the community.

Sustainability also can be stimulated and nurtured at the staff level through small-scale programs that are created as precursors to larger efforts. Often, federal grants and state money are available for pilot programs that can be used to build momentum within the community. Staff initiatives are powerful in getting specific projects and programs off the ground. Although the effort will be much more powerful with leadership from a high-level champion, it takes staff to create and implement viable programs. Even when there is no support from the top, a ground-level approach that subtly implements some components of sustainability can ultimately result in a change of mindset from leadership as the benefits become clear.

Action Plans

A vision has no meaningful value unless it is pursued with passionate action. A plan is needed to enable and guide that action—to harness and direct the energy and momentum created through visionary leadership. That plan is a strategic document that encompasses sustainability goals for the organization and the community, identifies the project leaders, notes tangible action items and measurable outcomes, and provides a timeline for accomplishing sustainability goals. Once created, the plan should be presented to the city council for adoption. This is a visible step forward that documents the support of elected leadership and helps garner the support of the community at large.

The impetus to create a plan can come from the community or the local government:

- In Hayward, California, for example, informed, engaged, and inspired leaders were elected to the city council. Those individuals, particularly the mayor, worked hard to engage the community and push for tangible staff initiatives. The professional staff heard from citizens, businesses, and organizations across the city, signaling legitimate community support. Staff then identified the highest priorities based upon the problems facing the city. A steering committee led by the mayor contributed to the effort, ensuring that the public's voice continued to be heard. Ultimately, the city council adopted Hayward's Climate Action Plan.

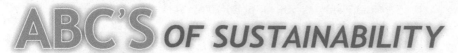

ABC'S OF SUSTAINABILITY

ADJUST CODES AND ORDINANCES
BUILD GREEN STANDARDS
COMMUNITY INVOLVEMENT
SIMPLE SOLUTIONS

Successful sustainability education starts with these building blocks.
Susan J. Daluddung

- In Peoria, Arizona, a cross-functional staff team developed a sustainability action plan over a six-month period. The process included analyzing the community's strengths and weaknesses in the area of sustainability; clarifying city council priorities; identifying available financial and staff resources; and seeking partnerships that could help achieve sustainability goals. The process not only created a viable plan, but also created organizational buy-in—an important step toward ultimate success.

HAYWARD'S CLIMATE ACTION PLAN

In 2006, the City of Hayward joined Alameda County Climate Protection Project and ICLEI's Cities for Climate Protection Campaign:

- Created a baseline greenhouse gas (GHG) inventory using 2005 as a baseline
- City staff presented the actions to several community groups
- Feedback was collected and actions were prioritized by calculating an overall score for each action
- The draft Climate Action Plan was presented to the community in March 2009

In 2008, at the same time the Climate Action Plan was developed by HDR, Inc. and Town-Green, the City Community and Economic Development Department worked with leadership to develop and adopt a Green Building Code.

PEORIA'S SUSTAINABILITY ACTION PLAN

In Peoria, Arizona, city leaders' vision of a sustainable future is articulated in a sustainability action plan that sets goals and measurements toward progress in eight specific areas that the community understands and appreciates:

- Rethinking energy use
- Reducing consumption, reusing materials, and recycling waste
- Managing water resources
- Promoting sustainable development and green-collar jobs
- Developing efficient and innovative modes of transportation
- Preserving open space and our natural environment
- Communicating ideas and opportunities
- Forging partnerships and encouraging growth of a renewable-energy sources

As a final step, a marketable identity for those efforts was created. The Sustain & Gain logo and tag line is the public identity for the City's efforts, and is central to the message that sustainable actions also mean short- and long-term financial savings.

The plan is simply a guiding document. To truly embrace sustainability, a community must have the active and willing support of its people: regular citizens, business leaders, and certainly those who manage and provide government services. Once the organization has committed to the vision and developed a plan of action, gaining the support of key stakeholders is critical. Nonprofits and business organizations provide a larger pool for spreading the costs, providing resources the city may lack, and offering more people an opportunity to be involved. The key is to identify "win-win" situations in which a partnership can accomplish more than any single entity can achieve on its own, and in which each partner has an interest. These kinds of partnerships can deliver results when the individual entities are too small or lack the financial resources to implement or fund their own activities—and in doing so, they make the plan real for the community.

Figure 12-3
The Sustain & Gain Program logo for the City of Peoria symbolizes sustainability in our City and throughout our community. *City of Peoria*

Results that Matter: Sustainability Offers Opportunity for Community Engagement

Community members will judge the success or failure of any sustainability initiative. A comprehensive communications strategy to engage and educate the public is elemental to the success of the effort. This strategy should include media outreach—news releases, interviews, op-ed columns, photo opportunities, and so forth—and grassroots community interaction, such as classes, special events, opportunities for participation that further the vision and bring the "green" message to the public in a practical, hands-on way.

Peoria partnered with local businesses to stage a "Green Your Ride" auto show on a Saturday morning in May, 2009. Organizers believed it to be the first such event in the greater-Phoenix area. Six Peoria auto dealerships displayed their "greenest" vehicles at the city's Park West outdoor lifestyle center in conjunction with a privately run farmers' market. The City's public works department staffed booths to educate the public on sustainable practices—and displayed its alt-fuel heavy work vehicles in a family-friendly "Touch-a-Truck" area.

Peoria First is a shop local program that encourages people to shop locally and reduce miles traveled. *City of Peoria*

Benefits included:

- Education for the public
- Opportunities for the car dealers, farmers' market, and shopping center to market to motivated, larger-than-usual audience
- Recognition for Peoria and its Public Works employees
- Extra city sales-tax collections from transactions stemming from the event

Results that Matter: Sustainability Saves Money

Demonstrating the benefits of sustainability with concrete numbers is imperative. It shows the dollars-and-cents savings that result from changes in personal behavior, and how simple actions can improve an individual or organizational bottom line. Results that Matter: Sustainability Improves the Environment

More and more, people accept the fact that the way we build and sustain our communities cannot compromise the ability of future generations to do the same, so accomplishments in these should be clearly communicated.

Results that Matter: Sustainability Improves the Quality of the Community

Efforts such as attracting green businesses and revitalizing depressed or blighted neighborhoods to encourage affordable and sustainable housing and jobs also are an opportunity to build strategic relationships. For instance, the City can attract and support green businesses by employing them in neighborhood-revitalization programs that, in turn, improve the quality of the community.

Recognizing Accomplishments

Beyond communication lies recognition and celebration of accomplishments. When progress is made—when actions make a difference—recognizing these accomplishments is a crucial way to keep the community energized and focused toward achieving sustainability. Recognition can take a variety of forms. Regional organizations, as well as local and state (or provincial) governments, may establish awards to recognize the accomplishments of businesses and individuals in their constituencies.

The bestowing of those awards then becomes news, and media coverage can increase the attention on successful sustainable programs and make people want to take part. Recognizing accomplishments also is a great way to energize stakeholders. Media attention and community feedback help maintain support for sustainability among elected officials. Politicians, even more than most people, like to see their names in print and their faces on TV. They also like pleasing their constituents. By celebrating successes in a high-profile manner, whether through television programs, newspaper articles and editorials, or award ceremonies, leadership keeps the topic in the public eye and creates rallying points for further actions.

Stirling Energy Systems' solar plant, a public/private partnership, received recognition in the *Wall Street Journal*. A successful collaboration between Stirling Energy Systems (SES), the U.S. Department of Energy, and Sandia National Laboratories has resulted in an optimized SunCatcher power system. These SES Sun-Catcher systems were recently deployed in a Tessera Solar facility in Peoria, Arizona, known as Maricopa Solar, the first commercial-scale SunCatcher Dish Stirling power plant. More than a decade of innovative engineering and validation testing readied the SunCatcher for commercialization and deployment in utility-scale power plants. Staff from the City of Peoria and Salt River Project facilitated the land development for this new solar facility, as well as assisted with the organization of the ground-breaking event.

Finally, regular, formal presentations to the elected body are critical for maintaining effective leadership and support for sustainability. For example, cost savings from energy-efficiency measures enacted as part of a sustainability action plan should be presented to a city council not only to celebrate a successful, measurable outcome, but also to provide those elected officials with a basis for their continued support. After all, what elected official is against delivering quality service for less money?

Words of Wisdom

After identifying leaders, rallying support, developing a vision, and adopting an action plan, it is time to walk the talk. All eyes will be watching, anticipating the rewards of a more sustainable community.

But that need not be a daunting prospect, because the foundation has been set:

- The champion has created a vision and inspired staff and the community alike to come along.
- A group of dedicated staff has committed to achieving the vision.
- An inventory of accomplishments has been taken and presented to City Council and to the community, demonstrating action on the vision and establishing a positive track record.
- The same group of dedicated staff developed a measurable, achievable plan of action that has the approval of the community and elected body.
- The plan elements were integrated into the City's General Plan.
- The General Plan sustainability elements are subject to voter approval.

The result should be business as usual. The people are on board, informed, and inspired. The plan is in place, and staff is acting on its priorities. Sustainability is now real—it is not a pie in the sky, or a pipe dream. Before long, execution of the plan becomes a matter of routine and a City Council priority.

Figure 12-5
Stirling Energy Systems and SunCatcher Technology employees with the Peoria sustainability team during a visit at the Tessera Solar Plant in the City of Peoria. *City of Peoria*

GREEN YOUR RIDE

Dr. Susan J. Daluddung, Deputy City Manager
City of Peoria, Arizona

INTERVENTION TYPE: PROGRAM

Description

In May, 2009, the City of Peoria held its first Green Your Ride alternative-fuel vehicle show. The event commemorated Public Works Week by demonstrating, in
cooperation with private-sector partners, how Peoria fosters sustainability in its
operations and how individuals can do so in their daily lives.

The Green Your Ride event provided the City of Peoria with an opportunity to
educate the public as to its sustainable fleet management practices. The City
partnered with the local auto dealers to display the greenest vehicles that both
parties maintain.

Managers and supervisors from the Public Works Department volunteered
their time on a Saturday morning to staff Green Your Ride, in order to show
their customers—the public—the personal dedication, industry best practices,
and top-of-the-line equipment that recently made it the first Public Works
Department in the West Valley to be accredited by the American Public Works
Association.

New advances in alternative fuel technology for autos were showcased as part
of the event. Six of Peoria's Bell Road auto dealerships displayed their greenest
vehicles (with representatives available to answer questions) at the City's Park
West outdoor shopping center.

SUPPORTS GOALS AND OBJECTIVES

The City of Peoria maintains the goal of improving access to government and
increasing citizen participation. The Green Your Ride event improved access
to the City government by demonstrating to Peoria's residents what they can
do to foster sustainable practices at home. Green Your Ride helped develop
a sustainability partnership between the City and its residents. Peoria's
leaders believe renewable energy should be the core of the City's industrial
strategy going forward, so Green Your Ride complemented a larger agenda—
to marshal natural resources, improve city services, and attract forward-
looking businesses that bring intellectual capital and conveniently located,
high-quality jobs.

Figure 12-6
Citizens and families enjoying Peoria's farmers' market and learning
about sustainability through the
City of Peoria's Public Works Department. *City of Peoria*

Performance Characteristics

The success of this event was evaluated by media exposure and community attendance at the Green Your Ride program.

It will also be evaluated based on whether alternative-fuel vehicle use increases in Peoria, and whether communitywide emissions are reduced over the long term.

Conceptual Strategy

The City's broad strategy is to encourage the use of alternative- and renewable-fuel vehicles through outreach events, in partnership with auto dealers and other businesses in the community. The Green Your Ride program helped in addressing this goal.

Synergism

The coordination that was done as part of the public-private partnership for this event created an effective synergism. The City will continue to partner with the private sector in an effort to educate the public in the wide variety of City sustainability programs, such as city recycling, signage, stormwater, streets, trip reduction, and water conservation programs. The methods in which the City and auto dealers provide resources to encourage the public to manage resources responsibly in their daily lives will prove invaluable as a resource to be shared with other organizations.

IMPLEMENTATION TIMELINE

This project required about three months of planning to successfully launch. The business model for the program has since been replicated by the Chamber of Commerce.

BENEFITS

The Green Your Ride event provided the City of Peoria with an opportunity to educate the public. Increased citizen awareness helped the City address economic and environmental interests in that citizen engagement is a necessary and vital component of ensuring communitywide sustainability.

This event benefitted the Peoria Public Works employees, whose everyday contributions were recognized in conjunction with national Public Works Week. The event also supported the City's Peoria First initiative, which aims to increase sales-tax revenue by encouraging residents to shop in Peoria. It was a creative approach to making Public Works Week relevant to the general public.

DRAWBACKS

Some of the obstacles were related to the coordination of the event. Due to the fact that so many players were involved—the City, the retailers/shopping center management, farmers' market, and six auto dealers—ensuring that everyone knew their role and the role of others was trying at times, but attainable in the end. Another obstacle was ensuring a high level of even coverage and publicity. Extra efforts were conducted by the communications team to assure television coverage, press presence, editorials, and a radio interview of the Public Works director.

FIRST COSTS

Green Your Ride costs were limited to staff time to prepare and execute the event. Besides the assistance from volunteer labor, several of Peoria's Bell Road auto dealerships sent their "greenest" vehicles, along with representatives to answer questions.

ESTIMATED QUANTITATIVE PERFORMANCE

The number of people who were exposed to the event on TV is a positive outcome. According to Nielsen, the "Good Morning Arizona" audience ranged from 48,502 to 57,484 viewers over three hours; "12 News Weekend Today" ranged from 57,895 to 62,404 viewers over two hours. Information about the level of newspaper coverage shows that Arizonans were interested in this event. Green Your Ride netted approximately 150 free column-inches of news/editorial content with an estimated ad-equivalent value of $2,471.65.

Outreach efforts through social media methods were monitored. A message from the Peoria's Twitter account reached 390 people, five of whom "re-tweeted" it for a total audience reach of 3,982. The City will determine the number of first-time visitors who came to the relatively new Park West shopping center and its weekend farmers' market on the date of this event.

At the event, Peoria's Fleet Division provided information as to the fact that more than a quarter of the City's 720-vehicle fleet runs on B-20 (20 percent biodiesel, 80 percent diesel), E-85 (85 percent ethanol, 15 percent unleaded), gas/electric hybrid technology, propane, or electricity alone.

Will Peoria's efforts help to reduce pollution? An increase in the number of clean-running vehicles will result in a reduction of carbon emissions, and improve the air quality of the community. In a region beset by traffic congestion and air pollution, Peoria's Green Your Ride event promoted clean-running vehicles, but the City management is hoping the event will have the positive effect it was intended to. This remains to be seen and will have to be evaluated on a long-term basis.

Figure 12-7
Local news coverage of the Green Your Ride event with reporter and citizens exemplifies the unique community engagement strategies used by the City of Peoria. *City of Peoria*

INFORMATIONAL SOURCES

- City of Peoria News Release on the Green Your Ride Event: Peoria Brings Eco-Friendly Vehicles to Park Westwww.peoriaaz.gov/News/NewsPR.asp?PID=734

- "In Energy Innovation, Everything New Is Old Again." *Wall Street Journal,* December 11, 2009. Available at http://online.wsj.com/article/SB126048948482786623.html?mod=WSJ_hpp_LEFTTopSt.

REPORTS AND STUDIES

- The Environmental Protection Agency's green-fuel economy estimates for vehicles www.epa.gov/greenvehicles/Index.do;jsessionid=9d5a38 3393ddaa2fddc5c1bab88e1617351316410e7ea51405772526cccfb9a1. e34MbhqOa3uSbyoRa3uSb3aLaN1on6jAmljGr5XDqQLvpAe

Ambient Outdoor Air Quality: Community Health

Anthony Bernheim, FAIA, LEED AP BD+C
Sustainability Principal for AECOM

Concept

What you cannot see has a major impact on your health, your community's health, the environment, and property. However, little attention has been paid to air quality. The air we breathe is not labeled with its constituent chemicals as is done for the food we purchase at the supermarket, so we have no way to understand the air quality that we take into our bodies. Multiple sources contribute to the quality of the ambient outdoor air which we breathe every day.

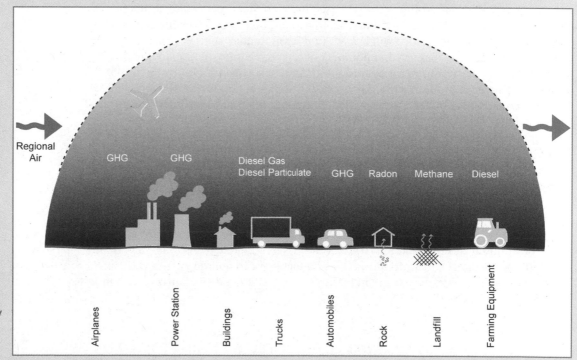

Figure 13-1
The types of air quality contaminant sources include both mobile and stationary emission contributors. *Anthony Bernheim, AECOM*

The ambient outdoor and indoor air causes short-term acute and long-term chronic health effects, and exposes humans to carcinogens and reproductive toxicants. While the acute effects are experienced almost immediately, the chronic, carcinogenic, and reproductive effects generate health impacts over time. Recent research documents increases in asthma, allergies, and respiratory symptoms in the population and particularly in children who live or go to schools located close to busy roads, where they are exposed to traffic-related air pollution.[1]

Community planning, urban design, and to a large extent, building design have ignored good or improved air quality as a design criteria. Comparative community air quality data is available but has not yet been compiled into a functional and usable system. The result is that communities have at best anecdotal air quality information. A recent study ranked the top 50 U.S. green cities in terms of air quality (based on average air quality indexes and nonattainment areas for the U.S. Clean Air Act data obtained from the Environmental Protection Agency (EPA)).[2]

America is a sedentary nation.[3] The U.S. EPA data show that Americans spend on average 89 percent of their time indoors, 6 percent in transit, and 5 percent outdoors. A more recent study by the California Environmental Protection Agency, Air Resources Board, found that California's children spend 85 percent of their time indoors (at home and in school), 4 percent in transit, and 11 percent outdoors.[4] A building's indoor air quality is largely dependent on outdoor air chemical concentrations, and indoor air chemical concentrations are two to five times higher than the outdoor air. Children, older adults, and the population at large are exposed to high chemical concentrations that their bodies were not designed to accommodate. Children are particularly vulnerable to air pollution as their bodies are developing, and chemical exposure will impact that development.

Another area of concern is the impact of climate change on human health.[5] Climate change results from an increase in greenhouse gases (GHG) in the troposphere (the layer of air above the Earth's surface). Ozone (O_3) is formed through a series of complex chemical reactions involving sunlight on nitrogen dioxide and hydrocarbons. Ozone is desirable in the upper atmosphere, but is undesirable in the troposphere, where it is responsible for respiratory health effects such as asthma. More importantly, ozone is an oxidizing agent. It reacts with other chemicals in the outdoor and indoor air to form secondary chemicals that include strongly irritating compounds, aldehydes, formaldehyde (a known carcinogen and respiratory irritant at small concentration levels), and fine particles[6] (suspected to increase the severity of asthma symptoms in children[7]).

Another source of air pollution is radon which occurs from the natural breakdown of uranium in soil, rock, and water. Radon is a radioactive gas that emits from the Earth and is most concentrated in the breathable air in buildings. The U.S. Surgeon General has warned that radon is the second leading cause of lung cancer in the United States.[8]

Proposed Solution

Start by understanding the community ambient outdoor air quality, its potential to impact the community's health and environment, and by developing integrated planning and community strategies to improve outdoor and indoor air quality. A

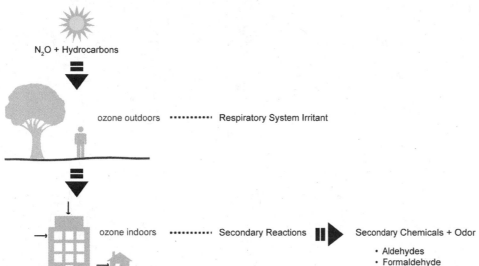

N₂O + Hydrocarbons

ozone outdoors ·········· Respiratory System Irritant

ozone indoors ·········· Secondary Reactions ▌▶ Secondary Chemicals + Odor
- Aldehydes
- Formaldehyde
- Fine Particles

Figure 13-2
Poor air quality continues to adversely affect human health in both indoor and outdoor environments, exacerbated by secondary impacts from indoor chemicals and odor. *Anthony Bernheim, AECOM*

community is a complex entity that is part of many larger regional and global ecosystems.[9] Positive solutions require a holistic approach with an understanding of the interrelationships between ecosystems[10] including the local geography, climate, vegetation, ground rock and soil composition, mobility and transportation, industry, and the built environment. Restorative and regenerative solutions may also be found by using community-scale biomimicry as a way to emulate nature's ecological solutions.[11]

What are the factors that determine outdoor air quality, and how can they be modified to produce improved air quality with reduced risk to human health? The process for improvement requires the understanding of the determining factors, the acceptable safe and desirable chemical concentrations, and the actions needed for improvement.

The principles for creating more sustainable and healthy communities are as follows:

1. *Community context:* Establish the current baseline community context by researching and assembling the community ambient outdoor quality and health data

2. *Acceptable air quality standards:* Research current national, state, and local standards for acceptable outdoor air quality

3. *Integrated sustainable community systems:* Develop an understanding of the integrated community systems that impact air quality

4. *Improvement strategies:* Develop outdoor air quality improvement strategies that support restorative and regenerative ecological solutions:

   a. Policy

   b. Planning and building codes

   c. Planning and building guidelines

   d. Immediate actions

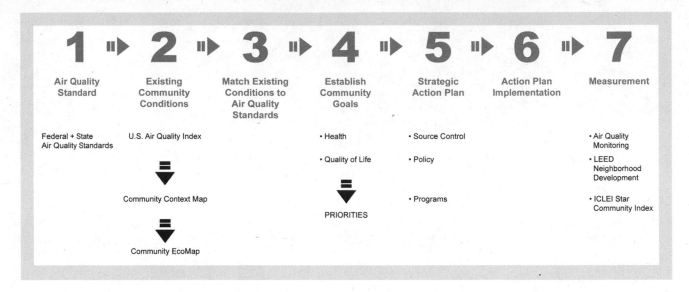

Figure 13-3
The Seven Steps for improving community ambient air quality match the process for improving comprehensive sustainability. *Anthony Bernheim, AECOM*

5. *Measurement of success:* Develop the procedures for annual measurement to evaluate success and allow for program refinement

In summary, as shown in Figure 13-3, there are seven basic steps to improving ambient community air quality.

Prepare the Team

Many challenges present themselves when addressing community sustainability from an air quality perspective. These challenges require attention and focus in several key areas.

1. *Awareness and understanding of the issue:* It is hard to comprehend the fact that air—something that is primarily invisible—has a profound effect on human health and well-being. Additionally, we know that some health impacts generate over time. This can complicate the relationship between cause and effect.

2. *Finding the data and using it:* Most communities and their planners do not have direct access to historic and current ambient air quality data. Available data would need to be interpreted to be useful.

3. *Interpreting the regulations and guidelines:* The U.S. EPA and some state EPAs are now making available recommended ambient outdoor air quality standards, but the research indicates that these standards may be insufficient to protect community health. A recent study on the adequacy of current O_3 regulations in the United States finds that "even low levels of tropospheric O_3 are associated with increased risk of premature mortality. Interventions to further reduce O_3 pollution would benefit public health, even in regions that meet current regulatory standards and guidelines."[12]

4. *Regional community collaboration:* Air moves from one community to another so it is very likely that pollutants in one community will move to adjacent communities. Improving air quality will require regional community collaboration.

5. *Political support:* Changes involving pollutant source reductions are necessary to improve the air quality and living conditions. Political, business, and public support will be vital to facilitate change.

Relating outdoor and indoor air quality to human health is a relatively new discipline and much research is still needed to verify and confirm the links. A community should attempt to build a team of appropriately qualified specialists with multiple skills. At the community level, a specialist consultant should bring skills and knowledge on the following:

- The potential human health impacts and risks of airborne chemicals and fine particulate matter
- The current federal, state, and local acceptable ambient air quality standards
- The information sources for local ambient air quality data
- The practical strategies to improve the ambient air quality
- Integrated sustainable systems knowledge
- Public process and participation
- Planning and building codes

At the building level, an architect and a building engineer should bring indoor air quality skills and knowledge about the potential health impacts and risks of airborne chemicals and fine particulate matter, as well as design principles that improve indoor air quality. The four principles[13] needed by architects and building engineers are:

- Source control
- Ventilation design
- Building commissioning
- Building maintenance

Improved air quality can be achieved by including members of the air quality research community in the discussions. There are a number of researchers and scientists who have a comprehensive knowledge of air chemistry, the impact of outdoor air on indoor air, and the relationship between air chemistry and air quality. This knowledge can be a powerful tool when working with public officials whose support will be needed for public policy implementation. Knowledge is also very useful when presenting information to the public and when seeking collective and creative solutions.

Prepare the Tools

New environmental concerns require new quantitative and qualitative performance-measuring tools. Few such tools currently exist and will need to be developed. The Healthy Development Measurement Tool (HDMT), recently developed by the San Francisco Public Health Department, provides communities with a customizable Web-based qualitative tool to help evaluate a community's health. The section "Preserve Clean Air Quality" provides benchmarks for evaluating key elements of a community and gives directions for improvement.[14]

Many cities, public agencies, and design professionals use Geographic Information Systems (GIS) to map community information. These tools are ideal for mapping community ambient air quality, land uses, air pollution sources, and ground radon areas. The City of San Francisco has developed an urban EcoMap[15] to illustrate community air quality by Zip code districts. This is a useful graphic representational tool of the current conditions.

Minimum acceptable air quality standards were developed by the U.S. EPA and also by state EPAs based on the scientific evidence connecting air pollution exposure to human health effects; damage to agricultural crops, forests, and other plants; damage to buildings; and reduced visibility. The U.S. EPA[16] has identified six common air pollutants, developed National Ambient Air Quality Standards[17] with maximum outdoor air concentrations for these air pollutants, and set the minimum acceptable ambient air quality levels. The State of California EPA Air Resources Board (CARB) has expanded on the work of the U.S. EPA by adding to the list of common air pollutants[18] and by providing information on their potential health effects.

The CARB also provides a complete list of the California Ambient Air Quality Standards[19] with a comparison to the Federal Air Quality Standards. Refer to Figure 13-4 for a summary of this list.

Once a community agrees on the use of the federal, California, and possibly local ambient air quality standards, the historical and current local ambient air quality data will be needed. This data is available from various agencies, will form the community's baseline air quality measurements, and should be assessed against the acceptable standards. Current and historical ambient air quality data is available from the following resources:

- U.S. EPA provides an Air Quality Index[20] with detailed historical and current information on actual air quality, ozone, and particulates for the United States by state and county.

- California EPA Air Resources Board provides California historical and current information on actual air quality and ozone using their AQMIS2-Air Quality and Meteorological Information System.[21]

- The American Lung Association State of the Air, 2010 Report[22] provides valuable ambient air quality and related health information by state, county, and Zip code. Based on the ozone and particulate matter in the air, their data identifies the community groups at risk for significant health impacts.

Current regional information on ground source radon emissions is available for use by communities to help evaluate their potential exposure to radon gas:

- The EPA Map of Radon Zones[23] provides general information on potential exposure to radon gas for the United States. Counties are rated by zone with potential for radon exposure: Zone 3 with low potential exposure, Zone 2 with moderate potential exposure, and Zone 1 with the highest potential for exposure.

- Most states within the United States have their own radon program that provides more detailed local radon location information. The U.S. EPA provides the links to these state radon programs.[24]

Ambient Air Quality Standards				
Pollutant	**Averaging Time**	**Federal Standards**		**California Standards**
		Primary Concentration	Secondary Concentration	Concentration
Ozone (O_3)	1 Hour	—		.09 ppm (180 µg/m³)
	8 Hour	0.075 ppm (147 µg/m³)		.070 ppm (137 µg/m³)
Respirable Particulate Matter (PM 10)	24 Hour	150 µg/m³		50 µg/m³
	Annual Arithmetic Mean	—		20 µg/m³
Fine Particlate Matter (PM2.5)	24 Hour	35 µg/m³		No Separate State Standard
	Annual Arithmetic Mean	15.0 µg/m³		12 µg/m³
Carbon Monoxide (CO)	8 Hour	9 ppm (10 mg/m³)	None	9.0 ppm (10 mg/m³)
	1 Hour	35 ppm (40 mg/m³)		20 ppm (23 mg/m³)
	8 Hour (Lake Tahoe)	—		6 ppm (7 mg/m³)
Nitrogen Dioxide (NO_2)	Annual Arithmetic Mean	.053 ppm (100 µg/m³)		0.030 ppm (57 µg/m³)
	1 Hour	—		.18 ppm (339 µg/m³)
Sulfur Dioxide (SO_2)	Annual Arithmetic Mean	0.030 ppm (80 µg/m³)	—	—
	24 Hour	0.14 ppm (365 µg/m³)	—	.04 ppm (105 µg/m³)
	3 Hour	—	0.5 ppm (1300 µg/m³)	—
	1 Hour	—		.25 ppm (655 µg/m³)
Lead	30 Day Average	—		1.5 µg/m³
	Calendar Quarter	1.5 µg/m³		—
	Rolling 3-Month Average	.15 µg/m³		—
Visibility Reducing Particles	8 Hour	No Federal Standards		Extinction coefficient of .23 per km—visibility of ten miles or more (.07 — 30 miles or more for Lake Tahoe) due to particles when relative humidity is less than 70%.
Sulfates	24 Hour			25 µg/m³
Hydrogen Sulfide	1 Hour			0.03 ppm (42 µg/m³)
Vinyl Chloride	24 Hour			0.01 ppm (26 µg/m³)

Notes: 1. Information obtained from http://www.arb.ca.gov/research/aaqs/aaqs2.pdf on 1 December 2009.
2. Refer to website for most up to date standards and clarifying notes.

Figure 13-4
This comparison of Federal and California Ambient Air Quality
Standards illustrates the range of differences of compliance
requirements. *Anthony Bernheim, AECOM*

Prepare the Place

Data should be collected, reviewed, evaluated, and documented to understand a community's ambient air quality and the related community's health. It is recommended that significant information and data be assembled to help build a picture of a community's environmental context:

1. *Climate data:* Prepare a report on the community's climate with data on temperature, humidity, and prevailing winds.

2. *Historic and current ambient air quality data:* Access the federal and local data on historic and current ambient air quality data.

3. *Community health:* Research data on community health to include significant incidences of a particular health condition in the community, or possibly local data on airborne health conditions.

4. *Local ecology:* Obtain maps that indicate the local vegetation, forests, and community green zones.

5. *Pollution sources:* Research current data on known and potential pollution sources.

6. *Community context map:* Prepare a diagram of the community to show:
   - The current climate, including prevailing winds
   - Potential or known air pollution sources, such as major roads and intersections, industry, fossil fuel power plants, landfill sites, and ground radon sources
   - Community health conditions related to airborne contaminants
   - Local vegetation, trees, and community green zones

Analysis of the community context map will give the planners and community a visual representation of the current and future potential air quality contamination problems. Once the sources of air contaminants are understood, solutions can be developed to mitigate and solve the problems. This is an opportunity for a community to learn more about the quality of its environment and to initiate air quality improvement programs.

Significant constraints will emerge from this endeavor since air quality problems result from industry and utility combustion of fossil fuels, and the use of gas and diesel-powered vehicles. Solutions may be costly, and will involve political and regional collaboration, as well as public lifestyle changes.

Additional studies that would contribute to a better understanding of a community's ambient air quality and opportunities for improvement could include the following:

1. Greenhouse gas inventory with identification of the concentrations of major greenhouse gases

2. Traffic study with identification of the major routes, intersections, and vehicle miles traveled (VMT)

3. Local ground source radon emission research to indicate locations where radon gas is being emitted into air and into buildings

Prepare the People

Outdoor air contamination has many causes and impacts the health of the entire population. Therefore, many stakeholders with an interest in this issue include community leaders, elected public officials, public agency staff, industry leaders, utility companies, institutional education leaders, and the community at large.

A number of strategies should be considered to engage a community in protecting its health and the local environment:

1. Many cities have formed a Department of the Environment or Environmental Services. The establishment of such a department will provide a community with staff to focus on the community's ecology and air quality, provide local environmental and ecological educational services, and implement an air quality action plan.

2. The Department of the Environment could prepare a community air quality map to indicate ambient outdoor air quality in the community (e.g. the San Francisco Urban EcoMap[25]). Such a map could be further developed to show other outdoor air chemical concentrations and particulates. (See Figure 13-5.)

3. Workshops should be held during the community planning process to provide usable data to the community and its stakeholders. At this time physical plans of the community with climate data and pollution sources should be studied to understand the problem, and preliminary ideas for solutions should be developed.

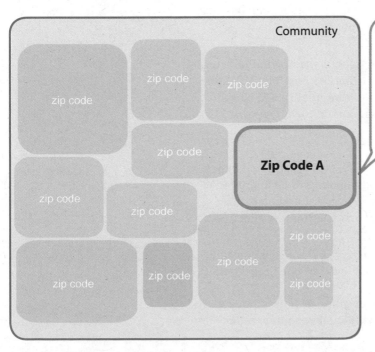

Develop Goals, Objectives, and Performance Metrics

The goals are to improve community health, reduce environmental and building-related illnesses and costs, improve human productivity, and generally improve the quality of life. At a minimum, a community should strive to achieve the California Ambient Air Quality Standards, with improvement beyond these standards as a secondary goal.

The formation of a community action group will help the local population understand the issues and empower the community to participate in the solutions. Community groups work closely with public agencies to effect change within their community and the region. Voting citizens also have the power to bring about political changes that support community needs.

Develop the Strategic Plan

Strategies for improving a community's ambient outdoor air quality should focus on the following:

1. Source Control:

   a. Reduce or preferably eliminate the source of pollutants.

   b. Dilute or absorb pollutants: Use integrated ecological systems to develop strategies for air pollutant absorption and oxygen production.

   c. Encapsulate pollutant sources: Encapsulate pollution sources such as radon that cannot be reduced or eliminated.

2. Policy: As future community developments are planned, modify planning and building codes to guide and regulate these developments.

   a. Planning Codes
      * Locate future schools and residential developments upwind of major traffic corridors and as far from these corridors as possible. Facilities located in areas with good ambient outdoor air quality will benefit from passive ventilation systems such as operable windows and skylights.

   b. Building Codes
      * In areas with poor ambient outdoor air quality, modify local building codes to require renovated and remodeled buildings to be upgraded to include mechanical ventilation with appropriate air filtration.
      * Modify local building codes to address radon exposure reduction.

   c. Schools
      * Conduct health surveys to determine if there is an increased prevalence of asthma and other illnesses in schools and to determine the potential causes.
      * Implement programs in school districts to upgrade facilities (particularly those facilities closest to freeways) and ventilation systems to reduce the infiltration of polluted outdoor air.

d. Integrated Pest Management Programs
- Develop integrated pest management programs for planting adjacent to public buildings, schools, parks, and roadways to control pests without the use of airborne pesticides.
- Provide integrated pest management educational programs for citizens on techniques that can be used in residential neighborhoods.

e. Transit and Mobility
- Develop a transit-oriented community plan.
- Develop policies to support safe pedestrian and bicycle paths throughout the community.
- Develop policies to encourage public agencies to procure low-emitting vehicles as they replace their fleet vehicles.
- Develop policies to encourage the public to replace current vehicles with low-emitting vehicles through tax incentives, access to high-occupancy vehicle traffic lanes, preferential parking, or other incentives.
- Create and support policies that reduce diesel particulates and gases by reducing the streets usable by diesel trucks, and eliminating diesel trucks from residential neighborhoods. Enforce no-idling rules at loading docks, bus stops, and transit facilities.

3. Programs: Current data collection is needed to update knowledge about air quality and to indicate positive and negative trends.
a. Air Quality Monitoring
- Expand outdoor air quality monitoring to include more locations in communities close to highways, freeways, airports, and ports.
- Consider regular collection of ambient outdoor air quality data from the federal and state sources.
- Provide updated air quality data on a community, city, or project websites.

b. Air Quality Warnings
- Consider establishing a communication system to notify the public when the ambient air quality does not meet locally acceptable air quality standards. Prioritize high-impact areas and vulnerable populations.

c. Free Transit Days
- Offer free transit days to deter private vehicle use when the ambient air quality exceeds specific acceptable healthy levels.

Develop the Action Plan

The next step is to assess the efficacy of the proposed measures, and select which ones will fit into the action plan. Assemble the proposed measures to improve a community's ambient air quality into one list ready for evaluation and prioritization. These measures should have been identified in community workshops. The community should then develop an importance and weighting level for each measure, followed by a scoring exercise to determine the appropriate implementation priority for each proposed measure.

Proposed Measures	Importance of Weighting	Community Votes				Total Votes	Total Votes x Important Weighting
		Impact on Improved Ambient Outdoor Air Quality	Impact on Improved Indoor Air Quality	Cost to Community	Political Support Available		
Source Control							
Reduce or eliminate pollutant sources							
Use integrated ecological systems							
Radon encapsulation							
Other							
Policy							
Planning codes							
Building codes							
School upgrade program							
Integrated pest managment							
Transit and mobility							
Other							
Programs							
Air quality monitoring & reporting							
Air quality warnings							
Free transit days							
Department of Environment							
Other							

To obtain votes on the measures, request that participants vote on the measures using ballots and then count the votes for each measure. Measures are then prioritized based on the score. (Refer to Figure 13-6.)

There are several methods for securing technical resources and funding. Local communities are advised to form partnerships with national organizations to further share and obtain technical support. Such organizations include:

1. The U.S. Green Building Council (USGBC)26
2. ICLEI-Local Governments for Sustainability[27]

Technical resources can also be obtained from research institutions that are themselves positioned to obtain grants to assist communities with energy and air quality improvements. Such organizations include:

1. Lawrence Berkeley National Laboratories, Berkeley, California28
2. National Renewable Energy Laboratory (NREL), Golden, Colorado[29]

Communities should research and seek federal, state, and local programs that provide funding for improved air quality. While funding for such programs may change with political and policy changes, it is advantageous to know what might be available. Examples of grants include:

1. U.S. EPA Grants and Funding. The EPA provides access to information on funding opportunities available from the EPA Office of Air and Radiation on their website.

Figure 13-6
A simple matrix can help the community, staff, and officials assess and prioritize air quality measures. *Anthony Bernheim, AECOM*

2. U.S. EPA State Indoor Radon Grant (SIRG) Program.[31] The EPA provides matching grants to states for programs aimed at radon reduction by local governments, schools, residential developers, homeowners, and other related professional organizations.

While it might take about five years to develop and implement an action plan to improve community sustainability, there needs to be a continuous community ambient outdoor air quality monitoring program in place within this five-year period. This program should span several seasons and years so that air quality patterns can be measured, documented, understood, and evaluated. Once comparative data is available it will be possible to evaluate the performance of the proposed implementation strategies.

Another method to monitor and measure performance of the proposed measures is to collect annual data on the community's health focused on environmentally caused illnesses. The data collected over the months and years should indicate visible health trends as measures are implemented.

Communities should be measured regularly to verify the level of sustainability. Two communitywide measurement tools are mentioned here as they both include some air quality measurement tools:

1. U.S. Green Building Council Leadership in Energy and Environmental Design (LEED®) green rating system for neighborhood development, LEED-ND.[32] The USGBC states that "the LEED for Neighborhood Development Rating System integrates the principles of smart growth, urbanism and green building into the first national system for neighborhood design." The LEED-ND rating system provides credits for improved walking, cycling, and public mobility which are strategies that improve air quality.

2. ICLEI—Local Governments for Sustainability, in collaboration with the USGBC and the Center for American Progress (CAP) have developed the STAR Community Index.[33] It is intended to "provide a national, consensus-based system with indicators and metrics that will help local governments set priorities and maximize their investments in strategic actions."

3. ICLEI Clean Air and Climate Protection (CACP) software 2009.[34] This downloadable software is used to prepare air quality emissions inventories and climate action plans. The tool calculates and tracks emissions and proposed reductions of greenhouse gases and air pollutants associated with power generation, fuel use, and waste disposal.

Implement the Action Plan

Outdoor air quality is a complex issue and it will not be easy to launch short-term actions. Long-term actions are more productive and include:

1. Developing a community healthy development measurement tool

2. Preparing a Web-based community air quality map indicating the most important GHG concentrations

3. Establishing a public interagency team representing local city agencies including the City Planning, Public Health, and Building Permit and Inspection departments

4. Establishing a local community action group

A Holistic Public Health Approach

Karen Mendrala
Senior Planner, City of Holyoke, Office of Planning &
Development

The Holistic Approach

Many people have worked to improve public health in the United States for a long time with little or no long-term results. Obesity rates among both youth and adults have more than doubled over the last 30 years, with more than one-third of those over the age of 20 considered obese, according to the CDC. At the same time, the percentage of physical leisure activity for those ages 18 or older has not increased over the last ten years.[35] In order to create a successful change in health at the local level, we need a holistic approach across all sectors living and working in a community. This effort requires gathering representatives of all sectors, from school food providers to engineers, many of whom may have never worked together in the same room. The greatest impacts are achieved by bringing these groups together and enabling them to speak the same language, all working toward improvements in public health with coordinating funding sources. Foundations and even the federal government's Sustainable Communities Initiative are beginning to focus on the importance of leveraging funding and investments across sectors.

These efforts can have significant effects and yield incredible successes on the health of communities as a wide range of residents and professionals collaborate on strategies and actions, benefiting from a common understanding of the issues and goals. The most critical requirement is a holistic approach to community involvement. A truly successful plan for a sustainable, healthy, energy-efficient environment is created for everyone, by everyone.

Historically, improvements in community health were completed in silos of sectors, based on funding opportunities within each. The school community, health providers, and city representatives worked in their own worlds. This methodology continues to cause disjointed and ineffectual results as demonstrated by the continuing decline in the health of Americans. Working at cross-purposes means efforts counteract each other.

A cross-sector issue such as the quality of food within the school systems seems like a simple problem to solve: Secure better food. Yet, the constraints to providing healthy food in schools may include not only a lack of proper equipment, but also food service provider policies that require main warehouse food distribution. This type of distribution policy precludes obtaining fresh produce from local farmers because of the coordination, cost, and shipment time involved. However, when given opportunity and encouragement to work together, school districts and departments, food service providers, and local farmers can easily arrange to ship directly to the local school's new salad bars. Community involvement alone is insufficient; residents and businesses need to be engaged together with the city in the continuing delivery of the solutions.

Prepare the Team

A substantial challenge to working together on a systems-wide change means learning to speak the same language. Literally, this means linguistically, in Spanish, for example, or Chinese, communicating across the divide between the well-educated and those who lack high school diplomas, and bridging the health care to engineering language gaps. Throughout the process, set ground rules by defining the appropriate "language" that will be spoken. Agency members should refrain from the use of technical lingo that community members, youth, and other agency sectors will not understand, and maximize opportunities for questions and comments.

Another major hurdle, distrust between sectors, requires relationship building and the development of methods that allow participants to get to know each other as "people," not just sector represents. A personal example in my community, I was stereotypically viewed as "The City" by residents and even by nonprofit agencies. I broke the stereotype byparticipating in a conference and getting to the leaders of the initiative on a personal level while they were able to see me as a person and began to trust me and the process. Creating social occasions to foster those connections and bonds is key to the success of a long-term planning project. Meet individually, in groups, and as gatherings of groups, though the logistics can be difficult. Agency members prefer to meet during the day, while residents and youth often cannot, so compromise on locations and times is necessary.

Understanding what the barriers are for community residents to be healthy is the first step in defining the players who need to be involved to realize success. Once the goal is defined, the next step is to establish who needs to be involved in order to realize that goal. Through the collection of data and research that is done on a community and the problem, it can be determined what the key areas are that need to be focused on to create your plan. An example of the barriers to the improvement of the health of a community could be:

- Infrastructure/Built Environment
- Food Access
- School Wellness
- Family Fitness

A project can then organize itself around those strategy teams which should be comprised of representatives from agencies, youth, and community members. These groups can then work together to examine their needs for expert involvement in their strategies.

An important lesson is not to involve all key players before those preliminary goals and objectives are established. Be strategic about when and who is involved when in the process. Many players should only be drawn into the process during the phase of developing the implementation strategies and during the actual implementation.

Throughout the process be sure not to create independent silos that work on their own. Work hard to ensure that this does not happen through the mixing of participants at different levels throughout the process. An example can be to have the strategy teams act as subcommittee work groups that consist of each of youth, community, and agency members working together, but also keep regular meetings within the individual sectors to be able to discuss all of the strategies within a sector, and be sure to gather all participants together to break down the barriers of sectors altogether. There will be strategies that cross sectors and strategy committees. This is why it is important to emphasize the cross-pollination between groups of ideas in as many ways as possible. For example, some fitness strategies require improvements to infrastructure as well as programming to be successful; food access requires providing locally grown vegetables in schools and bodegas, changing policies for food assistance to promote the purchasing of produce, as well as teaching residents how to cook that food.

The relationships established between all of the participants of the process will yield amazing results throughout the entire project. When this strategy is followed, an awesome power emerges from so many people working together and learning about one another.

Prepare the Tools

Baseline data from the community needs to be collected in order to have a benchmark of the current condition and to quantify successes over time. A common tool used by the health community is the Community Health Assessment (CHA), which uses GIS along with health and population data for use in spatial analysis. However, the evidence says that health professionals have a tendency to think more statistically in charts and graphs, not spatially as planners often do.[36] Working across sectors will allow for spatial analysis to become a stronger component in CHA in the future.

When conducting a community-driven process, it is easier for residents to visualize a concept than it is for them to think of ideas through words. Many large maps illustrating the target area, with a variety of colored markers, can help to stimulate ideas and conversations about areas and the connectivity of those areas. For example, a barrier to people walking to improve their health is the condition of the sidewalks. It is important to use GIS to be able to mark those areas that have problems.

Surveys are also a useful tool in collecting the data needed to develop a systems-changing plan for a healthier community. There are many different types of surveys that should be used to ensure the proper collection including one-on-one interviews, paper surveys, and surveying of conditions of infrastructure and parks. This data is necessary to have the tools to make informed decisions about the barriers preventing residents from being healthy.

No technology available can surpass the benefits of getting out on the streets and walking or riding to collect data on the built environment. Conducting walking audits using a combination of community, youth, and agency members will ensure a holistic look from different users of the space. Likewise, talking to community members directly about the barriers to a healthier lifestyle in their experience is important to realize the extent of the problem and potential solutions in a real life light.

Prepare the Place

Using residents to conduct the surveys is an effective way to use the tool for both data collection as well as education. Residents have credibility and trust in the neighborhoods and, in turn, are able to learn first-hand what the concerns are in

Sidewalk Conditions

Holyoke Sidewalk Walkability Assessment

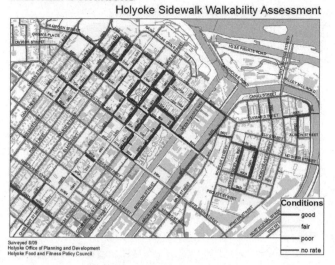

Surveyed 8/09
Holyoke Office of Planning and Development
Holyoke Food and Fitness Policy Council

Conditions
— good
— fair
— poor
— no rate

Shade Trees

Holyoke Sidewalk Walkability Assessment

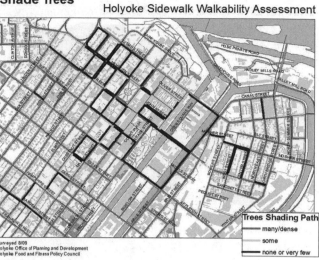

Surveyed 8/09
Holyoke Office of Planning and Development
Holyoke Food and Fitness Policy Council

Trees Shading Path
— many/dense
— some
— none or very few

Cleanliness and Building Maintenance

Holyoke Sidewalk Walkability Assessment

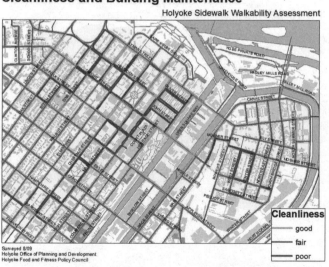

Surveyed 8/09
Holyoke Office of Planning and Development
Holyoke Food and Fitness Policy Council

Cleanliness
— good
— fair
— poor

Least Walkable Segments

Holyoke Sidewalk Walkability Assessment

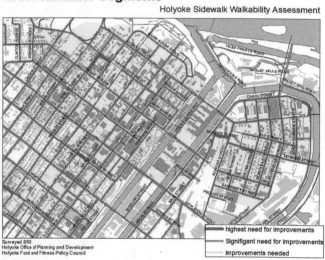

Surveyed 8/09
Holyoke Office of Planning and Development
Holyoke Food and Fitness Policy Council

— highest need for improvements
— Signifigant need for improvements
— improvements needed

their own community. The best way to get useful sidewalk data is to use people who use those sidewalks every day. This data can then be put into a modified pavement management system that can be used by the city to keep track of the conditions of the sidewalks and prioritize where the most need is for repairs.

The other useful tool is a more technical sidewalk inventory, using a pavement management software program. The data that it collects in the target area can be entered into the software to help to graphically illustrate the worst areas, as well as prioritize which areas need to be repaired next. This program can assist the municipality to have a focused plan for the future that can counteract political pressures to invest in sidewalks that may not be a priority.

Figure 13-7   Figure 13-8
Figure 13-9   Figure 13-10
Walkability assessments completed with residents and input into GIS illustrates the areas of most need. *Holyoke Office of Planning & Development*

Policy analysis is an often overlooked component of the barriers to a healthy community. The zoning ordinance in the community should be analyzed for policies that could be preventing people from having mobile food markets, or from developing community gardens within an urban setting. Also, city transportation policies historically do not consider all modes of transportation in their construction projects. Advocating locally for transportation projects to follow the Complete Streets framework of ensuring that pedestrians, bikers, and vehicles all have a place on the roadway can be an effective way of making change. In addition, advocating at the state level or higher for change to food assistance programs to increase allocations and to restrict allowable purchases to healthier choices is also a beneficial practice.

Prepare the People

For all systems-changing plans, it is important to think strategically about the best expert players to involve in your process in order to successfully realize your goals. Nothing can be done without the buy-in of those who will need to make the changes. In the case of a plan to improve the overall health of a community, it is important to have city planning, parks, engineering, DPW, health departments, state health representatives, school representatives in policy and food supply, nonprofits, residents, and youth all involved.

Stepping back and brainstorming throughout the process for stakeholders who are not yet part of the process is a useful exercise. As strategies emerge, new stakeholders often come to the forefront who would not have been considered at the beginning. It is also important to think strategically about when the stakeholders are brought into the process. Making sure that the people who are asked to participate have a need to share their expertise when you invite them could make or break a long-term relationship. A lesson learned is not to include the full range of stakeholders at the beginning

Figure 13-11

Developing a set of values by the participants of the project, to be used in establishing the final goals and objects, is a useful exercise early in the project. *Photo taken by Sandy Ward.*

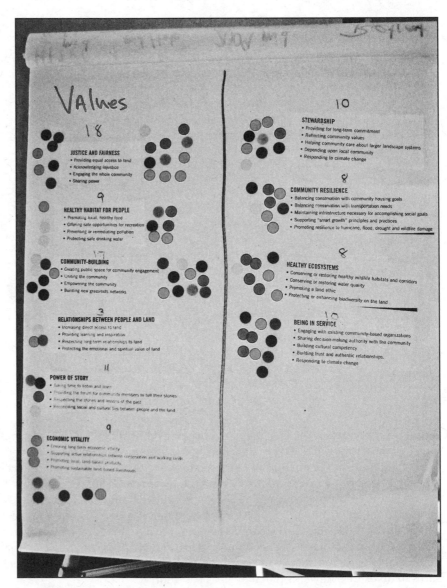

Figure 13-12
Farmers' markets in urban centers can be a useful way to provide fresh produce during the growing season. *Holyoke Office of Planning & Development*

organizational meetings or you *will* lose them. Wait until the project is at the point of brainstorming ideas to bring those people into the process.

Community leadership will be one of the most important components of any successful plan. Members of the community have respect in their community, can spread the word easier about the project, and can continue the good fight through changes in staffing and administrations. However, often community members do not have the tools to be the best leaders that they can be. They have not been given those tools, but a good project can also train their resident participants to be good leaders and advocates for the project. Examples of trainings that can be useful are basic knowledge of government and advocacy, leadership trainings, use of media, public speaking, and others. These new skills should be directly used in relationship to the project to learn how each item can be used in seeing the project to success.

The long-tested, best way to keep community members involved in a project over an extended period of time is to see results. Without results community members as well as agency members will lose faith in the project. An easy way to accomplish this is to determine the low-hanging fruit to start with small, early successes throughout the entire process.

Develop Goals, Objectives, and Performance Metrics

A case study example in the complexity of discovering a comprehensive solution to removing barriers to a healthy community is access to food. There are many components to being successful in increasing the amount of healthy foods that a community, as a whole, purchases. It is not just having the fresh produce available. Below is a case study on the necessary aspects of creating true change.

The goal for a community is to increase the consumption of healthy food of its lower-income residents. Once the goal is established, the research is then done to discover why the lack of consumption exists, and where the residents shop. The data gathered showed that within the target neighborhood there is only one grocery store, which does not have regularly fresh produce, and the remaining sources of food are small bodegas that focus on fast and unhealthy food. Researching where residents shop and why can help provide the tools to the existing stores to provide better foods and increase their business. It can also attract healthier businesses into the neighborhood by showing data that the residents travel to a store in a neighboring community to get their food instead of their own neighborhood. The community does have two other grocery stores outside of the target neighborhood, but they are only accessible by bus and are much higher priced. A key strategy to realize the goal is to give the bodegas the tools to provide fresh fruits and vegetables throughout the year, including refrigerated displays and potential subsidies to allow for affordable produce.

The cost of fresh produce is the most significant barrier to the proper consumption of produce. No increase in consumption will occur until state and federal policies are changed that involve food subsidies such as food stamps. When a person is faced with the decision of providing enough food for their family, although unhealthy, and not being able to buy enough healthy food, it is impossible to change the habit. The only way to increase the consumption of healthy foods for those on food subsidies is to limit the types of food that can be purchased with those subsidies.

A low-cost method to increase fresh produce supply is to provide opportunities to grow vegetables within community gardens which allow for residents in urban areas to grow their own vegetables as well as potentially create an income through the sale of their produce at the local farmers' market.

The availability of fresh produce will not necessarily increase consumption, however. Another necessary component is teaching people how to cook with healthy food. Many people have been raised on prepared, boxed, and fast food. We no longer cook "from scratch," as everything is easy and prepared in a rush. In order to give people the tools to be healthier, it is critical to provide lessons on how to prepare healthy meals.

Develop the Strategic Plan

Once the research is completed on what the barriers are to success, and the team is established, the key strategy areas can begin to be brainstormed. Strategy teams need to be organized around the key strategies and include members of the community, youth, and agency organizations. Be sure to include any other stakeholders at this point who can add expertise to each of those strategy groups. For instance, for an infrastructure strategy team, it would be important to be sure that the city engineer, public works and planning department of the community are involved in the strategy team. These strategies will most likely be the most long term and costly and require the buy-in and knowledge of the city departments.

A very useful tool in developing and evaluating a large number of strategies is to use a standard ranking and evaluation sheet that all participants must fill out. The teams could be given color coded sheets by strategy team to enter each implementation strategy on a consistent form.

The goals and values that were determined early on in the process can be used as "deal breaker" questions in the sheets that everyone has agreed upon. The forms should be presented with questions ranked on a scale of their importance. This method can remove some of the personal emotion out of the strategies when it comes time to prioritize and cut items out. Examples could include such things as:

- Does the community support this strategy? (based on the data gathered through the surveys)
- Does it meet the values of the group? (values that were established by the full group)
- Is the community ready? Does the community have information and skills already to advocate for their interests?
- Is there research, evidence, and/or logic that support this strategy? Is there a proven best practice, or is there no research but it makes sense based on local knowledge?

Other items that should be included, but should not preclude a strategy from being considered are:

- What is the timeframe to complete the item? (short, medium, or long term)
- What is the cost to complete the item? Is it a "low hanging fruit" or high-cost item?
- What partners will be needed to accomplish the goal?

Creating a successful plan to change a community to be healthier is challenging and thought provoking. Many questions will arise throughout the process on how to give people to tools to be healthier, as well as how to make them use the tools. The solutions to the crisis of health in our country cannot be solved by one sector, or by one strategy.

Develop the Action Plan

Once the implementation strategies are determined, the difficult part of the process is putting it into a meaningful, practical plan. The strategy sheets can be the mechanism to create a meaningful method of fairly prioritizing the many implementation strategies that were developed.

In creating a plan, it is important to pay attention to developing a holistic approach to accomplishments. The colored sheet method is a useful tool in visually displaying the sectors that each implementation strategy represents. The entire compilation of strategy sheets that passed the above mentioned "deal breaker" questions, can then be mixed together and organized first by score, then by timeline. The score of each sheet is based on the key evaluation criteria that were determined through the process of developing goals and objectives.

This method is best accomplished by holding a meeting of all participants and gathering around a large table to organize the strategies to form a matrix, as seen in Figure 13-13. The first exercise is to organize the sheets by their score, and the second is to organize them into timeline order of short-term, medium-term, and long-term goals.

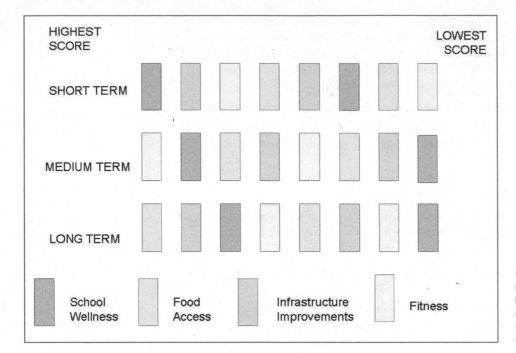

Figure 13-13
Using colored strategy sheets provides the ability to visualize if each primary strategy area is being equally represented. *Holyoke Office of Planning & Development*

The final check on the resulting matrix should be if there is a good mix of strategies from each key implementation area. If there is not, there should be efforts to include strategies to fill out the strategic plan. This matrix can be used to organize the strategic plan in terms of cost restraints to allow for "low hanging fruit" items throughout the length of implementation, timed with the beginning work on long-term costly strategies to ensure that there are continual success stories throughout the process.

The most useful ways to secure political and technical resources and funding for your project is to involve those key stakeholders in the process so that they are a part of the solution and have buy-in. The agencies are an important sector to focus on for participation. Unless the project group is willing to go through the process of becoming its own 501c3 nonprofit agency, many funding sources are not available. The power of collaboration is awe-inspiring. Funding is possible for most anything when people work together to both pool their possible resources as well as their human capital.

Implement the Action Plan

In order to maintain progress in a long-term project, an action plan needs to be established with responsible parties and timelines. Those strategies need to be regularly visited and responsible parties must be held accountable. Without regular checks, items will fall by the wayside and the project will loose focus. A project director is an important component to keeping the multisector project focused. Without one point person, it will be difficult to keep track of the process with so many people involved.

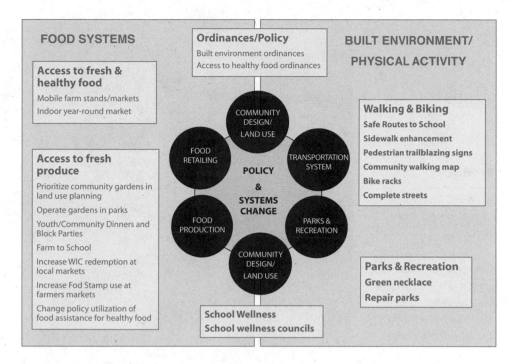

FOOD SYSTEMS

Access to fresh & healthy food
Mobile farm stands/markets
Indoor year-round market

Access to fresh produce
Prioritize community gardens in land use planning
Operate gardens in parks
Youth/Community Dinners and Block Parties
Farm to School
Increase WIC redemption at local markets
Increase Fod Stamp use at farmers markets
Change policy utilization of food assistance for healthy food

Ordinances/Policy
Built environment ordinances
Access to healthy food ordinances

BUILT ENVIRONMENT/ PHYSICAL ACTIVITY

Walking & Biking
Safe Routes to School
Sidewalk enhancement
Pedestrian trailblazing signs
Community walking map
Bike racks
Complete streets

Parks & Recreation
Green necklace
Repair parks

COMMUNITY DESIGN/ LAND USE

FOOD RETAILING

TRANSPORTATION SYSTEM

POLICY & SYSTEMS CHANGE

FOOD PRODUCTION

PARKS & RECREATION

COMMUNITY DESIGN/ LAND USE

School Wellness
School wellness councils

Figure 13-14
Creating a visually appealing strategy plan can be useful in getting the word out to the community and to potential funders. *Holyoke Office of Planning & Development*

A well-thought-out strategic plan will help in this process. Creating a graphic representation of the project's goals and objectives that illustrates the overall plan to the participants as well as potential supporters and funders will be extremely valuable.

The key to ensuring continued interest in the project over the years is to make sure that there are continual success stories. These successes need to be celebrated to create more momentum. Below are some examples of low-hanging fruit that can be completed even during the process of creating an action plan.

- **Farm to school:** Participation from local farmers, school department, and the school food service provider are needed to accomplish this goal. The largest barrier is to change the policies of the food service provider to allow for local farmers to deliver their produce directly to the schools. The purchase of a salad bar, if not already obtained, is another equipment requirement.

- **Walking school bus:** This strategy can begin immediately in a community that is working on creating safe routes to school, even prior to any formal adoption of the program. The strategy requires one adult leading students from a neighborhood to a school. There can be pick-up points along the way at determined times. Once established, parents can rotate to share the responsibility.

- **Community meals:** The organization of community meals by community members to share information about the strategic process can also be used as a tool to teach residents healthy recipes, how to cook fresh produce, as well as ways to develop new strategies and recruit new participants.

A well-thought-out, communitywide plan will attract funding. There is a multitude of potential funding sources depending on the efficiency of the strategies.

CREATING HEALTHIER COMMUNITIES THROUGH POLICY CHANGE

Karen Shore, Ph.D.
Center for Health Improvement

INTERVENTION TYPE: POLICY, STRATEGY

Description

Many of today's public health challenges—such as global warming, obesity, and pandemic flu—require multilevel solutions. Because public health solutions are designed to cover whole populations rather than individuals, there is an opportunity to address these multisectoral problems through changes in policies at the local, regional, state, and national levels. Building up to the local level, policies can be changed in homes, schools, and workplaces to help create healthier communities.

Efforts focused solely on changing individual behaviors, have not succeeded in addressing public health problems such as tobacco use or obesity. Thus, many of today's efforts to address such problems build on the concept of creating healthy communities. This approach requires commitment from diverse organizations and multiple sectors including education, health care, housing, transportation, city planning, parks and recreation, and public health, as well as the engagement of residents in discussions of community transformation. Community-level changes to support healthy environments may include ensuring access to safe, green open spaces; free, safe drinking water; and affordable, desirable, locally grown fruits and vegetables.

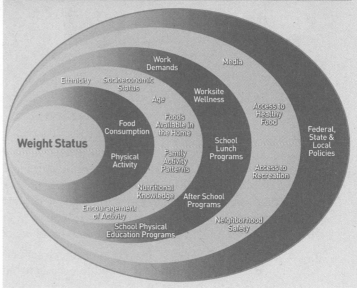

▲▲ A Worksite Wellness Program allows access to a new farmers' market in downtown Sacramento. *Center for Health Improvement, 2008*

▲ Individual and environmental factors are determinants of weight status. *Center for Health Improvement, 2009*

SUPPORT GOALS AND OBJECTIVES

The overall goal is to create healthier communities and environments in which all residents have the opportunity to thrive. As an example, if the goal is to create a community in which more residents have a healthier weight status, it is essential to identify the various determinants of weight status and the policy umbrellas under which many of those determinants fall. The determinants of weight status range from individual behaviors related to food consumption and physical activity, to individual characteristics such as age, ethnicity, socioeconomic status, and nutritional knowledge, to work and school environments (school lunch programs, after-school programs, school physical activity programs, worksite wellness programs, work demands), to community environments including the media, access to healthy foods, access to recreation, and neighborhood safety.

In many communities, children and adults do not have safe places to exercise. Several communities have recently begun efforts to establish "joint use agreements" for local schools—allowing access to playgrounds so that community residents can engage in physical activity during nonschool hours. Others have implemented "complete streets" that are safe and convenient for all users, so that community members can walk or ride bicycles safely to school, work, or recreation—this may represent a win both in terms of increased physical activity for the individual and reduced vehicle miles traveled/lower greenhouse gas emissions.

PERFORMANCE CHARACTERISTICS
Performance characteristics differ and should be tailored to each type of policy change.

POTENTIAL SYNERGISM
The development and implementation of policies often involves multiple agencies or organizations. In the case of community-level policy change, for example, to make healthier beverage choices easily available, schools, worksites, and retail stores may all be involved. In addition to new policies requiring that healthy beverage choices be available in various locations within the community, there may be opportunities to influence consumption of beverages by implementing or increasing taxes on sugar-sweetened beverages at the state or national level.

IMPLEMENTATION TIME
The timeframe for a community to successfully change policies affecting health ranges from a few weeks to several months to multiple years, depending on the level of change, complexity of change, and institutions and entities involved.

BENEFITS
All residents have the potential to benefit from living in healthier communities, and policy changes have the potential for much more widespread benefits than can be realized when one or more individuals change their own behavior. Benefits from policy change vary widely and can range from having safe walking paths for exercise, to having access to fresh produce at local farmers' markets, to having enhanced public transit leading to fewer greenhouse gas emissions.

DRAWBACKS
It can be challenging to engage and motivate individuals and organizations to change policies. Proponents of long-standing policies may be reluctant to embrace change.

First Cost

The initial costs will vary widely depending on the policy change. These costs will include those related to personnel, with time being spent researching policy options, along with the costs and benefits of those options, and identifying implementation and evaluation approaches.

Lifecycle Costs

Lifecycle costs will also vary widely depending on the policy change. These costs will include those borne by the affected entities, such as homes, schools, workplaces, and so forth.

Estimated Quantitative Performance

Quantitative performance must be measured separately for each policy change and be relevant to the policy. For example, the performance of a change in policy to impact global warming by supporting public transit in lieu of individuals operating passenger vehicles should be measured by individual vehicle miles traveled, number and percent of the population using mass transit, aggregate greenhouse gas emissions. By contrast, measuring the performance of a policy change designed to impact childhood obesity should be measured by the number of schools with healthy lunch programs and the number of participants in those programs, the number of and participation by youth in school physical education classes, the percent of children eating a certain number of servings of fruits and vegetables per day.

Implementation Supports and Constraints

The path to policy change typically has several steps:

1. Identification of a problem
2. Formulation of a policy change to solve the problem (involves identifying potential solutions and the pros and cons of each, as well as champions for change)
3. Communicating with stakeholders about the policy change
4. Implementation of the policy change (involves working with all affected parties to ensure smooth implementation of the change)
5. Evaluation of whether the solution is working as desired

Informational Sources

- Central California Regional Obesity Prevention Program www.ccropp.org
- The City Project (Los Angeles) www.cityprojectca.org

Reports and Studies

- Trust for America's Health. July 2008. "Prevention for a Healthier America: Investments in Disease Prevention Yield Significant Savings, Stronger Communities." http://healthyamericans.org/reports/prevention08/
- "Tackling Obesity by Building Healthy Communities: Changing Policies Through Innovative Collaborations," Center for Health Improvement, California Health Policy Forum Brief, December 2009. www.chipolicy.org/pdf/Issue_Briefs/CHIObesityBriefFinal.pdf

Chapter 2: The Process of Transformation

PUBLIC UTILITY PROGRAMS

Some public utility programs offer a statewide rebate program that promotes the more efficient use of electricity and renewable energy, funded by electricity consumers, in addition to residential and commercial energy audit and retrofit opportunities.

PUBLIC SERVICE FEES

Revenues from municipal public service fees, such as parking meter and utility fees, can fund transit improvements and water use efficiency. In some states, municipalities, and counties, increased water and wastewater use fees can cover efficiency improvement costs without direct voter approval.

TAX AND BOND REVENUES

Revenues can be generated through a bond secured by the proceeds of a specific tax whose rate cannot be raised if it becomes insufficient to pay the bonds. General obligation bonds and special purpose taxes and property assessments provide another funding source.

IMPACT FEES

Some county and municipal governments retain the authority to include emissions mitigation fees as impact fees on new development. The City of Chula Vista, California, funds energy retrofits of existing buildings with revenues generated from mitigation fees developers pay when new buildings do not meet a minimum energy performance threshold.

GRANTS AND LOW-INTEREST LOANS

Federal, state, and regional agencies provide grants and loans for investments in a variety of energy and climate-related projects.

SELF-FUNDING AND REVOLVING FUND PROGRAMS

Self-funding loan programs provide direct cash savings after an initial investment in energy efficiency retrofits and green building standards. Loan payments are designed to be equal or proportional to the cost savings. A revolving fund for an energy management program and reinvestment program can fund energy-efficiency retrofit improvements with savings, reinforcing a city's general fund to help render the energy program self-supporting.

PRIVATE INVESTORS

Private investors can provide funding to local governments. For example, energy service companies (ESCOs) can finance the up-front investments in energy efficiency. Local governments reimburse the companies over an agreed time period; private companies may finance solar power installations, recouping the investments by selling generated power to building owners.

CARBON OFFSETS

In the carbon trading future, the emerging carbon offset market could help fund projects that expect to significantly reduce emissions, providing U.S. institutes a national carbon cap and trade system. Jurisdictions may then be able to sell carbon offsets to other communities or businesses that have not been as successful at reducing GHG emissions.

CROSS-FUNDING

Cost sharing programs recognize that some programs will cost money and some will save money. Communities such as City of Roseville, California, can identify opportunities for cost sharing, borrowing against future energy savings to fund a comprehensive action plan.

Chapter 3: The Physical Built Environment

SUSTAINABLE COMMUNITY COMMERCE

The following is a list of organizations and websites that can provide information on tools, expertise, and funding in support of sustainable commerce:

- Center for Neighborhood Technology; the New Jersey Office of Sustainable Business
- EPA Office of Smart Growth: www.epa.gov
- Locavores.com; Slow Food USA: www.localharvest. org/csa/
- National Retail Federation Sustainable Retailing Consortium
- Sustainable Communities Network: www.missionlo-cal.org/street-food-news/; tnr.com/blog/the-avenue/budget-2011-joined-government-0.

BUILDING SUSTAINABLE COMMUNITIES: THE ECOLOGICAL TOOLKIT

- LEED-ND website on USGBC: www.usgbc.org/leed/nd/
- Congress for New Urbanism (CNU) website: www.cnu.org
- Natural Resource Defense Council (NRDC) website: www.nrdc.org
- Natural Step: www.naturalstep.org
- Green Globes: www.greenglobes.com
- One Planet Living: www.oneplanetliving.org
- Building Research Establishment Environmental Assessment Method (BREEAM): www.breeam.org

BIOCLIMATIC BUILDING DESIGN

- U.S. Green Building Council: www.usgbc.org
- Green Building Certification Institute: www.gbci.org/homepage.aspx
- Center for the Built Environment, University of California, Berkeley: www.cbe.berkeley.edu/
- National Institute of Building Sciences: www.nibs.org/
- International Living Building Institute: http://ilbi.org/countries/usa/united-states
- The Pharos Project: www.pharosproject.net/
- The Daylighting Collaborative: www.daylighting.org/

- BuildingGreen.com: www.buildinggreen.com/
- Database of State Incentives for Renewables & Efficiency: www.dsireusa.org/

Chapter 4: The Regulatory Environment

SUSTAINABILITY PLANNING AND THE LAW

- U.S. Green Building Council: www.usgbc.org/LEED
- Green Roofs for Healthy Cities: www.greenroofs.org
- SmartCode: www.smartcodecentral.org
- Form-Based Codes Institute: www.formbasedcodes.org
- Earthcraft House Program: www.atlantahomebuilders.com
- One Planet Communities: www.oneplanetcommunities.org
- Audubon International: www.auduboninternational.org
- NAHB Green Scoring Tool: www.nahbgreen.org/ScoringTool.aspx
- RMI: www.rmi.org
- Green Building Codes: www.dcat.net/about_dcat/staff.php
- Sustainable Design and Green Building Toolkit for Local Governments EPA 904B 10001 June 2010
- Innovative Energy and Sustainability Design: www.cleanair-coolplanet.org/images/EppingPressRelease.pdf.
- Pliny Fisk: www.cmpbg.org, www.archone.tamu.edu/college/news/newsletters/spring2005/fisk.html
- Sim Van der Ryn: www.vanderryn.com

TRANSFORMING THE BUILT ENVIRONMENT THROUGH FORM-BASED CODING

- Christopher Leinberger, Back to the Future: The Need for Patient Equity in Real Estate Development Finance, The Brookings Inst., January, 2007.
- Policy Guide on Smart Growth, (American Planning Association, Chicago, IL), (April 15, 2002), (Introducing land use planning history).
- Comprehensive Planning, (Ohio State University, Columbus, OH), (1999) at 1, (Describing the purpose of a land use plan in comprehensive planning).

Chapter 5: Transportation

SUSTAINABLE TRANSPORTATION AND TRANSIT PLANNING

- Reconnecting America and the Center for Transit-Oriented Development: www.reconnectingamerica.org
- Housing + Transportation Affordability Index: www.htaindex.org
- Center for Neighborhood Technology: www.cnt.org
- Smart Growth America: www.smartgrowthamerica.org
- Project for Public Spaces: www.pps.org

AN INCREMENTAL APPROACH: DEVELOPING A LONG-TERM COMPREHENSIVE REGIONAL TRANSPORTATION PLAN

- The Federal Transit Administration: www.fta.dot.gov/
- Moving Cooler—Moving Cooler analyzes and assesses the effectiveness and costs of almost 50 transportation strategies for reducing GHG emissions, as well as evaluates combinations of those strategies. www.movingcooler.info/
- The Federal Highway Administration (FHWA) Surface Transportation Environment and Planning Cooperative Research Program, STEP: A Federal Research Program—conducting research that links to practice www.fhwa.dot.gov/hep/step/proposal.htm

Chapter 6: Energy

THE ENERGY SHIFT

Federal, State, Regional, and Local Funding:

- Sources include federal and state funding for energy and infrastructure projects accessed directly or indirectly through state or regional energy offices that coordinate many programs.

Utilities:

- Utilities typically have a variety of renewable energy and energy-efficiency programs that cities can leverage, participate in, and promote.

Other Sources:

- Other potential funding sources include revolving loan programs and voluntary tax assessment funding districts. The private sector also provides a variety of funding and financing mechanisms.

Chapter 7: Water

STORMWATER MANAGEMENT—LIGHT IMPRINT DEVELOPMENT

Much of the traditional funding for stormwater management comes from municipal general funds and other funding mechanisms that include the following:

- Enterprise funding is based on a fee charged for providing stormwater management within the community, based, for example, on the amount of impervious surface on a tax parcel.
- Special districts within legal described boundaries might be assessed a stormwater management fee based on the services delivered to the area.
- Development fees are usually a one-time payment to a jurisdiction for the cost of designing and implementing stormwater management services to a new development.
- Finance through the sale of bonds can allow some jurisdictions to borrow the money necessary to fund major projects.
- Local and state agencies offer grants and funding for pilot projects in many communities. An example is the Community Action for a Renewed Environment (CARE) program through the Environmental Protection Agency. It is active in many areas to help fund local organizations implementing tools such as Light Imprint.
- Grants are also available through nonprofit organizations such as the Low Impact Development Center.

Some websites that provide information on funding include:

- U. S. Environmental Protection Agency: www.epa.gov
- U. S. Department of Housing and Urban Development: www.hud.gov
- Central storehouse for over 1,000 grant programs: www.grants.gov
- Congress for the New Urbanism: www.cnu.org
- Center for Applied Transect Studies: www.transect.org

Information, websites, and technical expertise:

- Atlanta Regional Commission, et al., "Georgia Stormwater Management Manual, Stormwater Policy

Guidebook and Technical Manual, Volumes 1 & 2." Atlanta: Atlanta Regional Commission, August 2001.

- Timothy Beatley. *Green Urbanism: Learning from European Cities.* Washington, DC: Island Press, 2000.

- Nate Berg. "Top-Down Greening in the Urban Core." Planetizen: The Planning & Development Network (July 27, 2006). www.planetizen.com/node/20612

- Craig Campbell and Michael Ogden. *Constructed Wetlands in the Sustainable Landscape.* New York: John Wiley & Sons, Inc., 1999.

- City of Abilene-Stormwater Utility Division. "Stormwater Ponds." Abilene, Texas: 2008. www.abilenetx.com/StormwaterServices/

- Richard A. Claytor, Jr., P.E. "Critical Components for Successful Planning, Design, Construction, and Maintenance of Stormwater Best Management Practices." Washington, DC: U.S. EPA, Office of Wetlands, Oceans and Watersheds (February 4, 2003). www.epa.gov/owow/nps/natlstormwater03/27Claytor.pdf.

- Herbert Dreiseitl and Dieter Grau. *New Waterscapes: Planning, Building and Design with Water.* Boston: Birkhauser, 2005.

- Andres Duany, Sandy Sorlien, William Wright, et. al. SmartCode, Version 9.0. Gaithersburg, Maryland; The Town Paper, 2007.

- Duany Plater-Zyberk and Company, Charlotte office.
  - Light Imprint New Urbanism: Integrating Sustainability and Community Design, v. 1.3. Charlotte, North Carolina: dpz charlotte, 2008.
  - "Case Study: Habersham, Beaufort County, South Carolina." Charlotte, North Carolina: dpz charlotte, 2007.

- Dave Elkin. "Sustainable Stormwater Blog: The place to share information about innovative stormwater management." Portland, Oregon: 2008. www.sustainablestormwater.com/blog/

- Bruce K. Ferguson. *Porous Pavements.* Boca Raton, FL: CRC Press, 2005.

- Jonathan Ford, PE. *Stormwater's Role in New Urbanist Development.* Providence, Rhode Island: Morris Beacon Design, 2008.

- David Gustafson, James Anderson, Sara Heger Christopherson, and Rich Axler. "Innovative Onsite Sewage Treatment Systems: Constructed Wetlands." St. Paul, MN: University of Minnesota: Extension Service, 2002. www.extension.umn.edu/distribution/naturalresources/DD7671.html

- Liz Guthrie. "The Sustainable Sites Initiative." Austin, Texas: Partnership of the American Society of Landscape Architects, the Lady Bird Johnson Wildflower Center and the United States Botanic Garden, 2007. www.sustainablesites.org/.

- William F. Hunt and Nancy White. "Urban Waterways: Designing Rain Gardens (Bio-Retention Areas)." North Carolina Cooperative Extension Service (June 2001). www.bae.ncsu.edu/stormwater/PublicationFiles/DesigningRainGardens2001.pdf.

- Heather Kinkade-Levario. *Design for Water: Rainwater Harvesting, Stormwater Catchment, and Alternate Water Reuse.* Gabriola Island, BC, Canada: New Society Publishers, 2007.

- Randel Lemoine. *Replicating Natural Runoff Through Retention and Dissipation.* Twin Lake, Michigan: Symbiotic Ventures, L.L.C., 2008. www.symbioticventures.com/.

- The Low Impact Development Center, Inc. *Sustainable Design and Water Quality Research.* Beltsville, Maryland: LID Center, 2008. www.lowimpactdevelopment.org/.

- Melbourne Water. *Water Sensitive Urban Design Engineering Procedures: Stormwater.* Collingwood, Australia: CSIRO Publishing, 2006.

- Lynn Merrill. "Finding the Money for Stormwater Management." *Stormwater: The Journal for Surface Water Quality Professionals,* Forester Media, Inc., Santa Barbara, California (September–October 2005).

- Metro: People Places Open Spaces. "GreenStreets: Innovative Solutions for Stormwater and Stream Crossings" Portland: Metro, 2002.

- Monmouth County Mosquito Extermination Commission. "Stormwater Management Basins and Their Maintenance." Monmouth County, New Jersey: MCMEC, 1999. www.shore.co.monmouth.nj.us/mosquito/water.html.

- Natural Resources Defense Council. "Rooftops to Rivers: Green Strategies for Controlling Stormwater and Combined Sewer Overflows." New York, New York: NRDC, 2008. www.nrdc.org/water/pollution/rooftops/contents.asp.

- New Jersey Department of Environmental Protection. "New Jersey Stormwater Best Management Practices Manual: Chapter 9.1," Stormwater and Nonpoint Source Pollution. Trenton, New Jersey (January 25, 2008). www.njstormwater.org.

- North Carolina Division of Coastal Management. "Wetlands: Their Functions and Values in Coastal North Carolina." Raleigh, North Carolina: Department of Environmental and Natural Resources (December 12, 2001). http://dcm2.enr.state.nc.us/wetlands/brochure.htm

- Pennsylvania Department of Environmental Protection. "Final PA Stormwater Best Management Practices Manual." Harrisburg: Commonwealth of Pennsylvania, 2006.

- Howard Perlman. "The Water Cycle: Streamflow." USGS: Science for a Changing World (August 24, 2007). http://ga.water.usgs.gov/edu/watercyclestreamflow.html

- Portland Bureau of Environmental Services. Portland, Oregon (2006–2008). Home Page: www.portlandonline.com/BES/

    - "Stormwater Management Manual," (2008). www.portlandonline.com/bes/index.cfm?c=47952&

    - "Stormwater Solutions Handbook," (2008). www.portlandonline.com/bes/index.cfm?c=43110

- Public Works. "Stormwater Maintenance: Wet Detention Facilities; Retention Ponds; Filter Ponds, Swale Ditches with Swale Blocks." Leon County, Tallahassee, Florida: (August 28, 2007). www.leoncountyfl.gov/lcswm/Maintenance_Practices.asp.

- Dr. Georgio Tachiev. "Sustainability and New Urbanism at the Regional Scale." Quoted in Light Imprint New Urbanism: A Case Study Comparison. Charlotte, North Carolina: dpz charlotte, 2006.

- U.S. Department of Agriculture. Washington, DC: USDA, Natural Resources Conservation Service (January 29, 2008), "Conservation Practice Standards: Subsurface Drain." www.nrcs.usda.gov/

- U.S. Environmental Protection Agency:

    - Robert Goo and Cathy Berlow. "EPA Headquarters Low Impact Development Program" (Washington, DC: USEPA, Greening EPA, July 2008). www.epa.gov/oaintrnt/stormwater/hq_lid.htm

    - David J. Hirschman and John Kosco. "Managing Stormwater in Your Community: A Guide for Building an Effective Post-Construction Program" (Washington, DC: USEPA, Center for Watershed Protection, July 2008). www.cwp.org/postconstruction

    - "Reducing Stormwater Costs through Low Impact Development (LID) Strategies and Practices" (Washington, DC: USEPA, Nonpoint Source Control Branch, December 2007).

    - "River Corridor and Wetland Restoration: Additional Funding Sources." Washington, DC: U.S. EPA, Office of Wetlands, Oceans and Watersheds (August 14, 2007). www.epa.gov/owow/wetlands/restore/funding.html

- B.C. Wolverton and John Wolverton. Growing Clean Water: Nature's Solution to Water Pollution. Picayune, Mississippi: Wolverton Environmental Services, 2001.

DECENTRALIZED WASTEWATER MANAGEMENT

References:

- T. Asano, F. Burton, H. Lerenz, R. Tsuchihashi, and G. Tchobanoglous, *Water Reuse: Issues, Technologies, and Applications*. New York: McGraw-Hill Books, 2009.

- R.H. Kadlec and S. Wallace. 2008. *Treatment Wetlands* 2d ed. CRC Press, Boca Raton, FL.

- T. Lohan (ed), *Water Consciousness*. San Francisco: Alternet Books, 2009.

- A. Vickers, *Handbook of Water Use and Conservation*. Amherst, MA: Water Plow Press, 2001.

Nonprofit Organizations:

- Water Environment Federation: www.wef.org

- The Pacific Institute: www.pac-inst.org

- Alternet Water Blog: www.alternet.org/water

Water Standards:

- U.S. Green Building Council: www.usgbc.org

- Cascadia USGBC and Living Building Challenge: www.cascadiagbc.org

- Alliance for Water Stewardship: www.allianceforwaterstweardship.org

Chapter 8: Natural Environment

SUSTAINABLE LANDSCAPING

- Green Industry BMPs for Florida; Florida Department of Environmental Protection, Tallahassee, FL, and Florida-IFAS at University of Florida, Gainesville, FL

- Tree City USA Bulletins: 1–43; National Arbor Day Foundation, Lincoln, NE
- Right Tree Right Place Bulletin; Florida Power and Light, Jupiter, FL
- Water-wise [Xeriscape] Landscape Principles; South Florida Water Management District, West Palm Beach, FL
- ANSI A-300 Principles for Maintenance of Trees and Woody Plants; International Society of Arboriculture, Champaign, IL
- Sustainable Sites Initiative; Lady Bird Johnson Wildflower Center, Austin, TX
- The Lawn Handbook; Cornell Cooperative Extension, Cornell University, Ithaca, NY
- Canopy Tree Benefits; McPherson, Greg; Center for Urban Forest Research, USDA Forest Research Station, UC, Davis, CA
- CANOPY: A computer-based tree benefits calculator; Center for Urban Forest Research, USDA Forest Research Station, UC, Davis, CA
- Energy Saving Landscapes; Parker, Jack; Florida International University, North Miami Beach, FL

Chapter 9: Food Production/ Agriculture

SUSTAINABLE FOOD SYSTEMS

- American Farmland Trust
- Community Food Security Coalition
- National Sustainable Agriculture Coalition
- Kellogg Food and Society Program
- Wallace International
- Local Research Universities
- Rodale Institute
- Organic Consumers Association
- Sustainable Agriculture and Food Systems Funders
- Food Policy
- Farmers Market Coalition
- Food Routes
- The Food Trust
- Public Health Law & Policy

Chapter 10: Solid Waste

SUSTAINABLE MATERIALS MANAGEMENT

- Grass Roots Recycling Network: www.grrn.org/zerowaste/zerowaste_faq.html
- U.S. EPA WARM Model: www.epa.gov/climatechange/wycd/waste/calculators/Warm_home.html
- U.S. EPA national waste characterization: www.epa.gov/waste/nonhaz/municipal/msw99.htm
- The California Department of Resources Recycling and Recovery has published several statewide waste characterization studies: www.calrecycle.ca.gov/WasteChar/WasteStudies.htm

Chapter 11: Economics

SUSTAINABLE ECONOMIC DEVELOPMENT: THE LONGER VIEW

- Urban Land Institute: www.uli.org
- National Trust for Historic Preservation
- American Planning Association
- Congress for New Urbanism
- New Market Tax Credits: www.cdfifund.gov/
- International City/County Management Association: http://icma.org/
- International Downtown Association: www.ida-downtown.org
- National Council for Public-Private Partnerships: http://ncppp.org/
- International Economic Development Council: www.iedconline.org

A SUSTAINABLE RETURN ON INVESTMENT

The following resources could be useful for communities looking for more information, technical expertise, and funding:

- Economic and Sustainability Benefits of Boston's ARRA Investments, Boston Redevelopment Authority, March 2010
- Determining the Right Shade of Green for a Specific Community: Using Interactive Value Analysis and the Risk Analysis Process for Assessing the Economic Value of Sustainability Initiatives, April 2008 (Sustainability: The Journal of Record)

- Four Steps to Sustainability, August 2009 (Sustainability: The Journal of Record)
- Sustainable Return on Investment (available through www.HDRGreen.com)
- Your Commitment to Serve is Now Measurable (available through SROI@HDRInc.com)

EPA Publications about Environmental Accounting:
- The Lean and Green Supply Chain: A Practical Guide for Material Managers and Supply Chain Managers to Reduce Costs and Improve Environmental Performance, January 2000 (EPA 742-R-00-001)
- An Introduction to Environmental Accounting as a Business Management Tool: Key Concepts and Terms, June 1995 (EPA 742-R-95-001)
- Valuing Potential Environmental Liabilities for Managerial Decision-Making: A Review of Available Technologies, December 1996 (EPA 742-R-96-003)

Enhancing Supply Chain Performance with Environmental Cost Information:
- Examples from Commonwealth Edison, Anderson Corporation, and Ashland Chemical, December 2000

Searching for Profit in Pollution Prevention:
- Case Studies in the Corporate Evaluation of Environmental Opportunities, April 1998 (James Boyd, Resources for the Future)

Environmental Cost Accounting for Chemical and Oil Companies:
- A Benchmarking Study, June 1997, University of Houston's Institute for Corporate Environmental Management in Partnership with the Business Council for Sustainable development—Gulf of Mexico (EPA 742-R-97-004)

Environmental Accounting Case Studies
- Full Cost Accounting for Decision Making at Ontario Hydro, May 1996 (EPA 742-R-95-004)

Environmental Cost Accounting for Capital Budgeting:
- A Benchmark Survey for Management Accounting, September 1995 (EPA 742-R-95-005)

Chapter 12: Engagement And Education

CREATING AND MANAGING SUSTAINABILITY FOR A MUNICIPALITY
- *Peoria Brings Eco-Friendly Vehicles to Park West.* News release by the City of Peoria, AZ, on the Green Your Ride Event. www.peoriaaz.gov/News/NewsPR.asp?PID=734
- "In Energy Innovation, Everything New is Old Again." *Wall Street Journal,* December 11, 2009. http://online.wsj.com/article/SB126048948482786623.html?mod=WSJ_hpp_LEFTTopSt
- *Green Vehicle Guide,* the Environmental Protection Agency's Green-Fuel economy estimates for vehicles. www.epa.gov/greenvehicles/Index.do;jsessionid=9d5a383393ddaa2fddc5c1bab88e1617351316410e7ea51405772526cccfb9a1.e34MbhqOa3uSby0Ra3uSb3aL-aN10n6jAmljGr5XDqQLvpAe

Chapter 13: Public Health

AMBIENT OUTDOOR AIR QUALITY: COMMUNITY HEALTH
- Warren Karlenzig, et al., "The Sustain Lane U.S. City Rankings, How Green is Your City?" New Society Publishers, 2007. The most current city rankings can be found at www.sustainlane.com/us-city-rankings/.
- California Environmental Protection Agency, Office of Environmental Health Hazard Assessment, "Traffic-Related Air Pollution near Busy Roads: The East Bay Children's Respiratory Health Study," published in *American Journal of Respiratory and Critical Care Medicine*, Vol. 170, pp. 520–526, June 2004.
- Douglas Farr, *Sustainable Urbanism: Urban Design with Nature,* New York: John Wiley & Sons, Inc., 2008.
- California Environmental Protection Agency, Air Resources Board, "California's Children: How and Where They Can Be Exposed to Air Pollution," Research Note 94-6, April 1994, available at www.arb.ca.gov/research/resnotes/notes/94-6.htm
- Interiors and Sources, "The Ozone Factor: The Health Implications of Climate Change," Anthony Bernheim, October/November 2008, pp. 58–63. www.interiorsandsources.com

- National Institute of Environmental Health Sciences, Environmental Health Perspectives, U.S. Department of Health and Human Services, Charles J. Weschler, "Ozone's Impact on Public Health: Contributions from Indoor Exposures to Ozone and Products of Ozone-Initiated Chemistry," 2006. Available at http://dx.doi.org, doi:10.1289/ehp.9256

- Janneane F. Gent, Ph.D., Elizabeth W. Triche, Ph.D., Theodore R. Holford, Ph.D., et al., "Association of Low-Level Ozone and Fine Particles with Respiratory Symptoms in Children with Asthma" *Journal of the American Medical Association*, Vol. 290, No. 14), October 8, 2003.

- U.S. EPA, "A Citizen's Guide to Radon," www.epa.gov/radon/pubs/citguide.html

- 7Group and Bill Reed, *The Integrative Design Guide to Green Building, Redefining the Practice of Sustainability*, New York: John Wiley & Sons, Inc., 2009.

- Isaac Brown and Steve Kellenberg, "Ecologically Engineering Cities Through Integrated Sustainable Systems Planning," vol. 4, no. 1, *Journal of Green Building*.

- Janine M. Benyus, "Biomimicry, Innovations Inspired by Nature" Perennial, 1997.

- Michelle L. Bell, Roger D. Peng, and Francesca Dominici, "The Exposure-Response Curve for Ozone and Risk of Mortality and Adequacy of Current Ozone Regulations,"Environmental Health Perspectives, Vol. 114, No. 4, April 2006.

- Robin Guenther, Gail Vittori, Sustainable Healthcare Architecture, Essay by Anthony Bernheim, "Good Air, Good Health," Chapter 2, pp. 40–43, John Wiley & Sons, Inc., 2008.

- San Francisco Department of Public Health, "Healthy Development Measurement Tool," www.thhdmt.org

- San Francisco Department of Environment, Connected Urban Development, Cisco, Leaptide LLC, "Urban EcoMap, San Francisco," http://sf.urbanecomap.org

- U.S. EPA, "What are Six Common Air Pollutants?," www.epa.gov/air/urbanair/

- U.S. EPA, "National Ambient Air Quality Standards," www.epa.gov/air/criteria.html

- CARB, "California Ambient Air Quality Standards" (CAAQS), www.arb.ca.gov/research/aaqs/caaqs/caaqs.htm - table

- CARB, "Ambient Air Quality Standards," www.arb.ca.gov/research/aaqs/aaqs2.pdf

- U.S. EPA AIRNOW, "Quality of Air Means Quality of Life," http://airnow.gov/index.cfm?action=airnow.main

- CARB, "AQMIS2-Air Quality and Meteorological Information System," www.arb.ca.gov/aqmis2/aqinfo.php

- American Lung Association, "State of the Air, 2009" Report, 2009, available at www.stateoftheair.org/. The report can be downloaded and data can be researched at this website.

- U.S. EPA, "EPA Map of Radon Zones," www.epa.gov/radon/zonemap.html

- U.S. EPA, "Where You Live: State Radon Contact Information," www.epa.gov/radon/whereyoulive.html

- San Francisco Department of Environment, Connected Urban Development, Cisco, Leaptide LLC, "Urban EcoMap, San Francisco," http://sf.urbanecomap.org/

- U.S. Green Building Council: www.usgbc.org/

- ICLEI-Local Governments for Sustainability: www.icleiusa.org/

- Lawrence Berkeley National Laboratory: www.lbl.gov/

- National Renewable Energy Laboratory: www.nrel.gov

- U.S. EPA "Air and Radiation Grants and Funding": www.epa.gov/air/grants_funding.html - trans

- U.S. EPA "State Indoor Radon Grant (SIRG) Program": www.epa.gov/radon/sirgprogram.html

- U.S. Green Building Council, LEED for Neighborhood Development: www.usgbc.org and www.usgbc.org/DisplayPage.aspx?CMSPageID=148

- ICLEI Local Community for Sustainability, Star Community Index: www.icleiusa.org/programs/sustainability/star-community-index

- ICLEI Local Community for Sustainability, Clean Air and Climate Protection (CACP) Software 2009: www.icleiusa.org/action-center/tools/cacp-software

A HOLISTIC PUBLIC HEALTH APPROACH

- U.S. Department of Health and Human Services, Centers for Disease Control, National Center for Health Statistics, "Health, United States: with special feature on Medical Technology," January 2010.

- Matthew Scotch; Bambang Parmanto; Cynthia S. Gad; and Ravi K. Sharma: "Exploring the role of GIS during community health assessment problem solving: experiences of public health professionals," *International Journal of Health Geographics*, September 2006.

Endnotes

Chapter 1

1. *Conventional Suburban Development* (CSD) describes the outward expansion of a city and its suburbs beyond its outskirts to low-density, auto-dependent development on rural land, with associated design features that encourage car dependence. http://en.wikipedia.org/wiki/Urban_sprawl.
2. *Traditional Neighborhood Development* (TND) refers to the development of a complete neighborhood or town using traditional town planning principles. TND may occur in infill settings and involve adaptive reuse of existing buildings, but often involves all-new construction on previously undeveloped land. http://en.wikipedia.org/wiki/Traditional_Neighborhood_Development_(TND)
3. "Livestock a Major Threat to Environment." Fao.org. 2006-11-29. www.fao.org/newsroom/en/news/2006/1000448/index.html. Retrieved August 7, 2009.Steinfeld, H., P. Gerber, T. Wassenaar, V. Castel, M. Rosales, and C. de Haan. 2006. U.N. Food and Agriculture Organization. Rome, Italy. "Livestock's Long Shadow—Environmental Issues and Options." Retrieved December 5, 2008.
4. *The Impact of Climate Change on America's Forests: A Technical Document Supporting the 2000 USDA Forest Service RPA Assessment.* Linda A. Joyce and Richard Birdsey, technical editors. Washington, DC: U.S. Department of Agriculture, Forest Service, 2000 (www.fs.fed.us/rm/pubs/rmrs_gtr059.pdf).
5. Jeff Vail. Net Monday, September 21, 2009, The Diagonal Economy 3, Growth and Sustainability, www.jeffvail.net/labels/Diagonal%20Economy.html.

Chapter 2

1. Best practice is any design, technique, process, technology, practice or operation that has been deployed, activated, and operated or used at a stationary source site for a reasonable period of time sufficient to demonstrate that the design, technique, process, technology, practice or operation is reliable when deployed, activated, or operated in a manner that is recommended and typical for the process.
2. The National TOD Database is a project of the Center for Transit-Oriented Development. Intended as a tool for planners, developers, government officials, and academics, the Database provides economic and demographic information for every existing and proposed fixed guideway transit station in the U.S. http://toddata.cnt.org/db_tool.php. The Center for Transit-Oriented Development is a collaboration of the Center for Neighborhood Technology, Reconnecting America, and Strategic Economics. The original version of the TOD database was funded by HUC in 2004; it is currently funded by the Federal Transit Administration.
3. Drupal is a free and open-source Content Management System (CMS) written in PHP and distributed under the GNU General Public LIcense. Although Drupal offers a sophisticated programming interface for developers, no programming skills are required for basic website installation and administration. Source: Wikipedia.
4. Stephen Abley, "Walkability Scoping Paper," March 21, 2005. Retrieved 4/21/08.
5. The Climate Registry, a nonprofit collaboration among North American states, provinces, territories, and native sovereign nations that sets consistent and transparent standards to calculate, verify, and publicly report greenhouse gas emissions in a single registry. www.theclimateregistry.org.

Chapter 4

1. The DPZ Transect, www.dpz.com/transect.aspx
2. The Form-Based Codes Institute, a nonprofit corporation engaged in research, standards setting, outreach, and education related to its mission of advancing the use and acceptance of form-based codes. The FBCI offers courses across the United States in partnership with leading academic institutions and creates and administers courses and special programs tailored to the needs of municipalities, public agencies, and private organizations. Go to www.formbasedcodes.org.
3. The nonprofit Center for Applied Transect Studies (CATS) was founded in 2007 to promote understanding of the built environment as part of the natural environment, through the planning methodology of the rural-to-urban transect. The SmartCode is the foundational tool for implementation of this methodology, and can be found at www.transect.org/.
4. The SmartCode is a model unified land development ordinance. www.smartcodecentral.org/.
5. Version 10, released in 2010, has only six articles.
6. To view the SmartCode Modules, see: www.smartcodecentral.org/.

Chapter 5

1. Planned stations include those planned transit corridors that have a Full Funding Grant Agreement with the Federal Transit Administration through the New Starts or Small Starts programs.

Chapter 6

1. For example, California's Assembly Bill 375, signed by Governor Schwarzenegger in 2008, is the nation's first law aimed at controlling greenhouse gas emissions by curbing urban sprawl. http://gov.ca.gov/press-release/10697/.
2. California recently unveiled its Long Term Energy Efficiency Strategic Energy Plan which lays out "big bold" goals for all new residential buildings to be zero-net energy by 2020 and all new commercial buildings to be zero-net energy by 2030. www.californiaenergyefficiency.com/docs/EESStrategicPlan.pdf.
3. National Renewable Energy Laboratory, *"Lessons Learned from Case Studies of Six High-Performance Buildings,"* 2006. www.nrel.gov/docs/fyo60sti/37452.pdf.
4. Information on 377 building software tools for evaluating energy efficiency, renewable energy, and sustainability in buildings is provided. http://apps1.eere.energy.gov/buildings/tools_directory/.
5. www.ctgenergetics.com.
6. www.energy.ca.gov/places/.
7. http://apps1.eere.energy.gov/buildings/tools_directory/subjects.cfm?pagename=subjects/pagename_menu=whole_building_analysis/pagename_submenu=renewable_energy.
8. www.usgbc.org.
9. The California Attorney General's Office provides a variety of resources including frequently asked questions and examples of general plan policies, www.ag.ca.gov/globalwarming/ceqa/generalplans.php.
10. Office of the California Attorney General, Local Government Green Building Ordinances in California. 9/22/09, http://ag.ca.gov/globalwarming/pdf/green_building.pdf.
11. For example, New York City's GHG inventory is available online at www.nyc.gov/html/planyc2030/html/emissions/emissions.shtml.
12. http://sf.solarmap.org/.
13. www.epa.gov/cleanenergy/energy-resources/egrid/index.html.
14. The Commercial Buildings Energy Consumption Survey (CBECS) is a national sample survey that collects information on the stock of U.S. commercial buildings, their energy-related building characteristics, and their energy consumption and expenditures. www.eia.doe.gov/emeu/cbecs/.
15. www.energystar.gov/index.cfm?c=evaluate_performance.bus_portfoliomanager.
16. http://poet.lbl.gov/cal-arch/.

Chapter 7

1. The SmartCode is a model unified land development ordinance. www.smartcodecentral.org/.
2. The DPZ Transect, www.dpz.com/transect.aspx.

Chapter 8

1. *Biodiesel* is "a domestic, renewable fuel for diesel engines derived from natural oils like Camelina, canola and soybean oil, and which meets the specifications of ASTM D 6751, "a fuel comprised of mono-alkyl esters of long chain fatty acids derived from waste vegetable oils or animal fats..." (National Biodiesel Board). Biodiesel is made through a chemical process called transesterification "whereby the glycerin is separated from the fat or vegetable oil. The process leaves behind two products—methyl esters (the chemical name for biodiesel) and glycerin (a valuable byproduct usually sold to be used in soaps and other products). (NBB).

    Fuel crops like Camelina are high in oil content and low in saturated fat. In contrast to most biofuel crops, Camelina is drought-resistant and immune to spring freezing, requires less fertilizer and herbicides, and can be used as a rotation crop with wheat.
2. Sources: P. Smith, J. Brenner, K. Paustian, G. Bluhm, J. Cipra, M. Easter, E.T. Elliott, K. Killian, D. Lamm, J. Schuler and S. Williams, *Quantifying the Change in Greenhouse Gas Emissions Due to Natural Resource Conservation Practice Application in Indiana.* Final report to the Indiana Conservation Partnership. Fort Collins: Colorado State University Natural Resource Ecology Laboratory and USDA Natural Resources Conservation Service, 2002; David A. Kroodsma and Christopher B. Field, *Carbon Sequestration in California Agriculture,* 1980–2000. Ecological Applications 16 (5):1975–1985.

Chapter 9

1. *Livestock's Long Shadow: Environmental Issues and Options.* Food and Agriculture Organization of the United Nations, 2006.
2. Branden Born and Mark Purcell, "Avoiding the Local Trap: Scale and Food Systems in Planning Research." *Journal of Planning Education and Research,* 26:95–207.
3. Drake University Agricultural Law Center, *State and Local Food Policy Councils,* 2009.
4. "Good, clean and fair food" is the philosophy of the organization Slow Food.
5. Illinois Food Marketing Task Force, *Stimulating Supermarket Development in Illinois,* 2009.
6. Popularized by the book, *Plenty,* by J.B. Mackinnon and Alisa Smith.
7. Jack Kloppenburg Jr., John Hendrickson, and G. W. Stevenson, "Coming in to the Foodshed." *Agriculture and Human Values* 13:3 (Summer): 33–42, p. 34.

Chapter 10

1. The USEPA has calculated that 42 percent of the nation's GHG emissions stem from the provision of food and goods. USEPA, 2009, Opportunities to Reduce Greenhouse Gas Emissions through Materials and Land Management Practices. U.S. Environmental Protection Agency, Office of Solid Waste and Emergency Response, September 2009. Accessed at: www.epa.gov/oswer/docs/ghg_land_and_materials_management.pdf.
2. USEPA, *Municipal Solid Waste Generation, Recycling, and Disposal in the United States Detailed Tables and Figures for 2008.* U.S. Environmental Protection Agency Office of Resource Conservation and Recovery. November 2009. This publication provides information on waste characterization and generation rates going back to 1960.

3. The 2008 LGO protocol was jointly developed by ICLEI, California Air Resources Board (CARB), California Climate Action Registry (CCAR), and The Climate Registry (TCR).

Chapter 13

1. California Environmental Protection Agency, Office of Environmental Health Hazard Assessment; and Atmospheric Sciences Department and Indoor Environment Department, Environmental Energy Technologies Division, Lawrence Berkeley National Laboratory, Berkeley, California, Janice J. Kim, Svetlana Smorodinsky, Michael Lipsett, Brett C. Singer, Alfred T. Hodgson, and Bart Ostro, "Traffic-Related Air Pollution Near Busy Roads: The East Bay Children's Respiratory Health Study," published in *American Journal of Respiratory and Critical Care Medicine*, Volume 170, pp. 520–526, June 2004.
2. Warren Karlenzig, et al, "The Sustain Lane U.S. City Rankings, How Green is Your City?" New Society Publishers, 2007. The most current city rankings can be found at www.sustainlane.com/us-city-rankings/.
3. Douglas Farr, "Sustainable Urbanism: Urban Design with Nature." New York: John Wiley and Sons, 2008.
4. California Environmental Protection Agency, Air Resources Board, "California's Children: How and Where They Can Be Exposed to Air Pollution," Research Note 94-6, April 1994, available at www.arb.ca.gov/research/resnotes/notes/94-6. htm.
5. Interiors and Sources, "The Ozone Factor: The Health Implications of Climate Change," Anthony Bernheim, October/November 2008, pp. 58–63. www. interiorsandsources.com.
6. National Institute of Environmental Health Sciences, Environmental Health Perspectives, U.S. Department of Health and Human Services, Charles J. Weschler, "Ozone's Impact on Public Health: Contributions from Indoor Exposures to Ozone and Products of Ozone-Initiated Chemistry," 2006. Available at http://ehp03.niehs.nih.gov/ article/info%3Adoi%2F10.1289%2Fehp.9256
7. Janneane F. Gent, PhD., Elizabeth W. Triche, Ph.D., Theodore R. Holford, Ph.D., et al, "Association of Low-Level Ozone and Fine Particles with Respiratory Symptoms in Children with Asthma," *Journal of the American Medical Association*, Vol. 290, No. 14 , October 8, 2003.
8. U.S. EPA, "A Citizen's Guide to Radon," www.epa.gov/ radon/pubs/citguide.html.
9. 7Group and Bill Reed, *The Integrative Design Guide to Green Building, Redefining the Practice of Sustainability*, " Hoboken, NJ: John Wiley & Sons, Inc., 2009.
10. Isaac Brown and Steve Kellenberg, "Ecologically Engineering Cities Through Integrated Sustainable Systems Planning," *Journal of Green Building*, Vol. 4, No. 1.
11. Janine M. Benyus, *Biomimicry, Innovations Inspired by Nature*,New York: Perennial, 1997.
12. Michelle L. Bell, Roger D. Peng, and Francesca Dominici, "The Exposure-Response Curve for Ozone and Risk of Mortality and Adequacy of Current Ozone Regulations," *Environmental Health Perspectives*, Vol. 114, No. 4, April 2006.
13. Anthony Bernheim, "Good Air, Good Health," in *Sustainable Healthcare Architecture*, by Robin Guenther and Gail Vitorri, essay in Chapter 2, pp. 40–43. New York: John Wiley and Sons, 2008.
14. San Francisco Department of Public Health, "Healthy Development Measurement Tool," www.thehdmt.org/.
15. San Francisco Department of Environment, Connected Urban Development, Cisco, Leaptide LLC, "Urban EcoMap, San Francisco," http://sf.urbanecomap.org/.
16. U.S. EPA, "What are Six Common Air Pollutants?," www. epa.gov/air/urbanair/.
17. U.S. EPA, "National Ambient Air Quality Standards," www. epa.gov/air/criteria.html.
18. CARB, "California Ambient Air Quality Standards" (CAAQS), www.arb.ca.gov/research/aaqs/caaqs/caaqs.htm - table.
19. CARB, "Ambient Air Quality Standards," www.arb.ca.gov/ research/aaqs/aaqs2.pdf.
20. U.S. EPA AIRNOW, "Quality of Air Means Quality of Life," http://airnow.gov/index.cfm?action=airnow.main.
21. CARB, "AQMIS2-Air Quality and Meteorological Information System," www.arb.ca.gov/aqmis2/aqinfo.php.
22. American Lung Association, "State of the Air, 2009" Report, 2009, available at www.stateoftheair.org/. The report can be downloaded and data can be researched at this website.
23. U.S. EPA, "EPA Map of Radon Zones," www.epa.gov/radon/ zonemap.html.
24. U.S. EPA, "Where You Live: State Radon Contact Information," www.epa.gov/radon/whereyoulive.html.
25. San Francisco Department of Environment, Connected Urban Development, Cisco, Leaptide LLC, "Urban EcoMap, San Francisco," http://sf.urbanecomap.org/.
26. U.S. Green Building Council, www.usgbc.org/.
27. ICLEI-Local Governments for Sustainability, www.icleiusa. org/.
28. Lawrence Berkeley National Laboratory, www.lbl.gov/.
29. National Renewable Energy Laboratory, www.nrel.gov.
30. U.S. EPA "Air and Radiation Grants and Funding," www. epa.gov/air/grants_funding.html - trans.
31. U.S. EPA "State Indoor Radon Grant (SIRG) Program," www.epa.gov/radon/sirgprogram.html.
32. U.S. Green Building Council, LEED for Neighborhood Development, www.usgbc.org and www.usgbc.org/ DisplayPage.aspx?CMSPageID=148.
33. ICLEI Local Community for Sustainability, Star Community Index, www.icleiusa.org/programs/sustainability/star- community-index.
34. ICLEI Local Community for Sustainability, Clean Air and Climate Protection (CACP) software 2009, www.icleiusa.org/ action-center/tools/cacp-software.
35. U.S. Department of Health and Human Services, Centers for Disease Control, National Center for Health Statistics, "Health, United States: With Special Feature on Medical Technology," January 2010.
36. Matthew Scotch, Bambang Parmanto, Cynthia S. Gadd, Ravi K. Sharma, "Exploring the Role of GIS During Community Health Assessment Problem Solving: Experiences of Public Health Professionals." *International Journal of Health Geographics*, September 2006.

Contributors

Raoul Adamchak is the Market Garden Coordinator at the UC Davis Student Farm, where he teaches organic agriculture and manages a five-acre market garden. He has served as the president of the board of California Certified Organic Farmers, and worked as an organic farm inspector. He is the co-author of *Tomorrow's Table: Organic Farming, Genetics and the Future of Food.* He has a Master's in international agricultural development from UC Davis.

Anthony Bernheim, FAIA, LEED AP BD+C, Sustainability Principal, AECOM, a global provider of architecture and engineering services, is a pioneer in integrated sustainable building practices and indoor air quality. Currently a member of the National U.S. Green Building Council Board of Directors, he received the 2004 AIA California Council's Nathaniel A. Owings Award in "recognition of a lifetime of service, commitment, and advocacy for the principles of sustainable design and preserving the Earth's natural resources."

Nora Black, Associate AIA, CNU-A, is a designer with Duany Plater-Zyberk & Company's Charlotte office with experience in town planning and traditional neighborhood development focusing on Light Imprint and New Urbanism. Black is a contributor to the Light Imprint Handbook. She works with clients and travels to workshops and conferences as part of the Light Imprint team. She holds a B.A. in architecture and a B.S. in geography from the University of North Carolina–Charlotte.

Monica Carney-Holmes, AICP, CNU-A, is a designer with DPZ Charlotte. She received a B.A. in architecture and history from North Carolina State University, and a Master's in city and regional planning from Clemson University.

Jeff Caton, PE, LEED, is director of ESA's Renewable Resources Group, specializing in resource management, climate change and other sustainability issues. He assists clients with planning, strategy development, benchmarking, performance measurement, and communications. His project experience includes community climate action planning and all aspects of carbon management including inventory design and development, management systems, energy efficiency and reduction strategies, lifecycle analysis, target setting, and preparing for emerging regulations and carbon markets.

Paul Crabtree, PE, CNU-A, is president of Crabtree Group, Inc. (www.crabtreegroup.net) a civil engineering and town planning firm with offices in Salida, Colorado, and Ventura, California. Paul holds registration as a Professional Engineer (Civil) in five states: is a member of NSPE, ASCE, LGC, APA, ULI, CNU and the Transect Codes Council; orchestrated the first SmartCode adoption in Colorado in 2009, and won a CNU Charter Award in 2010.

Erin Cubbison, LEED, Assoc. AIA, a sustainable design specialist at Gensler, has expertise at a variety of scales, including architecture, master planning, and infrastructure. Erin sees the cycles of energy, water, materials, and transportation as design generators. She has a specialization in on-site water and energy strategies and has applied this in master planning projects in the United States, China, and India, with significant experience guiding teams through LEED certification, including portfolio-scale assessment of sustainable strategies.

James M. Daisa, P.E., a transportation planner and traffic engineer specializing in planning and designing walkable, transit-oriented, and sustainable urban communities for the past 20 years. He has authored award-winning design guidelines for street design including the Institute of Transportation Engineers' Recommended Practice for designing walkable urban thoroughfares. He currently is employed by Kimley-Horn and Associates, Inc.

Susan J. Daluddung, PhD, joined the City of Peoria, Arizona in 2008. She has over 30 years' experience including positions in economic and community development in Oregon and California. Dr. Daluddung has a PhD in Urban Studies and a Master's degree in Urban Planning from Portland State University, and a Bachelor's degree from Mankato State University, Minnesota. She is a member of the American Institute of Certified Planners, the International City/County Management Association, and the Arizona City/County Management Association.

Cyane Dandridge is the executive director and founder in 1997 of Strategic Energy Innovations (SEI), a non-profit organization that establishes new business concepts and combines a technical and a policy-oriented approach to clean energy, green buildings and energy efficiency. SEI enables communities, especially underserved market sectors, to embrace clean energy, energy efficiency, green buildings, economic development, and sustainable communities.

Daniel Dunigan, AICP, LEED AP, collaborated closely with Steve Coyle on the creation of this book. Dunigan is a city planner with a wide range of professional experience, including climate action planning, public outreach and charrette facilitation, urban design master planning, detailed architectural specification, and all phases of design/build project management.

Norman Garrick, PE, PhD, is associate professor of civil engineering at the University of Connecticut and a member of the national board of The Congress for the New Urbanism (CNU) and the Tri-state Transportation Campaign. He specializes in the planning and design of urban transportation as they relate to sustainability and urban revitalization. He is a 2008 recipient of the Transportation Research Board's Award for Best Paper and 2004 Fulbright Fellowship to Jamaica.

John Harris of Earth Advisors is a landscape economist with qualifications including certified landscape inspector, certified forester, certified arborist, certified nursery tree grader, registered consulting arborist, and membership in Lambda Alpha International Honorary Land Economics Society. He has over 25 years of experience in the green industry doing projects across the United States, Canada, the Caribbean, and most recently, Brazil. Earth Advisors provides landscape, forestry, and environmental consulting for public, commercial, and private properties.

Seth Harry, AIA CNU, architect, urban designer, and retail/economic development consultant, has worked around the world for 25 years on urban mixed-use projects. Seth Harry and Associates, Inc. Architects and Planners, consults on projects for both public and private clients, from regional planning projects, such as a new transit-oriented regional urban center for Queensland, Australia, to major suburban infill mixed-use developments. He assisted Prince Charles' Foundation on revitalizing Britain's Historic Urban Centers, based on the principles of sustainable commerce.

Sara N. Hines, Architect, CNU, principal and owner of Hines Design Associates, Ashland, MA, has been a registered architect for 37 years and an urbanist working with communities on comprehensive planning and sustainability issues. She has been involved with affordable housing, housing for the homeless, existing town center redevelopment and retrofit, and design of urban mixed use projects in New England and the Southeast. She is currently writing a book called *Cottage Communities, the Camp Meeting Movement in America.*

Monica Carney Holmes, AICP, CNU-A, a designer with Duany Plater-Zyberk & Company, has experience in town planning and traditional neighborhood development focusing on Light Imprint urbanism. Holmes is a contributor to the Light Imprint Handbook. She works with clients and travels to conferences as part of the Light Imprint team. Holmes holds Bachelor's degrees in architecture and history from North Carolina State University and a Master's in city and regional planning from Clemson University.

Will Kirksey, PE, is vice president of engineering for WWT. Prior to joining WWT, Kirksey has worked for the Florida Governor's Office, Battelle Labs, and the Civil Engineering Research Foundation. WWT has been developing advanced wetland wastewater treatment systems called Living Machines for ten years.

Sibella Kraus is president of SAGE (Sustainable Agriculture Education) a nonprofit organization that develops AgParks and Agricultural Conservancies at project and landscape scales. SAGE is also initiating a New Ruralism framework, as a bridge between smart growth and regional food systems. Kraus collaborates on regional agricultural planning efforts and with the Agriculture in Metropolitan Regions program at UC Berkeley. Previously, she directed the Center for Urban Education about Sustainable Agriculture (CUESA) and created its signature project, the Ferry Plaza Market.

Dave Leland, Urban Strategist, is a national advisor to the public and private realms on matters of implementing mixed-use, transit-oriented, and sustainable development. Having advised on more than 3,000 project engagements in his career, he is an expert in downtowns and urban centers, revitalizing urban corridors and large-scale private community development.

Trent Lethco, AICP, leads the Arup Urban Planning team in New York and has 14 years of experience. He has worked locally, nationally, and internationally on projects seeking to create more sustainable forms of living and mobility in existing and new communities. He received his Master's of Architecture in urban planning (transportation) from UCLA and a Bachelor of Arts with Honors in History from the UC Berkeley.

Eric Lohan is research manager for Worrell Water Technologies (WWT). He has worked for ten years on the development of the Living Machine® technology and is co-author of five patents on advanced wetland technologies.

Thomas Low, AIA, AICP, CNU-A, LEED, is director of Duany Plater-Zyberk's Charlotte office and a partner in the Miami-based firm. His projects received awards from AIA, Sierra Club, National Association of Homebuilders, Environmental Protection Agency for Smart Growth Achievement, and others. He lectures on town planning, sustainability, urbanism, slow food, environmental infrastructure, and civic engagement and design. In 2007, Low developed the Light Imprint Initiative for environmentally sensitive engineering using New Urban community design principles.

Wesley Marshall, PE, a PhD candidate in transportation engineering at the University of Connecticut, assists Dr. Normand Garrick and others in transportation planning, safety, and sustainability, multi-modal transportation, congestion pricing, street networks, and parking. A Dwight D. Eisenhower Transportation Fellow, recipient of the Charley V. Wootan Award for Outstanding TRB Paper in the field of Policy and Organization, and co-chair of the TRB Parking Management Subcommittee, he received his Professional Engineering (PE) license in Connecticut.

Jane Martin, AIA, is founding principal of the architecture and landscape design firm Shift Design Studio, and founding director of Plant*SF, a non-profit organization in San Francisco focused on stormwater diversion through public space gardens.

Michael Mehaffy, CNU-A, a sustainable urban development consultant, researcher, author, and educator, works internationally from his Portland, Oregon, office as research associate with Christopher Alexander at the Centre for Environmental Structure, Europe. He directs the Sustasis Foundation, a small catalytic think tank that researches and develops the link between climate change and urban form, assisted in the recovery of post-Katrina New Orleans and Mississippi, and helped plan a new "toolkit" for the Portland region's sustainable development.

Karen Mendrala, senior planner, has worked for the City of Holyoke, Massachusetts Office of Planning & Development for 13 years. She graduated from Syracuse University Maxwell School in Policy Studies and Geography with a B.A. in policy studies and geography and attended the University of Massachusetts Amherst for her graduate education in planning. She specializes in grant writing and project management on projects from brownfields cleanup and redevelopment to infrastructure improvements.

Guy Pearlman, RLA, CNU-A, is a project manager at Duany Plater-Zyberk & Company. Pearlman has extensive experience in town planning and traditional neighborhood development focusing on the Light Imprint Initiative. Pearlman is a registered landscape architect having nearly fifteen years of experience in planning, permitting, and implementation. He is a member of the Light Imprint Handbook team. Pearlman works with clients during development and construction phases to implement environmentally sensitive practices using Light Imprint techniques.

Lynn Peemoeller is a U.S.-based food systems planner and consultant with degrees in urban planning, environmental science, and geology. She works on projects and policy in every aspect of the food system, from farm to fork. For over 10 years she has worked with farmers, communities, government agencies, non-profits, foundations, and students to help forge paths towards more sustainable food systems. She currently lives in Berlin, Germany.

Dana Perls is city planner with a diverse background in both international and local planning. Her professional experience ranges from infrastructure management, green affordable housing financing and policy, community outreach for regional transit plans, to technical water supply analyses. Prior to joining Town-Green, Dana worked with several nonprofits, a planning firm, and the City of Oakland on climate change research, green building policy, transit-oriented development education, and water supply assessments. All of the projects had a significant emphasis on public education and outreach. Dana received her Bachelor of Sciences from Cornell University, and Master of City Planning from University of California at Berkeley. She served as a Peace Corps volunteer in Panama, and worked closely with government agencies and local leaders on watershed protection, solid waste management, and water infrastructure development.

Gaither Pratt, AIA, a registered architect with experience in preservation, sustainability and urbanism, is director of the New Orleans Field Office of the National Trust for Historic Preservation and founder of Limehouse Architects. Pratt studied architecture at the University of Virginia and the University of Miami, and worked for the office of William McDonough and Partners and the office of Duany Plater-Zyberk. Pratt collaborated on the book *A Pattern Book of New Orleans Architecture* (Pelican Press, 2010).

Rick Pruetz, FAICP, Planning and Implementation Strategies, is a planning consultant specializing in Transfer of Development Rights (TDR). He has written three books on TDR, including *Beyond Takings and Givings; Saving Natural Areas, Farmland and Historic Landmarks with Transfer of Development Rights and Density Transfer Charges.* Rick has written about TDR for several publications, including the *Journal of the American Planning Association* and *Planning & Environmental Law,* conducted presentations throughout the country, and prepared TDR studies and/or ordinances for over 20 communities, from Santa Fe County, NM, to Livermore, CA. Rick, whose web site is www.BeyondTakingsAndGivings.com, received his Master of Urban Planning degree and was the City Planner of Burbank, California, for 14 years before devoting his practice exclusively to TDR in 1999. In 2004, Rick was honored with membership in the College of Fellows of the American Institute of Certified Planners.

Jeannie Renné-Malone, LEED AP, director of HDR's National Climate and Greenhouse Gas (GHG) Management practice, is an experienced program manager with extensive background in sustainability, climate change and renewable energy program development. She advises clients on policies and technologies that reduce GHG emissions, assists in interpreting and navigating anticipated climate change policies, and helps them explore carbon financing implement options. Jeannie previously managed the Latin America program for the National Renewable Energy Laboratory.

Jon Roberts is the director of building science and a principal consultant at CTG Energetics, a multi-disciplinary sustainability consulting company. Previous experience includes energy savings performance contracting and extensive international sustainability work. He received his PhD from the University of Colorado, and performed solar energy research at the National Renewable Energy Laboratory. He specializes in quantitative, systems-based approaches to optimizing sustainability of the built environment, and has significant community-level and programmatic energy and sustainability experience.

Karen Shore, PhD, is vice president for planning and health policy at the Center for Health Improvement in Sacramento, California. With 20 years of experience in health policy and health services research, she has led a variety of projects and teams with a goal of improving program and organizational effectiveness. Her doctorate in health services and policy analysis is from the University of California, Berkeley.

Daniel T. Sicular, PhD, principal with Environmental Science Associates (ESA), national leader of waste management, recycling, waste prevention, composting, program planning, design, implementation, evaluation, and environmental review, has planned and managed waste characterization studies, program implementation, and environmental impact reports for waste handling facilities. He has authored academic and professional papers on waste management industry, Third World low-cost recycling and composting systems, the history of recovery-based waste management systems; and the social geography of waste collectors and scavengers.

Dan Slone, Esq., a partner with McGuireWoods LLP, represents developers and localities in the creation of new, infill, and retrofit neighborhoods using innovative techniques of sustainable and "New Urban" development. Slone teaches the legal aspects of form-based codes and the SmartCode around the country and lectures widely on coding and overcoming impediments to sustainable urbanism. In 2008, Dan and co-author Doris Goldstein published *A Legal Guide to Urban and Sustainable Development for Architects, Planners and Developers*.

Sandy Sorlien is an advisor to the Center for Applied Transect Studies and was its director of technical research from 2008 to 2010. She was the managing editor of the model SmartCode for six years, working with principal author Andrés Duany. She currently serves on the Transect Codes Council.

John Williams is a senior vice president and national director/sustainable development for HDR Engineering, Inc. Since 1979 he has guided outreach, public-private partnership, and sustainable development programs for communities nationwide. He is an advisor to the U.S. Conference of Mayors, the Partnership for NYC and a board member for the New York Foundation for the Arts. He is a member of the Clinton Global Initiative and is on the faculty at Columbia University.

Chris Zahas, AICP, is managing principal of Leland Consulting Group, where he manages projects and multidisciplinary teams focusing on turning broad visions into prioritized and achievable action plans, with an emphasis on downtown revitalization, urban corridors, transit-oriented development, and public-private partnerships. Chris has managed more than 20 downtown and corridor development strategies and is frequently sought out for his understanding of the linkage between transit and land use, particularly for modern streetcar systems.

Sam Zimbabwe, LEED AP, is an urban designer with a background in transit-oriented development and pedestrian-oriented design. He is the Director of the Center for Transit-Oriented Development (CTOD), a partnership among Reconnecting America, Center for Neighborhood Technology (CNT), and Strategic Economics dedicated to providing best practices, research and tools to support equitable market-based transit-oriented development.

Index

A

Actions, modeling, 50–51
Actions, team recommendation, 25
Agriculture, 2, 269
Alliance for Water Stewardship, 231
Ambient outdoor air quality, 357
  action plan development, 367–369
  action plan implementation, 369
  community context map, 364
  goals/objectives/performance metrics,
    development, 366
  integrated pest management
    programs, 367
  people preparation, 365
  place preparation, 364
  solutions, 358–360
  source control, 366
  strategic plan development, 366–367
  team preparation, 360–361
  tools preparation, 361–362
American Recovery and Reinvestment
  Act, 200
Anchor institutions, 154
Attainable/resilient housing, 96
  benefits/drawbacks, 98
  first cost/lifecycle cost, 98
  goals/objectives support, 97
  implementation supports/constraints,
    99
  implementation time, 97
  information sources, 100
  performance characteristics, 97
  quantitative performance, estimation,
    99
  synergism, 97
Automobile mode share, strategies, 174
Awareness for Communities about the
    Environment (ACE), 201
  benefits/drawbacks, 202
  first costs/lifecycle costs, 203
  goals/objectives support, 201
  implementation supports/constraints,
    204
  implementation time, 202
  informational sources, 204
  performance characteristics, 201–202
  quantitative performance, estimation,
    203
  reports/studies, 204
  synergism, 202

B

Best management practices (BMPs), 214
Best practices, 28, 49
Big picture strategies, defining, 48
Bioclimatic building design, 77
  building facilities/management
    teams, 83
  building occupants/tenants, 83
  comparable buildings, survey, 80
  design development, 84–85
  energy consumption, analysis, 80
  goals/objectives/performance metrics,
    development, 83
  infrastructure research, 81
  key stakeholders, 82
  market research, 81–82
  occupant survey, 80
  people preparation, 82–83
  place preparation, 79–82
  program study, 79
  site environmental analysis, 80
  team preparation, 77–78
  tools, preparation, 78–79
  utilization analysis, 80
  waste audit, 80
Black box method, 38
Boundaries, 32
Building information modeling (BIM), 79
Buildings
  energy codes, 195–196
  energy simulation software, 193–194
  standards, 27
Built environment, 29
  code administration/monitoring, 128
  code development, 124–125
  code implementation, 126–128
  code refinement/adoption, 126
  code strategies, development, 122–124
  coding strategies, 123
  defining, 1
  goals/objectives/performance
    measures, development, 121–122
  investigations, 32
  people preparation, 120–121
  place, preparation, 119–120
  supporting systems, 1
  team preparation, 118
  tools, selection, 118
  transformation, form-based coding
    (usage), 114
  types, 3–12

C

California, legislation, 196
California Academy of Sciences
  building, 209
California Building Energy Reference
  Tool, 198
California EPA Air Resources Board
  (CARB), 362
California Green Building Standards
  (CALGREEN), 79
Cellulosic Biofuels and Oilseed Biodiesel
  (CBOB), 264
  benefits/drawbacks, 266
  first cost/lifecycle costs, 266–267
  goals/objectives support, 264–265
  implementation, 266
  implementation supports/constraints,
    268
  informational sources/reports/studies,
    268
  performance characteristics, 265–266
  quantitative performance, estimation,
    267–268
  synergism, 266
Center for Applied Transect Studies
  (CATS), 118, 120
Center for Transit-Oriented
  Development National TOD
  Database, 150
Centralized composting, conventional
  disposal-based system variation,
  297
Change tools, 171
  benefits/drawbacks, 173–174
  first cost/lifecycle costs, 174–175
  goals/objectives support, 171
  implementation supports/constraints,
    175
  implementation time, 173
  informational sources, 175
  performance characteristics, 172
  quantitative performance, estimation,
    175
  synergism, 173
Chicago Community Trust, 280
Cities for Sustainable Community
  Protection (ICLEI), 30–31
Clean Air and Climate Protection
  (CACP), 316–317
Climate action plan (CAP), 27–28
Coded elements, components, 124–125

WILEY BOOKS ON Sustainable Design

For these and other Wiley books on sustainable design, visit www.wiley.com/go/sustainabledesign

Alternative Construction: Contemporary Natural Building Methods
by Lynne Elizabeth and Cassandra Adams

Biophilic Design: The Theory, Science, and Practice of Bringing Buildings to Life
by Stephen Kellert, Judith Heerwagen, and Martin Mador

Contractor's Guide to Green Building Construction: Management, Project Delivery, Documentation, and Risk Reduction
by Thomas E. Glavinich and Associated General Contractors

Design for Flooding
by Donald Watson and Michele Adams

Design with Nature
by Ian L. McHarg

Ecodesign: A Manual for Ecological Design
by Ken Yeang

Environmentally Responsible Design: Green and Sustainable Design for Interior Designers
by Louise Jones

Green BIM: Successful Sustainable Design with Building Information Modeling
by Eddy Krygiel and Brad Nies

Green Building Materials: A Guide to Product Selection and Specification, Third Edition
by Ross Spiegel and Dru Meadows

Green Development: Integrating Ecology and Real Estate
by Rocky Mountain Institute

Green Roof Systems: A Guide to the Planning, Design and Construction of Landscapes Over Structure
by Susan Weiler and Katrin Scholz-Barth

Guide to the LEED Green Associate Exam
by Michelle Cottrell

Guide to Green Building Rating Systems
by Linda Reeder

The HOK Guidebook to Sustainable Design, Second Edition
by Sandra Mendler, William O'Dell, and Mary Ann Lazarus

The Integrative Design Guide to Green Building: Redefining the practice of Sustainability
by 7group and Bill Reed

Land and Natural Development (Land) Code
by Diana Balmori and Gaboury Benoit

A Legal Guide to Urban and Sustainable Development for Planners, Developers and Architects
by Daniel Slone, Doris S. Goldstein, and W. Andrew Gowder

Materials for Sustainable Sites: A Complete Guide to the Evaluation, Selection, and Use of Sustainable Construction Materials
by Meg Calkins

Modern Sustainable Residential Design: A Guide for Design Professionals
by William J. Carpenter

Packaging Sustainability: Tools, Systems, and Strategies for Innovative Package Design
by Wendy Jedlicka

Sustainable Commercial Interiors
by Penny Bonda and Katie Sosnowchik

Sustainable Construction: Green Building Design and Delivery
by Charles J. Kibert

Sustainable Design: Ecology, Architecture, and Planning
by Daniel Williams

Sustainable Design of Research Laboratories
by KlingStubbins

Sustainable Healthcare Architecture
by Robin Guenther and Gail Vittori

Sustainable Preservation
by Jean Carroon

Sustainable Residential Interiors
by Associates III

Sustainable School Architecture: Design for Elementary and Secondary Schools
by Lisa Gelfand with Eric Corey Freed

Sustainable Site Design : Criteria, Process, and Case Studies for Integrating Site and Region in Landscape Design
by Claudia Dinep, Kristin Schwab

Sustainable Urbanism
by Douglas Farr

 Environmental Benefits Statement

This book is printed with soy-based inks on presses with VOC levels that are lower than the standard for the printing industry. The paper, Rolland Enviro 100, is manufactured by Cascades Fine Papers Group and is made from 100 percent post-consumer, de-inked fiber, without chlorine. According to the manufacturer, the use of every ton of Rolland Enviro100 Book paper, switched from virgin paper, helps the environment in the following ways:

Mature trees	Waterborne waste not created	Water flow saved	Atmospheric emissions eliminated	Soiled Wastes reduced	Natural gas saved by using biogas
17	6.9 lbs.	10,196 gals.	2,098 lbs.	1,081 lbs.	2,478 cubic feet